The Ivory Tower, Harry Potter, and Beyond

The Ivory Tower, Harry Potter, and Beyond

More Essays on the Works of J. K. Rowling

Edited by Lana A. Whited

UNIVERSITY OF MISSOURI PRESS
Columbia

Copyright © 2023 by
The Curators of the University of Missouri
University of Missouri Press, Columbia, Missouri 65211
Printed and bound in the United States of America
All rights reserved. First printing, 2023.

Library of Congress Cataloging-in-Publication Data

Names: Whited, Lana A., 1958- editor.
Title: The ivory tower, Harry Potter, and beyond : more essays on the works of J. K. Rowling / edited by Lana A. Whited.
Description: Columbia : University of Missouri Press, 2023. | Includes bibliographical references and index.
Identifiers: LCCN 2023024904 (print) | LCCN 2023024905 (ebook) | ISBN 9780826223005 (hardcover) | ISBN 9780826274960 (ebook)
Subjects: LCSH: Rowling, J. K.--Characters--Harry Potter. | Rowling, J. K.--Characters--Criticism and interpretation. | Children's stories, English--History and criticism. | Fantasy fiction, English--History and criticism. | Potter, Harry (Fictitious character) | Harry Potter films. | Wizards in literature. | Magic in literature. | LCGFT: Essays. | Literary criticism.
Classification: LCC PR6068.O93 Z7343 2023 (print) | LCC PR6068.O93 (ebook) | DDC 823/.914--dc23/eng/20230607
LC record available at https://lccn.loc.gov/2023024904
LC ebook record available at https://lccn.loc.gov/2023024905

∞™ This paper meets the requirements of the American National Standard for Permanence of Paper for Printed Library Materials, Z39.48, 1984.
Typefaces: Lapture and Garamond

If you found anything in these stories that resonated with you and helped you at any time in your life—then that is between you and the book that you read, and it is sacred. And in my opinion nobody can touch that.

—Daniel Radcliffe,
    comments on behalf of The Trevor Project, June 8, 2020

Contents

Acknowledgments		xi
Introduction J. K. Rowling: The First Twenty-Five Years *Lana A. Whited*		3

SECTION 1: MAGICAL DIRECTIONS AND MISDIRECTIONS

1.	Muggle Worthy: Deceptive Exteriors and Outsized Interiors in the Wizarding World *Elizabeth Baird Hardy*	21
2.	London as a Magical Location in the Harry Potter Series *Madison McLeod*	35
3.	Secrecy and Segregation in the Wizarding World's Hidden Histories *Kathryn N. McDaniel*	49

SECTION 2: INTERTEXTUAL READINGS

4.	Harry, Aeneas, and the Foundational Text *Mitchell H. Parks*	67
5.	From Sword to Sorcery: The Medieval(ist) Juxtaposition of Magic and Might in Harry Potter *Laurie Beckoff*	83
6.	Shakespearean Romantic Comedy and Hogwarts Couples *Heather Murray*	99

Contents

SECTION 3: SOCIAL AND PSYCHOLOGICAL APPLICATIONS

7. Why S.P.E.W. Was Doomed to Fail:
   Exploring Systemic Inequity through Rowling's
   Racialized House-Elves 115
   Alyssa Lowery

8. "The Ghost of His Last Laugh":
   Evolving Humor in Harry Potter 133
   Louise M. Freeman

SECTION 4: NARRATOLOGICAL READINGS

9. Pensieve Lessons in Critical Reading 155
   Leslie Bickford

10. Quidditch as Narrative Mirror in the Harry Potter Series 169
    Caitlin Elizabeth Harper

11. Eye Wonder? Reflecting Harry in Animal Eyes 185
    Catherine Olver

12. The Otter and the Stag: Narration
    and Objectification in Harry Potter 201
    Patrick McCauley

13. "Perfectly normal, thank you very much":
    Exploitation of Hybridity in the Borderlands of Harry Potter .. 219
    Molly L. Burt

SECTION 5: HARRY POTTER AND BEYOND

14. Literary Alchemy in "The Fountain of Fair Fortune"
    from *The Tales of Beedle the Bard* 239
    Kris Swank

15. Hopelessness and Hope in *The Casual Vacancy*:
    The Cost and Joy of Discipleship 253
    M. Katherine Grimes

Contents

16. Parenting Models in the Potter Saga and *Cursed Child*:
    Human and Divine ... 269
    Emily Strand

17. The Snake Woman in Harry Potter and *Fantastic Beasts* ... 289
    Beatrice Groves

18. Politics of Suppression and Violence in *Fantastic Beasts* ... 305
    Carsten Kullmann

19. The Story Turn: Parallels in the Pivotal Texts
    of Harry Potter and Cormoran Strike ... 325
    John Granger

20. *The Ickabog*, Monsters, and Monstrosity ... 341
    Lana A. Whited

SECTION 6: THE FANDOM, 25 YEARS ON

21. "Accio Jo!" Woke Wizards and Generational Potter Fandom ... 363
    Rebecca Sutherland Borah

    Bibliography ... 381

    Contributors ... 407

    Index ... 415

Acknowledgments

I OWE A debt of gratitude expanded with *engorgio* to my team of contributors for this volume. The interval of preparing this book has been the most difficult in the brief era of Rowling scholarship, and while working to complete the volume, I sometimes woke up in the middle of the night and wondered if anyone would read it. Thanks to the very high quality of these scholars' work, I feel confident that readers will follow. But it still astonishes me that professional people write essays like these for a copy of the book and a few lines on a vita. All of them deserve to have their photos on Chocolate Frog cards.

Among those contributors, I have particularly depended upon Louise Freeman, Katy McDaniel, and Emily Strand for behind-the-scenes advice about matters great and small, and with remarkable promptness for people with full-time professional lives and busy families. Without question, the best thing about having spent twenty-five years in *Harry Potter* scholarship is the friendships I have developed along the way. Louise, Katy, and Emily are my Marauders.

My editorial and production team also deserve their own Chocolate Frog cards. I am grateful for Mary Conley's sound advice and persistence through a process that took longer than we anticipated and had unexpected twists. I both appreciate and envy Miranda Ottewell's keen eye and thorough knowledge of the *Chicago Manual of Style*. And I am indebted to Drew Griffith for his patience and calm assurance in the final stage of completion. Having Mary, Miranda, and Drew assigned to this project definitely involved a vial of Felix Felicis.

Receiving a semester's sabbatical from my Ferrum College responsibilities helped me complete the final stages of this project, and I'm also grateful to Rachel Walton of Stanley Library for efficiently fulfilling every interlibrary loan request I sent her.

Acknowledgments

This is my fourth anthology project with Katherine Grimes, my professional and life partner. I have been her editor and she has been mine, without damage to our personal relationship and family harmony. Katherine has now read hundreds of thousands of words on my behalf, and no one in the world gives me better (or more honest) advice. I'm also grateful for our sons' interest in my work and their patience when I'm facing a deadline. Now that they're all adults, I have renewed admiration for that Weasley family clock.

The Ivory Tower, Harry Potter, and Beyond

Introduction

J. K. Rowling: The First Twenty-Five Years

Lana A. Whited

SINCE THE 1997 publication of *Harry Potter and the Philosopher's Stone*, Joanne Rowling has achieved an astonishing literary output: seven volumes in the Harry Potter series and three companion books; a novel of social realism for adults, *The Casual Vacancy*; seven Cormoran Strike detective novels; the story basis for a London and Broadway play, *The Cursed Child*; a book-length fairy tale, *The Ickabog*; a holiday fable, *The Christmas Pig*, and three screenplays in the Fantastic Beasts film series. The Rowling library now runs to twenty-one volumes in twenty-five years, with *The Harry Potter Wizarding Almanac* scheduled for an October 2023 release. Twenty years after Bloomsbury issued a first-run printing of five hundred copies for *Harry Potter and the Sorcerer's Stone*, five hundred *million* copies of Harry Potter books are available in eighty languages, the eightieth being, fittingly, Scots.[1]

Rowling's commercial success has been no less impressive. When *The Ivory Tower and Harry Potter* appeared in 2002 as the first anthology of scholarly essays on the Harry Potter series, fifty-five million copies of the first four novels were in print.[2] By 2018 that number had soared to half a billion.[3] The impact of the series on the children's book market was so direct that a downturn in 2001 and 2002 was attributed primarily to the absence of a new Harry Potter hardback.[4] Thus began the series' domination of booksellers' and bestsellers lists, a phenomenon that led the *New York Times* to create its first Children's Bestsellers List in 2000 in order to make space at the top of the regular fiction lists for authors other than Rowling. In 2007, when the series concluded with the publication of *Deathly Hallows*, its author was a finalist for *Time* magazine's Person of the Year. The success of the Harry Potter books and films, along with Rowling's additional projects, has vaulted her into the pantheon of the world's wealthiest authors; in June 2022 Rowling's net worth was estimated at $1 billion.[5] And on April

12, 2023, Rowling announced a multiseason television series readapting the seven-novel series, one novel per season. For those who asked, while the novels were still new, whether Harry Potter would quickly lose its appeal, the answer twenty-five years on seems to be Not Anytime Soon.

The Harry Potter series' political, social, and cultural impact has also been well documented. In *Harry Potter and the Millennials*, political scientist Anthony ("Jack") Gierzynski and associates have demonstrated the impact of growing up reading the Harry Potter series on the ideology of young Americans who came of voting age in time for the 2008 US presidential election. Here are Gierzynski's conclusions about this group: "In short, we found that Harry Potter fans tend to be more accepting of those who are different, to be more politically tolerant, to be more supportive of equality, to be less authoritarian, to be more opposed to the use of violence and torture, to be less cynical, and to evince a higher level of political efficacy."[6]

The series' focus on corruption within the Ministry of Magic has inculcated young readers with a sense of urgency about replacing corrupt governments, says Gierzynski, who attributes the success of Barack Obama's 2008 US presidential campaign in part to the fact that the early generation of Harry Potter readers voted in their first national election that fall.

Half a decade following *Harry Potter and the Millennials*, Diana C. Munz correlated reading the Harry Potter novels with an aversion to Donald Trump and to policies and beliefs associated with Trump, attributing the reaction to three themes that essentially reflect the same belief system described by Gierzynski: "1) the value of tolerance and respect for difference; 2) opposition to violence and punitiveness; and 3) the dangers of authoritarianism."[7] These themes, Mutz notes, "are prominent in coverage of Donald Trump's 2016 presidential campaign."[8] A few of Muntz's findings are particularly interesting. First, the aversion was evidenced even when Trump was a real estate mogul and reality television star and had not yet become a political candidate. This result is less surprising than it may appear. Even as a private citizen, Trump was outspoken on social issues, and the values identified by Mutz and Gierzynski as repugnant to Harry Potter readers are aptly demonstrated in the full-page *New York Times* advertisements he sponsored to advocate the death penalty for the Central Park Five (to whom Trump never publicly apologized, even after their exoneration).[9]

Another interesting finding in Mutz's study is that the observed effects were incrementally boosted with each additional Harry Potter novel that a subject had read. Also, Mutz found that reading the novels had a significantly stronger effect than watching the film adaptations for several reasons, some having to do with the selective nature of adaptation.

Values of acceptance and tolerance found by Gierzynski and Mutz were also demonstrated as stronger among Harry Potter readers than among other young people by a team of Italian researchers led by sociologist Loris Vezzali, whose findings were released in the summer of 2014 with far more mainstream media interest than social scientists typically attract.[10] The effects of the series on the sociopolitical ideology of these first generations of Harry Potter readers may have been more pronounced due to the escalation during the same era of international terrorism, including the September 11, 2001, attacks on the World Trade Center and the Pentagon in the United States. Daniel Nexon describes the morning when he recognized the political impact of Harry Potter on students he was teaching at Georgetown University. The previous evening (May 2, 2011), US Navy Seals had killed Osama bin Laden, leader of the pan-Islamic militant organization al-Qaeda, in Pakistan. President Barack Obama announced bin Laden's death in a national address just before midnight. The next morning, Nexon asked his government students whether any of them had attended a celebration outside the White House gates, and one replied. "Of course. I mean, they got Voldemort."[11] One literature professor has likened the Harry Potter series' sociopolitical impact to that of *Uncle Tom's Cabin* during the Civil War era.[12]

The series has also reached a very broad range of readers. Surveys indicate consistently that about 18 percent of all Americans have read the entire series, and 61 percent have seen at least one film adaptation. But the number of series readers rises to one out of three for Americans eighteen to thirty-two.[13] Millennials and Generation Z members who grew up with the series recognize the magnitude of its impact on them. For Jake Brown, the series imposed the borders of his adolescence, thanks to the publication delays between volume 4 and later books: "The series stretched the entirety of our precollege adolescence, leaving a more poetic mark than if it had merely met the seven-year release window indicated by the release cadence of the first four books. . . . Closing the last pages of *Deathly Hallows* felt like

Introduction

closing a chapter in our own lives."[14] Brown went on to earn bachelor's and master's degree in literature, motivated in no small part by his early reading of Harry Potter. On a conference panel in Roanoke, Virginia, in 2018, Taylor Holden (then twenty-five) called the series "the myth of my youth," and Mary Beth Fisher (then twenty-nine) said she sobbed through almost all of the *Deathly Hallows, Part II* film adaptation because, in her words, "I knew when it ended, my childhood was officially over." For millennials in particular, the entire Harry Potter experience was so influential in shaping values that at least one writer has called the series "a foundational myth that threatens, at least among millennials and Gen Z, to replace the Bible. For politically progressive millennials in particular, 'Harry Potter' is more than a book series. It's an entire theology."[15]

And then, in December 2019, the entire universe finding its origin point with J. K. Rowling began to shift on its axis.

Prior to that date, Rowling's relationship with fans was largely positive, but it took a startling turn with a few tweets in support of a British woman, Maya Forstater, whose contract with a global think tank was not renewed in March 2019 following Forstater's own tweets concerning biological gender. On December 19 Rowling tweeted a rhetorical question implying that it is wrong to "force women out of their jobs for stating that sex is real," adding the hashtag "I stand with Maya Forstater."[16] Over sixty-five thousand people retweeted, and another thirty-five thousand quoted the tweet.[17] The firestorm was lit.

Over the next six months, Rowling herself fanned the flames as she became increasingly vocal and, in a few cases, flippant about gender identity. In perhaps her most ridiculous public comment on the subject, Rowling pretended to have forgotten the word *woman*, implying that the term had passed out of fashion. On June 6, 2020, Rowling retweeted a report on menstrual health and hygiene issued in the aftermath of the COVID-19 epidemic by the Devex independent news company, prefaced by the snide comment, " 'People who menstruate.' I'm sure there used to be a word for those people. Someone help me out. Wumben? Wimpund? Woomud?"[18]

Perhaps the final straw for some Rowling fans came on June 10, 2020, when Rowling posted a lengthy letter on her own website explaining her perception that women are endangered by policies welcoming transgender individuals into spaces such as restrooms and changing areas matching their gender identity.[19] Rowling's concerns about individuals entering same-gender spaces based solely on self-declaration were influenced, she avowed, by her history as a sexual assault victim.[20] In late 2022 and early 2023, as Scotland considered its own gender identity reform, Rowling continued to be a vocal opponent of self-designation, especially for those in early adolescence.[21]

But in June 2020, Rowling's manifesto led some people to label her as a trans-exclusionary radical feminist (TERF), a term first used in 2008 that has more recently evolved as "gender critical."[22] Many transgender persons felt shocked and betrayed by the author's public statements. Tolonda Henderson, a Harry Potter scholar who is also transgender, has written that they felt "brainwashed and gaslit at the same time" after reading Rowling's response.[23] Henderson subsequently removed the author's name from their essay for *Open at the Close*, writing that the change "gives me back a sense of power and agency in my scholarship."[24] At the time of that book's publication (2022), Henderson was also considering abandoning Harry Potter scholarship altogether. The only thing the author and those whom she has hurt, offended, or angered now seem to agree on is that the issue is "surrounded by toxicity."[25]

For many fans and scholars, there were at least two surprising aspects of the whole controversy. First, the 2020 tweets were inconsistent with statements of support for the transgender community Rowling had made previously. For example, she has said that transgender individuals "need and deserve protection" and "pose zero threat to others" and has voiced support for "every trans person's right to live in any way that feels authentic and comfortable to them."[26] Her public presence, from her early work with Amnesty International to her charitable projects, reflected a thoroughly liberal mindset of the sort that she is credited with fostering in young readers.

The second and perhaps most surprising aspect of the 2020 tweets was the shockingly simplistic understanding of gender identity reflected in them and the inconsistency of these seemingly concrete views with the ideology of her novels. The Harry Potter series presents human nature as complex and identity formation as a process; reading the series requires a reader's maturation as the novels progress. Characters presented through a

Introduction

mostly concrete lens in *Sorcerer's Stone* and *Chamber of Secrets* have more depth and nuance in later volumes. The Albus Dumbledore presented early on as a wise and flawless headmaster turns out to have been negligent (at best) or complicit (at worst) in his own sister's death; in the final novel, he is revealed as having planned to sacrifice Harry Potter all along to save the Wizarding world. The animosity that Severus Snape directs at Harry in his classroom is revealed to be motivated by bitterness that his childhood love, Lily Evans, chose James Potter rather than him. The Tom Riddle introduced as an ambitious and calculating villain in *Chamber of Secrets* turns out to be another of the series' many wounded children. No better explanation of the series' multiple layers of complexity has been offered than M. Katherine Grimes's essay "Harry Potter as Fairy-Tale Prince, Real Boy, and Archetypal Hero" in the original *Ivory Tower* volume. Yet Rowling's declarations about gender identity reject this more nuanced perspective, instead recalling her very early books in their absolute concreteness, their insistence that human gender and gender identity are simple concepts. Readers have been understandably baffled.

In January 2021, a high court judge ruled that Forstater's gender-critical views were protected under British equality law as "a genuine and important philosophical position" that "could not be shown to be a direct attempt to harm others."[27] But regardless of the outcome for Forstater, who has called Rowling her "fairy godmother,"[28] the damage to Rowling's reputation has proven extensive. Fans have found themselves no longer comfortable reading (or watching) Rowling's work, or comfortable only so long as they do not contribute to her income, and have boycotted Harry Potter–themed festivals, fancons, conferences, and sites (real and virtual). Scholars have declined to participate in publishing or other professional projects based on Rowling's work or reconsidered the offering of Harry Potter–related courses, and students have been reluctant to sign up for them. Publishing houses have withdrawn support for Harry Potter–related manuscripts in progress.

A case in point for publishing is the experience of Cecilia Konchar Farr, editor of two anthologies on the series.[29] In summer 2019 Konchar Farr was contacted by an acquisitions editor at the Modern Language Association about editing a volume on the Harry Potter novels for the MLA's Approaches to Teaching World Literature series. By December 2021 Konchar Farr had

8

reviewed proposals, selected contributors, read first drafts of essays, and discussed the external review process with her editor. Their correspondence suggested to Konchar Farr that the project was moving along typically, and the editor's enthusiasm combined with the MLA's solicitation of the project led her to trust that publication would result.[30]

But an email from an MLA editor four months later brought a shock: the organization was withdrawing support for the project. On May 4, 2022, Konchar Farr notified her contributors that the anthology manuscript was no longer affiliated with the MLA. The organization's Office of Scholarly Communication declined to comment to this author on the decision, but Konchar Farr surmises from her correspondence with her editor that "they would rather not engage in HP studies because of the volatility of the issues around Rowling."[31] Konchar Farr never received a contract from the MLA during the thirty-three months that she worked on the manuscript; thus, the MLA's decision was not legally a breach. Nevertheless, she believes that whoever made the decision "made a mistake—both ethically and professionally,"[32] adding that it is the role of literary scholars "to help readers negotiate the complex relationship between authors and texts."[33]

The tempest resulting from Rowling's dogged defense of Maya Forstater and the author's subsequent public writing about gender identity has run a gamut from civil disagreement with Rowling to threats of violence directed at her. During her nine hours of interviews with Megan Phelps-Roper for the 2023 podcast *The Witch Trials of J. K. Rowling*, Rowling said that she and her family have been the target of threats, and major newspapers in the United Kingdom and the United States have reported the involvement of law enforcement in investigating some of them. Rowling told Roper that she has been doxxed, with her home address posted online, and that strangers have shown up outside her house. Authorities have found at least some of these threats "credible," Rowling said.[34] Listeners to Phelps-Roper's podcast can hear the more outrageous of these threats for themselves and should be cautioned that some are both vulgar and misogynistic, including calls for Rowling to be raped or sodomized. Regardless of one's position on Rowling's personal statements, I hope we all agree that encouraging rape crosses a line.

Rowling's fall from near-universal approval has also irrevocably changed the author's relationship not only with fans, readers, and scholars of the series but also with her works themselves, hastening the phenomenon that French cultural critic Roland Barthes has called "the death of the author."[35] And despite the pain experienced by devoted fans who have had to reconsider or end their own relationships with the texts, the separation of writer from writings is a good, even necessary, development if the Rowling scholarship that is already well established is to mature and diversify. Surely nothing better underscores the necessity of severing text and author than a firestorm caused by a writer whose public views seem to contradict her literary themes. In a 1927 Supreme Court ruling, Justice Louis D. Brandeis delineated what has come to be called "the counterspeech doctrine." In the case of objectionable speech, Brandeis wrote, "if there be time to expose through discussion, the falsehoods and fallacies, to avert the evil by the processes of education, the remedy to be applied is more speech, not enforced silence."[36] Whether the best cure for bad speech is always more speech—to paraphrase Brandeis—is debatable, but it definitely seems to be the case where literary criticism is concerned. Otherwise, considering that authors are human, fallible, and sometimes downright offensive, the extant body of literary scholarship could be gutted.

On the principle of the counterspeech doctrine, then, this volume affirms that analysis focusing on J. K. Rowling's works is still a valid response to the author's prodigious literary output. I believe I speak for every contributor in also asserting that every reader has the absolute right to determine what involvement—if any—with Rowling's texts is comfortable for them, her, or him. For an eloquent statement of reluctance to continue in Harry Potter studies by a nonbinary transgender scholar for whom the wizarding saga was the "way in" to literary scholarship, seek out Tolonda Henderson's short essay "A Coda: She-Who-Must-Not-Be-Named" in *Open at the Close*.

An important reason for continuing in the vein of Rowling scholarship has been expressed eloquently by Lorrie Kim, author of *Snape: The Definitive Analysis of Hogwarts's Mysterious Potions Master* (2022):

> Into the future, people studying the mass split between a readership and this author are going to want to know what we [who have engaged in Harry Potter studies] thought while going through it, what things we considered, what range of 'walk away' to 'stay and fight' we experienced . . . , what supplementary scholarship we brought in

to make a more honest intellectual environment. This is a difficult but energetic crossroads where we have an opportunity to define and guide [while helping to create] an environment that takes the entire picture into account.[37]

Just as the Harry Potter "Generation Hex" experience was unique to the young readers who inhaled and embodied the series' original release during their childhood and adolescence, the Era of the Transphobic Tweets is a unique experience for those of us who were not merely enchanted by the series' magic but deeply invested in building a body of scholarly work around it. Who can better account for the conflict between our "walk away" and "stay and fight" impulses than we can ourselves? Who can better explain the disconnect between the antiracist ideology of the Harry Potter series and the animosity its author expresses in some of those tweets?

If the harsh criticism of Rowling's extracanonical opinions and apparent personal beliefs seems relatively recent, it is important to note that appraisal of her work has never been universally positive and that a rift between the author and her fans had begun developing even before the incident involving Maya Forstater. (For more on the evolution of Harry Potter fan culture, see the essay by Rebecca Sutherland Borah that concludes this volume.) It is doubtful that any assessment of Rowling's literary achievement is more skeptical than Farah Mendlesohn's "Crowning the King: Harry Potter and the Construction of Authority" in the first *Ivory Tower* volume. Mendlesohn finds the series to be ideologically "rooted in a distinctively English liberalism that is marked as much by its inconsistencies and contradictions as by its insistence that it is not ideological but only 'fair.'"[38] Locating Harry Potter in the vein of an "Old Englishness" also characteristic of J. R. R. Tolkien and C. S. Lewis, Mendlesohn finds in the series a disappointing affirmation of the notion that "leadership is intrinsic, heroism is born in the blood, and self-interest simply the manifestation of those powers that ensure a return to order." This, Mendlesohn argues, is the authoritarian structure "encoded throughout the Potter texts."[39]

Mendlesohn may also be the first scholar to indict Rowling's presentation of the entire subplot involving the house-elves' welfare, a topic that has drawn enough analysis for an entire volume of essays.[40] For Mendlesohn,

Introduction

this subplot is "of all the structures of authority within the Potter books... the one I find most difficult to accept."[41] Considerations of how Rowling depicts Otherness in her fiction began long before the recent dissection of the author's personal views on gender identity; these analyses have expanded to include discussions concerning gender, gender identity, sexual orientation, race, socioeconomic status, and other limitations to access, including those that are physical (the latter especially in the Cormoran Strike series).

One of the most recent developments in recent Rowling scholarship is the emergency of entire volumes concerning identity and difference in her work. Two notable examples are Christopher E. Bell's *Wizards vs. Muggles: Essays on Identity and the Harry Potter Universe* (2018) and Sarah Park Dahlen and Ebony Elizabeth Thomas's *Harry Potter and the Other: Race, Justice, and Difference in the Wizarding World* (2022). Whole volumes devoted to resistance and subversion have also recently appeared, including Vandana Saxena's *The Subversive Harry Potter: Adolescent Rebellion and Containment in the J. K. Rowling Novels* (2012) and Beth Sutton-Ramspeck's *Harry Potter and Resistance* (2023). It is worth noting that Bell's book predates recent controversies stemming from Rowling's public stance on gender identity, while Saxena's predates the recent global rise of populism encapsulated in US politics by Donald Trump.

Clearly, then, attention to the quality and value of Rowling's worldbuilding and to the ideological context of her work is not merely a recent development or an aftereffect of a turning tide in the Rowling fandom. These veins may, however, be broadening and branching, and the work would be aborted now at great loss. One notable example of how serious conversation about Harry Potter may have expanded the nature of literary criticism itself is the proliferation of high-quality podcasts devoted to the explication of Rowling's work. The conclusion of the Harry Potter book and film releases dovetailed with the swell of podcasting. MuggleNet has been a leader in this regard, beginning with the *MuggleNet Academia* podcast hosted by John Granger and Keith Hawk, which ran to fifty-six episodes between 2012 and 2016, and extending through the currently running *Potterversity* podcast hosted by Katy McDaniel and Emily Strand. Both shows have included guests who are leading voices in Harry Potter scholarship, as well as professionals from other industries, such as film. While numerous podcasts featuring literary studies now exist, most have a focus based on nationality (British literature), subject (working-class literature), or genre (fantasy). For sheer numbers, Potter studies podcasts lead the way among shows origination from a single work or series. The addition of podcasting and blogging to the critical toolbox has diversified what literature scholars do and perhaps helped general readers to understand our work.

Much scholarship on Rowling's oeuvre has been accomplished in these first twenty-five years, but the Rowling canon is so rich as to be likely inexhaustible, and some of it remains unexplored, in analytical terms. Very little scholarship on *The Casual Vacancy* exists, except for a half dozen articles focused on topics related to the social sciences, such as suicide, self-mutilation, and child abuse. M. Katherine Grimes's essay in this volume is the first peer-reviewed attempt to place *Vacancy* in a literary context, locating it in the subgenre of social realism. Grimes asserts that the novel is in one respect the antithesis of the Harry Potter series, which centers on a strong hero, while *Vacancy*'s title "might refer to the empty chair where the hero should sit."[42]

Thought-provoking analysis of the Cormoran Strike novels and the Fantastic Beasts film series has been available to date mostly in the blogosphere and podcasting world, on sites such as MuggleNet (especially in Beatrice Groves's blog *Bathilda's Notebook*), on MuggleNet's *Potterversity* podcast (hosted by Katy McDaniel and Emily Strand), and in John Granger and Louise Freeman's posts on Granger's blog *Hogwarts Professor*. This anthology contains the first peer-reviewed article on the Cormoran Strike series, Granger's exploration of parallels between *Lethal White* and *Goblet of Fire* as the fourth ("pivotal") novels in their respective series and in the context of Granger's extensive work on ring composition theory in Rowling's opus.

Two essays by contributors address the Fantastic Beasts films. In "Policies of Suppression and Violence," Carsten Kullmann explores how the films present an allegorical context for recent political developments predicated on populist rhetoric such as Donald Trump's successful 2016 US presidential campaign and the voices propelling the United Kingdom's 2020 departure from the European Union. In its deep analysis of the power dynamic underlying the Wizarding world, Kullmann's essay is a worthy descendant of Farah Mendlesohn's foundational essay "Crowning

Introduction

the King: Harry Potter and the Construction of Authority" in the original *Ivory Tower* volume.

Beatrice Groves, a major voice in Harry Potter studies, takes a deep historical look at the snake-woman legend as background for the character of Nagini, primarily as she appears in *Fantastic Beasts*. Groves's essay contains thorough exploration of both the European folktale of Melusine and John Keats's narrative poem *Lamia* (1819) as sources for Rowling's snake woman, discussions that will likely send readers searching for these earlier texts as well as, perhaps, A. S. Byatt's Booker Prize–winning novel *Possession* (1991).[43] And in keeping with themes of both creatures or beasts and power-hungry politicians, my own essay examines monsters and monstrosity in Rowling's 2020 fairy tale *The Ickabog*, a story cut from the same cloth as Hans Christian Andersen's "The Emperor's New Clothes."

Three other works derived from the Harry Potter canon inspired essays in this volume. Kris Swank explores Rowling's use of alchemical symbolism in "The Fountain of Fair Fortune," one of the stories in *Tales of Beedle the Bard*. The folk-tale collection has been the subject of only a smattering of articles, mostly in children's literature journals and primarily concerning the metafictional aspect of the work. Emily Strand discusses parenting models in both the Harry Potter series and the play *The Cursed Child*, along with these models' religious and spiritual implications. And Katy McDaniel examines the "hidden histories" that Rowling has provided via the J. K. Rowling Archive at wizardingworld.com, and how these "histories" intersect with themes of secrecy and secret-keeping in the main series. Thus, just over a third of this volume (eight of twenty-one essays) addresses Rowling texts other than the Harry Potter series, most of which have received little scholarly attention.

With reams of paper now devoted to analysis of the Harry Potter series itself, some readers may wonder what is left to say about Rowling's best-known saga. As it turns out in the works of these contributors, the answer is "Plenty," even about some topics tackled by previous writers.

Some approaches to the series appear here in full discussion for the first time: the use of physical London as magical location (Madison McLeod), how the use of humor evolves and matures in the novels (Louise Freeman), the perspective gained by readers who view Harry through the eyes of animals or creatures around him (Catherine Olver), the biological concept of hybridity, especially the concept's usefulness as a form of resistance to oppressive systems (Molly Burt), and the series' lessons in the importance of critical reading (Leslie Bickford).

Some contributors have enriched or expanded veins of inquiry tapped by previous scholars. Three of these concern the Harry Potter series' debt to classical and classic texts. Beginning with the first Ivory Tower volume in 2002, scholars such as Mary Pharr and Jann Lacoss have eagerly pointed to the influence of epic and folk literatures. But in "Harry Potter and the Half-Blood Trojan Prince," Mitchell Parks, a classics scholar, is the first to provide a full tour of the series' connections with the *Aeneid*. Laurie Beckoff, a medievalist, expands the small body of existing scholarship on Rowling's debt to Arthurian legend in an essay explaining how the series presents medievalism's unique blend of wizardry and violence. And Heather Murray embellishes the thread of Shakespeare-Rowling connections explored more generally by Beatrice Groves in a text that should be mandatory for every serious Potter scholar, *Literary Allusion in Harry Potter* (2017). Murray's particular contribution assesses similarities between Hogwarts couples, especially Ron and Hermione, and those in Shakespeare's romances.

The sport of Quidditch has drawn considerable scholarly attention, and since at least 2015 there has been a Quidditch entry in the *Oxford Companion to Children's Literature*. The foundational contribution for understanding how the wizarding sport symbolically reflects the series' spiritual themes is Emily Strand's "The Second War Was Won on the Quidditch Pitch at Hogwarts" in *Harry Potter for Nerds II* (2015). In "What Happens to the Snitch Doesn't Stay on the Pitch" in this volume, Caitlin Harper argues that Quidditch serves also as a metaphor for the narrative structure of the series, including its chiastic aspect, to such an extent that an astute reader could use the series' Quidditch matches to predict the progress of the plot.

Two of the most popular topics in extant Harry Potter scholarship also get new looks. In "Why S.P.E.W. Was Doomed to Fail: Exploring Systemic Inequity through Rowling's Racialized House-Elves," Alyssa Lowery provides an admonition against viewing the house-elves subplot in overly racialized terms. Lowery cautions that, in her campaign for house-elf liberation, Hermione "is employing antiracist strategies to approach

Introduction

an issue that is not in fact racial." Drawing on Ibram X. Kendi, Lowery encourages a more productive reading.

And one of the most popular topics of discussion in extant Harry Potter scholarship, magic itself, gets fresh treatment from Elizabeth Baird Hardy and Patrick McCauley. Hardy explores wizard physics in "Deceptive Exteriors and Outsize Interiors in the Wizarding World" to explain how some wizards manipulate space and time via the use of portkeys, Time-Turners, and containers such as Hermione's handbag and Newt Scamander's suitcase. McCauley delves into Rowling's employment of magic as a narrative strategy. An example is the characterization of Molly Weasley that is achieved when her attempts to dismiss the boggart in the Black family home turn it into various Weasley family members but also into Harry. McCauley discusses elements of magic present in the use of narrative voice as well.

This volume concludes, as did *The Ivory Tower and Harry Potter*, with an essay by Rebecca Sutherland Borah on fan culture. Here, Borah revisits and expands upon her earlier work, drawing on new primary research as well as the work of popular culture scholar Henry Jenkins to provide insight about Harry Potter fandom and how fan culture itself, especially online fandom, has changed since the "birth" of the Boy Who Lived. Borah's conclusion, in a nutshell, is that "growing pains can be messy."[44]

It is interesting to imagine how and where Harry Potter fandom will evolve next and how Rowling's work will be regarded at the end of the next twenty-five years, when the series enjoys its golden anniversary, by which time Rowling will be eighty-one years old. Agatha Christie, still the bestselling novelist of all time, published five novels after turning eighty-one, the last of which, *Sleeping Murder*, appeared nine months after the author's death.[45] One thing is clear: Rowling's imagination is a fount that appears as unlikely as Christie's to run dry. We who were involved in the preparation of this volume hope to be around to assess the second quarter century of her career and its popular and critical reception.

NOTES

1. Gunelius, *Harry Potter*, 6; "500 Million Harry Potter Books."
2. Whited, *Ivory Tower and Harry Potter*, 2.
3. Watson, "Potter Unit Sales."

4. Roback and Bean, "Adding Up the Numbers."
5. Wallin, "20 Richest Authors."
6. Gierzynski, *Millennials*, 6.
7. Mutz, "Deathly Donald," 723.
8. Mutz, 723.
9. On April 19, 1989, Trisha Meili was jogging in Central Park when she was brutally assaulted and raped. Five black and Latino boys ages fourteen to sixteen who were also in the park that night were arrested by New York City law enforcement authorities. Although DNA evidence from semen found at the location of the attack did not match any of the boys, they were convicted and sentenced to six to thirteen years in prison. Donald Trump, at the time a New York City real estate mogul, reportedly paid $85,000 for four full-page advertisements advocating the execution of the five boys. In 2002 Matias Reyes, then serving a sentence for murder and rape, told authorities he was responsible for the assault on Meili and had acted alone. The Netflix film *When They See Us* is the best-known account of the Central Park Five's ordeal. BBC, "Central Park Five."
10. Vezzali et al., "Greatest Magic."
11. Nexon, "Terror."
12. Gibbs, "Person of the Year 2007."
13. Henderson, "18% of Americans."
14. Brown, "Scraping the Bottom," 2, 7.
15. Burton, "Millennials' Foundational Text."
16. Rowling (@jk_rowling), "Dress however you please. Call yourself whatever you like. Sleep with any consenting adult who'll have you. Live your best life in peace and security. But force women out of their jobs for stating that sex is real?" Twitter, December 19, 2019, 7:57 a.m., https://twitter.com/jk_rowling/status/1207646162813100033.
17. Rowling.
18. J. K. Rowling (@jk_rowling), " 'People who menstruate.' I'm sure there used to be a word for those people. Someone help me out. Wumben? Wimpund? Woomud?" Twitter, June 6, 2020, https://twitter.com/jk_rowling/status/1269382518362509313.
19. In September 2020, in a statement written by Women and Equalities minister Liz Truss, the government announced that medical diagnosis would continue to be required to change gender on identity documents, but the cost of the necessary certificate would be lowered significantly. Murphy and Brooks, "UK Government."
20. Rowling, "J. K. Rowling Writes."
21. "JK Rowling Backs Protest over Scottish Gender Bill," *BBC News*, October 6, 2022, https://www.bbc.com/news/uk-scotland-scotland-politics-63162533.
22. For an explanation of how the term *TERF* originated and how its use has evolved, see Flaherty, " 'TERF' War." Those who labeled Rowling as a TERF include both those who read her lengthy "J. K. Rowling Writes" blog post and those who read *about* the post on social media but did not actually read it.
23. Henderson, "She-Who-Must-Not-Be-Named," 224.
24. Henderson, 225.
25. Rowling, "J. K. Rowling Writes."

26. Quoted in Pamela Paul, "In Defense of J. K. Rowling," *New York Times*, February 16, 2023.

27. Dominic Casciani, "Analysis," *BBC News*, June 10, 2021, www.bbc.com/news/uk-57426579.

28. Forstater, "Joss Stone, Maya Forstater."

29. Cecilia Koncharr Farr's books on the Harry Potter series are *A Wizard of Their Age: Critical Essays from the Harry Potter Generation* (2015) and *Open at the Close: Literary Essays on Harry Potter* (2022). She is also the author or editor of six or seven other books.

30. Cecilia Konchar Farr, email to author, April 22, 2022.

31. Konchar Farr, email to author, May 4, 2022.

32. Konchar Farr.

33. Konchar Farr, email to author, July 5, 2022.

34. Paul, "In Defense."

35. The phrase "The death of the author" is derived from Barthes' 1967 essay by the same name.

36. Quoted in Hudson, "Counterspeech Doctrine." Justice Brandeis's words were in the US Supreme Court decision *Whitney v. California* (1927).

37. Lorrie Kim, comment on Lana Whited, "The past two weekends (LeakyCon and CHC conference) were a balm to me on that front," Facebook, October 24, 2022, 8:40 a.m., https://www.facebook.com/lana.whited.

38. Mendlesohn, "Crowning the King," 159.

39. Mendlesohn, 166, 161.

40. Analysis of the house-elves subplot has become a rich vein in Harry Potter scholarship and includes essays by the following authors (all listed in the bibliography): Brycchan Carey, Megan Farnel, Haley Herfurth and Clair McLafferty, Jackie C. Horne, Rivka Temima Kellner, Hannah Lamb, Alyssa Lowery (in this volume), Katy McDaniel, Susan Peppers-Bates and Joshua Rust, Christine Schott, and Jasmine Wade.

41. Mendlesohn, "Crowning the King," 178.

42. See Katherine Grimes, "Hopelessness and Hope in *The Casual Vacancy*," chapter 15 of this volume.

43. The tale of Melusine also figures prominently in A. S. Byatt's 1990 novel *Possession*.

44. See Rebecca Sutherland Borah, " 'Accio Jo!': Woke Wizards and Generational Potter Fandom," chapter 21 of this volume.

45. "Agatha Christie Books: The Complete List," *Biblio Lifestyle*, accessed August 21, 2023. https://bibliolifestyle.com/agatha-christie-books/.

SECTION I

MAGICAL DIRECTIONS AND MISDIRECTIONS

1. Muggle Worthy

Deceptive Exteriors and Outsized Interiors in the Wizarding World

Elizabeth Baird Hardy

J. K. ROWLING'S WIZARDING world has a marvelous propensity to defy the laws of time and space. From Time-Turners allowing people to be in two places at once to entire communities hidden from Muggle eyes, exceptions to the laws of physics abound. Throughout the Hogwarts and Fantastic Beasts adventures, settings and objects are frequently more than they seem. Fabulous portkeys, capable of instant transportation, look like rubbish, and magical real estate hides behind run-down shop windows and ordinary railroad station barriers. The combination of deceptively ordinary exteriors and vast, space-defying interiors appears throughout the texts of the Wizarding world, serving practical purposes and delivering powerful meaning with mythic and literary connections.

A fundamental lesson learned by Hogwarts students is missing from the standard curriculum: Do not trust architecture. Even if they fail to learn this lesson from riding to school on a train whose platform is reached only by walking into a barrier, Hogwarts students should find the castle itself an effective object lesson in disregarding face value. Stairways move, paintings are doorways, and the ceiling mimics the sky. While first-year Harry is fascinated, and sometimes stymied, by these structural oddities, they come as no shock to students from wizarding families. The Muggle-born students, with the notable exception of Hermione Granger, who has read *Hogwarts: A History*, are the only ones surprised by the castle's deceptions. Wizarding children accept that their surroundings are more than what they seem. Some, like the Weasley twins and their mischief-making predecessors, the Marauders, have even learned to manipulate the school's physical flexibility to their advantage. The Marauders' Map is an impressive artifact, and its creation springs from a wizard's acceptance of deceptive structure, allowing Peter Pettigrew, James Potter, Remus Lupin, and Sirius Black, all from wizarding families, to document and monitor the illogical space of the castle and grounds.

1. Muggle Worthy

Some buildings exist in an illusory space. Sirius Black's childhood home is just one of these locations. Wizards use a variety of methods to cloak homes and businesses, but 12 Grimmauld Place demonstrates that wizard home interiors can be out of all proportion to their exteriors. When anyone perceives the location of the Order of the Phoenix's secret headquarters, the house materializes: "A battered door emerged out of nowhere between numbers eleven and thirteen, followed swiftly by dirty walls and grimy windows. It was as though an extra house had inflated, pushing those on either side out of its way.... Apparently the Muggles inside hadn't even felt anything."[1] The House of Black, with its many floors, rooms, and furnishings, not only exists in a space far too small to logically accommodate it but also "inflates," rather than merely being hidden like Platform Nine and Three-Quarters. Dumbledore states that the Order has added protections, such as making the house Unplottable, but Sirius's description of his late father's extensive security measures implies that the house could mask its true size well before becoming the epicenter of the Resistance.[2]

Even when buildings don't visibly expand, they frequently boast interiors that exceed their exterior size. One of Harry's first encounters with the Wizarding world teaches him that outer and inner space are not always connected. Upon his first visit to Diagon Alley through the Leaky Cauldron (which passing Muggles also appear not to see), Harry notes the pub's size and unremarkable appearance: "tiny," "grubby-looking," "dark," and "shabby."[3] The emphasis on size continues as Hagrid takes Harry to a "small, walled courtyard" and creates a "small hole"[4] by tapping the correct brick. Once the opening to Diagon Alley appears, emphasis shifts from small to large, with an archway large enough for the immense Hagrid, revealing a street so big and twisted that it stretches "out of sight." The countless shops and the bulk of Gringotts Bank emphasize the vast space reached via a tiny pub and a small hole. Diagon Alley has so many tenants that no space is available for St. Mungo's Hospital for Magical Maladies and Injuries, "and we couldn't have it underground like the Ministry—unhealthy."[5] The hospital is large, but masks its true nature with bad marketing rather than deceptive size. The outdated, shabby exterior and unappealing window displays of Purge and Dowse Ltd. conceal a sophisticated medical facility. Muggles see the exterior, whose dreariness implies a magical power to induce disregard: "Not one of them seemed to have a glance to spare for window displays as ugly as Purge and Dowse Ltd.'s, nor did any of them seem to have noticed that six people had just melted into thin air in front of them."[6] Ironically, despite the external deception, the inner space of St. Mungo's retains a sort of badly managed department store air, with a bored receptionist waving patients and visitors toward the sign that lists maladies by floors; she might be directing traffic to Housewares or Ladies' Lingerie rather than Spell Damage.[7]

The Ministry of Magic's entrances are downplayed with a similar strategy, employing subtle references to government bloat and bureaucracy. Hidden underground, the Ministry can be reached via Apparition or the Floo Network, but the visitors' entrance is a vandalized phone booth that Harry immediately assumes must be out of order, suggesting the long waits familiar to anyone who has telephoned the government. The new security measures under Pius Thicknesse require Ministry staff to enter via pay toilets, certainly alluding to the associations of government operations with both money and excrement.

A Ministry of Magic employee supplies one of the series' most intriguing spaces with an interior disproportionate to its exterior. Perkins, who shares Mr. Weasley's pitiful excuse for an office, gets little mention, but his tent, loaned and then given to Arthur Weasley, becomes a crucial player. First appearing in *The Goblet of Fire*, the tent's spacious interior surprises Harry, but Ron "seemed completely unimpressed by its extraordinary inner proportions."[8] The trio later spends months in the tent, which Hermione has wisely packed. While its size and amenities certainly defy its external appearance, the tent's shabbiness and pervasive cat smell still reflect the character of its outer form.

Deceptive size and function are at play in all these spaces, but one of the most remarkable spaces in the Wizarding world, the Room of Requirement, goes a step further by also shifting its contents depending on the visitor. Entering St. Mungo's, one always finds the same hospital; the Ministry's interior is altered only by administrative changes; Harry knows the tent immediately by its smell; and as long as prospective shoppers use Floo powder cautiously, they always reach Diagon Alley and Gringotts. By contrast, the Room of Requirement conceals its existence from the uninitiated and also alters both its size and its purpose, depending on the user's needs. While desperate students may find a vast warehouse to store illicit goods or damaged items, a headmaster in need of a restroom may find only chamber pots. Fred Weasley reminds his twin George that it is "just a broom closet" when they need to hide from Mr. Filch.[9] The room shrinks or expands, adding space and resources as the user requires. These characteristics are certainly practical, providing practice space for Dumbledore's Army or a haven for drunk Winky to sleep off a hard night of butterbeer consumption, but the room's capabilities hint at far more than a simple deus ex machina or a bathroom joke. Other tricky exteriors hide surprising interiors, but the room's interior is an uncharted and fluid space that only takes form as it is needed.

The Room of Requirement can also detect its potential visitors' needs. Harry concentrates on what he needs the room to become as he paces by its location three times, yet it can also detect the user's unexpressed primal needs, from a full bladder to annoyance with chatter during defense practice: "I need a whistle," Harry thinks, and one appears.[10] Thus the room is malleable, like a boggart, which, as Professor Lupin explains, does not assume a form when it is alone, "but when I let him out, he will become whatever each of us most fears."[11]

The room's ability to detect and meet needs also parallels the function of the Mirror of Erised. The mirror is not exactly a storage space but nonetheless serves as a magical container for hiding the Sorcerer's Stone from the unworthy. However, it differs from the Room of Requirement in that its primary role is much more visual and psychological than spatial. On first encounter, Harry immediately assumes that the people he sees are contained within the mirror. Although he realizes that his family members are only reflections, he doesn't understand how the mirror really operates until he encourages Ron to use it. Ron's desire to outshine his stellar brothers is very different from Harry's hunger to be part of a loving family, so their visions in the mirror differ, attuned to their hearts' desires. Likewise, the Room of Requirement detects and meets the user's needs, even when not consciously expressed.

The Room of Requirement is also morally neutral, serving anyone in need, so that it assists Neville and his merry band as well as a dark wizard hiding a Horcrux and a terrified probationary Death Eater trying to assassinate the headmaster. One wonders if the lost diadem of Ravenclaw, bearing a torn fragment of Voldemort's soul, has some influence on the room. That may explain the way that Harry, himself a Horcrux, is able to connect with the space, particularly when he is "up to no good." While the diadem may not always be physically present in the room, it is there for Harry, whether he is inadvertently using the room to mark the hiding place of his troublesome potions book or seeking to destroy a Horcrux and save the Wizarding world. Harry's knack for getting into trouble is one reason he connects well with the room, when Dumbledore does not, inviting speculation about who else knows of its existence. While the room has aided Dumbledore when he needed a bathroom, Harry assumes the headmaster is not familiar with its true nature: "Of course, Dumbledore and Flitwick, those model pupils, had never set foot in that particular place, but he, Harry, had strayed off the beaten path in his time at school."[12] It seems likely that another Hogwarts alumnus could have used the room during his own academic career. Newt Scamander may once have had cause to hide something, as evidenced by the room's dragon eggshells and five-legged caged skeleton. Perhaps the room even inspired Newt to create his own home, a place that includes a vast substructure accommodating each of the creatures in his care—even a sizable lake for the kelpie—in the Fantastic Beasts series. More impressive than his home rehabilitation space, though, is the portable version, his iconic case, one of many small portable objects concealing large spaces.

The Wizarding world has any number of portable items whose interior spaces exceed their exterior parameters. Hagrid's seventeenth-birthday present to Harry is a rare pouch made of mokeskin: "Hide anythin' in there an' no one but the owner can get it out."[13] Although it is a secure and useful wallet, it does not seem to have an unusually large interior, as Harry notes when he adds his damaged wand: "The pouch was now too full of broken and useless objects to take any more."[14] Even items that may not be specifically magical, such as Hagrid's pockets and Harry's school trunk, seem to be capable of containing an impressive amount, disproportionate to their sizes.

None of these slightly expanded containers can compete with the remarkable holding power of Hermione's beaded bag. The tiny purse is literally a lifesaver in *Deathly Hallows*, as it transports all the supplies required in the Horcrux hunt: from the tiny bottle of dittany with which Hermione treats Ron after he is splinched to the massive painting of Phineas Nigellus

1. Muggle Worthy

Black, as well as a small library of books, several months' worth of clothes, and the fully furnished tent. The bag first appears as a mere accessory, part of Hermione's ensemble for Bill and Fleur's wedding. Only when the trio goes on the lam is it clear that the bag has been altered with an Undetectable Extension Charm. In order to heft all the supplies while Apparating all over the British Isles, Hermione has also presumably used a spell similar to one Harry once considered. When he ponders escaping on his broom after accidentally inflating Aunt Marge, he plans a spell "to make [his trunk] feather-light."[15] Ironically, Hermione's warehouse of supplies includes the tent with its disproportionately spacious interior, creating a "nesting doll" effect within the innocuous-looking purse. Besides providing resources for the trio's extended exile, the handbag also reminds readers of Hermione's resourcefulness and preparedness. She has "had the essentials packed for days" before the wedding, carefully selecting books and supplies, and adding Harry's rucksack the morning before, as she "just had a feeling."[16] In addition, by choosing the bag that she will carry to the wedding, Hermione shows an uncanny ability to think like her adversaries; she rightly guesses they will choose to attack at a moment of celebration. Hermione also uses the cultural expectations that she knows from both her childhood in the Muggle world and her education in the magical one to conceal her resources from prying eyes: the exquisitely feminine bag is unlikely to draw attention.

By trading on the fact that few would suspect something tiny and decorative to be so remarkably useful, Hermione is also making a statement about herself. Like the bag, she is far more complex than her bushy hair and bad posture indicate. Within, she is a vast repository of knowledge and resources, largely responsible for Harry's survival and success. Similar to the library she totes with her, Hermione provides the knowledge necessary to solve riddles, plan magical heists, and master complex spells and potions. Appearances are also deceiving where Hermione herself is concerned, so her brilliant pocketbook is both practical and metaphorical.

Perhaps the only other bag in the Wizarding world with as much hidden potential as Hermione's beaded bag is Newt Scamander's battered traveling case, using innocent "Muggle-worthy" contents to conceal its true nature as the portable version of his home, a portal into his workspace. As a man who fears a desk job above all else, Newt has crafted a working environment distinct from any mundane office. In addition to the shop/garage where he can create potions, repair tools, and prepare food for his charges, the case encompasses a multi-ecosystem outdoor habitat to accommodate creatures from every corner of the magical world. Newt can, like Hermione, reach into the case for whatever he seeks, usually one of his creatures, or push one inside when necessary. However, unlike Hermione, he can enter his case, even bringing guests. Newt's case resembles the entrance to a magical location such as Diagon Alley or Platform Nine and Three-Quarters, serving as a portal to an entirely different locale with its own weather, geography, and, of course, inhabitants.

These inhabitants include the Niffler, one of Newt's creatures without a pet name, unlike Picket the Bowtruckle, Dougal the Demiguise, or Frank the Thunderbird. It is simply "the Niffler," but it is also distinct as a living being with characteristics similar to the case and Hermione's purse. Upon stuffing shiny objects into its pouch, the animal appears to expand, struggling with the weight of these items. Because the Niffler is a live creature with its own free will, not simply a bag or a box that can be carted, it is an unreliable repository, but one invaluable in Newt's efforts to stymie Grindelwald's plans for world dominion. Its capacious pouch also makes Newt's case or his home into another of those "nesting" objects, like Hermione's bag when it contains the tent. Because the Niffler also becomes a parent, the pocketed baby Nifflers create yet another layer of outsize internal spaces in the multidimensional layers of these objects. By its nature, then, the Niffler can be both concealer and concealed; it can be carried about in the case or can store the case, with its vast internal contents, within its pouch.[17] Like Hermione's bag, Newt's case reflects its owner, connecting to misperceptions about the rumpled yet brilliant magizoologist who is far more capable than he seems.

The case is also "Muggle Worthy"; for the nonmagical viewer, it reveals normal luggage contents, with the most magical visible item being Newt's Hufflepuff scarf. In this regard, it resembles the trunk of a certain auror who is also not always what he seems. When Mad-Eye Moody comes to teach at Hogwarts, it is in fact Barty Crouch Jr. wearing the distinctive magical eye and artificial leg, while the real Alastor Moody is imprisoned but kept alive in a traveling case so that his hair can be regularly used for his captor's Polyjuice Potion. The trunk, which Harry first notices in Moody's office before the first Triwizard Tournament task, has seven keyholes. After the third task, Dumbledore subdues the false Moody and opens each lock in succession. With the turn of the first key, the trunk opens to reveal books. Dumbledore closes it, turns the second key, and opens it again, revealing parchment, quills, sneakoscopes, and an Invisibility Cloak. With each key, the trunk produces different contents until Dumbledore turns the seventh key to reveal the prison of the actual Moody, a pit ten feet deep and far exceeding the trunk's external parameters. In addition to explaining Mad-Eye Moody's location, the seven-layered trunk serves as a reminder of the way in which the seven Hogwarts adventures themselves function, revealing new wonders to sharp-eyed readers upon each reading.

While certainly an original, Rowling is also a master at weaving in threads from the vast compost pile of myths, images, and references she has collected. Her masterful use of reimagined familiar themes and elements is just one of the keys to the success of the Hogwarts saga. The remarkable luggage her characters use often alludes to other fantastic containers in literature and lore. One of the more recent of these is the Luggage in Terry Pratchett's Discworld novels. Several of the dozens of Discworld novels predate the publication of *Harry Potter and the Philosopher's Stone*, but the similarity between the Luggage and the containers used by Rowling's characters is not an issue of influence so much as of shared mythic themes that each author employs differently. Originally owned by uber-tourist Twoflower and introduced in 1983's *The Colour of Magic*, the Luggage later becomes devoted to the endearingly cowardly failed "wizzard" Rincewind and also operates independently. Made of sapient pearwood, the intensely loyal and virtually indestructible Luggage resembles a regular traveling trunk but sometimes sprouts little legs to walk. Although it devours all manner of creatures that threaten its owners, it also transports items just like ordinary luggage and always has room for more. Like Hermione's bag and Newt's case, it proves useful for the traveling magical practitioner, but like the trunk co-opted by the false Moody, the Luggage is also a weapon. Barty Crouch Jr. uses the trunk to imprison the true Moody, and the Luggage frequently breaks down doors and fights enemies for its owners. Its useful interior is also flexible; like Mad-Eye Mooney's trunk and Newt's case, it does not always reveal the same contents when it opens.[18]

Newt's case, Moody's trunk, Hermione's handbag, and the Luggage all represent the traditional trope of magical tools that have both practical purposes and symbolic power. Certainly, Hermione's bag is not a novel concept to most readers, particularly those who recall Mary Poppins reaching into her carpetbag to withdraw items larger than the bag itself. Readers familiar with Lloyd Alexander's Prydain series likely remember Gurgi's magic wallet that constantly provides "crunchings and munchings" without emptying. As far back as ancient mythology, bags with remarkable holding capacity have been used by mythic and supernatural characters: to transport dangerous items, such as the head of the Medusa; to collect resources and confine one's adversaries, such as the bag used by Welsh hero Pwyll in the Mabinogion; or to contain items for distribution, such as one used by a jolly old elf to carry a vast array of gifts every year on Christmas Eve.[19] Magical containers appear everywhere from fantastic literature to gaming, with magic bags of holding, handy haversacks, and other containers allowing characters and players access to needed materials, or simply providing comic possibilities in worlds not limited by the laws of physics.

Some Wizarding-world items appear to bridge the functions of deceptive architecture and useful luggage, defying both space and time. Such objects are in some ways gateways rather than mere containers. Examples include Platform Nine and Three-Quarters, Diagon Alley, the Pensieve, and, to a lesser degree, Tom Riddle's diary. While they may appear to be portable containers like Newt's case, the Pensieve and diary are actually entry points to both spaces and times, revealing memories. Harry and Dumbledore can enter the Pensieve much as Newt enters his case, but the destination changes depending on the deposited memories. Riddle's diary is limited, taking Harry to the specific dates on the calendar pages, and the control of the soul fragment that makes the diary a Horcrux means that Harry only sees what Riddle wants him to see; in *Chamber of Secrets*, that is the implication of Hagrid fifty years previously when the Chamber of Secrets was opened. While the visitor can move within them, the memories are only artifacts; they cannot be altered or expanded, and once the memory has reached its end, the viewer is wrenched back into the present time and the place of entry. The Pensieve and diary only give the illusion of containing large areas within them.

1. Muggle Worthy

A number of tools can move wizards rapidly from one place to another and allow them to stay there, but no such object is as thought-provoking or fraught with literary significance as the Vanishing Cabinet. Portkeys must be activated, but they are portable, and Floo powder converts otherwise ordinary fires into temporary modes of transportation. Yet the Vanishing Cabinet is a space one can enter for travel to the partner cabinet, wherever that might be. Long before its name and function are known, the Vanishing Cabinet (more properly, cabinets, as they are twins, like Fred and George) makes two brief appearances in *The Chamber of Secrets*: when Harry hides from the Malfoys in Borgin and Burkes and later when Nearly Headless Nick convinces Peeves to smash the Hogwarts cabinet, distracting Filch so that Harry can escape from his office. Like those who use it in its broken condition, the damaged Vanishing Cabinet crops up periodically, sometimes in odd places. In *Order of the Phoenix*, Fred and George force Montague, part of Professor Umbridge's Inquisitorial Squad, into the cabinet, which transports him into a toilet on the fourth floor. More than another bathroom joke, Slytherin Montague's unpleasant journey both emphasizes the cabinet's malfunction and echoes the time Peeves broke it, in a book whose greatest mystery, Salazar Slytherin's Chamber of Secrets, is reached through a bathroom. The real shining moment for the Vanishing Cabinet, however, comes in *The Half-Blood Prince* when, once again, the undamaged half of the pair appears in Borgin and Burkes, and the damaged one, eventually repaired by Draco Malfoy, plays a crucial role in the death of Albus Dumbledore when Draco uses it to bring Death Eaters into the school. A year later, it is presumably destroyed in the Fiendfyre that scours the Room of Requirement.[20] Of course the cabinet is a brilliant plot device, planted, like so many of Rowling's best tricks, early in the series, only to bloom in a later book.

The cabinet is more than a tool to advance the plot. It is an allusion to another item whose literary influences resonate throughout Harry's and Newt's adventures. Surely no reader who has ever journeyed to Narnia has passed a large cabinet without thoughts of climbing inside it, but hopefully those readers remember the wise observations of Lucy Pevensie, who notes what a foolish thing it is to shut oneself up in a wardrobe. C. S. Lewis's heroine of *The Lion, the Witch and the Wardrobe* enters a piece of furniture more benign than the Vanishing Cabinet, only to find a snowy, enchanted country beyond the fur coats. The wardrobe is in the house of a professor, Digory Kirke, both of whose names are used in the Hogwarts saga: Digory, with an extra *g*, becomes the ill-fated Cedric Diggory of *The Goblet of Fire*, while Andrew Kirke is one of the replacement Beaters brought in when Fred and George are banned from Quidditch in *Order of the Phoenix*. Digory Kirke's rotten Uncle Andrew, an inept magician, indirectly instigates the comings and goings to Narnia before loaning his name to a Quidditch player. The other Beater, Jack Sloper, shares a first name with Narnia's creator, as Lewis always went by "Jack."[21] Although the wardrobe does not always reveal the entrance to Narnia, when it does, the Pevensies realize that "this whole country is in the wardrobe,"[22] just as Newt's entire portable wildlife preserve is in his traveling case, or all of Diagon Alley is in the back of the Leaky Cauldron. Although the older Pevensies are originally puzzled by the wardrobe, Professor Kirke, without revealing his own Narnian history, challenges their assertion that "if things are real, they are there all the time,"[23] thus affirming the possibility of a space like the Room of Requirement, where things are both real and not there all the time. The Diadem of Ravenclaw is a very real object, doing its job of keeping Voldemort alive, whether or not it is visible, so in a sense it is always "in" the room, only manifesting when someone needs a hiding place for a questionable item. In like fashion, the four Pevensies only find the wardrobe willing to connect to Narnia when they, too, seek a hiding place.

In the last installment of the Narniad, the concept of an "inside bigger than its outside" takes on even more power with the stable through which the Narnians enter Aslan's Country, and are urged to go "further up and further in": "The Stable seen from within and the Stable seen from without are two different places."[24] Gateways, places leading from one space, or world, to another, are common in the Chronicles of Narnia. The "door in the air" Aslan makes to relocate the Telmarines and to send home the Pevensies at the end of *Prince Caspian* creates an effect similar to the one Montague experiences when he is shut up in the Vanishing Cabinet and can hear sounds from Hogwarts or from Borgin and Burkes. The Pevensies walk through the door, one branch laid across two uprights, and briefly glimpse the Telmarines' island destination, then their own railway station, which they have only just left. The Wood between the Worlds in *The Magician's Nephew*, whose many pools are gateways to other worlds, is

1. Muggle Worthy

another in-between place. Those who travel through there with the aid of magic rings are briefly in a transitional zone that, more than anything else, defines all the unreliable space and objects of the Wizarding world.

These reality-bending places and objects are all liminal spaces, existing between times and locations, and it should not be surprising that Rowling's Wizarding world contains so many of them. Harry and Newt are, after all, both liminal figures. Each straddles the Muggle and magical worlds, operating with more or less ease in both, but each also stands astride other worlds. Newt, often more at home with creatures than with people, is a bridge between the human and animal worlds, striving to bring understanding. He sees creatures and humans as equally valuable. Leta Lestrange asserts that he has never "met a monster he couldn't love," and thus he is not repulsed by her as are their fellow Hogwarts students. He compliments Tina Goldstein by comparing her eyes to a salamander's, flattering her in a way that makes sense to him, and which she recognizes as high praise.

Harry, too, has a foot in two worlds, but rather than standing in the liminal realm between animals and humans, he exists in the space between life and death. In each book, Harry undergoes symbolic or actual death and resurrection, and although he only realizes it upon accessing Snape's memories, Harry is himself a Horcrux, carrying a fragment of Voldemort's soul from the Dark Lord's attempted murder of "the chosen one." Although his confrontation with Voldemort in the Forbidden Forest releases him from his role as a Horcrux, Harry remains a man who has known both life and death, possessor of all the Deathly Hallows and heir of Ignotus Peverell, who, alone among his brothers, succeeded in both evading and accepting death.

These liminal figures, the objects they own, and the places they visit remind us, throughout the Hogwarts and Fantastic Beasts scripts and films, that very little of the Wizarding world lacks meaning. The unreliability of appearances is not a stage trick for comic effect; it is the core of the story. While Rowling draws upon literary and mythic themes, some employed by other texts, she is clearly using the environment and props of her narrative to convey a very specific meaning. By setting Harry's story in a world of spaces whose outsize interiors completely belie their external dimensions and by littering that world with a vast array of containers with paradoxical inside and outside parameters, Rowling demonstrates one of the central pillars of Harry's journey: external appearances can be deceiving. The scary half-giant is a maternal dragon lover, the pink-clad administrator with cutesy cat plates is a sadistic monster, and the sneering, mean-spirited teacher is the bravest and most loving of people. That theme is one that readers struggle to accept alongside Harry, who, despite his many gifts, can be fooled by appearances. Yet it is a theme he ultimately embraces and embodies by naming his son after the man he once judged as his worst enemy.

It is essential that so many elements of the saga are bigger on the inside than they are on the outside because, although events of the Wizarding world happen inside Harry's head, or inside a trunk, or inside a very small beaded bag, Professor Dumbledore might well ask, Why on earth should that mean that they are not real? Like all of the important stories, the ones that stay with readers, these stories convey insights that are very real indeed, no matter the size of the boxes that contain them. By embracing these stories, by allowing them to take place inside their own heads, readers thus become part of this same magical process. Once readers have visited these places with their outsize interiors and have encountered these objects with their extraordinary carrying capacity, these places and items are then carried inside their minds. Those vast spaces and objects can reside comfortably within the confines of an individual person, a reader. As readers, we ourselves are magical containers, somehow carrying with us on our own journeys the vast and extraordinary worlds J. K. Rowling has created and invited us to share.

NOTES

1. Rowling, *Order of the Phoenix*, 59. All Harry Potter book citations in this essay refer to the original Scholastic (US) editions.

2. There is a slight discrepancy about who made the House of Black Unplottable. While Sirius says Unplottability was one of the security measures put in place by his father, before the addition of Dumbledore's extra security measures, Dumbledore, in explaining Harry's inheritance, indicates that this was an addition by the Order of the Phoenix: "We do not know whether the enchantments we ourselves have placed upon it, for example, making it Unplottable, will hold now that ownership has passed from Sirius's hands." Rowling, *Half-Blood Prince*, 50. It is possible that the original spell placed by Orion Black was altered or improved by Dumbledore and the Order.

3. Rowling, *Sorcerer's Stone*, 68.
4. Rowling, 70–71.
5. Rowling, *Order of the Phoenix*, 482.
6. Rowling, 484.

1. Muggle Worthy

7. Mad-Eye Moody explains that the hospital's placement is, in part, to allow "sick wizards [to] come and go and just blend in with the crowd" (*Order of the Phoenix*, 482), but it seems unlikely that most of the patients visiting St. Mungo's would be able to blend in with a Muggle crowd. Harry sees a child with wings, a wizard whose shoes make him dance in place as he tries to get them off his feet, and patients "sporting gruesome disfigurements such as elephant trunks or extra hands sticking out of their chests" (484). It seems probable that these patients would be brought into the hospital some other way than via the display window entrance, where they would doubtless draw the attention of those unseeing Muggles walking past the department store facade.

8. Rowling, *Goblet of Fire*, 81.
9. Rowling, *Order of the Phoenix*, 391.
10. Rowling, 394.
11. Rowling, *Prisoner of Azkaban*, 135.
12. Rowling, *Deathly Hallows*, 620.
13. Rowling, 120. There is a slight variance from the description of the moke and its skin's uses in *Fantastic Beasts*, as noted in Thomas, *Rowling Revisited*, 100.
14. Rowling, *Deathly Hallows*, 351.
15. Rowling, *Prisoner of Azkaban*, 32.
16. Rowling, *Deathly Hallows*, 162.
17. Yates, *Fantastic Beasts*. The niffler's lack of a name may be to mask whether it is male or female, thus preserving the surprise of the baby nifflers in *Fantastic Beasts: The Crimes of Grindelwald*, but it is also possible that the niffler's parent roles are complicated, like those of that other pocketed species, the seahorse, whose male parent carries the young in his pouch.
18. For more on the origins and adventures of the Luggage, see *The Colour of Magic*, the first in the long-running and beloved Discworld series, which features a different sort of magical school, the Unseen University, whose library is home to the L-Space, a mysterious other dimension that allows vast areas to be shunted behind shelves.
19. For more on the history of bags, including Santa's and its connection to the far less cuddly figure of Krampas, see Munson, "Christmas in Austria."
20. *Chamber of Secrets* and *Half-Blood Prince* are mirrored texts, as outlined beautifully in Lee, "There and Back Again," and Granger, "On Turtle-Back Tales."
21. Lucy has come to Professor Kirke's house because she has been sent away from London to escape the World War II air raids. London is also home to Knockturn Alley, and thus Borgin and Burke's, where one part of the pair of Vanishing Cabinets is located. The other is in a castle, which is also a school. By the end of *The Lion, the Witch, and the Wardrobe*, Lucy is a queen living in a castle. When she is on her way to school a year after returning to Narnia, in *Prince Caspian*, she finds Cair Paravel in ruins, much like the disguised Hogwarts.
22. Lewis, *Lion*, 52.
23. Lewis, 45.
24. Lewis, *Last Battle*, 140.

2. London as a Magical Location in the Harry Potter Series

Madison McLeod

INTRODUCTION

IN BOTH FAIRY tales and many foundational children's stories, forests used to be the dangerous location into which children would venture to find adventure.[1] However, as the world and children's literature have evolved, the woodlands have increasingly been replaced by urban environments as the city has taken on this slightly hostile role and become a place of both danger and discovery for children. The city becomes the location through which young protagonists find themselves and mature, where they self-actualize. One urban landscape of particular current significance is London, a location of magic that prompts self-actualization in the protagonist of the Harry Potter series. London is quintessentially a locationally cryptic city, partially familiar to so many children, while also the site for a strange new topography where magic occurs.[2] These locations are familiar to children in the literary sense, as they are regularly encountered while reading and depicted in films. In *Children's Fantasy Literature: An Introduction*, Michael Levy and Farah Mendlesohn argue that stories set in urban locations "are overwhelmingly intrusion fantasies [where] the fantastic breaks into the world and disrupts it," and that the "best . . . locationally cryptic fantasies make use of [and blend the] archaeological and legendary layers of the world around them."[3] In the Harry Potter series, London becomes the place where wizarding children learn to manage their magical abilities in nonmagical spaces. Much like the heroes of mythology, Harry must choose to return to London at many crucial moments within the series in order to realize his full apotheosis. Through this process of return, London becomes a location of magic; a site of formative transitions during Harry's journey to a particular form of heroism.

To clarify the lines that tie the map of London to the Harry Potter series, this chapter will assess the role of London as a location of magic within the series. The magical locations set within London—the Leaky Cauldron, Diagon and Knockturn Alleys, the Ministry of Magic, Grimmauld Place and Platform Nine and Three-Quarters—spur Harry's self-actualization. Further, as Harry navigates each of these locations, he gradually comes to control and understand his own magic. The locations that bookend the Harry Potter series mark the beginning and end of Harry's process of self-actualization.[4]

SPACE AND PLACE IN DIAGON ALLEY

At the start of the first novel, Harry is skeptical about his own magical abilities. He asks Hagrid if they can "buy all [his magical school supplies] in London," doubtful that they will be able to find a shop with magical goods within the city.[5] Hagrid is quick to assure Harry that what he needs can be found only "if yeh know where to go,"[6] thereby stressing that special knowledge about London is needed to find its magical shops. Yi-Fu Tuan, in *Space and Place: The Perspective of Experience*, makes a crucial distinction between space and place that is relevant to Harry's negotiation of London. Space implies freedom and a sense of exploration, while place offers security,[7] Tuan argues: " 'Space' is more abstract than place. What begins as undifferentiated space becomes place as we get to know it better and endow it with value."[8] At the start of the series Harry is unfamiliar with London, but once he comes to London through magic, a distinction between space and place can be made. Hagrid uses the word *place* to describe the Leaky Cauldron when he introduces the pub to Harry, because Hagrid is already familiar with it: " 'This is it . . . the Leaky Cauldron. It's a famous *place*.' "[9] To Harry, not yet aware of its importance or magic, the pub is still a "space," so he describes it as "a tiny, grubby-looking pub" that, "if Hagrid hadn't pointed it out, [Harry] wouldn't have noticed."[10] The Leaky Cauldron comes to mean more to Harry as the series progresses and the pub moves from unfamiliar space to a place he knows well.

The reader comes to know magical London through the novel's many fantastical portals. The Leaky Cauldron serves as a perfect example. In a portal fantasy, a hero or heroine finds a doorway to another world, ventures into that world, and becomes a hero there before returning to his or her own world, having been changed for the better. At first the Leaky Cauldron seems to represent the quintessential British pub, "dark and shabby" with "a few old women . . . sitting in a corner, drinking tiny glasses of sherry."[11] After passing through it into the alleyway in the back, Hagrid performs the greatest act of magic in the novel thus far to reveal to Harry magical London, and how to access it: he "tapped the wall three times with the point of his umbrella. The brick he had touched quivered—it wriggled—in the middle, a small hole appeared—it grew wider and wider."[12]

Harry is struck by the abrupt change between nonmagical and magical London. These two versions of London aptly coexist "diagonally." Diagon Alley, by its very presence and name, creates for the reader a dichotomy between the real and the unreal.[13] This diagonal coexistence contrasts with the "verticality" of the high-rises of the nonmagical city that Harry has just experienced. The verticality of the nonmagical world makes the diagonal seem all the more unusual, and in crossing from the modern vertical space of a well-known street to the ancient diagonal and nonvertical space of Diagon Alley, readers begin learning the differences between magical and nonmagical locations.

Furthermore, as an orphan raised by an abusive aunt and uncle, Harry has never experienced the verticality of biological parent-child relations. The biological verticality is absent from Harry's experience of Diagon Alley; he experiences it diagonally through friends of his parents rather than with his own kin. Initially, he experiences it with Hagrid. Later, he experiences it through the Weasleys. Cynthia J. Hallett and Peggy J. Huey state that "Freud suggests . . . this combination of strangeness and familiarity resonates most strongly in relation to the mother's body, the original home, which is a 'forgotten' place (as a site of trauma) but still familiar."[14]

It is in Diagon Alley that Harry has this "uncanny experience."[15] Because Harry experiences London and the magical world as a newcomer, just as Lily Potter did, the city becomes a way in which he comes to know his mother.[16] Thus, Harry's return to the magical world through London is like a return to his origins. Until his first trip to the Leaky Cauldron, Harry was ignorant of his magical heritage, but by re-entering the magical world, he has returned to a world where his parents lived and learned.

Diagon Alley is for Harry a place of both trauma and safety. It is a site of trauma as a part of the world in which Voldemort killed Harry's parents, and where he will realize that Voldemort is also trying to kill him. The safety of the magical world comes from the knowledge of his newfound magical abilities as well as his relationships with the magical family and friends he gains there. Harry has few memories of his mother's death, and it is only after his return to the Wizarding world that he starts to remember his traumatic past, to learn more about it, and to begin to heal from it. Therefore, his experiences in magical London launch his journey toward self-actualization.

Magical and diagonal Diagon Alley is intentionally placed somewhere along the very vertical and real Charing Cross Road; it is thus represented in the Harry Potter films as well as Rowling's description in the novels. Harry travels from the mundane—"book shops and music stores, hamburger bars and cinemas"—to the magical, where there are "shops selling robes [and] telescopes and strange silver instruments [and] windows stacked with barrels of bat spleens and eels' eyes."[17] Not only does Harry seem to go back in time to a place that uses parchment, bottled ink, and candles, but he is also simultaneously experiencing it alongside the technology of modern London. By moving between nonmagical and magical London, Harry seems to be moving in both time and space, an experience unavailable to nonmagical Londoners.

In the novels, magic is real, but it is also something that is controlled and regulated. Young wizards need to be taught how to enter the magical world and how to use magic with the help of their wands. London—its nonmagical section—creates another parameter for both young wizards and their magic, as they can only show the full extent of their abilities within magical parts of London. Magic also necessitates specificity in both speech and action. As Fran Pheasant-Kelley points out in *J. K. Rowling: Harry Potter*, "Kristeva's notion of the semiotic and symbolic is relevant to the chanting of spells in the Potter [series]. Here, the student's conjuring skills not only rest on the successful swish of a wand but also on a mastery of enunciation, for in lectures the students are told, 'just swish and flick, and enunciate.'"[18] This notion that enunciation is a part of magic is exemplified in Harry's initial experiences with magic, such as his discovery of Diagon Alley with Hagrid, the Weasleys teaching him how to get onto Platform Nine and Three-Quarters and into the Ministry of Magic, and members of the Order of the Phoenix showing him how to "see" Grimmauld Place. All of these experiences occur in London. These locations are tangible precisely because

Rowling sets them in London, a city that readers can find simultaneously familiar and magical.

London thrusts Harry not only into a new magical world but also into a new socioeconomic status when he gets there. Harry only realizes this change when he comes to learn of the money he has at Gringotts Bank. Readers come to learn that Diagon Alley is the place where the magical community keeps its riches. Rowling integrates the bank into the topography of London by explaining through Hagrid that the tunnels and vaults of Gringotts are "hundreds of miles under London, see. Deep under the Underground."[19] The bank towers "over the other little shops," denoting its importance and making the building more intimidating to those who might have sinister motives. The grandeur of its white marble exterior within the shabby alley gives it the appearance of power, as do its burnished bronze doors and its "vast marble hall."[20]

Two items of large importance to the story are kept at Gringotts. Aptly, these items—the philosopher's stone and the Hufflepuff cup (a Horcrux)—are important in the first and last novels of the series. The objects are essential for both the start and end of Harry's journey of self-actualization, and both items are found in London at Gringotts, which Harry enters first as a welcome customer and later as a thief. At the beginning of his experience in the Wizarding world, Harry lacks the magical control to handle the stone and thus Hagrid must retrieve the object, a "grubby little package wrapped up in brown paper," that he tucks "deep inside his coat."[21] Only when Harry has passed a series of tasks within Hogwarts and reached the end of his academic year is he prepared to find the stone himself and protect it from Voldemort. While Harry achieves possession of the stone at Hogwarts, it is crucial that the highly magical object is initially located in London.

In the last novel of the series, Harry, Ron, Hermione, and the goblin Griphook set out to steal the Hufflepuff cup from the vault of Bellatrix Lestrange to aid in their defeat of Voldemort.[22] This movement from customer to thief occurs as a result of Voldemort's dastardly influence on the magical world and the behavioral changes required of decent people to stop him. This creates a complete contrast from Harry's first experience within Gringotts as Harry, Ron, Hermione, and Griphook must trick their way into the bank and retrieve an object that is not theirs. While Harry's mission to retrieve the Hufflepuff cup is successful, it is also disastrous for the bank. The trio's mastery of complex spells such as the Imperius Curse is needed to enter the magically protected Gringotts, and their control of a dragon is necessary to facilitate their escape. The escape impacts the whole of Diagon Alley as they "[blast] their way out of the passage into the marble hallway," where the dragon turns "its horned head towards the cool outside air," destroying parts of the bank in the process.[23] Harry and his friends not only work toward their self-actualization by besting the magical protections of Gringotts, but they also go about changing the landscape in order to do so. The dragon destroys the bank's facade, and thus the aesthetic of Diagon Alley as a whole, when it forces "its way through the metal doors [of Gringotts], leaving them buckled and hanging from their hinges."[24] The destruction of Gringotts' entryway, like the demolition and devolution of Diagon Alley, parallels the destruction of the containment and restrictions put on magic and propels Harry toward the final battle at Hogwarts, the end of the series, and his own self-actualization.

THE PLATFORM, DEATH AND THE IN-BETWEEN

Platform Nine and Three-Quarters at King's Cross Station becomes another launching point for Harry's forays into magical learning. Although both the platform and Hogwarts are sites of schooling, they do not focus "in the conventional training of social and cultural norms. Rather, [they encourage] the orchestration of objects in space, and the moral and physical navigation of the self through space."[25] Therefore, Harry must learn to master different, other spaces in order to learn to control and manage his magic. This skill in magical management and spatial awareness is the key to Harry's self-actualization.

This is particularly true of Platform Nine and Three-Quarters, which readers see Harry master, both magically and spatially, little by little each year. When Harry is first confronted with the platform, he "[tries] hard not to panic" and realizes that "Hagrid must've forgotten to tell him something you had to do" to get onto the platform.[26] As a result, he has to find a magical family to help him discover how to get through the barrier. Mrs. Weasley is happy to explain to Harry how to transcend this magical boundary: "All you have to do is walk straight at the barrier between platforms nine and ten. Don't stop and don't be scared you'll crash into it, that's very important."[27] Mrs. Weasley's advice is a manner of saying, "Just have confidence that you can do it."

Harry is quick to follow Mrs. Weasley's advice and runs straight into the wall, expecting to crash. Once he reaches the magical side, the contrast with the Muggle platform is evident. The Muggle world is "packed with Muggles, of course," and Harry stands out "with a trunk he [can] hardly lift, a pocket full of wizard money and a large owl."[28] The wizarding side of the platform, on the other hand, contains a "chattering crowd" and "cats of every colour [winding] . . . between their legs. Owls hooted to one another," and "the scraping of heavy trunks" is audible despite the chaos.[29] Harry is no longer the only one with a trunk, an owl, and wizard money. On the wizarding side, the details that previously made him stand out now render him normal, and Harry becomes incorporated with his magical peers only when he reaches magical London. In this moment, as Barbara Klinger describes it, "the forward motion of the narrative slows down or temporarily halts, allowing the spectacle to fully capture our attention."[30] Rowling halts time in a literary manner by using strategically placed dashes and ellipses on top of having Harry close his eyes when he believes he's about to crash into the platform. The crash doesn't come; "he [keeps] on running," and the reader feels relief alongside the protagonist when Harry realizes that he has made it.[31] Fran Pheasant-Kelly maintains that the platform achieves an "unusual temporal status, often appearing outside of time in a fantasy or dream-like dimension."[32] This particular entrance into the magical world is arresting because it is "juxtaposing incongruous elements" and "conferring a surreal quality" on London and King's Cross Station by adding in Platform Nine and Three-Quarters.[33] "The narrative's temporality [distorts] those images," Pheasant-Kelly writes, by pairing the incongruous elements of the nonmagical and, therefore, technology-filled version of London—which includes high-speed trains and electronic ticket machines—and the magical version of London that includes owls, cats, and trunks so heavy that one would need magic to lift them.[34] This difference is evidenced by Uncle Vernon's reaction to Harry's reappearance at King's Cross Station at the end of the first novel: Vernon is "looking furious at the nerve of Harry, carrying an owl in a cage in a station full of ordinary people."[35]

Harry's experience with the barrier at Platform Nine and Three-Quarters changes over the years. The barrier refuses them during their second year.

2. London as a Magical Location in the Harry Potter Series

Unlike their previous experience with the barrier, this time nonmagical "people all around them stared and a guard nearby yelled, 'What in the blazes d'you think you're doing?'"[36] Ron and Harry are not undetectable, and do not possess enough magical power or knowledge to become so. When Harry returns to the barrier for his third year at Hogwarts, he chooses to imitate Mr. Weasley to make sure he makes it through the barrier: "Mr Weasley strolled towards the barrier between platforms nine and ten, pushing Harry's trolley and apparently very interested in the InterCity 125 that had just arrived at platform nine. With a meaningful look at Harry, he leant casually against the barrier. Harry imitated him. Next moment, they had fallen sideways though the solid metal onto platform nine and three-quarters."[37] By his fourth year, Harry is "used to getting onto Platform Nine and Three-Quarters"; it is "a simple matter of walking straight through the apparently solid barrier dividing platforms nine and ten."[38] He even seems to be explaining to readers how to go about following him across the barrier, even going so far as to warn them that "the only tricky part was doing this in an unobtrusive way, so as to avoid attracting Muggle attention."[39] The audience watches Harry, Ron, and Hermione lean "casually against the barrier, chattering unconcernedly, and [slide] sideways through" it with ease.[40] It is evident that in this moment the Golden Trio have started to master the magic of the barrier and of the liminal space that is King's Cross Station.

Magical management is demonstrated every time Harry crosses the barrier. Hogwarts students are taught to control their magic up to a point, to keep their magic *three-quarters* under control. In the same way, Harry and other magical children are sent to Hogwarts for three-quarters of the year, and left out of control and in the real (or in some cases Muggle) world for the last quarter. Magic is essentially chaotic, but magical mastery is the control of most, not all, of that chaos. Platform Nine and Three-Quarters is aptly named; it too controls magical children and the chaos they create only up to a point, and then releases them back into the Muggle world.

The barrier between the Muggle and magical worlds bears some resemblance to ancient mythical barriers between the mortal and immortal realms, or between the realms of death and the realms of the living. Ancient myth often parallels portal fantasy: its heroes frequently have to experience the world of death, learn something from it, and return to the world of the living to achieve heroic status.[41] This particular experience marks such a hero as greater than human or, at the very least, amongst the greatest of humans. It seems particularly poignant that Harry's acceptance of his destiny and fate at the hands of Voldemort due to the prophecy occurs in London at King's Cross Station, right at the edge of the same barrier. Harry quietly accepts his fate as he gets "into the back of the Dursley's car" and realizes that "there [is] no point in worrying yet. . . . As Hagrid had said, what would come, would come . . . and he would have to meet it when it did."[42] Harry is no longer avoiding his duty toward the Wizarding world as its savior. While he is not yet cognizant of the prophecy, he is mature enough to think about his fate as an opponent to Voldemort and accept it. As Jack Zipes points out, "Fairytale films [and books] are concerned with profound human struggles and seek to provide a glimpse of light and hope despite the darkness that surrounds their very creation and production."[43] Pheasant-Kelly expands upon this notion and makes it relevant to the end of the Potter series. The series, like the fairy tales Zipes references, "inevitably [seeks] to deliver such hope, portraying recovery and regeneration" while simultaneously using mythological parallels and magic to portray death as "a transient state from which one can return."[44] Harry is the first to point out the similarities between King's Cross Station and the doorway to the realms of dead. It is a mystical place filled with "clouds of steam" that carries with it a feeling of being in between places, just like being in between life and death.[45] Harry remarks in *Goblet of Fire* that through the "clouds of steam billowing" from the Hogwarts Express, "the many Hogwarts students and parents on the platform *appeared to be dark ghosts*."[46] Ghosts, too, are trapped in a space between life and death.

Harry also finds himself trapped between life and death. Most importantly, Harry's death scene occurs within London at King's Cross Station. After he dies in the Forbidden Forest, he finds himself "waking" from death: "A long time later, or maybe no time at all, it came to him that he must exist, must be more than disembodied thought, because he was lying, definitely lying, on some surface. Therefore, he had a sense of a touch, and the things against which he played existed too. Almost as soon as he had reached this conclusion, Harry became conscious that he was naked."[47] Harry's experience here parallels that of first creation and Eden, where something comes from nothing due to mere thought as thoughts

2. London as a Magical Location in the Harry Potter Series

materialize. Harry, like Adam and Eve before him, realizes that he is naked: "For the first time, he wished he were clothed. Barely had the wish formed in his head, than robes appeared a short distance away."[48] These heavenly robes are "soft, clean and warm" and to Harry it is "extraordinary how they had appeared, just like that, the moment he wanted them."[49] It is at this moment that Dumbledore walks toward him: "He spread his arms wide, and his hands were both whole and white and undamaged."[50] It is due to Dumbledore's appearance that Harry begins to wonder about his own state and whereabouts. As Dumbledore is dead, Harry questions both where he is and the state of living he is in:

> "But you're dead," said Harry.
> "Oh yes," said Dumbledore matter-of-factly.
> "Then . . . I'm dead too?"
> "Ah," said Dumbledore, smiling still more broadly. "That is the question, isn't it? On the whole, dear boy, I think not."[51]

In a version of London projected from his consciousness, Harry inhabits the space between life and death. By allowing himself to die and accepting death, Harry ensures that only the part of Voldemort residing within him does not survive.

In Rowling's fictional world, the person who is currently between life and death chooses the in-between's location or setting. The space then reflects the wants and needs of the individual faced with the decision between living and dying. Harry is the one who chooses King's Cross Station as his limbo. While he asks Dumbledore, "Where are we, exactly?" Dumbledore responds, " 'Well, I was going to ask you that. . . . Where would you say that we are?' "[52] Harry realizes that "until Dumbledore had asked, Harry had not known. Now, however, he found that he had an answer ready to give. 'It looks,' he said slowly, 'like King's Cross station. Except a lot cleaner, and empty, and there are no trains as far as I can see.' " Dumbledore is quick to point out that the location is Harry's doing, saying, "This is, as they say, *your* party," and Harry becomes aware that he has chosen their location to be within London.[53]

This fictional version of London also provides Rowling with the space for a chapter, as in each of her Potter novels, that serves to unravel the mysteries that have been built throughout the novel. Rowling uses this in-between space to give readers the time to understand Harry's death as well as his decision to continue living and fighting for those he loves. Harry initially believes that he has "got to go back"; however, Dumbledore clarifies that he can choose to return to life or go "On."[54] It is particularly important that this choice occurs in a location familiar to Harry and his readers and in the space where a portal separates the wizarding and Muggle realms. It is in his own imagined version of London that Harry achieves self-actualization. There he chooses to return to the land of the living as a fully-fledged hero and wizard, and as a result he ensures Voldemort's—and uncontrolled magic's—destruction.

CONCLUSION

In a close reading of Diagon Alley and King's Cross Station, what becomes clear is that the city of London participates not only in Harry's self-actualization but also in the literary self-actualization of his readers. This close reading of the novels is necessary to find meaning in Rowling's London locations. It is her use of mundane locations within London and the magical backstory for each of them that makes these locations spellbinding.

London in Harry Potter is not only a real location but also a conceptual space of childhood, a city that is a location of childhood growth and exploration separate from the adult reality/version of the city.[55] However, the London of the series moves beyond the scope of that conceptual space. By showing young wizards gaining gradual control of their magical abilities, the series not only eases children toward self-actualization and adulthood but also helps readers come to terms with acts of terrorism both as the series gets darker and as these acts occur within our own borders and across the world. Twenty-five years after the first publication of *Philosopher's/Sorcerer's Stone*, London has seen numerous terrorist attacks. Thus, new readers of the anniversary editions experience the fabric of London being torn apart both in the city itself and by Death Eaters and giants in the final installments of the series. While they do not completely distract readers from the harsh realities of modern-day terrorism, the novels do teach children how to navigate an unfamiliar "space" that is at once ambiguous and dangerous while also being a familiar "place" of fantasy and escape. By learning to

2. London as a Magical Location in the Harry Potter Series

relate to Rowling's London, a purely architectural and manufactured space, children assimilate the lived experiences of their own cities. Therefore, as Harry achieves full control over his magic and reaches self-actualization, so too does a child reader feel prepared to navigate the city with new vigor and a thirst to find the magical within the mundane.

NOTES

1. For more see Bettelheim, *Uses of Enchantment*, 94–95.
2. Levy and Mendlesohn, *Children's Fantasy*, 179.
3. Levy and Mendlesohn, 179–80.
4. For more on the locations in between, see McLeod, "Critical Survey."
5. Rowling, *Philosopher's Stone*, 53. All Harry Potter book citations in this essay refer to the original Bloomsbury (UK) editions.
6. Rowling, 53.
7. Tuan, *Space and Place*, 3.
8. Tuan, 6.
9. Rowling, *Philosopher's Stone*, 53 (emphasis mine).
10. Rowling, 53.
11. Rowling, 53.
12. Rowling, 55–56.
13. Diagon Alley, said aloud quickly, becomes "diagon-ally."
14. Hallett and Huey, *Rowling: Harry Potter*, 54.
15. Strange or mysterious, especially in an unsettling way (Oxford English Dictionary).
16. Lily Evans was a Muggleborn, a witch born to nonmagical parents, unaware of the magical world and experienced it similarly to Harry.
17. Rowling, *Philosopher's Stone*, 53, 56.
18. Pheasant-Kelly, "Bewitching," 53.
19. Rowling, *Philosopher's Stone*, 51.
20. Rowling, 56, 57.
21. Rowling, 59.
22. Rowling, *Deathly Hallows*, 436.
23. Rowling, 438.
24. Rowling, 438.
25. Pheasant-Kelly, "Bewitching," 49.
26. Rowling, *Philosopher's Stone*, 69.
27. Rowling, 70.
28. Rowling, 69.
29. Rowling, 71.
30. Pheasant-Kelly, "Bewitching," 49.
31. Rowling, *Philosopher's Stone*, 71.
32. Pheasant-Kelly, "Bewitching," 49–50.
33. Pheasant-Kelly, 50.

34. Pheasant-Kelly, 50.
35. Rowling, *Philosopher's Stone*, 223.
36. Rowling, *Chamber of Secrets*, 55.
37. Rowling, *Prisoner of Azkaban*, 57.
38. Rowling, *Goblet of Fire*, 145.
39. Rowling, 145.
40. Rowling, 145.
41. For more about the hero's journey, see Campbell, *Hero with a Thousand Faces*.
42. Rowling, *Goblet of Fire*, 636 (ellipsis in original).
43. Zipes, *Enchanted Screen*, 350.
44. Pheasant-Kelly, "Bewitching," 71.
45. Rowling, *Goblet of Fire*, 145.
46. Rowling, 145 (emphasis mine).
47. Rowling, *Deathly Hallows*, 565.
48. Rowling, 565–66.
49. Rowling, 565–66.
50. Rowling, 565–66.
51. Rowling, 567 (ellipsis in original).
52. Rowling, 570.
53. Rowling, 570.
54. Rowling, 578.
55. Cecire et al., *Space and Place*, 1.

3. Secrecy and Segregation in the Wizarding World's Hidden Histories

Kathryn N. McDaniel

J. K. ROWLING PLAYS wizard historian on her Wizarding World fan site (formerly Pottermore), revealing the context of everything from characters' love lives to the arcane workings of magical plumbing in the fantasy realm she created through the Harry Potter novels. Certainly more interesting than the lectures of ghostly history teacher Professor Binns, these "ghost plots," as Rowling calls them, expose her world-building and reinforce key themes of her fantasy series.[1] Since the publication of the seventh Harry Potter novel, she has made her backstory public by increments through essays on her fan website (currently collected under the appropriately historical heading "J. K. Rowling Archive" at the Wizarding World website) and through a series of e-book publications.[2]

For Harry Potter's Muggle readers, there is something delightfully appealing about learning of the hidden histories of the Wizarding world.[3] Rowling does not approach her world-building without literary art. As John Granger has noted, Rowling is a talented genre parodist. In the Harry Potter series she parodies schoolboy novels, Gothic romance, detective whodunits and, of course, fantasy fiction, among other popular genres, with the ultimate aim of subverting them.[4] Her ghost plots likewise are parodic histories, mimicking the tone and content of historical narratives characteristic of the late nineteenth through mid-twentieth century, in particular. Rowling's pitch-perfect narrative mimicry of Muggle histories, as well as the revelation of previously hidden information about the Wizarding world, create an opportunity to merge her fantasy world's past with our own.

Rowling illustrates through these short stories the contradiction that, on the one hand, wizards have sought to keep themselves and their history secret from Muggles, for safety's sake, while on the other, the two societies remain deeply entwined. Wizard and Muggle history intersect, despite the antipathy of the former and the ignorance of the latter. They share the same world. Explaining the quite desperate need for secrecy felt by witches and wizards, Rowling nevertheless highlights the problematic consequences of wizard separatism, namely harmful ideologies, personal tragedies, and authoritarian government. These ghost plots demonstrate not only that secrecy and segregation fail in keeping the two groups separate, but also that the keeping of secrets poses dangers to the values of inclusion and liberty.

Rowling's gift for parody extends to these parodies of historical writing, but she is not completely successful in subverting this genre. She adopts the proper third-person tone of smug all-knowingness, situates events and developments in context, and even references Wizarding-world primary-source documents as evidence. There is a strong hint of the ridiculous in many of her histories as her officious tone competes with fanciful topics like the Knight Bus, the game of Gobstones, or wizard plumbing, as well as the often patently silly arguments and personalities at the center of historical developments. Rowling is self-conscious of the pomposity of her historical prose; this is the main source of her parody. Too often, though, she falls into the traps of Western colonialist narratives of which she appears unaware, especially their tendency to universalize Western developments and essentialize Western imperial domination.[5] Particularly Rowling's histories of magic in North America expose her own colonialist blind spot and lead her into problematic portrayals of the Wizarding world that naturalize European global expansion.

THE INTERNATIONAL STATUTE OF SECRECY AND THE WIZARD-MUGGLE DIVIDE

Rowling's histories trace the segregation of the magical and Muggle communities to the International Statute of Secrecy passed in 1692, the year of the Salem witchcraft trials. Before the wizarding community created the Statute of Secrecy, Muggles and magical people intermixed regularly without much difficulty. The Leaky Cauldron was "initially visible to Muggle eyes," and "Muggles were not turned away or made to feel unwelcome."[6] Rowling explains that the Ollivanders came to Britain with the Roman invasion; the Malfoys came with the Norman Conquest (and a Malfoy may have proposed to and then jinxed Queen Elizabeth I); Sir Cadogan was a knight at King Arthur's Round Table; Nearly Headless Nick was a victim of Henry VII's court.[7] Even the Malfoys regularly engaged in business with Muggles, making most of their money this way, and routine intermarriage between Muggles and magical people did not arouse much concern.[8] Rowling explains that prior to the Statute of Secrecy, wizards commonly lived among Muggles and worked Muggle jobs.[9] The discovery of a witch or wizard born into a Muggle family was also typical; "Magbobs," as they were called, were even thought to be "particularly gifted" with magical talent.[10] This relatively benign intermingling ceased, however, with the advent of the Statute of Secrecy.

Although Rowling acknowledges the danger posed to witches and wizards by American Puritans, she blames the Salem witchcraft trials primarily on an international group of "wizarding mercenaries" she calls "Scourers," who came to the Americas to hunt down criminals and "anyone who might be worth some gold." The Scourers became corrupt, "indulged a love of authority and cruelty," and "even went so far as trafficking their fellow wizards."[11] In response to the trials in Salem, which were presided over by at least two Scourer judges, many American witches and wizards fled. But it was the international response to this tragedy that created the most lasting impact on wizard-Muggle relations: the passage of the Statute of Secrecy by the International Confederation of Wizards. Although this statute policed segregation of the magical community and enforced magical secrecy, Rowling cannot seem to decide whether to characterize this as a "voluntary" measure designed to ensure wizard protection against Muggles or a mandate that "forced" wizards into hiding.[12] In considering their options for response to the Salem witchcraft trials, some wizards demanded war against Muggles in retaliation, but cooler heads prevailed, and magic went underground instead.

Interestingly, Rowling sets the impetus for the worldwide repression of magic in the seventeenth-century British North American colonies, an environment she characterizes as harsher toward magic than other places in the world, partly because of the colonies' religious atmosphere. It's curious that Rowling uses the Salem trials as her catalyst; relatively few (twenty) "witches" died in this event, compared to the century-long European witch craze, in which tens of thousands of people perished. The Salem incidents occurred about thirty years after Europe's witch craze ended, and so might be considered one of the last of these persecutions. Perhaps Rowling sees the

Salem witch hunts as an appropriate line of demarcation between a magical/religious world and a scientific one. Even as wizards felt more secure in the rest of the world, their continued persecution in the American colonies may have reminded them of the perpetual hazards of being magical.

In a way, magic did go "underground" in the eighteenth-century era of the Enlightenment, as rational, natural, and scientific principles came to predominate over supernatural or religious ones. Britain's Witchcraft Act of 1735 punished individuals who *pretended* to have magical abilities, on the assumption that such a claim was necessarily fraudulent. As Owen Davis has explained, "The fight was now not against the evil of witchcraft, but, instead, against the evil influence which such 'ignorant' and 'superstitious' delusions had on the mindset of the uneducated masses."[13]

Rowling hints that part of what makes the Statute of Secrecy so successful is Muggles' willful denial of the existence of magic. She explains that Muggle-wizard mixed marriages have become more common in recent times, and yet the Wizarding world remains hidden, a phenomenon explained by Professor Mordicus Egg in his book *The Philosophy of the Mundane: Why the Muggles Prefer Not to Know*.[14] According to Egg, Muggles no longer needed magic nor acknowledged its existence from the late seventeenth century on. By revealing the hidden properties of substances and the hidden laws of the universe, scientific discoveries allowed Europeans to develop new technologies that were more effective in empowering (Muggle) humanity than any kind of magic.

The Statute of Secrecy segregated wizarding society in ways that affected its technological, ideological, and political evolution. As David M. Martin has demonstrated, the sharp division of wizarding from Muggle society after 1692 meant that wizards were isolated (and isolated themselves) from technological developments that emerged after that point. So many of the "old-fashioned" ways of writing, traveling, and communicating that readers find irritating about the Wizarding world reflect Rowling's deliberate choice to emphasize the divergence of wizard and Muggle societies from the eighteenth century forward.[15] Unlike Muggles, her witches and wizards still champion and depend upon magic. In fact, Rowling says, "To fill one's house with tumble dryers and telephones would be seen as an admission of magical inadequacy."[16] Several of her histories reveal wizard fear and scorn of adopting new technologies, including the Knight Bus and the very controversial Hogwarts Express, which was opposed by "pure-blood families" as an "unsafe, unsanitary, and demeaning" way to travel.[17] These technological divisions became a source of identity and a means of othering Muggles, which further entrenched the wizard-Muggle divide.

SEGREGATION AND RACIAL IDEOLOGY IN THE WIZARDING WORLD

Designed to be self-protective, the statute nevertheless had serious negative consequences for the magical community. It created heartache for individual characters like Minerva McGonagall, who rejected her Muggle first love,[18] and it allowed for the development in the magical world of racist ideologies that parallel those in the Muggle world. Rowling's essays "The Malfoy Family" and "Pure-Blood" make direct connections between the Statute of Secrecy and antipathy toward Muggles among wizards and witches. Despite the Malfoys' initial opposition to the statute, after it became law, the Malfoy family performed "an abrupt volte-face, and became as vocally supportive of the Statute as any of those who had championed it from the beginning, hastening to deny that they had ever been on speaking (or marrying) terms with Muggles." Their historic disdain for the poor translates quite easily into an adoption of the pureblood doctrine, which provided them in the twentieth century with a "source of untrammelled power."[19]

Although the pureblood doctrine is often connected with Salazar Slytherin's refusal to teach anyone with Muggle heritage, Rowling emphasizes that this attitude was unusual until the statute came into effect. She explains that the trauma of this era led to a historic decline in Muggle-wizard marriages due to fears that discovery could lead to prosecution under the statute. An editor's note on this point references Egg's book on Muggle denial to suggest this was an unfounded fear.[20] In this climate of "uncertainty, fear and resentment," the pureblood doctrine gained followers and developed into a pervasive ideology that maintained a fiction of wizard purity and thus superiority. Instead of being seen as a breach of the law, intermarriage with Muggles would now be considered "shameful, unnatural," leading to "a 'contamination' of magical blood." The next paragraph in "Pure-Blood" assures us that there was no real foundation for any notion of genetic purity among wizards, who had been marrying Muggles for centuries: "To call oneself a pure-blood was more accurately a declaration of political or social intent . . . than a statement of biological fact." Early eighteenth-century wizard scholarship nevertheless sought to codify the signs of wizard purity, through genetic science, classification, and several "tests" that might demonstrate pureblood status (all of which, we are told, proved to be bogus). With pureblood fever reaching a peak in the early 1930s, the anonymously published "Pure-Blood Directory" listed out the "truly" pure families, the "Sacred Twenty-Eight." This list evoked protest from both so-called pureblood families who did not espouse this doctrine (like the Weasleys) and especially those left off the list.[21]

With this history, Rowling shows readers how, despite segregation, there were common trends in the historical development of wizarding and Muggle society. Rowling's history of the wizard purity concept hews fairly closely to the development of scientific racism in Europe and the Americas since the eighteenth century. The scientifically justified fiction of racial separation and hierarchy created by Europeans like Carl von Linné (or Carolus Linneaus)[22] mirrors Rowling's explanation of how fear and a desire for domination led to the development of the Wizarding world's equivalent, the pureblood doctrine. The 1930s "Pure-Blood Directory" is certainly a reference to the era of German fascist racial identification—and the delusion of German racial superiority—which facilitated the rise of Adolf Hitler and his eugenic policies. Rowling tells us that those families who first embraced the concept of "pure" wizarding blood were typically descended from those who had argued for war against Muggles in the wake of the Salem trials. The ideology became a substitute for physical dominance.

The decision to go into seclusion instead of making war (or peace?) with Muggles had, therefore, unintended negative consequences: segregation produced both isolation and fear, and brought previously marginalized ideas of wizard superiority into the mainstream. Some wizards and witches continued to interact with Muggles, however.[23] Rowling includes tales of wizards arguing (nobly, she suggests) for wizard involvement in Muggle conflicts like World War I. On the other side, wizard warfare obviously affects Muggles in the Harry Potter series, despite their denial of the magic in their midst or the power of the spell Obliviate.

Rowling appears very much to regret the absence of magic among the Muggles, seeing the dangers in Muggle ignorance of magic, as well as wizards' self-imposed isolation. Suppression, seclusion, denial, racism—each of these resulted from fear of the other created in response to historical events. Moreover, segregation did not prevent these two groups from sharing the same world. Rowling's use of historical rhetoric to convey these points causes them to ring with the promise of factuality.

SECRECY AND AUTHORITARIANISM IN BRITAIN AND NORTH AMERICA

Rowling's Wizarding World histories point out that both the Ministry of Magic and MACUSA formed in direct response to the Statute of Secrecy, and that both governments used secrecy—and segregation of magical and nonmagical folk—to create states with authoritarian tendencies. Several scholars have discussed the totalitarian elements of wizard government that emerged in the British Ministry of Magic, including putting the "trace" on young wizards and witches to ensure that they do not practice magic outside of school, press censorship, the relatively unregulated use of *veritaserum*, and the quite unjust practice of modifying Muggle memories when they have been exposed to magic.[24] Wizard government justifies these commonplace infringements on individual liberties as being necessary to maintain magical secrecy.[25] The Statute of Secrecy led to administrative structures that prioritized silence, which became the government's most central imperative. As Kamillea Aghtan argues, the government became an "administration of silence" used for social discipline and repression, creating a smooth transition into power for Voldemort because the Ministry "create[d] the conditions for only an impossible response," that is, "the silence of the unspeakable response."[26] The developments of the Harry Potter series from the fifth to seventh books reveal both the magical government's vulnerability to totalitarian takeover and the difficulty of speaking openly in the face of this catastrophe. Both were fostered by the Statute of Secrecy.[27]

Although Rowling asserts that pureblood ideology did not gain as many followers in the United States as it did in Europe,[28] she also explains that MACUSA was even more severe than the British Ministry of Magic in maintaining magical secrecy. Discriminatory and controlling policies were designed for security but impinged on individual rights. Such laws developed in America largely because of the shared fear initially generated by the Salem witchcraft trials in the British North American empire, codified in Rappaport's Law, which expressly prohibited intermarriage and even friendship between wizards and No-Majs.[29] Huge numbers of No-Majs were Obliviated. Wands had to be licensed, and students could not receive wands until they went to Ilvermorny School, where their wands were kept during summer and winter breaks to minimize risk of exposure. Rowling notes that MACUSA was "more intolerant of such magical phenomena as ghosts, poltergeists, and fantastic creatures than its European equivalents."[30]

Unlike the Ministry of Magic in Britain, MACUSA would have no contact with the United States' No-Maj government, nor does it appear to mimic the democratic structure of the USA. Wizarding law enforcement is the central priority of MACUSA and therefore the main organizing feature of its governing institutions. The first Fantastic Beasts film suggests that individuals can be sentenced to execution without trial, and the manner of execution steals individuals' free will so they voluntarily plunge into a deadly potion rising up from the floor of a chasm.

In Britain and North America, therefore, secrecy developed as a political policy to promote security of the wizarding community. But it lingers as a fertile ground for racist ideology and as a tool of social regulation and authoritarianism. Rowling rejects these as negative consequences of misguided segregation policies, showing that MACUSA, with its commitment to total secrecy and radical segregation, has developed institutions that are vulnerable to takeover by authoritarian leaders embracing racist (pureblood) ideology. Instead of working with the No-Maj government of the USA, MACUSA maintains its magical, colonial ties overseas, to the detriment of diversity, liberty, and security. Despite Rowling's claims to the contrary, her magical North America is less free, more segregated and intolerant, and more open to authoritarian exploitation than its colonizing mother country.

J. K. ROWLING'S UNCONSCIOUS ORNAMENTALIST IMPERIALISM

These historical parodies by and large support the central themes of the Harry Potter novels: the importance of inclusion, the insidiousness of othering via racial ideologies, and the ability of evil forces to use separation as a vehicle for inhumanity and destruction. It becomes challenging for Rowling to maintain her parody in the face of these themes she wants to affirm (not undermine) through the historian's authoritative voice. While

Rowling seems quite intentional about these messages, her ghost plots about North America reveal her own blind spot when it comes to British imperialism, neatly expressed through the Western-style historical narrative form. Postcolonialist scholars have noted how Western historians shaped a Eurocentric global history that denied non-Western people agency or ignored them entirely.[31] Rowling's desire to create a freer, more egalitarian magical world outside Britain reflects an imperialist goal of which she is apparently unaware: the replication of one's own culture in a new landscape. Historian David Cannadine has labeled this reflexive imperialist mindset "ornamentalism," seeing this as an inherited way of viewing Britain's nineteenth-century colonies, dominions, and mandates as an extension of self.[32] In mimicking the rhetoric of colonialist history, Rowling's History of Magic in North America series actually reinforces a British imperial worldview. As Amy H. Sturgis has noted, "Most of Rowling's depiction of magical North America is merely magical Britain 2.0, and she either erases or appropriates everything else. An odd nostalgia permeates her writings, as if Brexit-era Rowling is trying to recapture the safety and stability of the now-lost British Empire."[33]

Unconsciously, Rowling's parody histories have adopted Western historical prejudices regarding the centrality of Europe and European peoples to global historical development, the technological backwardness of non-Western societies, and the inevitability that these societies would adopt Western ways. This is evident in Rowling's choice of the Salem witchcraft trials (centered on Europeans in North America) as the catalyst for the *International* Statute of Secrecy. A crisis involving European people in European imperial territory became the impetus for a global movement of wizards into hiding. Rowling's faux sports history *Quidditch through the Ages* likewise describes uncritically the rise and spread of Quidditch as a process of colonization through sport culture and characterizes non-Western societies as unsophisticated because of a lack of European broom technology.[34] The History of Magic in North America series especially was roundly criticized by fans for its portrayal of American history and Native American peoples.[35]

Rowling's story of magic in North America establishes a Eurocentric frame for the history of the continent, envisioning "magical" and "natural" early inhabitants who all shared common traditions and approaches

3. Secrecy and Segregation in the Wizarding World's Hidden Histories

to spirituality ("skin walkers" and "medicine men"). Despite Rowling's assertion that, unlike Muggles, European and American magical peoples knew each other before the fifteenth-century, she also notes that Americans lacked a central technology (in this case, the wand) that could have made them more powerful.[36] Enter the European settlers. Native Americans (always a monolith in these stories) quickly wind up on the margins or entirely absent from the succeeding magical history of the continent. North America's past becomes the history of Europeans—wizards and witches as well as the No-Majs—who take over territory and set up institutions: schools, governments, and sports. Rowling does not seem to realize how her history naturalizes the story of colonization. She attempts to echo the Harry Potter book series' view of marginalized people, now within the North American context. Yet in laying her understanding of European history over non-European territory, she effects a kind of literary colonization.

The story of Ilvermorny's founding presents a good example of this ornamentalist imperialism. Rowling has the North American wizard school founded by a poor, abused Irish orphan girl named Isolt, who escaped from her pureblood-fixated aunt to America on the *Mayflower* in the early 1600s. (Bear in mind that Irish immigrants were racially stigmatized and much maligned in both Britain and North America even into the twentieth century.) Through persistence, kindness, and an adventurous spirit, Isolt creates a family—she marries a No-Maj and takes in two wizard orphans. She then begins to teach wanded magic, which attracts local Wampanoag and Narragansett people first to her home and then to the school she has founded, Ilvermorny. Inspired by Hogwarts, this school is named after Isolt's family's old home in Ireland. Native American families soon abandon their "home-schooling" in witchcraft and wizardry for the British-inspired institution. Ilvermorny, Rowling writes, "has the reputation of being one of the most democratic, least elitist of all the great wizarding schools."[37]

Rowling attempts a European underdog story here (the Irish orphan girl who makes good)—one that aims to be antidiscriminatory in its intentional egalitarianism and in the intermarriage between witch and No-Maj. But her heroine is still very much a European, marries a man of European descent, adopts children who are also European immigrants, and establishes a European style of schooling (named for a European house) which all

North American wizards and witches—of European descent or not—will now attend. Rowling ends Isolt's story this way: "They had hired staff, they had built dormitories, they had concealed their school from No-Maj eyes by clever enchantments: in short, the girl who had dreamed of attending Hogwarts had helped form the North American equivalent."[38] Rowling seeks to subvert a traditional history of a school's founding in choosing a racially marginalized young woman as the triumphant agent of historical change. By placing this tale in a colonial context, however, and focusing exclusively on British institutions and hierarchies, she has erased the colonized territory and its inhabitants. This is the essence of ornamentalist imperialism: re-creating a colony in the image of the colonizing country, replicating not only institutions but also social hierarchies. North America's history has become a mere reflection of Britain's. Rowling unwittingly colonizes North America, and Native Americans, all over again.

Just as radical segregation of wizards and Muggles enabled authoritarian policies, it also magnified colonialist tendencies in both the European and North American settings. The Statute of Secrecy required forming new wizard governments in both the mother country and the colony. In 1693 North American colonists named their government the Magical Congress of the United States of America (MACUSA) and modeled it after the Wizard's Council of Great Britain. It is impossible to read the history "The Magical Congress of the United States of America (MACUSA)" without remarking that Rowling appears to have very little working knowledge of American history.[39] Anachronistically, Rowling has the magical "United States of America" and its institutions predate the Muggle ones. The unity of the British North American colonies was in no way assured even in the revolutionary era, much less in 1693, when independence itself was hardly imagined by the settler colonials. Even as late as 1773, there was little discussion of independence, much less the name "United States of America." All of this mischaracterizes American independence and undermines the agency of the colonist-rebels. We might imagine that Rowling wishes to suggest that the magical realm influences the No-Maj realm, but her emphasis on secrecy precludes this possibility. This anachronism effectively naturalizes the entity "United States of America."[40] If two groups organized independently in this fashion, the formation of this nation seems inevitable, perhaps even a "manifest destiny."

3. Secrecy and Segregation in the Wizarding World's Hidden Histories

The memorial erected in the MACUSA headquarters in New York City by the 1920s illustrates the importance of the Salem trials to this new government. An image of this statue appeared in the first Fantastic Beasts movie, where its bronze figures depict those persecuted at the Salem trials, including a small child.[41] While the Ministry of Magic in Britain stands in tribute to wizard dominion over other magical creatures, given shape in the Fountain of Magical Brethren, the Salem statue signals that MACUSA is an institution built on fear of discovery by Muggles. So that persecution will not recur, the government prioritizes the protection of wizards and witches in North America through policing and rigorous enforcement of magical secrecy.[42] In other words, MACUSA as a government was founded to defend and conceal, not based on principles of self-government or the protection of natural rights, as with the Muggle United States Congress that formed a hundred years later.

As illustrated in the prominent positioning of the Salem statue, MACUSA constantly reminds its citizens of the potential for harm should magical secrecy be compromised. When the American War for Independence broke out, Rowling writes, wizards were on the fence about whether to participate or not. To settle the issue, they engaged in a "Country or Kind?" debate (1777) in which they disputed whether they owed loyalty to their fellow British wizards abroad or their fellow American No-Maj colonists. They opted, officially, to stay out of the conflict, as did—interestingly enough—the magical government of Britain.[43] Rowling notes that several individual witches and wizards in North America did participate in the war, though without governmental sanction. However, both wizarding governments chose secrecy—and continued colonial connection—over engaging in the conflict for independence or severing their strong ties with each other. Thus the imperial periphery of (magical) North America maintained ties with the metropolitan center in Britain, to the exclusion of the No-Majs and non-European peoples among whom they lived day-to-day.

PLAYING THE HISTORIAN'S PART TOO WELL

The merging of real and imagined history in these ghost plots allows readers to interrogate important currents in the history of Western civilization, not only the diminishment of magical thinking but also the development of scientific racism, the dangers of secrecy for democracy, and the effects of colonization. Rowling argues through her magical histories that secrecy and segregation are antithetical to humanistic and democratic values by building on the notion that the Salem witchcraft trials drove wizards underground, enabled racist ideologies to naturalize the wizard-Muggle divide, and forged governments that could use authoritarian measures to maintain secrecy. This message is in keeping with the themes of the Harry Potter novels. To articulate them in this quasi-historical form, she must in some respects drop the pose of subverting historical rhetoric and adopt its authoritative voice instead. Consequently, even as she wishes to reinforce these values, she ends up presenting contradictory ones that replicate attitudes of the historians she initially parodies, namely the view of global history as Europe's history and the emphasis of colonial connection over independence. Instead of subverting the imperialist histories of twentieth-century Europe, she has mirrored them in her magical world.

Rowling tells us that North America is a free and egalitarian space, but her evidence shows otherwise. Not only is wizard-Muggle separation enforced more severely than in Britain, but MACUSA's government also appears even more susceptible to authoritarian tendencies than Britain's Ministry of Magic. Within the closed circuit of secrecy, Rowling's North America, rather than being its own unique entity, represents a more constrained version of Britain. The origin history of magic in North America—which only begins once *European* magical people arrive—is designed to show the upward mobility of the underdog, but what it actually reveals is the exclusion of the non-European and nonmagical Other. America's history becomes a footnote to the European story of class striving rather than an independent narrative with its own internal logic. Rowling has followed the ornamentalist imperial paradigm, creating a world in Britain's image, one that can be simultaneously "the same" as Britain and perhaps even more fully embodying British social and political structures.

Rowling has created a literary replica of this imperial vision through her appropriation of the rhetoric of imperial-era histories. The global expansion of the British Empire is echoed in the magical realm with no critical insight into this distorted aspect of traditional historical narratives. Although Rowling pokes fun at some characteristics of traditional histories, she seems unable to see through one of the more insidious, hidden aspects of the field: the way it has presented Eurocentric history as universal and global, to the

3. Secrecy and Segregation in the Wizarding World's Hidden Histories

marginalization and exclusion of non-European people and places. The fan outrage over Rowling's History of Magic in North America series indicates that the view she unthinkingly advances contradicts the larger themes of inclusion, equality, and friendship across boundaries promoted so fully in the Harry Potter novels. Instead of subverting the historical genre, Rowling has been swept up in it, revealing her own obliviousness to the imperial legacy in historical storytelling as well as the power of historical rhetoric to communicate European global superiority.

Both fantasy writers and colonizers are world-builders, projecting their own identities on the worlds they create. Rowling, as a child of late British Empire and modern liberalism, exposes her internal contradictions through these pseudohistories. As a result, the ghosts of Britain's imperial past haunt the histories in Rowling's ghost plots in ways her fans recognize, even if she does not.

NOTES

1. Rowling, "Ghost Plots." Rowling stated that this phrase was "my private expression for all the untold stories that sometimes seemed quite as real to me as the 'final cut.'"

2. Rowling, *Short Stories of Power*; Rowling, *Short Stories of Heroism*; Rowling, *Hogwarts*.

3. J. R. R. Tolkien argued that world-building, which makes the author a "sub-Creator" in designing a secondary world to our own, is a requirement of fairy stories, allowing for a secondary belief in the fairy world's reality and producing one of the higher forms of art. Tolkien, "On Fairy Stories," 5–6.

4. Granger, "Russian Formalism."

5. Since the later twentieth century, historians have become more aware of the literary (and creative) qualities of historical narrative and historical sources, as well as the effects of narrative techniques on the perception of historical truth. See White, *Content of the Form*. White argues that historians and novelists have much more in common than most historians are willing to admit. See also Davis, *Fiction in the Archives*.

6. Rowling, "Leaky Cauldron."

7. Rowling, "Mr. Ollivander," "Malfoy Family," "Sir Cadogan," and "Hogwarts Ghosts." Even before the Statute of Secrecy, practicing magical arts could be a risky business. Nearly Headless Nick nearly lost his head because he augmented a lady's appearance, and we learn that the Fat Friar pulled one too many rabbits out of the communion cup and was—apparently—executed for it. Rowling, "Hogwarts Ghosts."

8. Rowling, "Malfoy Family."

9. Rowling, "Sir Cadogan."

10. Rowling, "Pure-Blood." Hermione Granger fits the description of a Magbob.

11. Rowling, "Seventeenth Century."
12. Rowling, "Pure-Blood."
13. Davis, *Witchcraft, Magic, and Culture*, 1.
14. Rowling, "Pure-Blood."
15. Martin, "Why So Old-Fashioned?"
16. Rowling, "Technology."
17. Rowling, "Knight Bus" and "Hogwarts Express."
18. Rowling, "Professor McGonagall."
19. Rowling, "Malfoy Family."
20. Rowling, "Pure-Blood."
21. Rowling.
22. Pratt, *Imperial Eyes*, 32–33.
23. Rowling, "Professor McGonagall" and "Potter Family."
24. See, for example, Swank, "Potter as Dystopian Literature"; and Castro, "Azkaban to Abu Ghraib."
25. Barton, "Half-Crazed Bureaucracy"; and Moline, "Introduction to Wizarding Law."
26. Aghtan, "Anticipating Exceptionalism," 49–58.
27. Consider how important the *Quibbler* becomes as a source of information and resistance—yet its marginal nature makes it suspect, and it too is vulnerable to the silencing effect of the Death Eater government in *Deathly Hallows*.
28. This seems a strange assertion, at odds with the total secrecy of the North American magical community, not to mention the United States' racist history, legacy of racial slavery, and dehumanization of people of African descent. See Swank, "House-Elves in Harlem."
29. The incident is a little too involved to relate here, but the daughter of MACUSA's Keeper of Treasure and Dragots (treasury secretary), Dorcus Twelvetrees, fell for a No-Maj and Scourer descendant, Bartholomew Barebone, who lured her to reveal the locations of MACUSA and Ilvermorny, among other secrets. Sanctioned by the International Confederation of Wizards, MACUSA enacted the law to drive the American wizarding community "still deeper underground." Rowling, "Rappaport's Law." Note that the name "Barebone" reminds us significantly of a famous English Puritan, Praise-God Barebone, from the English Civil War period.
30. Rowling, "1920s Wizarding America."
31. Tosh, *Pursuit of History*, 239–50.
32. Cannadine, *Ornamentalism*.
33. Sturgis, "Hogwarts in America."
34. McDaniel, "Quidditch and Cultural Imperialism." On Quidditch's role in the *Harry Potter* novels in demonstrating global power imbalances, see Long, "Quidditch."
35. There has been an outpouring of criticism regarding Rowling's writings about Native Americans. See Fallon, "Cultural Appropriation"; and Sturgis, "Hogwarts in America."
36. Rowling, "Fourteenth to Seventeenth Centuries." Sturgis provides an extensive critique of Rowling's portrayal of Native Americans in "Hogwarts in America."

3. Secrecy and Segregation in the Wizarding World's Hidden Histories

37. Rowling, "Ilvermorny."
38. Rowling.
39. Rowling's concept of historical chronology and geographical space also produces head-scratching. Noteworthy are her comments on how MACUSA moves its capital from Williamsburg, Virginia (1760), to Baltimore, Maryland (no date), and then to "Washington" (1777)—all before the major events of the Revolutionary War. The idea that a Washington existed at this point is ahistorical at best; the notion that Washington, DC, would be later overrun by Sasquatch makes one wonder if she bizarrely means Washington State, which certainly would have been far beyond the British imperial reach at this point. Of course, Rowling is not interested in North America as itself, but rather as a colonial mirror for Britain, and perhaps this explains the lack of care with its history. Rowling, "Magical Congress."
40. One also cannot help but wonder: What about Canada?
41. Bundel, "Salem Witchcraft Memorial."
42. Rowling, "Magical Congress."
43. Rowling. The Minister of Magic messages, "Sitting this one out," to which MACUSA replies, "Mind you do."

SECTION 2

INTERTEXTUAL READINGS

4. Harry, Aeneas, and the Foundational Text

Mitchell H. Parks

LOOK FORWARD TWO thousand years into the future. Some calamity has occurred—a natural disaster, say—involving great loss of life. A committee is appointed; a public memorial is planned. When it is finished, you go and visit it, and you find, inscribed on a broad surface, translated into your language, the following monumental text:

You think the dead we have loved ever truly leave us?[1] —Rowling

You might have an educated person's vague familiarity with the author or her work; you might know it well and be able to judge the appropriateness of the quotation in its new context; or you might just consider the sentiment, with its rhetorical invitation to reflection, and move along.

Now return to the twenty-first century. There are surely many who would find quoting Harry Potter in such a context undignified, perhaps even sacrilegious. There are, however, just as surely others—including many likely readers of this anthology—who even now would find this text meaningful in a somber, public context. How, then, will the reputation and wisdom of the Harry Potter series change through time? Since the novels were published, there has been endless speculation about how popular they will remain, on the scale of a decade, a generation, or even a century. It is even more difficult to assess how literature will age on the scale of millennia, and one cannot, of course, provide a firm answer to how readers will feel about Harry Potter in two thousand years—if, indeed, there will be anyone around to read anything at all. Nonetheless, it is possible to make conjectures on the basis of the fortunes of a text from the remote past: Virgil's *Aeneid*.

The choice to turn to the *Aeneid*, a Roman epic poem from the late first century BCE, is by no means arbitrary. It is a relevant text to put into

4. Harry, Aeneas, and the Foundational Text

dialogue with Harry Potter for two key reasons. First, the *Aeneid*, to an even greater extent than other ancient texts, provides a model for the self-conscious mining of earlier literature in the service of creating something new. The Harry Potter series, as Beatrice Groves, Richard Spencer, and John Granger have demonstrated, mines and deploys multifarious texts.[2] The *Aeneid* is not just useful for comparison here; in fact Harry Potter alludes directly to the *Aeneid*, and in ways similar to how the *Aeneid* itself performs allusion. The second reason for considering the *Aeneid* alongside Harry Potter is that, for almost two millennia, across diverse times and places, the *Aeneid* was the work of young adult literature par excellence, parallel to Harry Potter's place in contemporary society. Recognizing their shared cultural position allows us to read both texts in a new light: it may seem obvious that we can become more informed readers of a modern work such as Harry Potter by studying its literary predecessors, and yet it is equally true that what we learn from the series can help us see new facets of works that came before.

FOUNDATIONAL TEXTS

Scholarly readers of Harry Potter have frequently approached the series and its hero by way of the ancient Greek and Roman mythical traditions, and sometimes those cultures' epic traditions, which turn myths into literary narratives. For example, the first iteration of *The Ivory Tower and Harry Potter* contained essays by M. Katherine Grimes and by Mary Pharr that viewed Harry's heroism through a psychoanalytical lens, derived from twentieth-century studies of mythology; Pharr later took a more literary perspective on Harry's development as an epic hero.[3] Soon afterward, in 2015, Spencer catalogued references in the series to Greek and Roman material and analyzed these references with short essays. Even more recently, in the first chapter of *Literary Allusion in Harry Potter*, Beatrice Groves provided a magisterial analysis of storytelling patterns in Harry Potter and their analogues in the Homeric poems the *Iliad* and *Odyssey*, which later epic poets viewed as foundational texts for the genre.[4]

Nevertheless, Roman epic has not received the same attention as Greek epic and tragedy have in Potter studies: the *Aeneid*, which was viewed as a foundational epic in its own right almost immediately, has been largely ignored, except as a step on the road to Dante and, relatedly, as containing an example of katabasis, the trope of the hero's descent to the underworld.[5] One suspects that, at least in part, this is because the search for allusions to earlier literature has frequently been grounded in locating some "smoking gun"—or, better, *Priori Incantatem*—in extratextual sources such as Rowling's biography and interviews she has given. Aside from a few Virgil-derived epigraphs in *The Cuckoo's Calling*, these sources are absent regarding the *Aeneid*. But such evidence is not necessary to the process of literary criticism, especially when one uses the interpretive lens of intertextuality, which considers how literary works speak to and through each other. Rowling is, in the end, just one more reader of the series, and her biography is only one "text" among many available for intertextual analysis.[6] Moreover, assuming a reader-centric viewpoint has become all the more pressing given the growing divergence between Rowling's perspective on the values of the series and that of many fans, as evidenced by her public statements calling for limitations on trans rights.[7] If the literary branch of Potter studies is to avail itself of the full range of interpretive possibilities, scholarship on allusion in Harry Potter must reach the point at which we allow the novels to speak for themselves—to enter a conversation with other texts and with readers, and not solely with the author.

Without recourse to extratextual clues like author interviews, then, why should one bother to listen in on the dialogue between Harry Potter and the *Aeneid*? One initial response might be to cite the *Aeneid*'s status as a canonical "great text"—a status that would make it indisputably worth the attention. This, however, is yet another unnecessarily limiting approach, one prone to ending a conversation before it begins. In a world where diversity is increasingly recognized and valued, universal standards of greatness and appeals to what is "classic" and "canonical" are revealed as hollow. Instead, if we want to call a work "great," we must define the grounds for that praise, and not universally, but within the context of the conversation.[8] For the purposes of comparison with Harry Potter, the *Aeneid* is a classic in two senses: that it was a standard classroom text for centuries, and that it has been, and to some extent remains, culturally pervasive.

Regarding the latter criterion, just as it is hard to spend a day on the internet or look at bumper stickers in a college parking lot without encountering a casual reference to Harry Potter, so too is Virgil unavoidable. In the United States, for example, we encounter Latin mottoes daily on money,

4. Harry, Aeneas, and the Foundational Text

but it is remarkable that these mottoes—"Annuit coeptis," "Novus ordo seclorum," and even "E pluribus unum"—are not just Latin but specifically Virgilian.[9] For the framers of the US Constitution, the *Aeneid*, which narrates the start of Rome's history and empire, was a foundational text for authorizing a new republic.[10] Indeed, since Virgil was writing during the ascent of Augustus and the grafting of monarchy onto the Roman state, the *Aeneid* has often been understood as propaganda for the new regime.[11]

This is not, however, its only dimension. The futuristic vignette with which this chapter opened is based on a real-world example. The National September 11 Memorial contains, emblazoned on the wall of Memorial Hall, the following text:

No day shall erase you from the memory of time —Virgil

When the decision to use this text was made, modern readers of Virgil, and the public at large, exhibited the range of reactions depicted in this essay's opening vignette.[12] In this context, the *Aeneid* serves as a foundational text not for starting a nation but for how to mourn and remember the casualties of a national catastrophe. This is a thread woven so deeply into the epic that twentieth-century criticism of the poem was torn between viewing it as celebrating Augustus and as surreptitiously blaming him for the damage he wrought.[13] Grief and memory are, of course, key themes in Harry Potter, and the future reception of the series will depend on later cultures continuing to respond to them.

As for the texts' use in education, Harry Potter has begun to find a place in both the school curriculum and the curriculum of the household, now that many adults see the books as something culturally important to share with children. In terms of both its immediate popularity and its pedagogical potential, the Harry Potter series has much in common with the *Aeneid*.[14] In the Latin-speaking parts of the Roman Empire and, for over a millennium, in later cultures where Latin continued to be the language of the educated, adolescent learners took in the *Aeneid* in order to become better readers and orators, in addition to imbibing its moral lessons. In this sense, too, the *Aeneid* was a foundational text for the life of the active participant in society, just as researchers such as Anthony Gierzynski and Loris Vezzali have suggested that Harry Potter has been providing a political and cultural education to its younger readers.[15] For ancient, medieval, and early modern students and teachers, Virgil's epic was both for the young *and* serious literature: that was not a contradiction then, and one hopes it will cease to be for Harry Potter in the future.

BUILDING ON THE FOUNDATIONS

Part of how the *Aeneid* communicates this seriousness of purpose is by forging deep links to its predecessors as a foundational text: the *Iliad* and *Odyssey*. From the overall structure of the poem to the details of its individual lines, the *Aeneid* is suffused with Homeric elements.[16] It was obvious to ancient readers that the opening words of the *Aeneid*—*Arma virumque cano*, "I sing about arms and the man"—signaled that the epic would blend together the *Iliad*'s battle narratives ("arms") and the *Odyssey*'s story of a wandering hero ("the man").[17] Likewise, ancient and modern commentators have often analyzed the poem's structure into two halves: an Odyssean half (books 1 through 6), in which the Trojan hero Aeneas escapes from the Greeks at the fall of Troy and struggles toward his destined home in Italy, and an Iliadic half (books 7 through 12), in which Aeneas finds himself once again fighting a war like the one at Troy.[18] The *Aeneid* insinuates itself into the Homeric tradition not only by repeating plot elements but also by being a literal sequel, within the same continuity. Furthermore, the *Aeneid* does something that the Homeric poems do not do: telescoping the millennium of history between Aeneas and his descendant Augustus by way of prophecies and visions at key points in the narrative. In a sense it is all-inclusive, marking the end of history and, potentially, the end of epic by bridging distant myth and contemporary Rome.[19] It constructs itself not just as a sequel but as a conclusion.

For these reasons of structure and placement, the most specific comparisons can be drawn between the *Aeneid* and the final Harry Potter novel, *Harry Potter and the Deathly Hallows*, in which the prophecy at the heart of the series is fulfilled. This novel displays a structure parallel to that of the *Aeneid*: for a long stretch of the novel Harry and his friends, fleeing from their enemies, follow frustratingly incomplete clues in their quest for the Horcruxes, only to find themselves embroiled in the Battle of Hogwarts for its remainder. Aeneas is also the epic hero most closely aligned to Harry's mood in this novel: while the character of the *Iliad*'s Achilles is marked by

4. Harry, Aeneas, and the Foundational Text

an outsize wrath and that of the hero of the *Odyssey* by adaptability and duplicity, Aeneas, by contrast, inwardly grieves and seeks for absent parental figures, while outwardly displaying a drive to see the task through.[20] *Deathly Hallows*, with its refoundation of the Wizarding world after death and darkness, is in a way Harry's *Aeneid*.

The *Aeneid* begins seven years after the Trojan War, as the goddess Juno watches the Trojan remnant led by Aeneas journeying across the sea. An inveterate enemy of Troy, Juno causes a storm to scatter Aeneas's fleet. Our earliest glimpse of Aeneas himself comes as he expects imminent death by drowning. The first words he speaks in the poem show his mental state:

> All of you were three and four times more fortunate, whose lot it was to die before the faces of their parents under the high walls of Troy! Diomedes, mightiest of the race of Greeks, why could I not have fallen and spilled out my life at your hands on the fields of Ilium, where fierce Hector lies dead by Achilles' spear, where powerful Sarpedon lies, and where the Simois rolls beneath its waves so many lost shields, helmets, and strong bodies of men! (*Aeneid* 1.94–101)

He wishes to have died the death of an Iliadic hero, rather than facing anonymous death at sea because his destiny led him to survive Troy. Compare Harry, on learning from Snape's memories what fate awaits him in the Forbidden Forest:

> If he could only have died on that summer's night when he had left number four, Privet Drive, for the last time, when the noble phoenix-feather wand had saved him! If he could only have died like Hedwig, so quickly he would not have known it had happened! Or if he could have launched himself in front of a wand to save someone he loved.... He envied even his parents' death now.[21]

Harry, too, wishes to have died back at the beginning of the novel, in battle, instead of the very different kind of death he faces in this scene. Curiously, his internal monologue takes on a grander stylistic register, with the threefold "if he could" corresponding to Aeneas's three "where" clauses. His wand, which at this point has also died, so to speak, defending him as Hedwig had, even takes on an epic epithet, "noble," similar to "fierce" Hector and "powerful" Sarpedon. The echo of Aeneas in Harry's speech invites the reader to find points of overlap: the loneliness of both heroes in this moment; the number of deaths, often self-sacrificial, they have each already witnessed; the hint that Harry, like Aeneas, is destined to survive what seems to be certain doom.

This moment is illustrative not only of the heroes themselves but also of how both the Harry Potter series and the *Aeneid* interact with their models. Aeneas's words are in fact based on a speech of Odysseus in the *Odyssey* (5.306–12). Odysseus ends *his* speech, however, by stating that if he had died at Troy, he would have had a proper funeral and fame, which his prospective "wretched death" at sea prevents. There is nothing about burial and fame in Aeneas's version. His emphasis instead falls on wishing for death as a sacrifice for his community ("before the faces of their parents"), with no envisioned reward.[22]

Harry's lament picks up on this note from Aeneas's version, aligning him more closely with Aeneas than with Odysseus, while also adding something else to the chord: the wish for a swift, uncomplicated death. What is remarkable about this kind of literary conversation is that, in the process of comparison, these moments start to influence each other.[23] Even if the idea was already available in the text of the *Aeneid*, it is more likely, once we have read Harry's version, that we will hear that same request for an easy, comprehensible death in Aeneas's. Likewise, we can also hear, alongside Odysseus's selfish pursuit of glory, a regret for not having lost his life for others: he specifically wishes to have died on the day when he fought to reclaim the corpse of Achilles from the battlefield. These death wishes invite the reader to plot each hero on a sort of grid of heroism, calculating and, to some extent, collapsing the distances between them.[24] The ease with which Harry slips into this intertextual matrix shows that Harry Potter converses with its predecessors just as the *Aeneid* does.

BACK TO THE BEGINNING

Virgil and his contemporaries inherited from their Alexandrian Greek models and greatly developed the art of structuring long works, including through ring composition.[25] As an heir in their own turn to this tradition, the Harry Potter novels exhibit complex and meaningful structures. A

4. Harry, Aeneas, and the Foundational Text

comparison with the *Aeneid* illuminates additional structural elements. For example, the *Aeneid* can help the reader identify one particular moment in *Deathly Hallows* where the structure of the novel is not only aesthetically satisfying but also thematically relevant. This hinge is the moment mentioned earlier, the shift between the Odyssean and Iliadic portions of *Deathly Hallows*. Here the text makes a direct allusion to the *Aeneid*, by means of a character's name.

At the start of book 7, Aeneas reaches the shores of Latium, the region of Italy where his descendants Romulus and Remus will found Rome. The local king, Latinus, has received a prophecy that his daughter will marry a foreigner, and he initially welcomes the Trojans with an offer of marriage and many gifts. The final gift is the grandest: to Aeneas he sends fire-breathing horses that the enchantress Circe secretly bred from the horses of her father, the Sun (7.280–83). This detail would seem inconsequential, were it not for its sequel. It is at this moment that Juno calls up a Fury from the underworld to cause war between Aeneas and Latinus. First, the Fury bewitches Latinus's wife Amata—who shares her name with a character from "The Fountain of Fair Fortune" in *The Tales of Beedle the Bard*—by throwing a snake from her serpentine hair at the queen (7.346–47). The Fury then enchants an Italian prince, Turnus, Amata's preferred choice to be her daughter's husband. Amata and Turnus start rousing opposition to the Trojans: Aeneas in particular is painted as a version of his kinsman Paris, whose running off with another man's wife had sparked the Trojan War. From there, the situation spirals into all-out war between Aeneas's Trojans and Turnus's Italians, with the Trojans suddenly besieged in their camp, just as they had been besieged by the Greeks at Troy.

This repetition of the Trojan War was predicted earlier in the poem (6.83–97) by the prophetess known as the Sibyl—the eponym, as many have noted, of Professor Trelawney—and it is also foreshadowed by Latinus's gift to Aeneas right before the conflict breaks out, through the aforementioned detail about the horses. The explanation requires another look back at the *Iliad*. Aeneas's battlefield debut in the *Iliad* is in the scene in which he fought the Greek hero Diomedes, the same fight in which Aeneas, in his first appearance in the *Aeneid*, wishes to have died. In the *Iliad*, Diomedes attacks him in order to steal his horses, which were secretly bred by Aeneas's father Anchises from a stock given to Troy's king by Zeus himself (*Iliad* 5.265–73). The fact that in the *Aeneid*, Aeneas receives such similar horses from Latinus turns out to be an ill omen: they mark his personal reentry into the Trojan War by alluding to his debut in the *Iliad*.[26] From here, the plot of the Homeric model will keep reasserting itself, as Aeneas and Turnus replay the conflicts of the *Iliad* and suffer analogous losses.

To return to *Deathly Hallows*: although one could argue that Harry's very arrival at Hogwarts, like Aeneas's in Latium, sparks the chain of events that leads to war, there is only one direct inciting incident, in which Voldemort is alerted to Harry's location and battle becomes unavoidable. This occurs in the Ravenclaw Common Room, when the Death Eater Alecto Carrow catches Harry searching for the diadem.[27] Alecto's name is yet another whose most famous literary occurrence is in the *Aeneid*: it is the name of Juno's Fury.[28] In both works, the switch from quest narrative to war narrative is accomplished by a character named Alecto and, in both cases, by means of a snake, since Alecto summons Voldemort by means of her Dark Mark, "the skull and snake branded on her forearm." A reader of the *Aeneid*, recognizing the allusion, will become alert to the changes in tone, pace, and content in the remaining chapters of the novel, just as in the epic.[29]

That is not all, however: the allusion also prompts the reader to ask to what extent this is also a return to the beginning for Harry. He has certainly come back to Hogwarts—after a stop at Gringotts, just as in *Sorcerer's Stone*—but the battle, like the conflict between Aeneas and Turnus, will reawaken the preceding narratives by presenting them again in compressed form. Alecto's summoning of Voldemort essentially starts a timer: the battle will begin at midnight.[30] When it does, the reader is treated, in a few short pages, to a series of allusions to the previous six books.[31] The striking of midnight coincides with Hagrid crashing in through a window, just as Hagrid had burst through the door at midnight on their first meeting (*Sorcerer's Stone*). Next, Neville dashes by with Mandrakes (*Chamber of Secrets*), and the troops are rallied by Sir Cadogan (*Prisoner of Azkaban*). Shortly thereafter, Hermione and Ron's dramatic kiss is triggered by Ron's support for the rights of house-elves (*Goblet of Fire*). Then Grawp appears, and the life of one of the Marauders is imperiled by a Death Eater (*Order of the Phoenix*). Finally Harry arrives at his destination, the Room

4. Harry, Aeneas, and the Foundational Text

of Requirement in its guise as the "the place where everything is hidden" (*Half-Blood Prince*).[32] Just as Aeneas starts the Trojan War anew, so too do we see Harry's narrative in miniature as he approaches its conclusion.

PARENTS AND ROLE-MODELS

What does this return to the beginning mean, for Harry and for Aeneas? For both heroes, it means a chance to make different choices from those of their past selves and their models. As discussed earlier, it is well established that Aeneas rewrites the heroism of Achilles and Odysseus: Harry, in turn, does the same to Aeneas, and their parental influences are key to the comparison.[33] After Snape shares his memories with one last look into Lily's eyes, Harry undergoes a transformation: he has spent most of the series imitating the swashbuckling heroism of his father, but in order to meet his death he must recognize his mother's loving self-sacrifice as the better model. After his resurrection, he duels Voldemort with words and defensive magic, rather than violence.

The *Aeneid* also ends with a duel, but not between Aeneas and Juno: the goddess is not a foe to be defeated, like Voldemort, but a divine force to be propitiated and accepted, like Death. Instead, Aeneas faces Turnus at the poem's close. Aeneas is initially wounded and leaves the battlefield; he is resurrected, as it were, by his mother Venus. She does this by means of dittany, here in its most famous pre-Potter literary appearance (*Aeneid* 12.412), but even more important for connecting these works is Venus's identity as the goddess of love—the same divine force, in other words, that protects and resurrects Harry and whose source is also his mother. And this is not the first time Venus has saved Aeneas: in his first appearance in the epic "continuity," she had rescued him from his duel with Diomedes. The salvific power of love connects each hero's beginning to his story's end.

Throughout the poem, Aeneas has shared with Harry a powerful urge to rely on his parents' support, without much hope of receiving it. Unlike Harry, whose use of the Resurrection Stone enables this support in the end, Aeneas's final duel with Turnus finds the two of them alone on the battlefield, and it is here that Aeneas makes a choice that, for many readers of the poem, has defined Aeneas's character and the tone of the entire epic. He has Turnus at his mercy, and, unlike Voldemort, Turnus shows remorse.

Aeneas, however, suddenly reminded of a young ally—the *Aeneid*'s version of Colin Creevey—whom Turnus has slain, kills him in turn, and there the poem abruptly ends.

Readers have often turned to Aeneas's encounter with Anchises in the underworld at the poem's midpoint in order to interpret this finale. There, Anchises had offered to Aeneas advice on how to be truly Roman: "Spare the submissive and finish off the proud" (6.853). In killing Turnus, does he live up to his father's model? The answer has never been clear. Nonetheless, Harry Potter readers may find more clarity than others, because the series brings to the surface a conflict that may also underlie the *Aeneid*: tension between parental role models.[34] Like Harry, Aeneas tries to live up to his father throughout the epic, but in the end, a familiarity with Harry Potter makes it easier to identify Aeneas's realignment toward his mother, just as Harry adopts Lily's role. Throughout the epic, Venus's actions have been motivated by her desire to fulfill the imperial destiny of Rome. In the *Aeneid*, love is not patient and self-sacrificial but passionate and acquisitive. By reacting in the heat of the moment to avenge a friend and by taking the quickest means to remove an obstacle to Roman destiny, Aeneas becomes an agent of his mother's version of divine love. This difference in how the texts approach love and power marks Harry out as a transformation of his model, Aeneas.

If Aeneas founds the Roman empire, what does Harry found? That is a question that subsequent generations will answer and reanswer. For Virgil's contemporaries, it was by no means obvious that Augustus's restructuring of the state would last for centuries. Likewise, future readers of Harry Potter will find in the series the seeds of historical patterns and problems that are harder for us to pin down in the moment.[35] By looking to the *Aeneid*, however, we can start the process of identifying and, indeed, shaping the transhistorical dimensions of "the boy who lived."

The *Aeneid*'s reception suggests questions to ask and trends to follow: here are just three examples. First, the canonization of the *Aeneid* forced earlier works of Roman epic out of the schoolroom and out of readership. As information storage technology (i.e., books) evolved, those earlier epics ceased to be copied onto new media and are now lost. This raises questions

4. Harry, Aeneas, and the Foundational Text

about Harry Potter's place within its tradition. Has the Harry Potter series reduced the readership of any of its predecessors? Are people less likely to read Tolkien, or, for that matter, the *Aeneid*?

Next, the tragic love story of Aeneas and Dido in book 4 has exerted an outsize effect on the *Aeneid*'s reception, relative to the bulk of its narrative. Indeed, the North African bishop Augustine reports that his fourth-century schooling included "the wanderings of Aeneas," but he devotes more of that sentence to describing how he "wept for the death of Dido" (*Confessions* 1.13.20). The political questions raised by the *Aeneid* loom large for scholars, but they have not always been the central concern for readers in general. On this point, the Harry Potter fan community, members of which have engaged in "shipping wars" and rewriting relationships in fanfiction, provides a model for understanding the motives of historical readers of the *Aeneid*, while Dido provides a salutary reminder that Harry Potter scholarship should take note of readers' evolving interests.[36]

Finally, the *Aeneid* spawned centuries of transformative work based on it, starting with the poetry of Virgil's younger contemporary Ovid and continuing well beyond Dante to authors such as Ursula K. Le Guin. Just as one can ask how Harry Potter might displace earlier literature, it may also be useful to read subsequent works specifically as "post-Potter." Among traditionally published novels, *The Hunger Games* and *The Magicians* were some of the earliest Ovidian transformations of Potter themes, and doubtless there are already many others. This is not, however, the only kind of transformative work the *Aeneid* inspired: particularly because it lacks anything like the epilogue of *Deathly Hallows*, the *Aeneid* was prone to being continued and expanded in ways for which Harry Potter fanfiction and adaptation provide a model. The most famous example is Maffeo Vegio's fifteenth-century *Aeneid Book Thirteen*, which finds an analogue in *Harry Potter and the Cursed Child*: both works, like much fanfiction, return to a familiar text and make explicit themes and later events only adumbrated in the original.

What truly signaled the *Aeneid*'s cultural status, however, was the way that the story could be adapted by members of new identity groups to create their own *Aeneid*-like foundational moment, such as the medieval legend of Brutus, descendant of Aeneas and founder of "New Troy"—later known as London. Potter scholars should therefore keep an eye out for texts that hitch their wagons to Harry in order to foster group identities.[37] We will, moreover, know that Harry Potter has truly "arrived" as a foundational text when it finds its own version of Proba, a fourth-century Roman poet. Her mode of transfiguring Virgil was to make a "patchwork poem" (*cento*) out of his verses: she rearranged Virgil's exact words so that they told stories from Genesis, Exodus, and the New Testament. Ancient, medieval, and modern readers have even performed a kind of divination called *sortes Virgilianae* by opening Virgil's works at random and taking the words they find as a prophecy. Just as Virgil's words have proven, to quote Dumbledore, "an inexhaustible source of magic," so too may future generations find similar inspiration in Harry Potter.[38]

NOTES

The author would like to thank Lana Whited for her thoughtful suggestions and assistance with this essay.

1. The quotation is from Rowling, *Prisoner of Azkaban*, 427. All Harry Potter book citations in this essay refer to the original Scholastic (US) editions.

2. Groves, *Literary Allusion*; Spencer, *Classical World*; and Granger, *Potter's Bookshelf*.

3. Grimes, "Harry Potter"; Pharr, "In Medias Res"; and Pharr, "Paradox." Additional representative essays include Walde, "Graeco-Roman Antiquity"; Rogers, "Orestes and the Half-Blood Prince"; and Lovatt, "Metamorphoses of Classics."

4. Groves, *Literary Allusion*, 1–18.

5. The exceptions are Spencer, *Classical World*, 53–55; Walde, "Graeco-Roman Antiquity," 368–75; and Panoussi, "Harry's Underworld Journey," 42–68. Panoussi does focus on katabasis, but specifically as it appears in Virgil, and she compares the two texts on a broader scale in ways complementary with this essay.

6. Cf. Bishop, "Undead Author." Rowling, as is often noted, pursued Greek and Roman studies at the University of Exeter, where she probably did encounter the *Aeneid*, according to the reading list provided by one of her professors: see Wiseman, "Rowling and the Ancient World," 95.

7. See, among many other analyses and responses, Henderson, "A Coda"; Duggan, "Transformative Reading," 159–63.

8. Eliot, "What Is a Classic?," 116, serves as a model for providing a definition, even if one objects to the particulars.

9. Hardie, *Last Trojan Hero*, a good place to start for those investigating Virgil's later impact, surveys these mottoes on p. 1.

10. Panoussi also compares the *Aeneid* and *Harry Potter* as "foundational," but her usage is restricted to political foundation; by contrast, this essay takes a multivalent approach to what it means to be "foundational." Panoussi, "Underworld Journey," 44.

11. Cf. Granger, *Deathly Hallows Lectures*, 34.

12. Dunlap, "Grim Origins"; and Pandey, "Sowing the Seeds of War," 24–25.

4. Harry, Aeneas, and the Foundational Text

13. See Pandey, "Sowing the Seeds of War," 7–8 for definitions and qualifications.

14. Tarrant, "Aspects of Virgil's Reception." On the role of literature in ancient Greek and Roman education, as well as the *Aeneid*'s place in particular, see Lerer, *Children's Literature*, 17–34.

15. Gierzynski, *Millennials*, 63; and Vezzali et al., "Greatest Magic," 117. Whereas Vezzali used controlled experiments, Gierzynski's work is based on a retrospective survey, which is methodologically more similar to how one can judge the effects of reading Virgil among past societies.

16. This essay does not provide exhaustive references to Virgilian scholarship. Those engaging with the *Aeneid* for the first time can find much insight into ways of reading the text in Perkell, *Reading Vergil's Aeneid*.

17. All translations in this essay are the author's own.

18. On the history of the "two halves" question and its importance for intertextual readings of the *Aeneid*, see Farrell, *Juno's Aeneid*, 2–3, 7–28.

19. Cf. Hardie, *Epic Successors*, 12–13; Walde, "Graeco-Roman Antiquity," 371; and Panoussi, "Underworld Journey," 56.

20. Cf. Spencer, *Classical World*, 53; Walde, "Graeco-Roman Antiquity," 375; and Pharr, "Paradox," 14. On Aeneas's composite character, see Hardie, *Epic Successors*, 35.

21. Rowling, *Deathly Hallows*, 692.

22. Perkell, "Aeneid 1," 40; and Farrell, *Juno's Aeneid*, 66–70.

23. Cf. Hinds, *Allusion and Intertext*, 116–19, on the interplay between Aeneas's speech and an Ovidian reworking of it, in the mouth of Diomedes.

24. Farrell, *Juno's Aeneid*, analyzes the *Aeneid* itself as fundamentally concerned with raising, though not answering, the questions "Is this poem going to be an *Iliad* or an *Odyssey*?" and "Is Aeneas another Achilles or another Odysseus?" See especially Farrell, *Juno's Aeneid*, 35.

25. Duckworth, "Architecture of the *Aeneid*," is antiquated but illustrative.

26. Lyne, *Further Voices*, 139, identifies the allusion but assigns a different meaning to it.

27. Rowling, *Deathly Hallows*, 588.

28. The name is often spelled Allecto, but both variants are attested in Latin and Greek sources.

29. Nor is this the first time that a classical reference has performed a similar function in the Harry Potter works: the appearance of a sphinx right before Harry reaches the Triwizard Cup (Rowling, *Goblet of Fire*, 628–31) is a cue that he is about to meet the Oedipus-inspired Tom Riddle.

30. Rowling, *Deathly Hallows*, 610.

31. Rowling, 618–27.

32. Rowling, 627.

33. For another perspective on parental role modeling in Harry Potter, see Emily Strand, "Parenting Models in the Potter Saga and *Cursed Child*: Human and Divine," chapter 16 of this volume.

34. Cf. Farrell, "*Aeneid* 5," 109–10; and Panoussi, "Underworld Journey," 61.

35. Panoussi attempts an answer: "The world order that Harry represents is one of liberal democratic values." Panoussi, "Underworld Journey," 59, cf. 44.

36. See Duggan, "Transformative Readings," 154–9, for an overview of trends in Harry Potter fanfiction and their interaction with ways of reading the series.

37. Thomas, *The Dark Fantastic: Race and the Imagination from Harry Potter to the Hunger Games,* especially 152–64, describes models for "restorying," by means of which fan communities can make room in a narrative for greater diversity of perspectives.

38. Appropriately enough, Dumbledore's oft-quoted line derives not from the novel *Deathly Hallows* but from the film adaptation, which eloquently demonstrates how quickly the later tradition can entangle itself with our understanding of the original text.

5. From Sword to Sorcery

The Medieval(ist) Juxtaposition of Magic and Might in Harry Potter

Laurie Beckoff

IF KING ARTHUR and his knights of the Round Table were to attend Hogwarts School of Witchcraft and Wizardry, most of them would likely be sorted into Gryffindor: the house "where dwell the brave at heart," who possess "daring, nerve, and chivalry."[1] The protagonists of the Harry Potter series are mainly Gryffindors who undertake intrepid quests, slay monsters, and fight evil in epic battles like the heroes of old. However, such action, though commonly central in medievalist fantasy, constitutes a small part of Harry's adventures. While Arthurian violence has attracted attention for centuries in both medieval and modern literature, the magic of Potter has captivated, charmed, delighted, mystified, resonated, and inspired by echoing the magic of Arthurian myth: challenging norms, judging morality, and facilitating personal development that can inhibit violence.

SHADOWS OF THE PAST: MEDIEVALISM AND FANTASY

Medievalism has been defined by Louise D'Arcens as "the reception, interpretation or recreation of the European Middle Ages in post-medieval cultures," by Leslie J. Workman as "the continuing process of creating the Middle Ages," and by Tom Shippey as "any post-medieval attempt to reimagine the Middle Ages, or some aspect [thereof], for the modern world."[2] Underlying all of these definitions is the idea that a portion of history between antiquity and the Renaissance remains of interest to modern society and is constantly being recycled in literature, media, and culture.

Ranging from about 500 CE to 1500 CE, the medieval period is a suitable backdrop for fantasy due to the pervasiveness of magic in medieval literature and the fact that the era is, in Tison Pugh and Angela Jane Weisl's view, "an invention of those who came after it; its entire construction is, essentially, a fantasy," thus serving as a *"tabula rasa* always inviting new rewritings."[3] Fantasy literature is saturated with images of a premodern past. Consequently, the word *medieval* tends to conjure up myth, magic, and monsters.

A historical understanding of the medieval period as characterized by the omnipresence of war leads to an expectation for action-packed, sword-swinging, blood-spilling escapades alongside the mysterious and mystical. M. J. Toswell lists common tropes of medievalism:

> knights; heroes; swords; vast landscapes with castles and forests and mountains; handmade artifacts; treasure-hunting; quests; witches and warlocks; various representations of the Other, including giants, elves, dwarves, and so on; flowery speechifying to make declarations about honor and justice; medieval weaponry and armor; magic . . .[4]

Violence and the supernatural are common threads. J. R. R. Tolkien's *Lord of the Rings* (1954–55), C. S. Lewis's *Chronicles of Narnia* (1950–56), and George R. R. Martin's *Song of Ice and Fire* (1996–) offer secondary fantasy worlds with these echoes of medieval Europe. According to Edward James, Tolkien's work made the Middle Ages "the default cultural model for the fantasy world."[5] Many subgenres feature warrior heroes and the supernatural set against a quasi-medieval backdrop.

Andrew Lynch writes, "War lies at the heart of contemporary medievalism."[6] Whether it is highlighted in gory detail or raging in the background, condemned or glorified, war is present. In opposing villains, heroes can use any means necessary—usually physical violence—and those who do so are portrayed as heroic. While war may be depicted as evil, Lynch argues, "it is rare to see the use of medievalism to contest the basic association of fighting with goodness and with struggle towards a worthwhile goal."[7] Although certain characters and situations may call for a critical examination of the use of force, it is a given that battles will be fought and lives will be taken.

The Harry Potter series questions this necessity by removing the medievalist military backdrop while maintaining medieval allusions. Although Hogwarts exists in the late twentieth century, Heather Arden and Kathryn Lorenz observe that the school remains "rooted in the Middle Ages" through its castle, use of parchment, creatures, magical objects, and Latin-derived spells and names.[8] Unlike other heroic fantasy, the fates of the Wizarding and Muggle worlds rest in the hands of students, teachers, and families. Violence is present, but it is limited, gradual, and approached from a more critical standpoint.

WARRIORS AND WIZARDS: VIOLENCE AND MAGIC IN ARTHURIAN LITERATURE

One of the most widely adapted sources for medieval literature is Arthurian legend because it is, as described by Michelle Sweeney, "distant enough and mythologized enough to be more fantastic than real."[9] Thomas Malory's fifteenth-century *Le Morte Darthur* links encounters with magic to battles for the kingdom, making it a useful touchstone for examining magic and violence. A manifestation of violence as a defining feature of Arthurian literature is the focus on a knightly fellowship. Arthur is a great conqueror, and Lancelot is respected for his skill in battle, preventing uprisings by holding all Arthur's "cankered enemies in subjection and danger" (Malory, *Le Morte Darthur*, 21.2).[10] Sir Cador is pleased by a challenge from Rome, "for now shall we have war and worship"—the two go hand in hand (5.1). Gawain and Gareth, as well as Percival and Ector, fight automatically before speaking or recognizing one another. Jean E. Jost and K. S. Whetter both observe Malory's dismissal of fighting as normative and inevitable, despite its horrors.[11]

While Malory portrays military prowess as admirable, he also highlights the tragic consequences of warfare. Lancelot "increase[s] so marvellously in worship and honour" because "in all tournaments, jousts, and deeds of arms, both for life and death, he passe[s] all other knights" (6.1). However, he also sustains and inflicts many serious injuries during his escapades, eventually sparking Gawain's unquenchable thirst for vengeance by killing his brothers, which leads to the breaking of the Round Table. Violence can be a tool of power, esteem, stability, and justice, but it easily becomes a chaotic source of destruction.

While violence is the dominant activity of the genre, Arthurian romances frequently feature fairies, enchantresses, prophecies, mythical creatures, potions, and magical objects. Magic is often depicted as an alternative distinct from or in direct opposition to the violence dominating the courtly world, especially when it is used to cure injury. The Sangrail heals both physical and psychological ailments, and Lancelot distinguishes himself by healing Sir Urry's cursed wounds. The first literary appearance of Morgan le Fay is a flattering portrait in Geoffrey of Monmouth's *Vita Merlini* of a beneficent, knowledgeable, skilled healer who will cure Arthur's fatal wounds.[12] Carolyne Larrington notes that "enchantresses often work at an interesting tangent to the courtly world, challenging or unsettling its norms, making opportunities for other voices ... to be heard" in a society "where the supreme value is male honour, gained on the battlefield."[13] Merlin, who thrice prevents violence in the first section of *Le Morte*, also offers a magical alternative to traditional masculinity as, in Larrington's words, "an intellectual whose prowess is not physical and embodied but mental and abstract."[14]

In exploring the impossible and violating the laws of science and nature, the fantastic, according to Rosemary Jackson, "opens up, for a brief moment, onto disorder, onto that which lies outside the law, that which is outside dominant value systems," and thus "traces the unsaid and unseen of culture."[15] When magic is at the center of society rather than on the fringes, different values can be given voice and the dominance of violence can be questioned.

"TEACH US SOMETHING PLEASE": MAGIC AND EDUCATION

Harry and his friends simultaneously embody the roles of knights and enchanters. They are the central characters who undertake quests through which they achieve glory, learn about themselves, and protect their society, but they also have magical abilities. While Arthurian enchanters operate outside the court to challenge, aid, test, reward, or harm the protagonists, Harry Potter centers on students in a self-enclosed world of magic.

Because in medieval literature the ability to perform magic is often gained through study, Hogwarts School of Witchcraft and Wizardry is an apt setting. In both Arthurian legend and the Harry Potter books, magic is a practice to be honed and refined that necessitates an understanding of nature, including celestial bodies, magical plants, and fantastic beasts. Magic is not merely a newly discovered power for Harry but an opportunity and expectation to learn. Possessing magical blood or buying a wand does not a wizard make. Harry quickly finds that there is "a lot more to magic . . . than waving your wand and saying a few funny words."[16] The emphasis on learning and contemplation distinguishes enchanters from knights, whose training prioritizes the body over the mind and quick instincts over slow deliberation. It is T. H. White's young Arthur under Merlin's magical tutelage in *The Once and Future King* who is "Harry's spiritual ancestor."[17] Hogwarts essentially provides a glimpse into the kind of study Arthurian enchanters might have undertaken.

Like *Le Morte*, the Harry Potter books feature individual quests against a larger political backdrop, each task serving to develop the characters' skills, knowledge, and identities and connecting to the overarching narrative. Rather than a tale of violence punctuated by magic, they tell a tale of magic punctuated by violence. The impetus behind Harry's escapades is not fun or glory but necessity, and his heroics come from his sense of responsibility toward others. Born into violence, he strives for peace. Hogwarts trains him to be not a soldier but a thinker.

Even when the threat of Voldemort lingers overhead, Harry's priority is supposed to be learning, a peaceful pursuit upon which violence could suddenly intrude. It is only in the final book that Harry's struggle against Voldemort takes precedence and prevents him from returning to school. Even then, his mission to find and destroy Voldemort's Horcruxes involves reading, research, and understanding advanced magic. Harry cannot simply pursue an adventure or charge into battle. He is rarely given a straightforward task to accomplish; instead, each book poses a mystery for him to solve, so that it is the act of interpretation itself that constitutes the quest, Shira Wolosky argues.[18] The nature of the challenges he faces precludes the possibility of opposing evil through conventional methods. Sheer force cannot defeat a villain who has taken precautions to ensure his immortality; as Harry quips, "Has anyone ever tried sticking a sword in Voldemort?"[19] Complex problems demand complex solutions.

In a world with medieval constructions of magic that require gradual study and intricate puzzles that take time to solve, characters must work slowly and think creatively. The centrality of education and critical thinking provides a stark contrast to the bold and impulsive behavior of knights, thus establishing an approach to conflict resolution that prioritizes ethics and eschews violence whenever possible.

5. From Sword to Sorcery

MAGIC IS MIGHT IS RIGHT: MAGIC FOR AND AGAINST VIOLENCE

Corinne Saunders has observed the importance of intention in medieval magic, concluding that "the force of magic, its potential violence, is not straightforwardly moral or immoral."[20] Morgan is described as "the false sorceress and witch most that is now living," and the Lady of the Lake is "the destroyer of many good knights," but Nenive does "great goodness unto King Arthur and to all his knights," and Merlin frequently helps them too (8.34, 2.3, 18.8). The Potter series features a similar construction, in which, as in Saunders's analysis, "the human manipulation of magic . . . and especially the use of magical violence . . . often defines individual morality," allowing for a critical examination of motivation, ethics, and methodology.[21]

In the world of Harry Potter, magic is—in the author's own words—"morally neutral," and using magic for violence takes a concentrated effort.[22] Even when Harry is at his most emotionally vulnerable, he is unable to cast an Unforgivable Curse on Bellatrix Lestrange, who tells him, "You need to *mean* them, Potter! You need to really want to cause pain—to enjoy it."[23] The Killing Curse "needs a powerful bit of magic behind it."[24] In order for Voldemort to create Horcruxes to house pieces of his soul, he needed not only to kill and perform a horrific process six times but also to obtain obscure and restricted information. Violent magic is difficult to perform due to both social and legal sanctions as well as the nature of the magic itself, requiring dedication, study, and genuine resolve.

Although Arthurian enchanters can be violent and enable knightly violence, they are notably less so when separated from the court. Larrington argues that Morgan's violent magic is a response to chivalric violence, demonstrated by the fact that she is portrayed as benevolent in texts in which she resides outside of Camelot in Avalon.[25] While the Merlin of Geoffrey of Monmouth's *Historia regum Britanniae* partakes in political intrigue and military operations, the Merlin of Geoffrey's later *Vita Merlini* focuses on the natural world and the divine, creating a peaceful intellectual community in the wilderness.[26] It is among knights that violence is abundant.

While knightly duels result in bodily harm, a duel in Harry Potter need not involve injury. Although magic is potentially dangerous, it has more flexibility and utility than chivalric violence. *Expelliarmus* disarms an opponent of a wand, *Petrificus Totalus* freezes the opponent, and *Protego* creates a shield. Saunders sees magic in both medieval romance and Harry Potter as "exotic, surprising, full of possibilities beyond the natural, and thus liberating."[27] With his wand, Harry can confront evil without actively harming anyone and even becomes the master of the Elder Wand through nonviolent means, while Voldemort fails to win it through murder.

Even when the stakes are highest, Harry is reluctant to use violence, opting for Expelliarmus over more offensive measures and insisting, "I won't blast people out of my way just because they're there. . . . That's Voldemort's job."[28] He is dedicated to fighting on his own primarily defensive terms and refuses to compromise his values. After learning of the prophecy foretelling that either he or Voldemort must kill the other, Harry finds it "very hard to believe . . . that his life must include, or end in, murder," no matter the justification.[29] In Siobhan McEvoy-Levy's view, Harry believes that "peace should be achieved by peaceful means."[30] He employs other tools in his arsenal before resorting to violence.

The Potter books highlight the supposedly limited resources for conflict resolution in our society by imagining how difficult matters could be confronted with alternative methods. Jackson writes that by "presenting that which cannot be, but *is*, fantasy exposes a culture's definitions of that which can be."[31] This technique can cause disillusionment and dissatisfaction with reality and thus the subversive thought Jackson finds prevalent in fantasy. Magic offers new perspectives through solutions that seem desirable but unattainable and challenges the assumption that violence is inevitable. Although we may not have magic, our substitutes can be technology, philosophy, and innovation.

While intention alters the results of magic, knightly prowess leaves little room for variation from one knight or cause to another. The waters of Arthurian ethics are muddied by the association of physical prowess with God's favor and moral justice. Malory portrays the Round Table as using violence for good causes, but White criticizes this might-for-right agenda in *The Once and Future King*. Raymond H. Thompson notes that medieval romance and fantasy generally share happy endings, implicitly endorsing such an agenda, with Malory and White as tragic exceptions depicting violence as an unsustainable method of peacekeeping.[32] Malory's very title—"The Death of Arthur"—highlights his story's tragic structure, and White similarly concludes with the dissolution of Camelot and deaths of the heroes.

Danny Adams argues that "the *spirit* of Harry Potter is Arthurian at its best and anti-Arthurian to avoid the point when Camelot met its worst."[33] When the heroes have magic, the paradigm shifts from a might-for-right mission to a focus on methods that reflect intention and morals. When the Death Eaters infiltrate the Ministry of Magic, they advocate the weaponization of magic with the slogan "Magic is might," encouraging magical violence as a tool of oppression.[34] But Potter depicts magic as so much more than might and violence as particularly deplorable in a society wherein other options exist. Therefore, even with magical protagonists, Jules Zanger's observation about fantasy holds true: "Evil magic is defeated finally by human virtues: courage, skill, innocence, or love."[35] In Harry Potter, these virtues are reflected in the heroes' use of magic itself.

BATTLES WITHIN: MAGIC AND INTROSPECTION

In medieval romance, magic offers an escape from the real world for the exploration of difficult or taboo issues, both political and personal.[36] Sweeney argues that the purpose of magic is "evaluation of the characters' values, identities or moral beliefs," functioning "as a barometer for . . . emotional development" and allowing space for critique and growth.[37] Morgan le Fay devises the supernatural challenges of *Sir Gawain and the Green Knight* to test the honesty, courage, and virtue of the Round Table. In Chrétien de Troyes's *The Knight with the Lion*, Yvain's use of a magical ring to make him invisible connects to his need to reinvent himself after committing murder.[38] Magic provides opportunities for characters to examine their inner selves, to prove their moral worth, and to explore, express, and control their emotions in healthy, constructive, and productive ways.

The magic of the Harry Potter series similarly functions as a manifestation of internal circumstances, as Wolosky writes, "chart[ing] for us our inward experiences, giving us ways of bringing them to consciousness, recognizing and acknowledging them, and ultimately dealing with them and integrating them into our self-understanding."[39] If "the great theme of medieval romance is self-realization," as Thompson argues, Harry Potter upholds this tradition by giving characters opportunities to translate their thoughts, feelings, fears, and dreams into action.[40] Many forms of magic in the series fit with Wolosky's definition of psychological allegory as the externalization of internal states.[41] Boggarts, for instance, take the form of whatever the viewer fears most and can be defeated with humor using the *Riddikulus* Charm. Dementors embody depression and are combatted by using a happy memory to cast a Patronus. These metaphors can help readers make sense of their own feelings.

Magical objects also serve as sources of character development. The sword of Gryffindor can only be obtained by displaying the courage of a true Gryffindor, just as only Arthur as the true king can pull the sword from the stone. Arthur's valuation of the magical sword and scabbard from the Lady of the Lake presents an interesting parallel for two of the Deathly Hallows: the Elder Wand and the Cloak of Invisibility. Merlin scolds Arthur's folly in preferring the sword when the scabbard prevents him from losing blood. Although the Elder Wand is a powerful weapon, Beedle the Bard's "The Tale of the Three Brothers" demonstrates the superior value of the cloak's protective powers. Adams posits that it is "where Harry breaks the most from the Arthurian mold that he is allowed to succeed where Arthur failed."[42] Arthur loses the scabbard, while Harry becomes the master of all three Hallows by chance and ultimately surrenders the power of the Elder Wand because it is "more trouble than it's worth."[43] In both texts, the ability to acquire a magical object reflects the worthiness of the character, but while Arthur relishes the sword's violent potential, Harry's desire to survive and serve using the cloak, rather than dominate and conquer using the wand, leads him to triumph.

Encounters with magical objects in Harry Potter provide characters with a self-awareness that many of Malory's knights lack. The centrality of self-analytical magic means that Hogwarts students are in touch with their emotions and thus opt for the nonviolent options their training provides. Magic allows Harry to confront his fears, desires, and values in a safe environment. The knights of the Round Table never address their violent behaviors or underlying emotions—omissions that eventually lead to Camelot's fall.

HEARTS, HEADS, AND HANDS: EMOTIONS, ACTIONS, AND REACTIONS
Knights use violence in conscious efforts to conquer, win praise, punish crimes, and establish peace but also in their eagerness to act upon and

inability to control their emotions. Jost argues that violence "is a natural human shortcoming imperfectly kept in check by those who temporarily or permanently lack self-discipline, rationality, or perspective."[44] Violence tends to result from either a lack of appropriate feeling or an excess of feeling, so that internal balance is essential to external peace.

When violence becomes ubiquitous, its impact on both perpetrators and audiences can decrease. Malory often treats death casually, describing gory detail and abundant fatalities with little comment. He remarks as an aside that "there was no year that there failed but there were some dead" among the Queen's Knights and mentions a hundred thousand dead in Arthur's battles with Lucius and Mordred (19.1, 5.8, 21.4). Albrecht Classen sees knights in both fiction and history to be often "little but simple killing machines without any emotions for their victims."[45] Moments of consideration occasionally halt violence, and Galahad is known for being merciful, but knights frequently kill with little hesitation or empathy.

In Harry Potter, violence is employed sparingly and to great emotional effect. Harry's orphanhood is presented as a deep emotional wound, such as when he sees his parents in the Mirror of Erised, from Voldemort's wand, and by using the Resurrection Stone. Each death in the series comes with particular weight and has profound emotional and practical consequences. Harry cannot accept that war has casualties; rather, he is deeply affected by the idea of people he loves dying for him. The narrative gives Harry space to ponder, yearn, and grieve, while Arthur's knights immediately spring into action.

Although there are moments of weeping and woe in *Le Morte*, grief tends to be swiftly channeled into violent vengeance, perpetuating a vicious cycle. Gawain expresses himself through violence, for "where he hated he would be avenged with murder" (7.34). Arthur laments the harm that will come to the Round Table from Gawain's vengeance against Lancelot, but he nevertheless initiates the discussion of revenge for his brothers' deaths. Lynch writes that in *Le Morte*, "emotion is directly affiliated to physical action—deeds—and is displayed and perceived within them."[46] Malory rarely explains his characters' emotions because their actions speak for themselves and the characters do not take time to process.

Lynch declares, "To be great, like any Malorian knight capable of surpassing deeds is ... to feel greatly."[47] R. L. Radulescu notes Malory's frequent use of the phrase "oute of mesure" to demonstrate the excess of emotion that causes reckless violence.[48] Gawain's anger at the knight who killed his hounds leads him to accidentally behead the lady defending him (3.7). Gareth's dwarf companion warns his captors, "And if [Gareth] be angry he will do harm" (7.20). Tristram and Lancelot experience bouts of madness when overcome with emotion. Enchantresses, however, can control and conceal their emotions. When Morgan learns of her lover's death, she is "so sorrowful that nigh her heart tobrast; but . . . she kept her countenance, and made no semblant of dole" (4.14). Although treated as unnatural and suspicious in the Arthurian world, this power can be helpful in the Wizarding world.

Strength of feeling is essential to the protagonists of the Potter series, but the ability to confront, understand, and moderate one's emotions is a positive quality that can be channeled into nonlethal forms of magic. In *Order of the Phoenix*, Harry must learn to conceal his thoughts and repress his feelings in order to master Occlumency and prevent Voldemort from accessing his mind. Snape warns Harry, "Fools who wear their hearts proudly on their sleeves, who cannot control their emotions . . . they stand no chance against [Voldemort's] powers."[49] Failing miserably at Occlumency and allowing his feelings to overwhelm all logic, Harry falls prey to Voldemort's plot to lure him to the Department of Mysteries, resulting in Sirius's death.

However, Harry has further chances to think through his actions and learn the importance of self-control. Rather than spurring him to action, his grief over Dobby's death in *Deathly Hallows* leads him to learn "control at last," as it blocks Voldemort's rage from his mind and gives him the clarity to focus on destroying the Horcruxes rather than trying to beat Voldemort to the Elder Wand.[50] This is a rare moment for Harry, who "could not remember, ever before, choosing *not* to act."[51] Self-control thus serves, in Wolosky's words, as "the fundamental basis . . . of both moral action and freedom."[52] Dumbledore, concerned that Harry's "hot head might dominate [his] good heart," intentionally makes the quest for the Deathly Hallows difficult so that Harry cannot act too rashly.[53] By contrast, hot heads frequently dominate the good hearts of Malory's knights.

Both romantic and familial love drive knights to violence. Romantic love motivates knights to increase their worship and fight for their ladies.

Lancelot accidentally kills the unarmed Gareth and Gaheris when rescuing his beloved Guinevere. Gawain swears vengeance out of love for his brothers, eventually destroying the Round Table. Nenive, however, protects her husband, "and so he lived to the uttermost of his days with her in great rest" (21.6). While it may seem unknightly for Pelleas to be kept home by his wife, the context of Malory's comment—Arthur's tragic death—shows Pelleas as a fortunate foil who is spared from this miserable violence by his magical wife's love.

While love is usually an instigator of violence in Malory, it is the main inhibitor of and defense against violence in the Potter books. Wolosky observes the "incompatibility between love and power" demonstrated by Narcissa Malfoy betraying Voldemort to protect her son.[54] While Voldemort disparages love as a weakness that makes people vulnerable to manipulation, Potter shows how, in Wolosky's words, it "fuels resistance and joint effort against Voldemort's evil, and builds care, commitment, and strength."[55] Harry's love for his friends and family constantly motivates him to oppose tyranny and work toward peace.

Love in the Harry Potter series can also have physical effects through magic. Because his mother died to save him, Harry survives Voldemort's attempts on his life. Despite the importance of controlling his emotions, Harry's ability to love—and feel grief as a result—is his "greatest strength."[56] His love for Sirius prevents Voldemort from possessing him "because [Voldemort] could not bear to reside in a body so full of the force he detests," and Harry's willingness to sacrifice himself protects everyone opposing Voldemort just as Harry's mother protected him.[57] Magic allows the means to reflect the ends, and love emerges as a sustaining rather than destructive force.

CONCLUSION: THE KEY TO SURVIVAL

The Harry Potter series fits into the medievalist fantasy tradition in its use of medieval tropes and narrative structures. However, it ultimately departs from the tendency to romanticize violence in its use of Arthurian models of intentional magic to scrutinize the assumption that violence is appropriate and glorious in a struggle against evil and that conquest is righteous. Through a combination of inquiry, creativity, and introspection required and advanced by magic, the series tells a story not about a tragically bygone kingdom but about a bright, hopeful, attainable future.

While Arthur dies, Camelot falls, and the Round Table is broken, sorceresses continue to exist on the periphery of society. Larrington calls them "survivors all . . . protected by the power of their magic from the fate that overtakes" those without it.[58] Similarly, while medieval politics, warfare, and values can lose relevance or interest for modern audiences, magic possesses an inherent versatility, with lasting power that can be transplanted into many times, places, and styles.

As what Jackson dubs "the literature of subversion," fantasy teaches us not to accept things as they are. To borrow from medieval literature without considering its themes or to follow in the footsteps of medievalist fantasy without questioning its formula is not sufficient. It would be a mistake to ignore the great potential of magic in medieval literature and to view it as less serious or meaningful than warfare. Fantasy literature like the Harry Potter series that uses medieval modes of magic to challenge the inevitability and glorification of violence and to explore identity, emotion, education, and ethics is ultimately poised to play a role in curbing actual violence and creating a more peaceful reality. We may not be able to literally harness love to have physical effects on our surroundings, but we do have the ability to think creatively, show compassion, question, advocate, research, educate, discover, invent, build, cooperate, and make our world less violent and more magical.

NOTES

1. Rowling, *Sorcerer's Stone*, 118. All Harry Potter book citations in this essay refer to the original Scholastic (US) editions.

2. D'Arcens, introduction, 1; Verduin, "Founding and the Founder," 1; and Shippey, "Medievalisms," 45.

3. Pugh and Weisl, *Medievalisms*, 32, 1.

4. Toswell, "Tropes of Medievalism," 69–70.

5. James, "Explosion of Genre Fantasy," 70.

6. Lynch, "Ideology of War," 135.

7. Lynch, 148.

8. Arden and Lorenz, "French Arthurian Romance," 55.

9. Sweeney, *Magic in Medieval Romance*, 24.

10. Malory's *Le Morte Darthur* will be cited parenthetically with book and chapter numbers.

5. From Sword to Sorcery

11. Jost, "Why Is Middle English Romance," 263; and Whetter, "Warfare and Combat," 172.
12. Larrington, *Enchantresses*, 8.
13. Larrington, 2.
14. Larrington, 104.
15. Jackson, *Fantasy*, 2.
16. Rowling, *Sorcerer's Stone*, 133.
17. "JK (Joanne Kathleen) Rowling," *Guardian*, last modified July 22, 2008, https://theguardian.com/books/2008/jun/11/jkjoannekathleenrowling.
18. Wolosky, *Riddles*, 1–2.
19. Rowling, *Deathly Hallows*, 129.
20. Saunders, "Violent Magic," 239.
21. Saunders, 232.
22. Rowling, *Very Good Lives*, 56.
23. Rowling, *Order of the Phoenix*, 810.
24. Rowling, *Goblet of Fire*, 217.
25. Larrington, *Enchantresses*, 96.
26. See Chism, " 'Ain't Gonna Study.' "
27. Saunders, "Violent Magic," 226.
28. Rowling, *Deathly Hallows*, 71.
29. Rowling, *Order of the Phoenix*, 856.
30. McEvoy-Levy, "War and Peace," 128.
31. Jackson, *Fantasy*, 14.
32. Thompson, "Modern Fantasy," 222.
33. Adams, "Once and Future Wizard," 93.
34. Rowling, *Deathly Hallows*, 242.
35. Zanger, "Heroic Fantasy," 231.
36. Sweeney, *Magic in Medieval Romance*, 46.
37. Sweeney, 19, 71.
38. Sweeney, 84.
39. Wolosky, *Riddles*, 23.
40. Thompson, "Modern Fantasy," 212.
41. Wolosky, *Riddles*, 24.
42. Adams, "Once and Future Wizard," 93.
43. Rowling, *Deathly Hallows*, 749.
44. Jost, "Why Is Middle English Romance," 246–47.
45. Classen, "Violence," 21.
46. Lynch, *Malory's Book of Arms*, 138.
47. Lynch, 141.
48. Radulescu, " 'Oute of Mesure,' " 121.
49. Rowling, *Order of the Phoenix*, 536.
50. Rowling, *Deathly Hallows*, 478.
51. Rowling, 502.
52. Wolosky, *Riddles*, 95.

53. Rowling, *Deathly Hallows*, 720.
54. Wolosky, *Riddles*, 131.
55. Wolosky, 138.
56. Rowling, *Order of the Phoenix*, 823.
57. Rowling, 844.
58. Larrington, *Enchantresses*, 121.

6. Shakespearean Romantic Comedy and Hogwarts Couples

Heather Murray

MUCH HAS BEEN written about love stories—their energy, their humor, the way they anarchically reinvent the world in defiance of all attempts to reduce things to order and immobility, the way they mingle the frivolous with the solemn and light with darkness. Shakespeare famously mixed genres, and the observation that his comedies have romance at the center of their plots is so obvious as scarcely to require statement; similarly, scholars have discussed the ways in which J. K. Rowling integrates comedy into her darker themes. For example, Beatrice Groves says that *"Harry Potter* makes its readers laugh, and comedy is an essential part of how it handles its serious themes,"[1] and Amanda Cockrell observes, "Good does not always win in Harry Potter's world. . . . But against this sometimes queasy shifting of the ground, Rowling manages something . . . unusual in a tale with as dark a theme as hers: she is funny."[2] Rowling's couples laugh and tease and express their feelings for each other in ways both sympathetic and recognizable from Shakespeare's plays. These moments of romantic comedy in the works of both Rowling and Shakespeare are not distractions from the main narrative; rather, they are integral to understanding, as the more serious events unfold, all that is at stake: love and community.

Love in comedies typically follows established patterns, and readers familiar with the well-understood rituals of courtship may be amused by the ways in which both Rowling's and Shakespeare's couples flirt with each other and test each other's emotional responses. After all, such familiar scenes are often critical tests of the maturity and humanity of the characters who participate in them. As Catherine Bates says, "The timeless tale of boy meets girl was as hot a topic in the New Comedy of ancient Greece, the courtly romances of the Middle Ages, or the bawdy fabliau stories of folk tradition—all of which Shakespeare drew upon for his sources—as it continues to be to this day."[3] Perhaps less obvious is that these burgeoning

6. Shakespearean Romantic Comedy and Hogwarts Couples

romantic relationships are also the points where private and personal values intersect with public ones. These values may not be in the foreground in the works of Shakespeare and Rowling, but there is always recognition of the wider context in which love between individuals is necessarily placed. Characters are not allowed to indulge, at least not for long, in the illusion that all that matters is what they feel for each other.

HARRY AND GINNY

Early in *Sorcerer's Stone*, Ginny Weasley first sees Harry Potter as she waits with her family at King's Cross Station for the Hogwarts Express to take her elder brothers to the school that she is not yet old enough to attend. Harry does not pay much attention to Ginny at the time, but their bond grows when she joins him at Hogwarts and then deepens into a romance when they are teenagers. The pair are surrounded by sociopolitical events that threaten to crush freedom and dissent in the Wizarding world: the fall of the Ministry of Magic, the increasing intolerance of difference, fascism in the government and at Hogwarts, the return of Voldemort. Yet these two key members of Dumbledore's Army insist on personal freedom and choice in their own relationship as they fight for the broader good. Rowling finds in Shakespeare models of romantic and personal autonomy and draws upon his use of poetry and love potions.

Written declarations of love are common in Shakespeare's plays, often but not always to comedic effect. Examples include Orlando's love poems to Rosalind in *As You Like It*, Hamlet's passionate missive to Ophelia in *Hamlet*, Proteus's romantic letter to Julia in *The Two Gentlemen of Verona*, and the love letter forged by Sir Toby Belch, Sir Andrew Aguecheek, and Maria in *Twelfth Night* to trick the steward Malvolio into believing Lady Olivia, a countess, is in love with him. Similarly, love poetry is used to great comedic effect in *Chamber of Secrets* when a poem written by eleven-year-old Ginny, in her first year at Hogwarts, is delivered on Valentine's Day to Harry, who is about a year older. The narcissistic wizarding celebrity and Defense Against the Dark Arts teacher Professor Gilderoy Lockhart has dressed up dwarfs in cupid costumes for the occasion, and one of them pursues Harry, tackles him to the floor, and then proceeds to sing the following Valentine message while sitting on top of Harry as his classmates pass by in the hall:

His eyes are as green as a fresh pickled toad
His hair is as dark as a blackboard.
I wish he was mine, he's truly divine,
the hero who conquered the Dark Lord.[4]

    While poetry can be found throughout Rowling's series—examples include the Sorting Hat, the Triwizard Tournament sphinx, and Peeves's songs—this intense outpouring of feeling is simultaneously funny and earnest. It is a blazon, a tradition within love poetry in which specific features of the beloved such as eyes, hair, and lips are listed and compared with beautiful objects such as flowers, jewels, and celestial objects. Made popular by the Italian poet Petrarch and used extensively by the Elizabethan poets, the message is the kind of poem that Jacques, in Shakespeare's *As You Like It*, mockingly refers to as "a woeful ballad, / Made to his mistress' eyebrow" (2.7.148–49). Both Shakespeare and Rowling play up on the blazon's history, upending the traditional form for their own comedic purposes.

    As Beatrice Groves observes, the comparison of Harry's green eyes to freshly pickled toad also recalls a specific Shakespearean moment: Thisbe's unintentionally comic lament over Pyramus at the end of *A Midsummer Night's Dream*.[5] This blazon is part of the play-within-a-play that the Rude Mechanicals perform at Theseus and Hippolyta's wedding ceremony, and, like Ginny's, breaks with established convention by being addressed by a woman to a man. Thisbe mourns the death of her love, Pyramus, who recently committed suicide because he thought she had been killed by a lion, by speaking of his physical attributes:

This cherry nose,
These yellow cowslip cheeks
Are gone, are gone.
Lovers, make moan.
His eyes were green as leeks. (5.1.319–23)

    The comparisons in both blazons are so forced as to render them unsuccessful aesthetically, and neither brings about the desired romantic outcome. The would-be lovers are not rewarded but subject to mockery for their efforts. The Athenian nobility laughs at the Rude Mechanicals in *A Midsummer Night's Dream*, and Harry and Ginny's classmates "[cry] with mirth" in the hallway (238). As Ronald P. Draper notes, "Frequently ... love sentiment verges on sentimentality, and so becomes an apt target for mockery and satire. ... Romance, especially in romantic comedy, is invariably accompanied by features that are deflatingly anti-romantic."[6] Ginny's girlish efforts in this particular situation may have been unsuccessful, but she demonstrates a certain courage, and her ability not only to know her own mind but to speak it foreshadows the strong young woman who will declare her feelings to Harry again much later in the series.

Why should a poem matter so much in a seven-volume tale that spans thousands of pages? The answer may lie in the vexation of Egeus in the first scene of *A Midsummer Night's Dream* when he lists those items that Lysander, a young Athenian nobleman, has given to his daughter, Hermia:

> ... thou hast given her rhymes,
> And interchanged love-tokens with my child.
> Thou hast by moonlight at her window sung
> With feigning voice verses of feigning love,
> And stolen the impression of her fantasy
> With bracelets of thy hair, rings, gauds, conceits,
> Knacks, trifles, nosegays, sweetmeats—messengers
> Of strong prevailment in unhardened youth. (1.1.28–35)

The objects in themselves are insignificant, even trivial. The first "love token" of which Egeus complains is not an object of material value but poetry. "Thou has given her rhymes," he begins, judging poetry to be the most significant item in this list. This kind of "giving," Egeus argues further, is a form of taking, even of stealing, because he believes it is his right to give his daughter to the man of his choice, in this case not Lysander but a startlingly similar young Athenian nobleman, Demetrius.

Egeus is angry because he understands that the "gauds" themselves are valuable, like poems, largely for the spirit in which they are given and received. Near the end of the play, Demetrius comments, on awakening to a renewed love of Helena, his former sweetheart, that his "melted" love to Hermia now seems as "the remembrance of an idle gaud" (4.1.164–65).

Alan Ackerman, in an analysis of *Hamlet*, argues similarly: "Here, perhaps anticipating the 're-membrances' that Ophelia 're-delivers' to Hamlet, the fact that the love tokens amount to nothing in themselves is enabling rather than disabling. They are the transitory forms through which an idealist spirit or essence of love (or beauty or the good) has been inventoried and expressed."[7] In other words, the lack of material value is rather the point. Just as Hermia would choose Lysander over Demetrius and "would [her] father look'd but with [her] eyes" (1.1.56), Ginny repeatedly insists on her right to choose her romantic partners without interference from her six elder brothers.

Harry and Ginny do grow up, and their relationship becomes more mature and complex. But Rowling clearly depicts that development as real and natural, despite the ready availability of magic and love potions. While magic is both legitimate and a worthy tool that students must learn to master and control, it is not to be used by witches or wizards to impose their will upon others. As Greg Garrett states,

> But only three curses are classified as Unforgivable Curses, and these illegal curses can explain a great deal about the use of magic to protect personal power. Certainly the wizarding community treats these spells as the most serious violations; the imposter masquerading as Alastor Moody explains in his Defense Against the Dark Arts class in *Goblet of Fire*, "The use of any one of them on a fellow human being is enough to earn a life sentence in Azkaban." These three curses all represent the most onerous magical projection of one's power onto another, and so we might say that the Imperius Curse, the Cruciatus Curse, and Avada Kedavra are magic at its darkest and most dangerous.[8]

The Imperius Curse is used to control another, the Cruciatus Curse is used to torture, and the Avada Kedavra is used to kill. Since these spells are impositions of power by one wizard or witch over another, they are incompatible with love.

Love potions are not classified as Unforgivable Curses, but in *Half-Blood Prince* Rowling makes it clear that love cannot be compelled. First, it is revealed that Voldemort's mother, Merope Gaunt, used a love potion on Voldemort's father, Tom Riddle, with tragic results. Dumbledore supposes that Merope stopped using the potion because she was so "besotted" that she "could not bear to continue enslaving him by magical means," but once he was freed, Riddle left her and their child (Voldemort).[9] Second, despite the fact that love potions are banned at Hogwarts, Romilda Vane's spiked package of Chocolate Cauldrons (intended for Harry but consumed by Ron) nearly ends in catastrophe as well. In contrast, Harry's use of the Felix Felicis potion, which is not a love potion but "Liquid Luck," is more successful. While Harry uses it primarily to recover a memory from Professor Horace Slughorn at Dumbledore's request, it also brings about other things that Harry has been wishing to happen: Ron and Lavender Brown break up, as do Ginny and Dean Thomas. In both cases, according to Hermione, the couples had been "a bit rocky for ages" (514). Shira Wolosky asserts that this is because "Felix . . . works with natural circumstances, not against them."[10] These relationships had simply run their course.

For Shakespeare, potions and romantic relationships never seem to go well together either: examples include the sleeping potion in the deadly conclusion of *Romeo and Juliet* and Helena's medical concoction in *All's Well that Ends Well*, which she uses to heal the King of France in order to manipulate Bertram, count of Roussillon, into marriage. The play that revolves the most directly around the uses and misuses of a love potion is *A Midsummer Night's Dream*, in which Oberon, King of the Fairies, and the mischievous sprite Puck use love-in-idleness on Titania, the Queen of the Fairies, and two young Athenian noblemen. Matthew Steggle describes this work as "a play in which love—arguably the most profound operation of the human spirit—is firmly under the control of a material (and liquid) drug."[11]

In the second act of *A Midsummer Night's Dream*, Oberon, frustrated by Titania's refusal to give him for his retinue the little Indian boy she adopted after the death of her friend, commands Puck to fetch a specific flower:

> the herb I showed thee once:
> The juice of it on sleeping eyelids laid
> Will make or man or woman madly dote
> Upon the next live creature that it sees. (2.1.169–72)

This magical herb, love-in-idleness, is derived from a plant and applied externally, and it seems to offer Oberon a remedy for the problem (as he sees it) of Titania's willfulness. In a manner similar to the love potions used by Merope Gaunt and Romilda Vane, love-in-idleness will cause Titania to lose control and surrender her affections to the will of another. The unintended consequences of this action and several subsequent mistakes cause chaos in both the fairy and mortal worlds.

Oberon believes that additional drugs will solve the problems that resulted from using love-in-idleness. He mentions with reference to Titania that there is an antidote that will "take this charm from off her sight—/ As I can take it with another herb" (2.1.183–84), and he eventually uses this antidote to undo the drug's effects on his wife. Likewise, the four young lovers are put by Puck into a "death-counterfeiting sleep" (3.2.364); the second herb is applied, and Lysander once again loves Hermia. Tanya Pollard observes that "as a substitute for the real death that would be the endpoint for a tragedy, 'death-counterfeiting sleep' allows for a hiatus and another transformation: this time toward the matched couplings conventional to comedy."[12] All would seem to be well. The young lovers are correctly matched and on their way to a triple wedding, alongside Theseus and Hippolyta. Marital harmony is restored between Oberon and Titania, and the fairies are at peace once more. However, many questions remain. Demetrius receives no antidote, so is he doomed to remain bound by a magical love potion to a woman he didn't choose? Or, since he previously was in love with Helena, is the reader to believe that his brief affection for Hermia was the aberration? What happens when Titania learns—as she undoubtedly will—that her husband drugged her and humiliated her? And Ronald P. Draper observes that Bottom is also duped (although not drugged): "It is true that [Bottom] loses his power to act independently: he would like to see his 'wit' (=intelligence, good sense) to get out of the irrational world symbolized by the wood . . . but Titania, with her supernatural powers, will not allow him."[13] Bottom, while he may remember the experience as a pleasant dream, never chose his brief affair with Titania.

Instead of using love potions, Harry shares the depth of his feelings with Ginny in *Half-Blood Prince* not long after they start to become romantically involved and as he decides to pursue Voldemort: "It's been . . . like something out of someone else's life, these last few weeks with you . . . But I can't . . . we can't . . . I've got things to do alone now."[14] When Ginny tells Harry that she does not care if Voldemort attempts to use her as a weapon against Harry, he responds simply with, "I care."[15] These words assure Ginny that Harry is not abandoning her, even if she disagrees with him. Ginny is intelligent and brave, which would seem to make her a worthy ally for Harry on his mission, but she is underage, and their deep affection does create a vulnerability that Voldemort would not hesitate to exploit. By contrast, Ron and Hermione, who do accompany Harry, have reached the wizard age of majority. Karley Adney compares Harry's behavior in this passage with the relationship between Snape and Lily, when they were roughly the same age: "Snape loses Lily because, essentially, of his *insensitivity* toward her, specifically when he uses a racial epithet to refer to her in public. Conversely, Harry's awareness of and respect for Ginny's needs dictate his actions. He does not lose the woman he loves, and his sensitivity to her needs is one reason for the success of their relationship."[16] Harry, who is only a teenager, responds to the extraordinary pressure he is under with (albeit imperfect) communication.

Ginny responds to Harry's declaration of love more fully early in *Deathly Hallows*. Harry turns seventeen at the Weasleys' house in the midst of planning for Bill Weasley and Fleur Delacour's wedding. Taking advantage of a private moment together, Ginny says that she has a birthday gift for him: "So then I thought, I'd like you to have something to remember me by, you know, if you meet some Veela when you're off doing whatever you're doing."[17] She then kisses him a way that reveals both the depth of her affection and the potential for a shared future. As the series concludes, they both fight to create a world big enough to encompass that possibility.

RON AND HERMIONE

Ron Weasley and Hermione Granger can be understood as following in a Shakespearean tradition of quarreling couples, such as Beatrice and Benedict in *Much Ado about Nothing*, Viola and Orsino in *Twelfth Night*, and Katherine and Petruchio in *Taming of the Shrew*, who bicker right up until they fall in love. Complicated by miscommunication, mixed signals, and emotional intensity, their burgeoning romance is observed by and occasionally a source of amusement (and frustration) for those characters around them. Hermione, the intelligent daughter of Muggle parents, needs to learn about herself and the Wizarding world she has joined; Ron, the pureblood son of magically powerful (if poor) parents, needs to learn about himself and to see his own world with fresh eyes. As a result of their arguments, they learn what they are fighting for, both personally and politically.

Throughout Rowling's series, Ron and Hermione, both as individuals and as a couple, are filtered through Harry's perspective, which is not so much unreliable as limited to what he knows and can understand; his observations throughout the series are shaped by his level of maturity and his feelings toward his friends. Harry and Hermione are not attracted to each other, although each is aware that their classmates find the other attractive. Perhaps for this reason, Harry simply pays little attention to Hermione's appearance, and so the series never offers a detailed description of her. When Hermione first meets Harry in *Sorcerer's Stone*, she is only said to have "lots of bushy brown hair and rather large front teeth."[18]

In contrast, Ron pays a great deal of attention to Hermione. In *Goblet of Fire*, Hermione's teeth are mentioned again after Malfoy hits her with a spell; her "front teeth—already larger than average—were now growing at an alarming rate . . . her teeth elongated, past her bottom lip, toward her chin."[19] Hermione's teeth are fixed, and several weeks pass before Ron, not Harry, notices that they look different, having become "straight and normal-sized."[20] (405). (Hermione admits that she let Madame Pomfrey "carry on a bit" when the spell damage was being reversed.) Not only does Ron observe such physical changes in Hermione but he also rushes to her defense whenever necessary. For example, Ron tries to curse Draco Malfoy after Draco calls Hermione a "filthy little Mudblood" in *Chamber of Secrets* (112), and he earns detention for challenging Professor Snape for humiliating Hermione in *Prisoner of Azkaban* (172).[21] Likewise, Hermione always seems to be aware of exactly when Ron needs help with his schoolwork, and she is better than Harry at understanding Ron's emotions. For example, in *Half-Blood Prince*, Ron's spell-check quill malfunctions while he is writing an essay for Professor Snape, and upon realizing that there are errors throughout, Ron is "horror-struck" and exclaims, " 'Don't say I'll have to write the whole thing out again!' "[22] Hermione understands how upset he is and says, "It's okay, we can fix it," to which Ron tellingly responds, "I love you, Hermione."[23]

In Shakespeare's *Much Ado about Nothing*, both Beatrice and Benedick are hyperaware of each other as well. For example, in the first scene, Beatrice hears about a recent military victory and immediately asks the messenger, "I

6. Shakespearean Romantic Comedy and Hogwarts Couples

pray you, is Signor Mountanto returned from the wars or no?" (1.1.25–26). Leonato, the governor of Messina and Beatrice's uncle, is so familiar with their repartee that he announces, "There is a kind of merry war betwixt Signor Benedict and her" (1.1.49–50). Benedick no sooner enters the stage after a significant absence than he calls her "my dear Lady Disdain," and in front of the assembled company they return to an argument they obviously have had many times before (1.1.96). If it is a war between Beatrice and Benedick, it might be best described as trench warfare, because they have dug deep into these predictable patterns of behavior, and neither side seems to be advancing in any particular direction.

Both Beatrice and Benedick (who knew each other "of old"; 1.1.118–19) and Ron and Hermione (who met on the Hogwarts Express as they were starting their first year) have established ways of interacting with each other. For both couples, a ball forces them out of these patterns and makes them see each other anew. The Yule Ball in *Goblet of Fire* is one of the most significant moments in Ron and Hermione's relationship. Ron does not ask Hermione to the ball, much to her frustration, but he is also unable to admit to himself that he is jealous of Hermione's soon-to-be boyfriend Victor Krum. As Katrin Berndt argues, "Ron . . . required a wake-up call to become aware of his romantic feelings for her."[24] Berndt's observations are supported by *Cursed Child*. During the time-traveling adventures of that play, it is revealed that Ron and Hermione's future relationship (and marriage and children, Rose and Hugo) derive from Ron's jealousy of Victor. Otherwise, according to *Cursed Child*, Ron marries Padma Patil and Hermione remains single.

During the masked ball in act 2 of *Much Ado About Nothing*, Beatrice and Benedick's "merry war" of wits turns into a much more hurtful competition. Initially, Beatrice enjoys her triumphs over Benedick. She sees through his disguise and his claim to be an unknown dance partner who can tell Beatrice that she is famed for being disdainful and having her wit "out of the *Hundred Merry Tales*" (2.1.115). Beatrice retaliates by saying that she thinks of Benedick as "the Prince's jester. A very dull fool" (2.1.122). Benedick now believes he knows what her candid opinion of him is, and he is hurt; Beatrice has wounded the man for whom she has a genuine admiration and even fondness, despite her mistrust of his affection for her. But they both learn from the experience. "Happy are they that hear their detractions and can put them to mending," Benedick declares in soliloquy after he has overheard his friends describing him as scornful and of "contemptible spirit" toward Beatrice (2.3.202–3,161). And Beatrice rethinks her attitude as well: "What fire is in mine ears? Can this be true? / Stand I condemned for pride and scorn so much? / Contempt, farewell, and maiden pride, adieu! / No glory lives behind the back of such" (3.1.107–110). As David Bevington argues, "Beatrice thereby becomes the perfect partner for Benedick, and on an equal footing, for both are duped and both are willing to admit their mistakes. Their love is based on generosity and mutual self-candor."[25] The capacity of the characters to grow becomes integral to their capacity to love.

Beatrice and Benedick, like Ron and Hermione, find that they are able to express their romantic interest in each other through banter and jokes; as Benedick says, he and Beatrice are "too wise to woo peaceably" (5.2.60). Both couples reject the elevated language of romantic love in favor of everyday speech. Benedick does try writing love poetry, but he soon gives up in frustration:

> Marry, I cannot show it in rhyme. I have tried. I can find out no rhyme to "lady" but "baby"; an innocent rhyme. For "scorn," "horn"; a hard rhyme. For "school," "fool"; a babbling rhyme; very ominous endings. No, I was not born under a rhyming planet, nor I cannot woo in festival terms. (5.2.30–34)

Beatrice and Benedick continue to communicate with each other in the way that they have all along because, as Michael Mangan observes, their witty exchanges can be understood "not only as a defense against desire, but also as a language of desire," and they "end the play more or less even on points, with the promise of frequent friendly rematches in the future."[26] Much the same could be said of Ron and Hermione.

Benedick and Ron are called upon by Beatrice and Hermione to right particular wrongs of their community and, in doing so, prove themselves worthy of their love. Beatrice wants Benedick's help to save her cousin Hero, who has been slandered; ultimately, they are successful. Hermione seeks Ron's support in her campaign to improve the lives of the house-elves, and here the results are decidedly more mixed. Hermione is, for most of the series, the only one who challenges the prevailing attitudes toward what is essentially the slavery of the house-elves. While many of the characters fight Voldemort and the obvious evil that he represents, she identifies and seeks to change problems within the Wizarding world. Katrin Berndt sees Hermione as uniquely positioned to do this work, stating that "as a Muggle-born outsider—and Hermione is the only major character apart from Harry's late mother who has no magical relatives at all—she persistently reminds the wizarding society of its inherent flaws."[27] She reminds those around her, as pureblood policies grow increasingly strict, that her Muggle status means the authorities are coming after her as well. Hermione is widely regarded as the best student in her year, but her many achievements and successes are erased in the Ministry's estimation by her undistinguished lineage. While Hermione is driven by her morality and compassion to help the house-elves, it quickly becomes evident that her own safety lies in protecting the freedoms of others, too.

Right before the Battle of Hogwarts, as those unable or too young to fight are being evacuated, Ron suddenly says that they've forgotten someone, and clarifies: "The house-elves, they'll all be down in the kitchen, won't they? . . . I mean we should tell them to get out. We don't want any more Dobbies, do we? We can't order them to die for us." Hermione then kisses Ron for the first time, and he responds "with such enthusiasm that he lifted Hermione off her feet."[28] Ron, of his own accord, has finally challenged the norms of the magical world that would have expected the house-elves to fight and die for their owners. Thus, he becomes a suitable partner for Hermione.

Hermione has lessons to learn as well, and she spends her time at Hogwarts studying to prepare herself to accept adult responsibilities in the magical world. She works so hard that she rises to the top of her class—her skill at schoolwork and spells is undisputed. However, Hermione must also ascertain the appropriate use of such knowledge. For her intelligence to mature into wisdom, Hermione must understand the underlying spirit of the world that she joined at age eleven, which can be found in the stories and tales told to children with magical parents from their earliest days. This is why Dumbledore leaves Hermione a collection of folktales in his will. Lana Whited states, "Dumbledore has bequeathed Hermione literature not just because of her tremendous intellect, but also because the stories are familiar to Ron from childhood. They were his bedtime stories, and he knows them by heart."[29] Hermione needs not just her intellect but her great heart to help fight the Battle of Hogwarts and to rebuild the Wizarding world in its aftermath.

CONCLUSION

Moments of romantic comedy in the works of both Rowling and Shakespeare illustrate the fundamental importance of love and community, particularly when the beloved and the communities depicted in these narratives are under attack. Harry and Ginny, alongside Ron and Hermione, succeed both in falling in love and in saving the Wizarding world because their public and private values align. Their growing affection for and acceptance of those who are marginalized in the Wizarding world, including non-purebloods, Muggles, half-giants, werewolves, house-elves, and Veela, and their insistence that relationships—including their own romantic relationships—be reciprocal leads to Voldemort's defeat and to their romantic success. As Cassandra Bausman puts it, the Potter story places an emphasis on "individual choice; on self-sacrifice and the use of power to protect and defend; on the preference to disarm rather than murder; to act, above all, from love."[30]

NOTES

1. Groves, *Literary Allusion*, 81.
2. Cockrell, "Secret Password," 16. For a discussion of humor in Harry Potter, see Louise M. Freeman, " 'The Ghost of His Last Laugh': Evolving Humor in Harry Potter," chapter 8 of this volume.
3. Bates, "Love and Courtship," 103.
4. Rowling, *Chamber of Secrets*, 238.
5. Groves, *Literary Allusion*, 85.
6. Draper, *Comedies*, 56.
7. Ackerman, "Spirit of Giving," 124.
8. Garrett, *One Fine Potion*, 26–27.
9. Rowling, *Half-Blood Prince*, 214.
10. Wolosky, *Riddles*, 94.
11. Steggle, "Humours," 227.
12. Pollard, *Drugs and Theater*, 144.
13. Draper, *Comedies*, 130.
14. Rowling, *Half-Blood Prince*, 646.
15. Rowling, 647.

6. Shakespearean Romantic Comedy and Hogwarts Couples

16. Adney, "Influence of Gender," 187.
17. Rowling, *Deathly Hallows*, 116.
18. Rowling, *Sorcerer's Stone*, 79.
19. Rowling, *Goblet of Fire*, 299.
20. Rowling, 405.
21. Rowling, *Chamber of Secrets*, 112; Rowling, *Prisoner of Azkaban*, 172.
22. Rowling, *Half-Blood Prince*, 449.
23. Rowling, 449.
24. Berndt, "Vindication," 163.
25. Bevington, "Lost and Won," 89–90.
26. Mangan, *Shakespeare's Comedies*, 200.
27. Berndt, "Vindication," 172.
28. Rowling, *Deathly Hallows*, 625.
29. Whited, "Hero's Journey," 20.
30. Bausman, "'Elder' and Wiser," 39.

SECTION 3

SOCIAL AND PSYCHOLOGICAL APPLICATIONS

7. Why S.P.E.W. Was Doomed to Fail

Exploring Systemic Inequity through Rowling's Racialized House-Elves

Alyssa Lowery

HERMIONE JEAN GRANGER, the brightest witch of her age, goes through a period of immense growth in *Harry Potter and the Goblet of Fire*. Her transformation from Harry's brainy friend and moral compass into a youth activist and media watchwitch has earned her a place in the proverbial pantheon of "strong girl characters." It has also contributed to some of the complexity surrounding activism in the books. When Hermione launches her Society for the Promotion of Elfish Welfare (S.P.E.W.) in *Goblet of Fire*, readers join her in one of the series' first real moral quandaries. Though the implied reader is expected to trust her judgment on issues of fairness, her organization is ill-received even by those closest to her, and it ultimately fades into obscurity. The otherwise brilliant heroine not only fails to liberate elves but cannot even convince them that they might benefit from liberation. That failure receives little attention in the novels, and Hermione's methods are never a serious topic of discussion within the narrative.

Is S.P.E.W.'s quiet death a result of poor management and problematic methods, or a situational inevitability? On one hand, Hermione does attempt to enact social change without actually involving those most affected. On the other, she is employing antiracist strategies to approach an issue that is not in fact racial. Other excellent essays have explored the clear parallels between Rowling's elves and representations of enslaved Africans in film and literature. Those resonances, along with the commentary of trusted characters like Hermione and Dumbledore, do encourage readers to associate house-elf labor with the African slave trade, even as other markers, like the use of a dialect that mimics stereotypical speech patterns of the British working class, draw parallels with other class-based systemic inequities. Even so, equivalencies between elvish labor and the mass enslavement of African people are deeply problematic, not only in their reifications of racist depictions of blackness but because they foreclose opportunities to examine Hermione's social justice organization in any useful way without significant pedagogical supplementation.

In this chapter I examine the problems that arise in readings that equate elves with enslaved Africans. As part of my framework, I use Stuart Hall's encoding/decoding model of communication and his related reception theory. Hall contends that producers of media (in this case, Rowling) encode meaning into texts, but that the audience decodes meaning in ways that may or may not align with the producer's intention. Dominant readings, or preferred readings, are those that align with the producer's intent. Negotiated readings acknowledge the producer's intent and accept some elements but reject others. Oppositional readings occur where the audience may understand the denotative and connotative meanings that were encoded but reject that meaning entirely.[1] I contend that a dominant reading of the text would see house-elves as analogous to enslaved Africans, but that such a reading perpetuates racist conceptions of blackness while also setting a would-be antiracist activist up for failure. Instead, I advocate for a negotiated reading that rejects the racialization of house-elves but still recognizes systemic inequity in the Wizarding world. Such a reading allows for a more nuanced discussion of S.P.E.W.'s failures and still leaves space for critical readers to explore themes of social justice and systemic inequity in the texts.[2]

PREVIOUS EXPLORATIONS OF RACIALIZED READINGS

Other scholars have neatly articulated the strong encoded relationships between house-elves and enslaved Africans and between S.P.E.W. and abolitionist organizations.[3] In the novels themselves, the term *slave*[4] is used rather infrequently, and it is only ever applied to house-elves by Dobby, Hermione, and Dumbledore.[5] Notably, these are also the only three characters who actively express dissatisfaction with the status of house-elves in the Wizarding world. Though Dobby, a mistreated house-elf, refers to his kind as "the lowly, the enslaved, we dregs of the magical world,"[6] Kreacher refers to himself instead as a servant, and both Mr. Crouch and Percy use the same terminology for Winky. Certainly, house-elves are unpaid workers and therefore fulfill the most basic, denotational definition of slaves. It is no surprise, then, that readers often decode house-elf labor as analogous to that historical atrocity.

Bethany Barratt makes a strong case for the linguistic and behavioral similarities that characterize house-elves in the Potter books and African slaves in film and literature. She first notes house-elf dialect, including frequent use of titles as terms of respect, use of the third person, removal of personal pronouns, and subject-verb disagreement.[7] Indeed, house-elf speech bears all of these hallmarks. "You is not insulting my master, miss! You is not insulting Mr. Crouch! Mr. Crouch is a good wizard, miss! Mr. Crouch is right to sack bad Winky!" cries a distraught elf in *Harry Potter and the Goblet of Fire*. These features of speech are similar to those used in caricature of southern American slave dialect, Barrett argues.[8]

Further, Barrett compares wizard attitudes toward house-elves to the paternalistic ones held by many American slaveowners. While slaveholders often regarded slaves as "equivalent to overgrown, frightened children who therefore needed to be told what to do," Ron, Hagrid, and other wizards in the novel express beliefs that elves are naturally subordinate and in need of protection. " 'Well, the elves are happy, aren't they?' Ron [says]. 'You heard old Winky back at the match . . . "House-elves is not supposed to have fun" . . . that's what she likes, being bossed around.' "[9] Barratt argues that this paternalism gives rise to characters' varying attitudes toward elfish enslavement. She likens Hermione's pity to that of American abolitionists who opposed slavery on the grounds that childlike slaves were "incapable of taking responsibility for their own actions."[10] She invokes that same paternalism as the root cause of Sirius's derision of Kreacher and of the Malfoys' mistreatment of Dobby.[11] These wizards regard house-elves as inherently inferior, internally justifying their actions by dehumanizing their laborers. Finally, Barratt claims that house-elves and enslaved Africans share the habit of "hiddenness." They are expected to be seen rarely and heard even less, and as a result, both groups are expected to internalize trauma and glorify their masters. In doing so they forgo hope, making them much easier to control.[12] Her apt observations are foundational to an understanding of a dominant reading of the house-elves as a racialized group relying on tropes of African enslavement, and they are indeed reflected in other critical works.

In her discussions of S.P.E.W., Bryccham Carey operates from a foundational assumption that elfish labor is akin to slavery in the antebellum American South. She also highlights some problematic dissonance with that representation, noting that "one forms the impression that Rowling intends us to understand that servitude is the natural and inescapable condition of house-elves."[13] As evidence, she points to Dobby's interpretation of freedom to mean that he can effectively choose his own master, not that he can leave servitude behind. Even his final act, accompanied by the assertion, "Dobby has no master! . . . Dobby is a free elf, and Dobby has come to save Harry Potter and his friends!" is in service of a chosen master. That sacrifice, Carey notes, mimics countless literary deaths of slaves in service of their own masters.[14] It also recalls the death of abolitionist hero Uncle Tom, who is beaten to death for refusing to betray his runaway compatriots.[15] The connection between Uncle Tom and Dobby is perhaps more resonant because, like Uncle Tom, Dobby becomes an abolitionist martyr whose death highlights injustice.

For Carey, Kreacher too echoes literary prototypes, coming to embody the "grateful slave" character through the events of *Deathly Hallows*.[16] He repays Hermione's kindnesses with devoted servitude both domestically and in battle: "Nothing in the room . . . was more dramatically different than the house-elf who now came hurrying toward Harry, dressed in a snowy-white towel, his ear hair as clean and fluffy as cotton wool, Regulus's locket bouncing on his thin chest. 'Shoes off, if you please, Master Harry, and hands washed before dinner,' croaked Kreacher, seizing the Invisibility Cloak and slouching off to hang it on a hook on the wall, beside a number of old-fashioned robes that had been freshly laundered."[17] Despite the fact that the trio inadvertently abandons him shortly after his rebirth as a happy slave, Kreacher still adopts their political perspectives and emerges during the Battle of Hogwarts leading a small army of elves armed with only carving knives and cleavers from the Hogwarts kitchens.[18] Although Kreacher's attitude changes spectacularly and he risks his life for the cause of his masters, he is not rewarded with freedom. In fact, the novel concludes with Harry's musing that perhaps Kreacher might bring his battle-weary master a sandwich. Carey's chapter again describes the historical and literary precedents for such behavior, suggesting two possibilities for its inclusion in the novels. One possibility is that the scene provides commentary on the unfair treatment of marginalized groups during wartime. Another is that the boundaries of the text simply prevent resolution to the house-elf issue. Ultimately, she concludes, "what seems clear throughout is that Rowling sees house-elf enslavement as an institution that is capable of much improvement but which cannot be eradicated. This is troubling since it militates strongly against the general message of the series, which is that great evils can be overcome, and should be overcome."[19] Carey's assessment acknowledges both the racial underpinnings evident in a dominant reading of the text along with some of the problematic implications of such readings.

That work is continued by Christine Schott, though she presents the argument that the ambiguity of S.P.E.W.'s failure is "one of the series' greatest strengths," promoting analytical thought and allowing readers "to ask questions they may not yet have addressed in their real lives but will one day need to."[20] Though she acknowledges "Rowling's perhaps unexamined but well-intentioned way of drawing the inescapable parallel between the house-elves and African-American slaves,"[21] Schott suggests that the context of the novel eliminates any need to critique the use of harmful tropes. All the elements of house-elf characterization that might be interpreted as racially problematic can also be extricated from their racial implications and still function as part of a social justice narrative. Similarly, readers can still critique Hermione's methods without viewing them as grand metaphors for the abolition movement. While true, this argument still relies on the assumption that the house-elves' predicament is reflective of African enslavement. Schott specifically calls on Hermione's comment that elves are "uneducated and brainwashed,"[22] confirming that elf labor is an old institution and that servitude "is not their natural state."[23] In this way, she reifies the connection between elves and enslaved Africans, ultimately complicating any effort to separate the two for the purposes of critical reading.

Jasmine Wade's discussion also approaches S.P.E.W., noting that house-elves "are particularly attractive for scholars thinking about race, as Rowling positions them as enslaved," calling on Farah Mendelsohn's assessment that Rowling's reliance on "the stereotype of the happy darky" causes her point to "[fall] flat."[24] Wade builds on Jackie C. Horne's argument that the series emphasizes individual responses rather than structural ones in the face of inequity, and advocates for a reading of the Potter texts in connection with organizations advocating for Black liberation, including the Student Nonviolent Coordination Committee (SNCC), the British

Black Power movement, and Black feminist organizations in the United States. Her persuasive and critically oriented chapter emphasizes S.P.E.W.'s unreached potential as a "student movement powered by love" like SNCC, its relevance to the British Black Power movement's conflation of race and class, and its commitment to consciousness raising as modeled by Black feminist organizations.[25]

I share Wade's interest in "an interdisciplinary structure that pulls fantasy and social movements together to strengthen each other's pedagogical power"[26] and celebrate her contribution to combating the "imagination gap" described by Ebony Elizabeth Thomas.[27] Her suggestion to consider literature along with infrequently told historical narratives about Black resistance to systemic racism constitutes an empowering response to the novels' clumsy parallels between house-elves and enslaved Africans. The argument I offer also attempts to supplement readings of the novels by filling some of the gaps left by Rowling's privileging of the individual over the systemic.

I attempt to isolate the systems oppressing house-elves from elements of real-world racial discrimination often projected into the text via Rowling's racial coding of house-elf oppression, drawing on readings of the main series as well as those texts included in the greater Wizarding World franchise to disentangle the plight of the house-elves from that of African enslavement. Finally, I offer questions for reading the house-elf narrative critically outside the racial paradigm in ways that still respond to the core issues of inequity that overlay systemic discrimination of many kinds. I hope that these suggestions, like Wade's, might enable critical readings of Rowling's house-elf problem, serving to approach very real systems of inequity alongside a narrative that in many ways fails to represent their nuances.

DERACIALIZING HOUSE-ELVES

In *Stamped from the Beginning*, his thorough and cogent history of racism, Ibram X. Kendi explores the origins of African enslavement and its relationship to the beginning of socially constructed racist thought. Slavery, he notes, preceded racism, and was initially a system wherein persons captured in wars or raids were held in bondage. However, as economic interests and religious beliefs changed, slave traders turned their attention almost solely to Africa and generated racist rhetoric to justify their actions.[28] Some posited that life in warmer climates produced inferior people built specifically to serve those from more temperate regions.[29] Others asserted that Africans were the cursed descendants of Ham, the biblical son of Noah who was punished for engaging in sexual relations while on the ark and for looking upon his father while Noah was drunk and naked.[30] Both of these racist concepts, termed "climate theory" and "curse theory," were used to justify the enslavement and maltreatment of a group of people who were truthfully no different from their captors.

In this regard, taxonomy is essential to any comparison between house-elf labor and African enslavement. The African slave trade was founded on the egregious dehumanization of an entire people group. That dehumanization has persisted in the form of racist thought and discriminatory practice even after the dissolution of the slave trade, and one of the long-reaching effects of African enslavement is the rhetorical othering of Black bodies. Active participants in the slave trade justified their actions with the argument that African people were beasts, "being utterly destitute of the use of reason, of dexterities of wit, and of all arts."[31] This denigration lies at the root of the problem of conflating elves with enslaved Africans.

As soon as a people group is designated as separate or other, a hierarchy is born. Though several hierarchies exist in the Wizarding world, the overlay of a real-world racial one onto a fantastical interspecies comparison is extremely unsteady. Elves, definitively, are of a separate species, and that species has its own separate mythology and history, separating it from the empowered wizards. Any conflation of enslaved Africans with house-elves immediately reifies the dehumanizing barrier at the very root of antiblack racism. In fact, it echoes the equally problematic mention on the now defunct Pottermore website of Yumboes, a type of racialized house-elf characterized as more malevolent and out of control than the European house-elf, despite the fact that both seem to belong to the house-elf species.[32] To equate black people with house-elves is to assign a shared set of behaviors to both groups, an act that automatically casts blackness as Other and as naturally suited to servility.

The mythology from which house-elves spring is wholly different from the historical reality of the African slave trade. While Schott argues that the elves of the Wizarding world cannot possibly be functioning in their natural state, their folkloric roots suggest otherwise. They are remarkably similar to brownies, legendary creatures from Scottish and English folklore known also as *urisks* in Lowland Scots, *brùniadh, ùruisg,* or *gruagach* in Scottish Gaelic, hobs in Northern England, *tomtar* in Swedish, *nisser* in Norwegian and Danish, *domovoys* in Russian, and *Heinzelmännchen* in German. The vast spread of their fabled lineage suggests that many readers might be familiar with the house-elf character type, offering an alternative schema through which to interpret elf labor. In *Popular Rhymes of Scotland*, Robert Chambers describes the brownie thus:

> [Every] farmhouse in the south of Scotland was supposed to be haunted by one. He was understood to be a spirit of a somewhat grotesque figure, dwarfish in stature, but endowed with great personal strength. It was his humour to be unseen . . . while the people of the house were astir, and only to exert himself while all the rest were asleep. It was customary for the mistress of the house to leave out work for him . . . and he never failed to have the whole done in the morning. This drudgery he performed gratuitously. . . . To have offered him wages, or even to present him with an occasional boon, would have ensured his anger, and perhaps caused him to abandon the establishment. . . . For instance, the goodman of a farm-house in the parish of Glendevon left out some clothes one night for the brownie, who was heard during the night to depart, saying in a highly offended tone, "Gie brownie coat, gie brownie sark, / Ye'se get nae mair o' brownie's wark!"[33]

Chambers also recounts tales of brownies as spies, reporting moral infractions on the part of servants to their masters:

> One of the principal characteristics of the brownie was his anxiety about the moral conduct of the household to which he was attached. He was a spirit very much inclined to prick up his ears at the first appearance of any impropriety in the manners of his fellow-servants. The least delinquency committed either in a barn, or cow-house, or larder, he was sure to report to his master, whose interests he seemed to consider paramount to every other thing in this world, and from whom no bribe could induce him to conceal the offences which fell under his notice.[34]

Much in the same way that Kreacher and Dobby act as Harry's agents, tailing Malfoy in *Harry Potter and the Half-Blood Prince* and Mundungus Fletcher in *Harry Potter and the Deathly Hallows*, brownies were traditionally thought to look after their masters' interests above all else.

The legendary brownie is the clear inspiration for Rowling's elves. Small and wrinkled with bat-like ears, house-elves are regarded as grotesque in appearance, and their "great personal strength" takes the form of exceptionally powerful magic. Also like brownies, elves are known for their hiddenness. As Sir Nicholas de Mimsy-Porpington reveals in *Goblet of Fire*, the mark of a good house-elf is that you don't know it's there: "They come out at night to do a bit of cleaning . . . see to the fires and so on. . . . I mean, you're not supposed to see them, are you?"[35] Another trait elves share with brownies is the desire to work voluntarily. That is, they enjoy the work they do and would choose to do it regardless of enchantments.

This explicit connection between the brownies of United Kingdom tradition and the domestically servile house-elves only strengthens a call for a class-based, nonracialized reading of the wizard-elf dynamic. Along with Hagrid, Mundungus Fletcher, and characters from outside the United Kingdom like those from Beauxbatons and Durmstrang, the house-elves are among the only characters whose dialogue is written in a nonstandard dialect or pronunciation. Though not fully Cockney, like the written speech of Mundungus, the speech of the elves is not unlike what the *Oxford Companion to the English Language* calls "literary and stage Cockney," placing them in a linguistic category with others who utilize such "working-class speech . . . generally viewed by both its speakers and outsiders as a liability for the upwardly mobile."[36] Their origins as elements of UK folklore, combined with the use of uniquely UK linguistic markers, bolsters an argument associating them with a population other than Africans enslaved in North America.

Admittedly, however, significant departures from brownie lore do separate house-elf servitude from the voluntary work of brownies. These embellishments to traditional tales are sites for critical social justice readings, as Schott suggests. Like brownies, house-elves can leave their families when they are given clothing, though such an action is apprehended as more of an intentional insult in the Harry Potter novels than as the well-meant gesture seen in Chambers's tale. In fact, when Mr. Crouch sacks

Winky after the events at the Quidditch World Cup, Winky remarks that she is "properly ashamed of being freed" and that "Mr. Crouch is right to sack bad Winky!"[37] When an elf is presented with clothes, it is the elf who suffers from the dissolution of the relationship and not the wizard.

Another departure from brownie tales comes with the enchantments that seem to bind elves to their masters. Dobby, Winky, and Kreacher are all physically and magically prevented from taking any action outside of their masters' commands, departing from the tradition that sees brownies exercising free will in their attachments. While brownies are offended by the presentation of clothes and leave willingly, house-elves are essentially fired from their homes through the ceremonial presentation of clothes, indicating that some kind of magical contract binds them to their masters. Significantly, the source of the magic tying elves to houses is elusive in the novels, diminishing the identification of wizards and witches as active participants in elf enslavement. Whatever spells bind elves to wizard families and estates are never shown, and readers are left to assume that elves are born enchanted, since they and their descendants stay bound to manors across generations.[38] One possibility, following the series' insistence that the greatest magic of all is love, is that elves' emotional investments in the lives and homes of their masters act as a force more binding than any spell. Whatever the case is, wizards are not shown actively binding elves to servitude, and it is perhaps this elision of culpability that makes it so difficult for many of the novels' characters to imagine elves as anything other than servants. Elves appear to have no other more natural state. They are not plucked from some elfish motherland and taken into captivity, but instead seem to voluntarily serve. The only hint that they may be unable to leave comes when they are treated unfairly but forced to remain with their families, as is the case with Dobby in *Chamber of Secrets*.

A look outside the seven Harry Potter novels provides only slightly more information about the history of elfish labor. Elves do not appear anywhere in the written volume *Fantastic Beasts and Where to Find Them*. Their exclusion from the rather colorful description of Wizards' Council meetings intended to establish categories of beast and being seems especially odd, though the omission does handily circumnavigate the very issue this chapter aims to address. The council eventually defines a being (as opposed to a beast) as "any creature that has sufficient intelligence to understand the laws of the magical community and to bear part of the responsibility in shaping those laws."[39] Given the absence of a "house-elf" or "elf" category in the main component of the text, readers might logically assume that they are afforded the status of being, constituting a full acknowledgment on the part of wizard governing bodies that elves are indeed intelligent and capable of participating in government.[40]

The only mention of that participation appears in the "About the Author" section of *Fantastic Beasts*, where it is revealed that Newt Scamander worked in the Department for the Regulation and Control of Magical Creatures, spending two years in the Office of House-Elf Relocation, which he describes as "tedious in the extreme."[41] The fact that such an office exists implies that elves do not have the freedom to choose new appointments when presented with clothing, but are instead relocated with government assistance. This policy represents a further departure from the brownie tradition, indicating that elfish labor is indeed partly systemic, at least in Britain. Elves of other nationalities do appear in the *Fantastic Beasts and Where to Find Them* film franchise and are all still in servile positions.

Two house-elves appear in the first film, *Fantastic Beasts and Where to Find Them*. One is seen polishing wands at the Magical Congress of the United States of America (MACUSA), and another bartends at the Blind Pig speakeasy.[42] A featured article titled "The Treatment of Intelligent Magical Creatures in *Fantastic Beasts* and *Harry Potter*," originally published on the Pottermore website, suggests that American house-elves might differ culturally from those in Britain.[43] Of the wand-polishing elf at MACUSA, the feature comments, "Since house-elves have their own, powerful brand of magic, this doesn't exactly seem like the best sort of work they could have been doing."[44] However, such an application of elfish magic is not so far outside the use of elves as domestic servants in Britain.

The feature goes on to consider the bartender elf. His appearance in the film comes as a surprise to Jacob, who turns to the bar and asks, "How does a guy get a drink in this joint?" A bottle flies into his hand, and the top of an elf's head becomes barely visible over the top of the bar. "What? Ain't you ever seen a house-elf before?" the elf asks. Jacob tries to hide his surprise and fumbles, "Oh, no, yeah, no, yeah, of course I have. . . . I love house elves. My uncle's a house-elf." The elf scoffs in response and turns his attention to another customer.[45] The Pottermore article describes this elf as "brash, rude to Jacob," and notes that he "certainly didn't seem to be serving anyone (except the customers, of course)."[46] Indeed, he lacks the scraping demeanor of the Hogwarts elves, though if readers have learned anything from Kreacher, it's that an elf doesn't have to be a gleeful servant. The article ultimately concludes, "Either way, it certainly seemed that the American house-elves didn't have the same reverence towards witches and wizards as British ones. But why? Could it simply have been a cultural difference, or were there circumstances that led house-elves to where they are now in the two different countries and time periods?"[47] With such a small sample size, it is impossible to generalize about the attitudes of American versus British house-elves. What is clear, however, is that the American elves in *Fantastic Beasts* are unarguably still in positions of servitude, albeit in the public rather than private sphere.

The only presumably wizard-bound house-elves in the *Crimes of Grindelwald* film are seen very briefly. One cleans the windows inside the Ministry of Magic, even though a very complicated but nonsentient machine has just finished with the floors. Another seems to be employed by Circus Arcanus and is responsible for packing up the festivities when the ringmaster leaves town. There are also part-elf characters whose existences have implications for elfish history. Their presence suggests that interspecies breeding has occurred, possibly suggesting consensual human-elf relationships, or more darkly suggesting the type of nonconsensual relations so often present in the real-world history of enslavement.

One half-elf, Irma Dugard, works as a housekeeper for the Lestrange family and signs the adoption papers for Credence Barebone. She appears briefly in the movie when Credence seeks her out to learn more about his family, and is marked as having elfish blood because she is small in stature and speaks with a high-pitched voice. Yusuf Kama, half-brother of Leta Lestrange, refers to her later, describing the circumstances through which Credence survived a shipwreck: "His servant, Irma Dugard, was a half-elf. Her magic was weak and therefore left no trace I could follow." It does seem unusual that her magic would be weak as a result of her part-elf pedigree—elves have especially potent magic, so unless her other parent is a Muggle, one would expect Irma to possess strong magic. Notably, she is still a servant to the powerful pureblood Lestrange family, remaining in the domestic service sphere like other elves. Part-elves also appear in Circus Arcanus, the magical traveling show from which Nagini escapes. Viewers might not connect the creatures that appear with part-elves, but the screenplay does indicate that half-elves and half-goblins juggle and tumble outside the circus tent when Tina Goldstein approaches.[48] Their positions are not technically in the domestic sphere, but their status as sideshow performers does relegate them to a kind of underclass.

Though house-elves face many of the same challenges as real-world minoritized populations, their backgrounds definitively prevent them from acting as sound metaphors for any particular people group, regardless of the encoded similarities in the text. There is no way to fairly represent a racial group as a separate species, and to do so begets further problems with textual interpretation.

WHY S.P.E.W. WAS DESTINED TO FAIL

In addition to problematically casting an entire people group as born for servility, reading house-elves as stand-ins for African slaves immediately prohibits any success on the part of S.P.E.W. At its birth, the Society for the Protection of Elfish Welfare does not intend to end elfish labor. When Hermione initially introduces her project to Ron and Harry, she explains, "I was going to put Stop the Outrageous Abuse of Our Fellow Magical Creatures and Campaign for a Change in Their Legal Status—but it wouldn't fit [on the badges]."[49] Such a title better encompasses the actual impetus of the coalition, emphasizing policy change. She cites three "short-term aims": to "secure house-elves fair wages and working conditions"; to "[change] the law about non-wand use"; and to "get an elf into the Department for the Regulation and Control of Magical Creatures." It is not her goal to remove elves from the domestic service sphere or to abolish elf labor, at least at the outset. She is campaigning instead for legal protections that would allow elves to continue the work they love without subjecting them to systemic inequities designed to disempower them. In essence, her organization (at its genesis) is what one might call antiracist.

In *How to Be an Antiracist,* Ibram X. Kendi divides conceptions about racial equity into three categories: assimilationist, segregationist, and antiracist. He describes an antiracist position as one "expressing the idea that racial groups are equals and none needs developing, and . . . supporting policy that reduces racial inequity."[50] In seeking to retain house-elves' natural inclinations to domesticity and servitude while eliminating policies that keep them subjugated, S.P.E.W. is antiracist. If it were to persist in that direction, the narrative arc might have become a more apt social justice parable. However, as the series wears on and Hermione takes on a more traditionally abolitionist rhetoric, that opportunity crumbles.

Hermione's methods and motives rather suddenly change in *Order of the Phoenix*, moving from antiracist to assimilationist. Defined by Kendi as "expressing the racist idea that a racial group is culturally or behaviorally inferior and . . . supporting cultural or behavioral enrichment programs to develop that racial group,"[51] assimilationist perspectives assume that a group must fundamentally change in order to earn equity. As she turns her attention to freeing unwilling elves by hiding clothes in the common room, Hermione pivots from her initial aims in a way that disempowers elves. At the same time, she reifies the house-elf problem as part of a problematic racial paradigm. She has ceased to recognize elves as disenfranchised, unfairly treated members of the service industry and has instead begun to see them as an ignorant racial group in need of a fundamental change to their ways of thinking and relating to the world.

At this point, then, S.P.E.W. is precluded from success. Because the dominant narrative has so firmly entangled house-elves with enslaved Africans, the only morally acceptable rhetorical move is to campaign for liberation. Because house-elves are not actually equivalent to enslaved Africans and actually want to continue working in the domestic sphere, however, liberation becomes a disempowering act. It places Hermione and S.P.E.W. in an ethical stalemate. Though she may have found success with her initial aims, all of which honored elves' cultural and social preferences, the organization's turn toward racialized assimilationist action necessitates failure. By reading elves as victims of race-based chattel slavery, readers back Hermione and S.P.E.W. into a corner. Abolition may have been the right thing to do in the face of real-world egregious human rights abuses, but it is not applicable here. In short, Hermione cannot win, so long as elves and slaves are conflated.

QUESTIONS FOR READING THE HOUSE-ELF NARRATIVE CRITICALLY OUTSIDE THE RACIAL PARADIGM

As Schott suggests and as Wade models, there is still great potential for analyzing the Harry Potter series through a social justice lens, especially through the use of critically oriented supplemental material. Though any attempt to overlay a real-life people group onto the house-elves will result in troubling and problematic inequivalences, there may be some value in reading S.P.E.W. and interspecies inequity as a sort of case study. Readers might practice critical skills in thinking about ethics and activism by exploring the fairly detailed social landscape provided in the text. Without equating Black people with house-elves, readers can still consider the events of the stories and ask important questions about justice, fairness, and equality that do affect systemic inequities of race, gender, class, sexuality, and more.

However real the stories of the Wizarding world may feel to countless readers around the globe, it would be a mistake to read them as allegories. One of the great triumphs of fantasy is its ability to transcend historical moments while challenging our capacities to think critically about our own worlds. In closing, I offer these questions as pathways to a critical reading of the S.P.E.W. narrative by asking the reader to approach social justice issues and systemic inequities in the texts, thus providing space to consider the implications of Hermione's efforts outside an undue racialized paradigm:

- *What is systemic oppression? How do policies keep certain groups in power and other groups out of power?* For example, the distinctions of beast, being, and spirit discussed in the book *Fantastic Beasts and Where to Find Them* are designed to create order, but they also function to exclude certain groups from exercising power. Elves and goblins are subjugated by legal decisions about wand use, and they lack governmental representation that might allow for changes to those laws.
- *How can members of oppressed groups advocate for change within their communities without patronizing their peers or appropriating the attitudes of oppressors?* Kreacher venerates those who oppress him, even when faced daily with evidence of his subjugation as he passes the heads of his own ancestors mounted on the wall of his

beloved Walpurgia Black. Why might he participate so willingly in his own oppression? On the other hand, Dobby alienates other elves by cheerfully collaborating with members of the oppressive group. How do his actions serve to inhibit actual systemic change? What might a positive example of elf-led advocacy look like? Could it possibly include cooperation from witches and wizards?

- *What are the responsibilities of the privileged in relation to those who are systemically oppressed?* Supposing that house-elves are happiest in service to families, are there ways that wizards could better support their well-being? What is the nature of the enchantments that bind them, and what would it mean to break them? How do the changes to Hermione's organization support or fail to support equity?
- *Does difference mean inequality?* The Wizarding world presents a rich tapestry of difference between magical beings and creatures. Are wizards and witches really inherently better than the others? If not, how have they positioned themselves to create that illusion?
- *Can individuals ever truly be spokespersons for their entire identity groups?* Does Dobby speak for all house-elves? Does Winky? Or Kreacher? What happens when we assign one person's (or creature's) behaviors and characteristics to an entire group?

NOTES

1. Rojek, "Stuart Hall," 54.
2. Other essays consider the house-elves outside of the racial paradigm, instead employing feminist lenses. See McDaniel, " 'Real House-Elves' "; and Kellner, "Rowling's Ambivalence."
3. See Barratt, *Politics*; Carey, "Hermione and the House-Elves" and "Hermione and the House-Elves Revisited"; Susan McWilliams, "The Problem of Slavery"; Schott, "House Elf Problem"; and Wade, "Black Liberation Movements."
4. And related terms *enslave, enslaved, enslavement*, and *slavery*.
5. One notable exception occurs in *Goblet of Fire* when Ron tells Hermione, "They. Like. It. They like being enslaved!" Rowling, *Goblet of Fire*, 224. All Harry Potter book citations in this essay refer to the original Scholastic (US) editions.
6. Rowling, *Chamber of Secrets*, 178.
7. Barratt, *Politics*, 48.
8. Barratt, 48.
9. Rowling, *Goblet of Fire*, 125. (ellipses in original).
10. Barratt, *Politics*, 48.
11. Barratt, 49.

12. Barratt, 50.
13. Carey, "Hermione and the House-Elves," 165.
14. Carey, 167.
15. Carey, 167.
16. Carey, 168.
17. Rowling, *Deathly Hallows,* 225.
18. Rowling, 734.
19. Carey, "Hermione and the House-Elves," 171.
20. Schott, "House Elf Problem," 260–61.
21. Schott, 262.
22. Rowling, *Goblet of Fire,* 239.
23. Schott, "House-Elf Problem," 262.
24. Wade, "Black Liberation Movements," 244.
25. Wade, 256.
26. Wade, 256.
27. Thomas, *Dark Fantastic.*
28. Kendi, *Stamped,* 19.
29. Kendi, 17.
30. Kendi, 31.
31. Kendi, 28. These words appear in the writings of Leo Africanus.
32. "Quidditch World Cup 1990–2014," Harry Potter Wiki, https://harrypotter.fandom.com/wiki/Quidditch_World_Cup_1990_-_2014.
33. Chambers, *Popular Rhymes of Scotland,* 325. Translated from Scots, "Give brownie [a] coat, give brownie [a] shirt / You'll get no more of brownie's work!"
34. Chambers, 327.
35. Rowling, *Goblet of Fire,* 182.
36. Tom McArthur, Jacqueline Lam-McArthur, and Lise Fontaine, eds., *Oxford Companion to the English Language,* 2nd ed. (Oxford: Oxford University Press, 2018), s.v. "Cockney."
37. Rowling, *Goblet of Fire,* 379-80.
38. See the grisly display of mounted elf heads at Grimmauld Place in *Order of the Phoenix.*
39. Rowling, *Fantastic Beasts,* xii.
40. For a fuller discussion of the implications of beast/being status in the series, see Valadão Lopes, " 'All Was Well'?"
41. Rowling, *Fantastic Beasts,* vi.
42. Though she appears elfish, the creature who sings at the Blind Pig is in fact a half-goblin, according to the screenplay, and not a house-elf or part-elf.
43. Accessible at the time of writing at WizardingWorld.com.
44. Wizarding World, "Treatment of Intelligent Magical Creatures," September 1, 2019, https://www.wizardingworld.com/features/the-treatment-of-intelligent-magical-creatures-in-fantastic-beasts-and-harry-potter.
45. Wizarding World.
46. Wizarding World.

7. Why S.P.E.W. Was Doomed to Fail

47. Wizarding World.
48. Rowling, *Crimes of Grindelwald* (screenplay), scene 41.
49. Rowling, *Goblet of Fire*, 224.
50. Kendi, *How to Be an Antiracist*, 20.
51. Kendi, 30.

8. "The Ghost of His Last Laugh"

Evolving Humor in Harry Potter

Louise M. Freeman

> *We did it, we bashed them, wee Potter's the one,*
> *And Voldy's gone moldy, so now let's have fun!*
> "Really gives a feeling for the scope and tragedy of the thing, doesn't it?" said Ron. —J. K. Rowling, *Harry Potter and the Deathly Hallows*

RON WEASLEY IS often unintentionally correct. Just as his made-up predictions in Divination sometimes come true, his sarcastic quip is an apt description of the role of humor in Harry Potter. Amanda Cockrell states that Rowling's "goofily skewed reality" makes readers forget the dark seriousness of the storyline, until "we are brought up short, heart pounding, on the precipice again."[1] Beatrice Groves notes that Rowling, like Shakespeare, uses comedy to both soften and highlight tragic themes.[2] Ron's understated response to Peeves's singsong "eases the transition from the excitement and peril of battle to the quiet contentment of the novel's conclusion."[3]

Fred Weasley's death illustrates the jarring juxtaposition of humor and horror.

> "Hello, Minister!" bellowed Percy. . . . "Did I mention I'm resigning?"
> "You're joking, Perce!" . . . Fred looked at Percy with glee. "You actually are joking, Perce . . . I don't think I've heard you joke since you were—"
> The air exploded . . .
> Then [Harry] heard a terrible cry that pulled at his insides, that expressed agony of a kind neither flame nor curse could cause.[4]

Fred lies dead, with "the ghost of his last laugh still etched upon his face."[5] Similarly, Sirius Black is confidently laughing when Bellatrix's fatal curse sends him through the veil. Mad-Eye Moody, Hedwig, Dobby, and Colin Creevey are other examples of characters that evoke laughter throughout much of the series, but ultimately die suddenly and violently.

Even as humor highlights terror, it can also help characters and, vicariously, readers cope with it. After Voldemort's return, Harry insists on funding the twins' joke shop with his Triwizard Tournament prize, which he won as a result of Cedric's ghastly murder. Harry reasons, "I could do with a few laughs. We could all do with a few laughs. I've got a feeling we're going to need them more than usual before long."[6] Harry proves prescient here; the twins' merchandise is eventually adapted into weapons against Voldemort.

The twins provide another example of the comforting power of humor when George is injured evacuating Harry from Little Whinging.

> "What's wrong with him?" croaked Fred, looking terrified. "Is his mind affected?"
>
> "Saintlike," repeated George, opening his eyes and looking up at his brother. "You see . . . I'm holy. *Holey*, Fred, geddit?"
>
> Mrs. Weasley sobbed harder than ever. Color flooded Fred's pale face.
>
> "Pathetic," he told George. "Pathetic! With the whole wide world of ear-related humor before you, you go for *holey*?"
>
> "Ah well," said George, grinning at his tear-soaked mother. "You'll be able to tell us apart now, anyway, Mum."[7]

The twins' ability to joke in the face of trauma brings comfort to both themselves and their mother. This effect is consistent with the association between humor and emotional resiliency seen in multiple studies.[8]

THE PSYCHOLOGY OF HUMOR IN THE WIZARDING WORLD

Psychological theories of humor explain why Rowling's series is fertile ground for comedy. Peter McGraw and Caleb Warren propose that humor emerges from violations of safety or moral standards that are ultimately benign.[9] Laughter becomes a "false alarm" message, signaling listeners that an apparent threat need not be feared.[10] Hogwarts students put the benign violation hypothesis into practice when they banish boggarts with the Riddikulus spell; they infuse humor into their worst fear, then render it harmless through laughter.

Because much, but not all, of Rowling's magic is reversible, violations that would endanger Muggles can be benign to wizards. Skiving Snackbox–induced sickness is funny because, once excused from class, the snacker can access an instant cure. Accidents and injuries are an expected part of a Hogwarts education, but melting cauldrons, overgrown teeth, and boneless arms are easily repaired by the wave of a wand or Madame Pomfrey's ministrations. The transience of harm both increases opportunities for day-to-day humor and accentuates the threat of the few spells, like Avada Kedavra and Sectumsempra, that do permanent damage.

Reversal theory, a comprehensive model of personality, motivation, and emotion, has also been applied to humor. Michael Apter argues that humor requires both cognitive synergy, the simultaneous perception of an entity in two contradictory states, and a paratelic state, a playful frame of mind that makes the incongruity enjoyable.[11] Magic normalizes the simultaneous perception of incompatible traits, allowing a small beaded bag to carry a full-size tent.[12] Rowling's most glaring example of synergy between real and illusory natures is the magical world itself, which exists under the Muggles' noses, but is invisible to them. Readers who follow Harry into Diagon Alley or Platform Nine and Three-Quarters enter an inherently playful realm, where contradictions and humor abound.

Apter and Mitzi Desselles add a third requirement to their application of reversal theory to humor: humor requires a target, or an entity to be diminished in some way.[13] They further classify humor into two categories, depending on whether the diminishment comes through the real or illusory components of the synergy: distortion humor and disclosure humor. Distortion humor occurs when the joke comes through the false element. Examples include caricature, parody, and sarcasm, where a genuine trait becomes unrealistic through exaggeration or inversion.[14] One example is Harry sassing Snape:

"Do you remember me telling you we are practicing *nonverbal* spells, Potter?"

"Yes," said Harry stiffly.

8. "The Ghost of His Last Laugh"

"Yes, *sir*."
"There's no need to call me 'sir,' Professor."[15]

Harry diminishes Snape by distorting Snape's actual demand (that Harry call Snape "sir") and presenting it as Snape calling Harry "sir."

Magic elevates the potential for distortion humor. Neville doesn't merely imagine Snape in his grandmother's clothes, which might evoke a private giggle. With Riddikulus, the boggart becomes a visible Potions Master in drag, and the entire class roars with laughter. Harry regularly ridicules his Muggle cousin Dudley through hyperbole, describing him as "roughly the size and weight of a young killer whale."[16] In the Wizarding world, magical beings such as giants exist, turning presumed exaggerations, like Hagrid's baby-dolphin-sized feet, into accurate descriptors. With magic, expectations of reality shift, allowing distortion humor reversals to themselves be reversed, with even funnier results.

In disclosure humor, diminishment derives from the real attribute, as the false entity is unmasked.[17] Umbridge falsely believes she can assert her authority over the angry centaurs by stating her Ministry credentials and quoting regulations, but instead she enrages them more, and is diminished when they attack. Slapstick humor falls into this category, when a character's intentions (Percy bringing Scrimgeor to the Burrow to recruit Harry) are foiled by the actual outcome[18] (Percy leaves covered with parsnips). Dumbledore demonstrates more subtle disclosure humor when he unmasks the Dursleys' pretense of courtesy:

"I don't mean to be rude—" [Vernon] began, in a tone that threatened rudeness in every syllable.
"—yet, sadly, accidental rudeness occurs alarmingly often," Dumbledore finished the sentence gravely. "Best to say nothing at all, my dear man."[19]

Rowling's slow narrative release[20] allows amplified humor through multiple and delayed disclosures. The twins bouncing snowballs off Quirrell's turban is funny; it is funnier still to learn they were actually hitting Voldemort. Another example is Harry's response to his friends' stealing the

Sword of Gryffindor: "'Snape might've thought that was a punishment,' said Harry, 'but Ginny, Neville, and Luna probably had a good laugh with Hagrid. The Forbidden Forest . . . they've faced plenty worse than the Forbidden Forest, big deal!' He felt relieved; he had been imagining horrors, the Cruciatus Curse at the very least."[21] Because Harry is apparently correct and Snape mistaken, the situation is initially interpreted as humor at Snape's expense. Later, Harry learns the truth about the Carrows' disciplinary practices and Snape's true loyalties. The Cruciatus Curse was a genuine, not imagined possibility; Snape was not a fool but a protector. Delayed disclosure reverses the humor, turning the joke on Harry.

RING STRUCTURE AND EVOLVING HUMOR AT PRIVET DRIVE

The magical and Muggle worlds regularly collide at Number Four Privet Drive, where the Dursleys' cartoonish excess makes them prime targets for distortion humor. Two plot points characterize the early Dursley scenes in each book: (1) Harry's magical allies rescue him from his miserable summer exile; and (2) the Dursleys receive some form of comeuppance for their maltreatment of Harry, often in the form of disclosure humor. Truths that the Dursleys would rather ignore, whether about the existence of wizards or their own shortcomings, become glaringly apparent and are usually quite funny.

The Privet Drive openings follow the same ring structure seen in the full series. John Granger shows that the seven books form a "turtle-back" cycle, with similar themes reflected between pairs of books.[22] *Philosopher's Stone* and *Deathly Hallows* are beginning and ending "latches," and both connect with the series' turning point, *Goblet of Fire*. The intermediate books form connections of their own, *Chamber of Secrets* with *Half-Blood Prince* through the exploration of Tom Riddle's history, and *Prisoner of Azkaban* with *Order of the Phoenix* by the focus on Sirius Black.

The Privet Drive sequences follow a similar pattern (fig. 1). The first and seventh books depict the Dursleys fleeing their home to escape wizards[23]; in the second and sixth, the Dursleys entertain houseguests. In the third and fifth, Harry performs underage magic, risks Ministry punishment, and attempts to flee.[24] The fourth book inverts the basic plot of the first and last, with wizards coming to Privet Drive, while simultaneously making

8. "The Ghost of His Last Laugh"

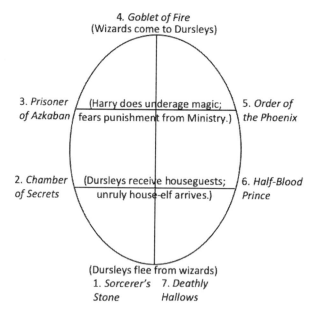

Figure 1.

thematic links to those books. For example, *Sorcerer's Stone* and *Goblet of Fire* both involve letters from witches that enrage Vernon.[25] Both *Goblet of Fire* and *Deathly Hallows* feature a rescuer indignant at the Dursleys' lack of a proper farewell to Harry. Dudley is "transfigured" in books 1, 4, and 7: by pig's tail, by engorged tongue, and finally by showing regard for Harry.[26]

Amid the plot parallels, the tone shifts in the second half of the series, becoming darker as the stakes become higher. The first three books rely on visual humor: escaped boa constrictors, persistent letters, levitating puddings and inflated aunts. There is less slapstick in the last three books, and more undertones of deadly seriousness. Books 5, 6, and 7 open with Harry grieving and traumatized, having witnessed murder at the end of the previous book. Humor is paired with more somber topics: criminal charges, the Dursleys' failure as parents, and genuine threats of torture and death.

As expected in the transitional book, *Goblet of Fire* is intermediate in tone. Harry witnesses Frank Bryce's murder, but only in a dimly recalled dream. Dudley's encounter with the Ton-Tongue Toffee begins as standard benign violation humor: a prank that Arthur Weasley could easily reverse. However, danger increases when Dudley's parents fight off Arthur's assistance, and Dudley starts to suffocate. Arthur, in an uncharacteristic temper, later chastises the twins: " 'It *isn't funny!*' Mr. Weasley shouted. 'That sort of behavior seriously undermines wizard-Muggle relations! I spend half my life campaigning against the mistreatment of Muggles, and my own sons—' "[27]

Genuine Muggle mistreatment will happen later at the Quidditch World Cup, where it is no laughing matter. The Dursleys' resistance also foreshadows their initial refusal of protection in *Deathly Hallows*, a choice that could have had fatal consequences. The echoes and contrasts of the Number Four Privet Drive scenes continue throughout the series, with the humor evolving from lighthearted slapstick to a literary device that spotlights greater dangers. For example, Dumbledore's witty banter with his would-be assassins heightens the tension on the Astronomy Tower and amplifies the shock of his death.

> "Good evening, Amycus," said Dumbledore calmly, as though welcoming the man to a tea party. "And you've brought Alecto too.... Charming..."
>
> The woman gave an angry little titter. "Think your little jokes'll help you on your deathbed then?" she jeered.
>
> "Jokes? No, no, these are manners," replied Dumbledore.[28]

Similarly, Ron's "IF WE DIE FOR THEM, I'LL KILL YOU, HARRY!"[29] is a rare flash of humor amid the horror of Fiendfyre and makes Ron's subsequent announcement of Crabbe's death more powerful.

"TRESPASSING ON YOUR AUNT AND UNCLE'S HOSPITALITY": *CHAMBER–PRINCE* CONNECTIONS

Chamber of Secrets begins with the Dursleys excitedly planning a dinner party, in hopes of securing Vernon a lucrative business deal. Their ridiculous extremes, such as Dudley's flattery of his father's boss ("We had to write an essay about our hero at school, Mr. Mason, and I wrote about you"[30]) exemplify distortion humor; Harry struggles not to laugh. The

8. "The Ghost of His Last Laugh"

Table 1. Parallels and contrasts in the opening Privet Drive scenes from *Chamber of Secrets* and *Half-Blood Prince*.

Chamber of Secrets	*Half-Blood Prince*
Dursleys are eagerly anticipating arrival of Masons. They are dressed up; Aunt Petunia has immaculately prepared house and meal.	Dursleys are not expecting Dumbledore to arrive. They are in pajamas; Aunt Petunia is cleaning kitchen. They offer no refreshments.
Dursleys are eager to impress Masons and practice complimenting them.	Dursleys are rude and barely speak to Dumbledore; he chides them for poor manners.
Petunia rehearses for the Masons' arrival; she says she is "waiting to welcome them graciously to our home."	Dumbledore enters without invitation and prompts Vernon, "Let us assume that you have invited me warmly into your house."
House-elf arrives who adores Harry, but will not obey his order to be quiet.	House-elf arrives who hates Harry, but must obey his order to be quiet.
Dursleys lock Harry in his room, refusing to let him return to Hogwarts. He considers the situation hopeless.	Harry gets to leave the Dursleys after only two weeks. He considers it "too good to be true."
Harry has to rush around his room and gather his things quickly when the Weasleys arrive.	Harry has to rush around his room and gather his things quickly when Dumbledore arrives.

party degenerates into hilarious calamity with the arrival of Dobby the house-elf, a character as funny as he is loyal. Dobby's hero worship of Harry is genuine, unlike the Dursleys' self-serving flattery of the Masons. Even so, Dobby refuses to obey Harry's order to be quiet, and takes steps to assure Harry will not return to Hogwarts. By the end, Harry resembles a classic pie-in-the-face victim, covered head-to-toe in whipped cream.

Soon Harry's plight becomes decidedly unfunny. The owl delivering the Ministry warning letter also delivers the death knell to the party, sending the guests of honor screaming from the house. Harry incurs full Dursley wrath once Vernon realizes his nephew cannot retaliate with magic, and the boy ends up imprisoned in his room. Happily, the Weasley boys engineer a jailbreak, with help from their father's flying Ford Anglia. Their liberation mission provides more visual humor: the car itself, the scramble to gather Harry's possessions, and Vernon's tug-of-war, using Harry as the rope. The boys aren't the only ones roaring with laughter as they pull Harry into the car and speed away.

The Dursleys receive a different kind of houseguest in *Half-Blood Prince*: Dumbledore (Table 1).[31] Instead of their company finest, they are wearing pajamas, and, in Petunia's case, rubber cleaning gloves. Dumbledore is greeted first with Vernon's "Who in the blazes is calling this time of night?"[32] and then mostly by stunned silence. The family that had been so eager to impress their Muggle guests is sardonically schooled on manners through Dumbledore's disclosure humor. "'I would assume that you were going to offer me refreshment,' Dumbledore said to Uncle Vernon, 'but the evidence so far suggests that that would be optimistic to the point of foolishness.'"[33]

Dumbledore both retrieves Harry and upbraids the Dursleys for their poor parenting. His quip to Vernon, "I must say, your agapanthus are flourishing,"[34] is a tongue-in-cheek early start on the second objective. *Agapanthus* is derived from *agape*, Greek for self-sacrificing love, a core value of Harry's but utterly absent in the Dursleys.[35] The plants' common name, lily of the Nile, evokes both Harry's mother and the river where baby Moses was protected from the ruler who wanted him dead.[36] Fans have speculated that Petunia secretly planted the flower in honor of Lily and as a reminder of her promise to care for her orphaned nephew.[37] Dumbledore may allude to the same sentiments in his compliment.

Another interpretation is potentially funnier. First, flourishing agapanthus are not a mark of a highly skilled gardener; they are easily grown and self-propagating.[38] Second, the common name is a misnomer; agapanthus are not true lilies.[39] Complimenting the "false lily" communicates that the Dursleys are poor surrogate parents, a point Dumbledore will make explicitly later.

Dumbledore's visit also includes some benign visual humor. He forces the Dursleys to sit and listen to him by magically sliding the couch. He conjures up glasses of mead, which knock insistently against their foreheads, and again corrects their manners when they refuse to drink it. But compared to the Masons' visit, Dumbledore's relies far more on verbal than visual humor, and some is quite subtle. The series has both darkened and deepened.

Half-Blood Prince has its own unruly house-elf arrival.[40] Kreacher is the antithesis of Dobby; he loathes Harry but must obey his order to "shut up!" Petunia's horrified reaction to the filthy, tantrumming elf contrasts with Dumbledore's "As you can see, Harry, Kreacher is showing a certain reluctance to pass into your ownership,"[41] demonstrating distortion humor based on understatement rather than exaggeration.

Harry's hasty trunk-packing is a final echo to *Chamber of Secrets*. Despite a letter confirming the pickup, Harry has postponed this task: "He could not shrug off the feeling that something was going to go wrong—his reply to Dumbledore's letter might have gone astray; Dumbledore could be prevented from collecting him; the letter might turn out not to be from Dumbledore at all, but a trick or joke or trap. Harry had not been able to face packing and then being let down and having to unpack again."[42] The excuse seems flimsy; why would the headmaster who effortlessly escaped Aurors have difficulty traveling to Little Whinging? But hurried packing is needed to make Harry's departure match his earlier Ford Anglia rescue. In contrast, in the first, fourth, and seventh books, Harry is packed and ready at the appointed hour.

Dumbledore's final words to the Dursleys are more sobering than his earlier banter; he explains the danger Harry is in, and the need to retain Lily's blood protection. He also sternly rebukes the Dursleys' parenting, citing not only their maltreatment of Harry but also the "appalling damage" their indulgence has inflicted on Dudley.[43] Thus the chapter ends on a bittersweet rather than purely comic note. The earlier humor Dumbledore pokes at the Dursleys contrasts with, and therefore highlights, the seriousness of his final disclosure.

"SURELY YOU DON'T *WANT* TO BE EXPELLED?": *PRISONER–ORDER* CONNECTIONS

Prisoner of Azkaban, like *Chamber of Secrets*, takes Harry through two rounds of cartoonish humor before depositing him safely in the Wizarding world. The first involves abuse from the figuratively—and soon to be

Table 2. Parallels and contrasts in the opening Privet Drive scenes from *Prisoner of Azkaban* and *Order of the Phoenix*.

Prisoner of Azkaban	*Order of the Phoenix*
Harry sees Sirius Black on the Muggle news, but does not connect him to the wizarding world.	Harry tries to listen to the Muggle news for information on what is happening in the wizarding world.
Harry is happy when he receives birthday presents from Ron and Hermione and keeps them.	Harry is angry when he receives birthday presents from Ron and Hermione and throws them away.
Harry tries to avoid Aunt Marge.	Harry picks a fight with Dudley.
Harry becomes enraged after Aunt Marge insults his parents.	Harry becomes enraged when Dudley taunts him about the nightmares Harry is having about his parents and Cedric.
Harry thinks of his birthday gift from Hermione to distract himself from Aunt Marge's abuse.	Harry thinks of Ron and Hermione to summon his Patronus.
Harry accidently does magic to punish Aunt Marge.	Harry deliberately does magic to save Dudley from dementors.
Harry runs away to Diagon Alley.	Harry tries to run away but is stopped by letters from Arthur and Sirius.
Stan Shunpike is introduced. Harry's decision to use *Expelliarmus* against Stan at the Battle of the Seven Potters reveals him as the real Harry.	Mundungus Fletcher is introduced. Mundungus's panicked Disapparation at the Battle of the Seven Potters reveals him as a decoy Harry.
Stan Shunpike, conductor, helps load Harry's trunk on and off the Knight Bus.	Tonks Locomotors Harry's trunk down the stairs, "holding her wand like a conductor's baton."
Harry is surprised by Fudge and the Ministry's leniency in light of his underage magic.	Harry is surprised by Fudge and the Ministry's harshness in light of his underage magic.
Harry winds up in Diagon Ally, where he enjoys a period of fun, freedom, and leisure.	Harry winds up confined in Grimmauld Place, where he must do many chores and worries about his Ministry hearing.

literally—overblown Aunt Marge, the only Dursley more loathsome than Vernon. Granger has argued that Marge is a caricature of Margaret Thatcher, and that her diatribes are a humorous slap at conservative politics.[44] Thus her presence is a ripe opportunity for distortion humor.

In a scene reminiscent of Oliver Twist's attack on Noah Claypole, Harry finally snaps on the last night of Marge's visit, when she declares Lily a "bad egg" who "ran off with a wastrel" and calls James a "no-account, good-for-nothing, lazy scrounger."[45] Losing control of both temper and magic, Harry inflates Marge until she is bursting from her clothes and floating on the ceiling. Once again, cartoonish mayhem ensues at Number Four Privet Drive, as Vernon struggles to pull Marge down, and her bulldog chomps down on his leg.

Harry runs away, fearing expulsion from Hogwarts and arrest for underage magic. He inadvertently summons the second comedic element of his escape, the Knight Bus, and boards under the pseudonym "Neville Longbottom." The magical bus ride adds careening car slapstick, reminiscent of the Keystone Cops era, with sudden jolts, sliding passenger beds, objects leaping out of the way, and Ernie, the myopic driver who "didn't seem to have mastered the use of a steering wheel."[46] The chaos sharpens the impact of Harry's increasing fear, as Ernie speaks fearfully of Azkaban, and Harry remembers that the wizard prison terrified even Hagrid.

Harry arrives at Diagon Alley intending to lie low, only to be greeted immediately, by name, by the Minister of Magic himself. Happily, his accidental magic has been reversed and Marge's memory wiped. Rather than punishment, Harry gets a three-week vacation of leisure and freedom in Diagon Alley. Amusingly, Fudge shows this leniency but refuses to sign Harry's permission form for weekend Hogsmeade trips.[47]

Order of the Phoenix is more than twice as long as *Prisoner of Azkaban*; unsurprisingly, Harry must overcome more obstacles to escape Privet Drive. The book opens with Harry again feeling mistreated, both by the Dursleys and by lack of news from his wizard allies. Harry endures a dementor attack, Arabella Figg's surprise revelation, a barrage of owl post, a period of confinement in his room, and finally, rescue by Mad-Eye Moody's Advance Guard.

As usual, the Privet Drive drama is punctuated by cartoonish distortion humor. Vernon channels Homer Simpson when he tries to strangle Harry in the flower bed, Mrs. Figg berates and batters Mundungus Fletcher, and multiple owls swoop into the kitchen, enraging Vernon. The disclosure humor of the slapstick is joined by the distortion humor of Harry's increasingly savage verbal jabs. He sarcastically informs Vernon that the news "changes every day, you see,"[48] and insults Dudley for looking "like a pig who's been taught to walk on its hind legs."[49]

The humor highlights very real peril, from dementors, Voldemort, and the Ministry. The first letter's threat to destroy his wand sends a "paralyzing dart" through Harry's mind; such a loss would not be reversible. Vernon's anti-owl rants contrast with Harry's stunned shock when Petunia recognizes dementors and receives the Howler. As her fear abruptly turns Vernon's bluster to timidity, Harry realizes there is extreme, unknown danger amid the mayhem.

The Advance Guard adds its own humor, largely from Moody's paranoid ravings amid the cheeriness and wisecracks of the rest of the team. But the sheer size of the eight-member evacuation team demonstrates the potential for attack, and Moody's fears will be all too justified in the parallel evacuation he leads in *Deathly Hallows*.[50]

Despite the common themes, there are contrasts to book 3 in book 5, many of which take the series in a darker direction (Table 2). Harry tries to avoid trouble with Marge but picks an intentional fight with Dudley. Inflating Marge is an accidental outburst in response to slander; casting the Patronus is a deliberate protective choice against deadly peril. Harry is pleasantly surprised at Fudge's leniency in Diagon Alley; after the dementor attack, he expects it, saying "I had to use magic—they're going to be more worried what dementors were doing floating around Wisteria Walk, surely?"[51] Harry is transported not to fun-filled Diagon Alley but to "grim old" Grimmauld Place,[52] to face screeching portraits, a nasty house-elf, arduous housework, and the looming dread of his Ministry hearing.

Books 3 and 5 introduce funny characters who will later play serious roles. On the Knight Bus, Harry meets Stan Shunpike, the none-too-bright conductor who, though delighted to learn that the famous Harry Potter is his passenger, continues to call him "Neville." The dementors attack when Order member Mundungus Fletcher abandons guard duty; a furious Mrs. Figg pummels him with her bag of cat food. Both Stan and Mundungus are

8. "The Ghost of His Last Laugh"

pivotal at the Battle of the Seven Potters in *Deathly Hallows*. Mundungus panics and Disapparates, revealing himself as one of the decoy Harrys, resulting in Mad-Eye's death. Harry's choice to disarm rather than kill Stan unmasks him as the real Harry.

A final connection again involves Harry packing for his journey. In *Prisoner of Azkaban,* Conductor Shunpike loads Harry's trunk onto the bus. In *Order of the Phoenix,* Tonks Locomotors his trunk down the stairs, "holding her wand like a conductor's baton."[53] Again, the turtle-back organization of books 3 and 5 extends to even minor details involving Harry's luggage.

"HE'S OFF WITH SOME OF YOUR LOT, ISN'T HE?": *STONE–GOBLET–HALLOWS* CONNECTIONS

Vernon and Petunia panic at the arrival of Harry's first Hogwarts letter. After an increasingly persistent postal barrage through windows, inside eggshells, and down the fireplace, Vernon decides they must flee, and goes to hilarious extremes that force even dim Dudley to conclude, "Daddy's gone mad, hasn't he?"[54] This escape is even funnier because it is completely unnecessary; the letter writers mean no harm. In a vain effort to escape the magical intrusion, materialistic Vernon and fastidiously clean Petunia take refuge in a shabby hut.

In *Deathly Hallows*, the family is in genuine danger, as the protective spell on their home breaks when Harry turns seventeen. Vernon, more troubled by association with benevolent wizards than torture by evil ones, keeps changing his mind about going into hiding. While there are comedic aspects of Vernon's bluster and repeated packing efforts, much of the humor is verbal and laced with bitterness. When Vernon accuses Harry of plotting to steal the house, Harry snaps back with another sarcastic distortion: "Why would I want this one? All the happy memories?"[55] For once, Vernon is silent.

Harry explicitly recalls the events of *Sorcerer's Stone*, saying, "If you remember the last time you tried to outrun wizards, I think you'll agree you need help,"[56] but there are more subtle reflections as well (Table 3). Vernon shouts "Hurry up!" as Harry picks up his first Hogwarts letter; Dedalus Diggle's pocket watch shouts "Hurry up!" as the Dursleys prepare to leave. In *Sorcerer's Stone*, Vernon takes refuge after letters stream

Table 3. Parallels and contrasts in the opening Privet Drive scenes from *Philosopher's Stone*, *Goblet of Fire*, and *Deathly Hallows*.

Philosopher's Stone	*Goblet of Fire*	*Deathly Hallows*
Harry is first seen in his cupboard. When confined after zoo trip, he remembers the pain from when he received the scar, and wishes for a relative to come take him away.	Harry is first seen in his bedroom, in pain from his scar. He remembers he has a godfather, Sirius, and writes him for advice, while wishing he could go live with him.	Harry is first seen in his bedroom, in pain from cut finger. He finds mirror shard, and feels "upsurge of bitter memories, stabs of regret and longing" for Sirius.
Uncle Vernon upset by excessive letters from wizards, some of which arrive via the fireplace.	Uncle Vernon upset by one letter that arrives with excessive stamps, and then by wizards who arrive via the fireplace.	Uncle Vernon is upset by the arrival of wizards assigned to be his bodyguards. One is named Hestia, which means "fireplace."
Vernon shouts "Hurry up!" at Harry when he is getting the mail.		Dedalus Diggle's pocket watch shouts "Hurry up!" at the Dursleys to keep them on schedule.
Dursleys pack quickly for sudden departure, as Uncle Vernon insists they leave.		Dursleys pack and unpack multiple times over a four-week period, as Uncle Vernon changes his mind about leaving.
Dudley tries to pack his electronics in bag; Uncle Vernon hits him.		Dudley packs his dumbbells in bag; Uncle Vernon hurts himself.
Uncle Vernon drives the family away in their car.		Uncle Vernon drives the family away in their car.
Something unexpected comes out of Dudley's bottom when Hagrid gives him a pig's tail.	Something unexpected comes out of Dudley's mouth when twins give him Ton Tongue Toffee. Aunt Petunia has emotional reaction.	Something unexpected comes out of Dudley's mouth when he thanks Harry for saving his life. Aunt Petunia has emotional reaction.
Hagrid is upset with Dursleys for Harry's lack of knowledge about Wizarding world.	Arthur is indignant when the Dursleys do not say good-bye to Harry. Harry responds, "It doesn't matter. Honestly, I don't care."	Hestia is upset at Dursleys' lack of knowledge of Harry's role in the Wizarding world. She is indignant when Dursleys do not say good-bye to Harry. Harry responds, "It's fine. It doesn't matter, honestly."
Harry packs all of his prized belongings in his trunk and is ready to go.	Harry packs all of his prized belongings in his trunk and is ready to go.	Harry packs all of his prized belongings in his rucksack and is ready to go.

through the fireplace; in *Deathly Hallows*, Hestia Jones, whose first name means "hearth" or "fireplace," escorts them to safety.[57]

Mail and fireplaces also connect the middle book to the first and last.[58] In *Goblet of Fire*, Vernon is again enraged by excess in a letter. "Every bit of it was covered in stamps except for a square inch on the front, into which Mrs. Weasley had squeezed the Dursleys' address in minute writing. 'She did put enough stamps on, then,' said Harry, trying to sound as though Mrs. Weasley's was a mistake anyone could make."[59]

The next day, the Dursleys' normality is again disrupted when the fireplace explodes to admit four Weasleys. The visitors are, if not harmless, at least willing to reverse any damage they cause. However, after Dudley eats the Ton-Tongue Toffee, there is another scene of comic chaos, with Dudley choking, Petunia yanking his tongue, and Vernon hurling ornaments at Arthur.

By *Deathly Hallows*, Dudley has become much less buffoonish, likely because of his dementor encounter in *Phoenix*. He alone shows some farewell affection for Harry, first saying, "I don't think you're a waste of space," then acknowledging that Harry has saved his life, then shaking hands.[60] Amusingly, this transformation of spoiled "Dudders" into a decent person sends Petunia into the same hysterics that the pig tail and jinxed tongue did.

Once the Dursleys depart, the guard arrives for the Seven Potters evacuation. Moody behaves much as he did in *Order of the Phoenix*, but this time no one is laughing at his fears.[61] The twins' jokes lighten the mood, and there is visual distortion humor as six people Polyjuice into Harrys, but tension mounts as they prepare to depart. As Harry takes his final glimpse of Privet Drive, the Death Eaters attack, abruptly killing Harry's beloved owl. Rowling claims that "the loss of Hedwig represents a loss of innocence and security. . . . Voldemort killing her marked the end of childhood."[62] After this, the series never returns to the sheer silliness of crashing puddings, engorged tongues, or head-clonking mead glasses.

CONCLUSION

Rowling crafted a magical world psychologically well suited to humor, particularly the benign violation, distortion, and disclosure types. Since wizardry reverses most harm, events that would otherwise be horrifying are instead funny, in accordance with the benign violation hypothesis. However, enough genuine danger remains for an exciting and sometimes terrifying tale. Pairing humor with danger puts extra emphasis on both, as many comic characters meet tragic ends. The Weasley twins, inseparable jokesters but tragically split by Fred's death, are the most obvious example of this pattern.

Magical transformations increase opportunities for distortion humor, while altered reality in the Wizarding world creates a playful environment that magnifies the humor in reversals. Rowling's gradual unfolding of her narrative expands the power of disclosure humor, allowing it to be reinterpreted and even reversed with new information. The opening Privet Drive scenes are particularly rich sources of humor, which Rowling evokes with the same organized approach that characterizes all her writing. Comedy emerges from ring structure, repetition, and contrast, even as the tone of the series darkens.

Finally, Rowling understands the power of humor to neutralize fear, as seen in elements like the Riddikulus spell and the weaponizing of joke-shop merchandise. The twins' "ear humor" response to George's injury, and Ron's ability to joke even in the aftermath of his brother's death, are reminiscent of trauma patients' use of humor as a therapeutic buffer.[63] In Harry Potter, humor functions as both a literary and a psychological tool, highlighting the increasingly tragic plot twists while also building resilience against terror.

NOTES

1. Cockrell, "Secret Password," 16.
2. Groves, *Literary Allusion*, 83.
3. Groves, 81.
4. Rowling, *Deathly Hallows*, 636–37. All Harry Potter book citations in this essay refer to the original Scholastic (US) editions.
5. Rowling, 637.
6. Rowling, *Goblet of Fire*, 733.
7. Rowling, *Deathly Hallows*, 74–75.
8. Cherry et al., "Spirituality, Humor, and Resilience," 492; and Cann and Collette, "Sense of Humor," 464.
9. McGraw and Warren, "Benign Violations," 1142.
10. Ramachandran, "False Alarm Theory," 352.
11. Apter, "Developing Reversal Theory," 4.

8. "The Ghost of His Last Laugh"

12. For a complete discussion of this phenomenon, see Elizabeth Baird Hardy, "Muggle Worthy: Deceptive Exteriors and Outsized Interiors in the Wizarding World," chapter 1 of this volume.

13. Apter and Desselles, "Disclosure Humor," 419.

14. Apter and Desselles, 422.

15. Rowling, *Half-Blood Prince*, 180.

16. Rowling, *Goblet of Fire*, 27.

17. Apter and Desselles, "Disclosure Humor," 422.

18. Apter and Desselles, 423.

19. Rowling, *Half-Blood Prince*, 46.

20. Granger, *Unlocking Harry Potter*, 13.

21. Rowling, *Deathly Hallows*, 302.

22. Granger, *Ring Composition*, 41. See also John Granger, "The Story Turn: Parallels in the Pivotal Texts of Harry Potter and Cormoran Strike," chapter 19 of this volume.

23. Granger, *Ring Composition*, 79.

24. Granger, "On Turtle-Back Tales," 48.

25. Granger, *Ring Composition*, 79.

26. Granger, 79.

27. Rowling, *Goblet of Fire*, 53.

28. Rowling, *Half-Blood Prince*, 593.

29. Rowling, *Deathly Hallows*, 633.

30. Rowling, *Chamber of Secrets*, 6.

31. Emily Strand highlights the irony of the Dursleys' kowtowing to the Masons, an unimportant Muggle family, while treating Dumbledore, an extremely important wizard, with disdain (personal correspondence, November 5, 2019).

32. Rowling, *Half-Blood Prince*, 45.

33. Rowling, 48.

34. Rowling, 46.

35. "Agapanthus," Harry Potter Lexicon, https://www.hp-lexicon.org/thing/agapanthus/.

36. "Agapanthus."

37. "Agapanthus."

38. "How to Grow Agapanthus," wikiHow, https://www.wikihow.com/Grow-Agapanthus#.

39. Kelch, "Consider the Lilies," 24.

40. Odell, "Second Guessing," 115.

41. Rowling, *Half-Blood Prince*, 52.

42. Rowling, 44.

43. For more on this point, see Emily Strand, "Parenting Models in the Potter Saga and *Cursed Child*: Human and Divine," chapter 16 of this volume.

44. Granger, *Unlocking Harry Potter*, 162.

45. Rowling, *Prisoner of Azkaban*, 28.

46. Rowling, 36.

47. Thomas, *Repotting Potter*, 92.
48. Rowling, *Order of the Phoenix*, 6.
49. Rowling, 13.
50. Freeman, "Diagnostic and Statistical Manual," 183.
51. Rowling, *Order of the Phoenix*, 22.
52. Thomas, *Repotting Potter*, 181.
53. Rowling, *Order of the Phoenix*, 53.
54. Rowling, *Sorcerer's Stone*, 43.
55. Rowling, *Deathly Hallows*, 32.
56. Rowling, 35.
57. "Hestia: Greek Goddess of the Hearth," Greek Mythology, accessed May 1, 2023, https://www.greekmythology.com/Olympians/Hestia/hestia.html.
58. Granger, *Ring Composition*, 79.
59. Rowling, *Goblet of Fire*, 30–31.
60. Rowling, *Deathly Hallows*, 40.
61. Freeman, "Diagnostic and Statistical Manual," 183.
62. Rowling, "Web Chat Transcript."
63. Sliter, Kale, and Yuan, "Best Medicine?" 267; and Üngör and Verkerke, "Funny as Hell," 80.

SECTION 4

NARRATOLOGICAL READINGS

9. Pensieve Lessons in Critical Reading

Leslie Bickford

CONDUCT A GOOGLE Image search for the *Daily Prophet*, and you are likely to see headlines like these: "Dumbledore: Daft or Dangerous?" "The Boy Who Lies?" and "Harry Potter: Undesirable No. 1." This type of fake news generated about Harry by the *Prophet*, the Wizarding world's primary news source, recently inspired one of my students to write a paper indicting J. K. Rowling for her portrayal of news media and reporters in the series. A reporter on our university newspaper, this student took Rowling to task for undermining her readers' trust in journalism, particularly in an age of increasing political divisiveness in both the United States and the UK. From an American perspective, the student's paper makes a solid point: in an age when former president Donald Trump has banned reporters from White House briefings and called the press at large "the enemy of the people," one would hope for a less biased portrayal of journalists in a series that transformed millions of millennials into avid readers. As my student astutely points out, Rowling's lack of positive examples of news media or those who create it could ostensibly lead her readers to develop a negative view of the press. In like manner, Amanda Sturgill, Jessica Winney, and Tina Libhart, authors of "Harry Potter and Children's Perceptions of the News Media," fear the series may engender negative real-world consequences: "The negative depiction of journalism in the series has the potential to greatly influence children's perceptions of the news media and the role of journalism in general."[1] Those of us who applaud Rowling for engendering a love of reading in an entire generation must also consider the consequences of her skewering perceptions of the news media in the minds of those same readers.

These negative appraisals are the logical outcome of analyzing the *Daily Prophet*'s machinations in isolation, but we must remember that Rowling's narrative weaves many complex topics and themes together over the course of a seven-book story arc made of individual narratives that grow along with readers. Viewed against this larger, more complex context, the deception of the *Daily Prophet* and its reporters becomes not an end but a means through which Rowling seeks to teach readers about the act of reading itself. Her authorial finger is pointed not at Rita Skeeter but at us. Readers read, after all, through a third-person narration mostly limited to Harry's experiences; we are never duped by Rita Skeeter's yellow journalism. This gives us an advantage: we can consider why and how some readers in the series are deceived and others are not. Shifting focus from writers to readers in the series, we receive instruction from Rowling about how to avoid the dangerous cycle of manufactured consent, the phenomenon whereby readers cede their agency to a dominating press. Throughout the series, her lessons in critical reading and thinking offer some very real solutions to the bleak real-world issues the books reflect. Rowling's negative portrayal of the press plays a crucial role in achieving these ends.

The need for critical thinking is highlighted by Rowling's unforgiving portrayal of the press; we therefore begin with a close analysis of the behaviors associated with reporters and the press in the books, exemplified nowhere better than in the character of Rita Skeeter. Ambitious to a fault, Rita's tactics are predatory: even the assonance of the hard vowels in her name is aggressive, and the plosives bite. In *Goblet of Fire* Harry falls victim to what Veronica Schanoes terms "Skeeter's treacherously slippery writing."[2] Interviewing Harry about being the youngest Triwizard champion, Rita shoves him into a broom closet, her "scarlet-taloned fingers [holding] Harry's arm in a surprisingly strong grip."[3] Along with her oft-mentioned crocodile-skin handbag, Rita's "talons" set her up as the consummate reptilian predator, and Harry is her prey. He watches as her "acid green" Quick-Quotes Quill spews lies about him.[4] The fact that the quill refuses to report exactly what Harry says and skates along the parchment, inventing facts and embellishing the truth, serves as a metaphor for both Rita's incompetence and the false nature of her reporting. As critic Leslee Friedman states, Rita "has absolutely no respect for the text itself" and "does not bother to so much as even take her own notes."[5] The absence of human agency in the use of the Quick-Quotes Quill, its disconnection from both Harry's statements and Rita's hand, points to the lack of humanity and scrupulousness in her reporting.

This "treacherously slippery writing," mirrored in the stories of other reporters for the *Daily Prophet*, has dangerous real-world repercussions: it leads to manipulation for rhetorical, political means. For an article about the Ministry inquest into Arthur Weasley's flying car, *Prophet* reporters choose to interview Lucius Malfoy, neither a confirmed employee of the Ministry of Magic nor in any way clearly connected to the car or the inquest. Lucius, who *is* a confirmed donor to the Fudge administration, is able to use the *Prophet* as a platform for his own political agenda, stating, "Weasley has brought the Ministry into disrepute. . . . He is clearly unfit to draw up our laws and his ridiculous Muggle Protection Act should be scrapped immediately."[6] The fact that he bewitched a Ford Anglia to fly may put Arthur Weasley on the wrong side of the Ministry's laws about magic and Muggle artifacts, but Lucius is clearly using the incident to his political advantage when he concludes that the Muggle Protection Act—completely unrelated to the flying car incident—should be "scrapped." That the unnamed *Prophet* reporter so willingly gives Lucius this platform to air his thinly-veiled anti-Muggle agenda points to the malleability of the press: the event that sparked the story—the flying car—is lost behind the desires of a wealthy, powerful man.

In like manner, Rita Skeeter's creation of fake news in *Goblet of Fire* points to a fundamental problem in the relationship of the wizarding press to its public. Arthur Weasley reads her report on the appearance of the Dark Mark at the Quidditch World Cup:

> "Listen to this: '*If the terrified wizards and witches who waited breathlessly for news at the edge of the wood expected reassurance from the Ministry of Magic, they were sadly disappointed. A Ministry official emerged some time after the appearance of the Dark Mark alleging that nobody had been hurt, but refusing to give any more information. Whether this statement will be enough to quash the rumors that several bodies were removed from the woods an hour later, remains to be seen.*' Oh, really," said Mr. Weasley in exasperation, "Nobody *was* hurt. What was I supposed to say? '*Rumors that several bodies were removed from the woods*'. . . well, there certainly will be rumors now she's printed that."[7]

9. Pensieve Lessons in Critical Reading

Arthur Weasley's complaint gets at the heart of the danger of misinformation perpetuated by the press. As Schanoes states, "Skeeter's writing . . . [may] have little or nothing to do with reality, but her writings *create* a reality of their own."[8] The fake news generated by Rita contains, ironically enough, given the name of her paper, a self-fulfilling prophecy: she generates rumors by falsely reporting that rumors exist.

This example points to a perilous cycle that the press has the power and the need to perpetuate: it can change and shape public opinion and actions, but, as Rita tells Hermione in *Order of the Phoenix*, it relies on the opinions and mood of the public for its very livelihood. It therefore *needs* to manipulate public opinion in its favor. Todd Ide, author of "The Dark Lord and the Prince: Machiavellian Elements in Harry Potter," describes the phenomenon: "The wealthy and political elites work hard to control not only *the way* information is presented, but also *what* information is disseminated for public consumption. In doing so, these elite individuals are able to *manipulate public opinion to fit their agenda*, a phenomenon described by Noam Chomsky and Edward Herman as 'manufactured consent.' "[9] In the Harry Potter series, the means to the ends of these political elites is most often the reporting in the *Daily Prophet*.

A perfect example of the emergence of "manufactured consent" appears during Hermione's aforementioned conversation with Rita in the Three Broomsticks. Arguing that the *Prophet* will not print an interview with Harry about the night Voldemort returned to physical form, Rita says, "There's no *market* for a story like that. . . . Nobody wants to read it. It's against the public mood. . . . People just don't want to believe You-Know-Who's back."[10] She callously tells Hermione, "The *Prophet* exists to sell itself, you silly girl,"[11] strongly implying that it must rely on and pay attention to public opinion, even as it manipulates said opinion through sensationalist reporting. Here we get the second play on the title of the wizarding paper: the *profit* manufactured by a story, its market value, is what drives the *Prophet* to print it. Hermione's scathing question, "So the *Daily Prophet* exists to tell people what they want to hear, does it?"[12] therefore has a double meaning: the *Prophet* tells people *only* those things they want to hear, for instance relating sentimental, untrue stories about Harry in *Goblet of Fire* but never reporting on the dementor attack he and Dudley suffer in Little Whinging at the beginning of *Order of the*

Phoenix. This relates the *Prophet* to its homonym, *profit*. At the same time, the *Prophet* tells people *what* they want to hear: it manipulates the truth in such a way as to manipulate public opinion and ensure its own existence, for instance, discrediting both Harry and Dumbledore in *Order of the Phoenix* as stark raving mad. The *Prophet* therefore takes on a *prophetic* function for society, telling people how to read the signs and act accordingly. The genius behind this cycle is that it keeps itself in perpetual motion. As Schanoes points out, readers of the *Prophet* lose agency as they "accept the text's version of reality"[13]; they are thereby made more dependent on that text.

Through their shared reliance on manipulating public opinion through manufactured consent, the *Prophet* and the Ministry of Magic have a complicated alliance that ultimately creates a more dangerous world for the public both are supposed to serve. The first time we see it being read in the early chapters of *The Sorcerer's Stone*, the *Prophet* evidently has run a negative story on the Ministry: "'Ministry o' Magic messin' things up as usual,' Hagrid muttered, turning the page."[14] However, as events in the series move toward an inevitable war between the forces of good and evil, the *Prophet* seems to be increasingly controlled by the Ministry. In the aforementioned conversation with Hermione, Rita Skeeter admits that Minister of Magic Cornelius Fudge is "leaning on the *Prophet*," a phrase that becomes nearly ubiquitous with any mention of the paper from this point forward. She further implies that the *Prophet* is willing to be controlled by the Ministry when their objectives align.[15] Fudge needs the public mood to be complacent, ignorant of the return of Voldemort, so that he can retain power. The *Prophet* needs to cater to the public mood to stay in circulation. The *Daily Prophet* essentially becomes the Ministry's mouthpiece, its means of manipulating public opinion; there seems to be, as Benjamin Barton observes, no free press in the magical world.[16] In book 5 alone, we see Fudge working through the *Prophet* to systematically discredit both Harry and Dumbledore, hush up the dementor attack in Little Whinging, and generally convince the public that Voldemort is not a threat. The effects of his actions ripple throughout the novel: Harry must endure the ridicule and disbelief of classmates and the sadism of Umbridge; Dumbledore loses his chairmanship of the International Confederation of Wizards, his position on the Wizengamot wizarding court, and ultimately his position as headmaster at Hogwarts; members of the Order of the Phoenix have a particularly hard time convincing individuals that Voldemort is back, which, as Lupin explains, "makes [people] easy targets for the Death Eaters if they're using the Imperius Curse."[17] In other words, by hushing up Voldemort's return, Fudge ensures it will happen: he aids the rise of Voldemort to power.

The *Prophet*'s complicity in perpetuating manufactured consent and reinforcing Ministry of Magic aims has some dangerous, potentially devastating outcomes. Rowling paints the press in a very negative light indeed, and it is possible to imagine young readers learning a distrust of all news media from the series. "The extremely negative depiction of journalism," Sturgill argues, "could have an adverse effect on child readers of the series as they may not have an understanding of journalism in a broader context. As a result of reading the series, they may infer that journalism is corrupt in general, deceptive, and would not make an attractive career choice."[18] One further negative impact could be exacerbated by the proliferation of conspiracy theorists like Alex Jones, who spread lies about the Sandy Hook school shooting as if they were news. Young American readers who buy into antagonistic rhetoric about the press may find themselves simply trading in a fictional manufactured consent (to the press) for a real one (to dangerous conspiracy theorists).

As mentioned before, however, we must temper critique of Rowling's treatment of the press with an understanding of our readerly experiences and lead young readers to do the same; readers are tied closely to Harry's point of view, which means we should not be duped by Rita or Fudge. In fact, most of the characters we get to know best are enabled to extract themselves from the vicious cycle of manufactured consent. Some, like Molly Weasley and Augusta Longbottom, simply stop taking the newspaper,[19] which could be instructional. Harry's plight at the beginning of *Order of the Phoenix*, however, points to how important it is to stay knowledgeable on what's happening, however slanted the reporting. Even Sirius, painted by the *Prophet* as a mass-murdering lunatic, admits to stealing papers out of trash bins to stay informed while hiding out in Hogsmeade in *Goblet of Fire*.[20] To remain engaged citizens, which Harry and his friends will need to be if they are to save both the Wizarding world and our own, characters and readers alike must know what is happening in the world.

When Harry asks Hermione testily in *Order of the Phoenix* why she's still taking the *Daily Prophet* and calls it a "load of rubbish," Hermione's response is instructive: "It's best to know what the enemy are saying."[21] Critical reading that circumvents manufactured consent involves a healthy dose of skepticism, which we see exemplified in both Hermione's continued patronage of the *Prophet* and Dumbledore's reading habits. Rather than eschew the press, Dumbledore reads not only the *Daily Prophet* but also Muggle newspapers,[22] which Rowling implies are no better at reporting the truth than wizarding papers (consider the infotainment that passes for news in *Order of the Phoenix*, when Harry hides behind a hydrangea bush to hear about Bungy the waterskiing budgie on the newscast in the Dursleys' living room[23]). It's the *way* Hermione and Dumbledore read that matters: they are skeptical, always aware of the Ministry's agenda, even propaganda, as they read. In *Harry Potter and the Millennials*, Anthony Gierzynski extrapolates six main political lessons that readers can learn from the series, the sixth of which is "Be Skeptical, Not Cynical."[24] This is difficult, coming hard on the heels of lesson five: "Government Leaders Are Corrupt, Incompetent, and Fixated on Maintaining Power,"[25] but, as Gierzynski points out, the entire Ministry is not evil: "The series' implicit critique of government, however, is limited to the individuals who are in charge"[26]; the integrity of characters like Kingsley Shacklebolt reassures us that not all politicians are corrupt. In like manner, all reading does not lead to manufactured consent. Leslee Friedman speaks to the way in which Hermione "makes magic happen when she reads . . . by entering into a relationship with the text where she not only receives information but finds ways of engendering action with that information."[27] One perfect example of the magic produced by Hermione's reading comes as she listens skeptically to Umbridge's welcome speech at the beginning of *Order of the Phoenix*. Where Harry and Ron glaze over and other students begin to whisper and giggle, Hermione, along with the faculty, listens attentively. She "[enters] into a relationship with the text" of Umbridge's speech by listening for what Umbridge is *not* saying and deducing that "the Ministry's interfering at Hogwarts."[28] Her understanding of the speech and her experience in Umbridge's class later lead Hermione to action. She talks Harry into teaching Defense Against the Dark Arts and essentially forms Dumbledore's Army, an alliance of students revolting against not only Umbridge but the Ministry itself. The lesson to readers is clear: rather than giving up agency, we can sharpen our critical reading (and listening) skills to become more active readers, which may lead to activism in our communities.

One of the best ways to retain readerly agency is to remain open-minded and consult alternative sources, for the complexity of the world cannot be filtered through a single viewpoint. While Sturgill argues that "references to the Wizarding world's only other newspaper, the tabloid *The Quibbler*, and references to other forms of media such as radio [are] minor and not of any particular significance when weighed against the references made to corrupt, underhanded journalism,"[29] the value of alternative sources is made clear in the series. During the course of *The Order of the Phoenix*, Harry's encounters with the *Quibbler* run from initially thinking it is a spoof to using it as his mouthpiece to broadcast a true account of the night Voldemort returned. As Friedman asserts, Umbridge's Educational Decree to expel students for reading the *Quibbler* "brings to the forefront [her] fear of what reading can accomplish."[30] The *Quibbler* continues in this role of alternative news source in *The Deathly Hallows*, right up until Xenophilius Lovegood is threatened by Death Eaters who have kidnapped Luna, further illustrating their fear of the power of the written word to disseminate the truth.[31] Xenophilius also serves to help the golden trio understand the importance of yet another unlikely print source, "The Tale of the Three Brothers." Although the ancient tale cannot be said to be news per se, it certainly supplies important information to the three on their quest, and it is instructive that this crucial puzzle piece comes to us and them through a source oft-demeaned by critics: children's literature. Overlooked for more than half of the novel, "The Tale of the Three Brothers" not only introduces the trio to the Deathly Hallows and reveals Harry's lineage and inheritance of the third hallow, it also serves a meta function for readers by illustrating the value of children's literature, specifically the Harry Potter series, in facing real evil. Finally, the alternative source of Potterwatch serves as a reminder that citizens may be called upon to broadcast news themselves. Members of the Order of the Phoenix and Dumbledore's Army risk their lives to bring the truth to the Wizarding world in much the same way people have used social media and mobile technology to speak truth to power and facilitate uprisings (the Arab Spring and the video of the murder of George Floyd being only two striking cases in point).

In addition to showing us the importance of an open mind, Rowling gives us experiential lessons in how to read not only skeptically but also recursively, using critical thinking skills to reflect on what we read and how we read it. More than any author I can think of, Rowling excels at enticing her readers to reread. She encourages the rereading of characters such as Snape, Kreacher, and Dumbledore; of objects such as invisibility cloaks, broken vanishing cabinets, and lockets. So many objects and people are reread throughout the series that Kate Behr has devoted an entire essay to this phenomenon, naming it "same-as-difference." Behr elaborates: "Core facts remain the same from first to last, but the reader's perceptions change as the stories and characters grow in complexity and acquire a history. Our understanding moves in a hermeneutic circle, as clues or references planted by Rowling in earlier books are only appreciated in the light of later events."[32] I argue that "hermeneutic circle" resembles the reflexive nature of critical thinking as defined by critical thinking expert Richard Paul: "Critical thinking is thinking about your thinking, while you're thinking, in order to make your thinking better."[33] Rowling's characters model this for readers, and her narratives engage us in such reading. We watch as characters revisit their own and others' memories through time travel and in Dumbledore's Pensieve, struggling to reinterpret past events and thus make sense of the present.

As Rowling directs readers to revisit characters and objects in the series, the text itself enacts the benefits of recursive reading and critical thinking by inviting us to do both. When Harry and Hermione use the Time-Turner in *Prisoner of Azkaban*, readers also travel back in time with them and reencounter some of the same phrases and descriptions of the action from an outside perspective. But this time, along with Harry and Hermione, we have new knowledge about the true identity of Scabbers. We, like they, are the same people, and yet, because time has passed and we've learned additional facts with the characters, we are different. This is highlighted in the text when Harry and Hermione watch their counterparts leave Hagrid's hut with Ron: "He, Ron, and Hermione had gone . . . but the Harry and Hermione hidden in the trees could now hear what was happening inside

9. Pensieve Lessons in Critical Reading

the cabin."[34] Watching our earlier selves reading by rereading causes us to think critically and assess our prior thought processes.

A second benefit of recursive reading is one all Harry Potter fans will recognize: the opportunity to gain new knowledge and reinterpret events. Like Harry and Hermione's change of perspective, the reader's new positioning in the forest allows us to fill in gaps through hearing and seeing things that happened after the characters left Hagrid's hut earlier. This gap-filling then leads to a same-as-difference moment when we see McNair swing his axe into the fence and hear Hagrid's cry. What at first we had interpreted as the beheading of Buckbeak, we now can reread and reinterpret. The experience of witnessing the scene again from a different point of view enables readers to learn more of the facts and interpret the scene accurately.

A third and very important development during this trip back to the past is that Hermione and Harry *change* the story. They are enabled to reread the axe thud and Hagrid's cry of joy *because* they have rescued Buckbeak. They have entered the story and changed it; they become coauthors, making the action happen, just as reader response theorists say readers participate in meaning-making through the act of reading. Despite Hermione's repeated injunctions that she and Harry "mustn't be seen,"[35] Harry understands that to rescue Buckbeak and Sirius, and later themselves, he must act, not just passively watch the events as they unfold. The rule that they cannot be seen seems to ensure that they cannot leave a mark on history, but the aforementioned same-as-difference was caused by their rescue of Buckbeak, proving they were participating in the story all along. Harry understands this just in time to save his own life: "And then it hit him—he understood. He hadn't seen his father—he had seen *himself.*"[36] Harry's same-as-difference realization here is of the utmost importance, for in it he finds not only his father metaphorically alive in himself but also the empowerment to cast the Patronus that saves his, Hermione, and Sirius's lives. He tells Hermione later, "I knew I could do it this time . . . because I'd already done it."[37] Harry's participation in the story has always already happened, just as our participation in meaning-making happens from the moment we open the book. This type of active, empowered reading obliterates manufactured consent.

Rowling's ingenious invention of the Pensieve helps to further illustrate the importance of rereading material and thinking recursively about our own relationship to it. Dumbledore's Pensieve is itself a metaphor for critical thinking, allowing users to "sieve" through thoughts to find focus and clarity; through it, readers also revisit textual passages such as the one in *Half Blood Prince*, describing the night Tom Riddle asked Slughorn about Horcruxes. Slughorn's fabrication in recalling his memory of this night is related in chapter 17, "A Sluggish Memory," while the true, factual memory is described in chapter 23, "Horcruxes." The first time Harry enters Slughorn's memory, Rowling spends eleven lines of text describing Slughorn's appearance and attitude. Along with Harry, readers take in an extraordinary amount of detail, down to the size of the bald patch on the back of his head.[38] We, like Harry, are "reading" the scene for the first time, and through his consciousness, we are naturally preoccupied with the youth of Professor Slughorn, the ways in which he differs in appearance from the Slughorn we know. The second time around, in chapter 23, neither readers nor Harry need to pay as much attention to *all* of the details of Slughorn's appearance. We are rereading a scene that we have experienced before and consequently know better what to look for. The description of Slughorn is much shorter in the replay, taking up only four and a half lines of text, and including only enough details to re-create the scene.[39]

Of course Rowling would want to make her writing more concise here; readers have read the scene before, and she wouldn't want to bore them. But the fact that she condenses five sentences into one and moves new information about Tom Riddle up into the paragraph that in chapter 17 had only described Slughorn signals a conscious effort on her part not only to condense the text but to get to the more pertinent details sooner.

Because Harry is rereading the scene, his mind can focus more acutely on what matters: the second time around, he sees Riddle earlier and knows where he is in Riddle's story. In each of the chapters, Harry's absorption of the scene before him ends with his recognition of Tom Riddle and Marvolo's gold and black ring (itself a same-as-difference object, as it contains the Resurrection Stone neither Harry nor we know to exist yet). Whereas before, the ring signals to Harry that Tom has already killed his father, an important interpretation that comes after nineteen lines of text in the book,[40] in his second reading of the scene Harry no longer needs to make this deduction: he mentions the ring after only seven lines of text and does not need to mention what its presence on Tom's finger signifies.[41]

9. Pensieve Lessons in Critical Reading

First readings, in other words, are not completely useless, nor are they only valuable in allowing us to achieve a second or third reading. Harry picks up valuable information during his first experience of the scene, regardless of the fact that Slughorn has tampered with the memory to obfuscate his own involvement in Tom Riddle's pursuit of immortality. That Harry is enabled to retain important information from the first reading of the scene while at the same time shifting his attention from Slughorn's changed appearance to obtaining important information about the number of Horcruxes Voldemort created points to the value of rereading material.

Harry's second "reading" of this scene is also the true one, of course, because his source, Slughorn, has finally divulged the facts. The truth comes out in the second reading in great part because both Harry and Dumbledore are skeptical enough not to buy Slughorn's first version of the story. Much like a dishonest journalist, Slughorn has "reported" his memory falsely to save his own skin and retain a favorable image of himself and with others. What is concealed in the fog that obfuscates his real memory is instructive: the first instance of fogging covers a compliment Slughorn pays Tom Riddle, and a possible quid pro quo offer to get him a job and help him advance at the Ministry of Magic.[42] It also covers a number of short paragraphs describing Tom's admirers, nascent Death Eaters, and their regard for and relationship with him.[43] Witnessing firsthand Riddle's charismatic nature and the relationships he forged while a student at Hogwarts is important for Harry as he builds his arsenal of understanding, equipping himself to defeat the man Riddle has become. The same thing happens again, of course, when Tom asks Slughorn about Horcruxes. In chapter 17, only two lines and two words from Slughorn's memory are devoted to Tom's question, "Sir, I wondered what you know about . . . about Horcruxes?"[44] But in chapter 23, three full pages of new information follow Tom's question.[45] By these comparisons, readers can see how Rowling seeks to promote the awareness that one reading of a person, situation, or even object is not enough. As knowledge accrues, as we grow and mature or become more aware of facts previously hidden, we understand that snap judgments are highly unlikely to be accurate, and we must be willing to reflect upon and revise our thoughts, which often means withholding judgment and seeking alternate or deeper sources of information or experience.

The power of reading, then, is affirmed through the processes of critical thinking that Rowling advocates. If we are to remain informed, engaged citizens, we must read and analyze our world, our politicians, and our news—and perhaps read it again. Perhaps Rowling only creates such terrible examples in Rita Skeeter and Cornelius Fudge to underscore her message more clearly; perhaps journalism is not so much the culprit as the backdrop against which her message of empowerment stands out. Rather than give away agency through manufactured consent—providing profit for the *Prophet*—we should engage in critical reading, remaining open-minded, and reading recursively—becoming pensive with the Pensieve. Only when we read situations, people, and the news actively, critically, and recursively will we be able to avoid giving away our readerly agency. Luckily, the Harry Potter series shows us how.

NOTES

1. Sturgill, Winney, and Libhart, "Children's Perceptions," 2.
2. Schanoes, "Cruel Heroes," 137.
3. Rowling, *Goblet of Fire*, 303. All Harry Potter book citations in this essay refer to the original Scholastic (US) editions.
4. Rowling, 304–5.
5. Friedman, "Militant Literacy," 198.
6. Rowling, *Chamber of Secrets*, 222.
7. Rowling, *Goblet of Fire*, 147–48 (ellipsis in original).
8. Schanoes, "Cruel Heroes," 142.
9. Ide, "Dark Lord," 185 (emphasis mine).
10. Rowling, *Order of the Phoenix*, 567 (emphasis mine).
11. Rowling, 567.
12. Rowling, 567.
13. Schanoes, "Cruel Heroes," 143.
14. Rowling, *Sorcerer's Stone*, 64.
15. Rowling, *Order of the Phoenix*, 567.
16. Barton, "Critique Bureaucracy," 54. Like me, Professor Barton is an American reader, which must certainly direct his reading of what constitutes a "free press." Where American print journalism typically prides itself on being objective and thereby free, print journalism in the UK (as opposed to visual media like the BBC) is more open about its political leanings. Rowling is therefore writing from a context that would consider the politicization of news through a more practical than moralistic or ethical lens. However, as the International Forum for Responsible Media reminds us in its comparison of US and UK print journalism, "impartiality is at any rate a relativistic term." International Forum for Responsible Media, "UK versus US—Comparisons of Media Standards," *Inforrm's Blog*, https://inforrm.org/2010/05/01

/uk-v-us-comparisons-of-media-standards/. American and British readers alike can benefit from Rowling's portrayal of a politicized press, regardless of whether we are scandalized by that portrayal or find it simply familiar.

17. Rowling, *Order of the Phoenix*, 94.
18. Sturgill, "Harry Potter," 11.
19. Rowling, *Order of the Phoenix*, 105, 291.
20. Rowling, *Goblet of Fire*, 522.
21. Rowling, *Order of the Phoenix*, 225.
22. Rowling, *Goblet of Fire*, 602.
23. Rowling, *Order of the Phoenix*, 4.
24. Gierzynski, *Millennials*, 25.
25. Gierzynski, 23.
26. Gierzynski, 24.
27. Friedman, "Militant Literacy," 193.
28. Rowling, *Order of the Phoenix*, 214.
29. Sturgill, "Harry Potter," 10.
30. Friedman, "Militant Literacy," 201.
31. Rowling, *Deathly Hallows*, 419.
32. Behr, "'Same-as-Difference,'" 113.
33. Nosich, *Learning to Think Things Through*, 2.
34. Rowling, *Prisoner of Azkaban*, 400.
35. Rowling, 405.
36. Rowling, 411.
37. Rowling, 412.
38. Rowling, *Half-Blood Prince*, 369.
39. Rowling, 494.
40. Rowling, 369.
41. Rowling, 494.
42. Rowling, 495.
43. Rowling, 495.
44. Rowling, 370–71 (ellipsis in original).
45. Rowling, 496–99.

10. Quidditch as Narrative Mirror in the Harry Potter Series

Caitlin Elizabeth Harper

IN QUIDDITCH, J. K. Rowling created a sport that required little traditional athleticism, could be picked up by Muggle-borns, and was played equally by both women and men. So inherently different from the sports readers know, Quidditch has been criticized, ignored, examined, and adored. About the invention of Quidditch, Rowling said she "had been pondering the things that hold a society together, cause it to congregate and signify its particular character and knew I needed a sport. It infuriates men . . . which is quite satisfying given my state of mind when I invented it."[1]

And yet Quidditch is so much more than just an "infuriating" sport; it is quite possibly the most important symbol set in the series. Emily Strand says of its symbolic significance, "Quidditch is an important symbol system that both prefigures and reflects the important events that will lead to the defeat of Voldemort and his Death Eaters, and the roles main characters will play in bringing about these events."[2]

By examining the plot mirroring within each book, readers will discover how Quidditch events in a book are reflected in that book's nonsporting events, showcasing the role Quidditch plays in Harry's evolution from child athlete to adult hero; what happens in matches and practices is reflected in the rest of his life, and he applies his sporting skills to nonsporting events. Following the chiastic structure or ring composition throughout the series allows readers to use Quidditch in earlier books to predict both Quidditch- and non-Quidditch-related events that occur later in the series, as well as gain greater insight into events in prior books. Additionally, the metaphorical Quidditch match Harry plays not only in each book but in the series as a whole reflects his hero's journey from game-playing student to leader in the fight against Voldemort.

10. Quidditch as Narrative Mirror

PLOT MIRRORING, RING COMPOSITION, AND QUIDDITCH PLAY AS A METAPHOR FOR HARRY'S JOURNEY

In the *MuggleNet Academia* podcast episode "The Wizarding War Was Won on the Quidditch Pitch of Hogwarts," host John Granger said that he couldn't wait to go back and reread the books to see how the "Quidditch games parallel the story as it plays out."[3] As a master of motif, Rowling of course uses and reuses images, actions, and other symbols to strengthen the story throughout the series, and a close reading reveals events happening in Quidditch matches are repeated in the rest of the plot; this pattern will be termed "plot mirroring." Rowling's use of plot mirroring is strengthened when this pattern falls in line with the chiastic structure of the series.

As J. Steve Lee states in his essay "There and Back Again," "chiasmus is a literary structure which mirrors key ideas or phrases in the reverse order of presentation. Sometimes called 'reverse parallelism,' 'ring structure,' 'palistrophes,' 'symmetric structure,' or 'concentric structures,' chiasmus has been a part of ancient literature such as the *Iliad* and the *Odyssey* as well as *Beowulf*, *Paradise Lost*, and the *Bible*."[4] Lee explains that the seven-volume series has a structure of A-B-C-X-C'-B'-A'. The first volume, *Sorcerer's Stone*, parallels or mirrors the seventh volume, *Deathly Hallows*. *Chamber of Secrets* parallels *Half-Blood Prince*, while *Prisoner of Azkaban* parallels *Order of the Phoenix*. *Goblet of Fire* is the center of the series and is itself split in two, the first half taking place at the Quidditch World Cup and the second half containing the Triwizard Tournament.[5]

Through these rings and mirrors, we see that symbolic Quidditch is played even when there is no Snitch in sight; what happens to Harry on the pitch will often occur in a similar fashion off the pitch later in the same book. Likewise, according to the series' chiastic structure, things that occur during a Quidditch match or season in earlier books occur in the non-Quidditch plot in their corresponding later books. This mirroring pattern also creates a main character who is not only a Seeker in all ways, but also a Snitch himself; we will see Harry seeking Horcruxes as he sought Snitches and Voldemort seeking Harry-as-Snitch as Voldemort plays the role of Seeker as well.

Following its British school story roots, the series has many sports-related themes like training, practicing, and coaching. Patti L. Houghton, author of "Harry Potter and the English School Story," writes, "Substitute rugby for Quidditch and Greek and Latin for Defense Against the Dark Arts and Transfiguration, and Hogwarts becomes a school at which Tom Brown would feel at home."[6] Harry's education both inside and outside the classroom is very physical, every action designed to prepare him in the fight against Voldemort, magically, mentally, and emotionally. It only makes sense that Harry would be an athlete.

Except that he isn't, in a traditional way. He's scrawny and not particularly fit, but he needs a place in the magical world, and he finds his niche in Quidditch as a Seeker who must capture the elusive Snitch—an ideal pursuit for a Chosen One. As the series unfolds, it is revealed that Harry's talents aren't just chance or luck. His father, James, was also a talented Quidditch player, and as a baby, Harry even had his own broom. But, as with most things, Harry doesn't start playing Quidditch with that knowledge. He doesn't even start playing Quidditch by actually playing Quidditch. He just goes along throughout the story, sharpening his instincts, his powers of observation, and his tolerance for pain on the training grounds of Hogwarts.

SORCERER'S STONE

In *Sorcerer's Stone*, Harry hears the word *Quidditch* for the first time from Draco Malfoy when they first meet in Madam Malkin's robe shop. When Draco asks him if he plays Quidditch, Harry says no, "wondering what on earth Quidditch could be."[7] This is the first of many times that Draco knows about things that are important to Harry before Harry knows them.

It is Ron who explains the game to Harry, although the reader does not get the full picture until Oliver Wood takes him out for his first practice. When Ron asks Harry what Quidditch team he supports and Harry says that he doesn't know any, Ron replies, "What! Oh, you wait, it's the best game in the world," and he explains the whole game.[8] While Harry's reputation as the Chosen One is often an issue for Ron, Harry's ignorance about the Wizarding world is never a problem for his best friend. Ron simply gives Harry the information he needs with no judgment.

Yet Harry has never seen Quidditch played. When he first mounts his broom and soars into the air to catch Neville's Remembrall, he's technically playing Quidditch for the first time, although he doesn't know it, just like he has been doing magic for years without actually knowing it. "Not a

10. Quidditch as Narrative Mirror

wizard, eh?" Hagrid asks him when they first meet. "Never made things happen when you was scared, or angry?"[9] Harry realizes that he has done plenty of magic without recognizing it. From birth, he has been training for a much larger game of which he has been completely unaware.

When McGonagall sees Harry catch the Remembrall, he ends up with a place on the Gryffindor Quidditch team; this is the first of many times readers see teachers break or bend rules on Harry's behalf rather than punish him. Wood gives Harry a crash course in Quidditch just as Hagrid gave him a crash course in the workings of the Wizarding world during their shopping trip to Diagon Alley. And just as Hagrid, Dumbledore, and McGonagall kept Harry's existence a secret for eleven years, "Wood had decided that, as their secret weapon, Harry should be kept, well, secret."[10]

Readers never see a Quidditch game played without Gryffindor in *Sorcerer's Stone*, nor in any of the subsequent novels. In his first year, Harry only plays two games; he misses the last match between Gryffindor and Ravenclaw because he's in the infirmary, and his missing matches becomes a frequent occurrence throughout the series. Thus, in *Sorcerer's Stone*, readers see only the Gryffindor versus Slytherin and Gryffindor versus Hufflepuff games. Later in the series, it becomes important to know that Gryffindor always plays Slytherin, then Hufflepuff, then Ravenclaw in a season of Quidditch at Hogwarts.

In Harry's first match ever, we begin to see how action in the Quidditch matches mirrors non-Quidditch events later in the same book and in other books in the series. For example, in the first Quidditch match, Quirrell tries to kill Harry, but Snape stops Quirrell, just as Snape stops Quirrell from getting the Resurrection Stone on Halloween. Then Harry, a natural flier and Seeker, ends the game by accidentally catching the Snitch in his mouth—the exact same Snitch that will present Harry with the stone in the final book. Furthermore, we see a trend emerge that Harry's accidents both on and off the pitch are, at least in his first few years at school, generally successful.

Harry's second game, played against Hufflepuff, is refereed by Snape, and Hermione and Ron bring their wands to the match to protect Harry. Everyone assumes Snape is refereeing in order to hurt Harry or penalize Gryffindor, but he's actually also trying to protect Harry. Similarly, the trio thinks Snape is trying to steal the Resurrection Stone, when he's actually helping to protect it. This is certainly not the last time the trio suspects Snape. Harry streaks past Snape and ends the match in less than five minutes by catching the Snitch. This solo effort is mirrored not only later in the novel as the trio tries to reach the Sorcerer's Stone, but throughout the entire series, and most significantly in the seventh book. Hermione and Ron are always ready to help, but only Harry can end the match.

Sorcerer's Stone also provides readers with the first opportunity to see Harry's opponent, Voldemort, as a kind of Seeker himself, always searching for objects that will help him "win." In the first book he seeks the Sorcerer's Stone, which is shaped very similarly to a Snitch. In later books, readers learn that Voldemort has been seeking objects his entire life. At the end of *Sorcerer's Stone*, Harry emerges as the winning Seeker (beating Voldemort, because Harry always beats Slytherin in Quidditch), catching the Sorcerer's Stone (or the Snitch) in his pocket and right out from under Voldemort's nose via the Mirror of Erised; these developments mirror both Harry's catch of the Remembrall and his first accidental Snitch catch in his mouth.

CHAMBER OF SECRETS

In *Chamber of Secrets*, only three Quidditch matches are depicted: Gryffindor versus Slytherin, Hufflepuff versus Ravenclaw, and Slytherin versus Ravenclaw. Readers are merely told that the latter two occur and do not see them, so a single match is described in the whole book. Still, a number of Quidditch events happen outside of the Quidditch matches themselves, and non-Quidditch mirrors of those Quidditch events appear throughout the book.

At the start, Draco Malfoy becomes Seeker on the Slytherin team because his father, Lucius, buys the entire team Nimbus Two Thousand and One brooms. Lucius also manages to get Tom Riddle into Hogwarts by slipping Tom's diary into Ginny's cauldron. In both instances, Lucius uses his power and money to get two young Slytherins where they are not supposed to be.

In the Gryffindor versus Slytherin match, Harry is stalked by a rogue Bludger. Fred and George Weasley try to protect Harry from it but eventually have to leave him to defend himself, just as they try throughout *Chamber of Secrets* to use their humor to defend him from accusations that he is the heir of Slytherin, another case in which Harry is ultimately left to

10. Quidditch as Narrative Mirror

defend himself. The Weasley twins continue to fulfill their beater duties in later books, both on and off the Quidditch pitch. The rogue Bludger in the Slytherin match finally smashes into Harry's elbow, leaving his broken arm dangling uselessly at his side, just as the basilisk fang does in the chamber in the novel's climax.

When Harry finally goes for the Snitch, Malfoy is unaware that the Snitch is next to his ear, and thinks Harry is attacking him. Later, when Harry and Malfoy duel, Harry speaks Parseltongue and Justin Finch-Fletchley thinks Harry is telling the snake to attack Justin; this misunderstanding makes everyone believe that Harry is the heir of Slytherin and that he's attacking the students. Gryffindor beats Slytherin in the match as usual, and then Lockhart shows up. He casts a spell to try to heal Harry's arm that seriously backfires, as does the spell he tries to use later to wipe Harry and Ron's memories in the chamber.

On her way to the Gryffindor versus Hufflepuff match, Hermione realizes how the basilisk is moving around Hogwarts and leaves the others to go to the library. She is then removed from the plot completely, and the remainder of the Quidditch season is canceled. In *Sorcerer's Stone*, Harry again goes up against his opponent with his team (Ron and Hermione), only to be alone at the end. A Seeker on and off the pitch, he is the sole player who can end the match. In *Chamber of Secrets*, Harry is again the sole "player" at the end of the book, up against the basilisk and Riddle, trying to save (or catch) Ginny, who, like Hermione, has disappeared from the narrative.

PRISONER OF AZKABAN

Prisoner of Azkaban is essentially all about Quidditch. Three chapters are dedicated completely to Quidditch: "Grim Defeat," "Gryffindor versus Ravenclaw," and "The Quidditch Final." One of the main plotlines of the book is Harry learning to fight dementors by producing a Patronus so they don't affect him while he plays. It is of course this skill that he develops to help him in Quidditch that ends up saving both him and Sirius from the dementors at the end of the novel.

In "Grim Defeat," the reader sees Harry lose a Quidditch match on his Nimbus Two Thousand for the very first time (it is worth noting that Harry loses to Cedric Diggory, so readers can be sure that Cedric will appear as an opponent again). In the first two books, Harry is able to defeat Voldemort with the tools he has, but now, in the first book without Voldemort, where Harry is battling something different, he needs new tools. In this book, he gains the Firebolt, a newly released racing broom that we later see the Bulgarian and Irish international Quidditch teams use at the Quidditch World Cup in *Goblet of Fire*, and the Marauder's Map, both of which aid him in many subsequent endeavors. Of course the Firebolt, a secret gift from Sirius, is assumed to be cursed but is not, just as Sirius Black is assumed to be a dark wizard but is not.

The appearances of both the dementors and (what appears to be) the Grim at the match against Hufflepuff mirror their appearances elsewhere. Harry sees the Grim when he leaves Privet Drive and almost gets run over by the Knight Bus, and when the Grim shows up to the Quidditch match, Harry almost dies falling off his broom. During the storm on the Hogwarts Express, the dementors show up where they are not supposed to be, and Harry loses consciousness; and during the stormy game against Hufflepuff, the dementors show up at the Quidditch match where they are not supposed to be, and Harry loses consciousness again.

In the second game of the season, played against Ravenclaw, Harry casts his first real Patronus, connecting him to his father, but unfortunately, he is battling what turns out to be a fake threat—the Slytherin team in dementor costumes. Harry also meets Lupin and Sirius, further connecting him to his father, and they are also both believed by others to be threats: Lupin as a dangerous werewolf and Sirius as a murderer.

When Malfoy says he's unfit to play in the Quidditch match against Gryffindor after Buckbeak injures his arm, the order of the Quidditch matches is changed to accommodate the Slytherin team. This is the only book in the series in which the order of the matches is changed. Slytherin swaps with Hufflepuff while Malfoy is injured so that Slytherin ends up playing Gryffindor in the last match of the season. Because *Prisoner of Azkaban* is the only book in which Voldemort makes no appearance, either as Tom Riddle or in his more snakelike form, it is conceivable that the purpose of the rescheduled season finale is to finish with Harry defeating Slytherin as a stand-in for Voldemort.

At the time of their eventual match, Slytherin is up by two hundred points. Wood repeatedly tells Harry that he must only catch the Snitch if

10. Quidditch as Narrative Mirror

they are more than fifty points up. As a Seeker, Harry knows timing is of the utmost importance, and this attention to timing serves a greater purpose during Harry and Hermione's travels back in time and the complicated order in which the events have to take place if they are, as Dumbledore says, "able to save more than one innocent life"[11] in one night. Following the chiastic structure of the series, where the third and fifth books parallel, Harry eventually "captures" the prophecy in *Order of the Phoenix*; the destruction of the Snitch-like object that holds the record of the prophecy and Sirius's death move Dumbledore to determine that it is finally time for Harry to know his fate.

In *Prisoner of Azkaban*, as the Gryffindor-Slytherin match approaches, Wood orders the Gryffindors to accompany Harry everywhere so no one does him harm, just as Ministry and Hogwarts staff make sure Harry is chaperoned everywhere so that Sirius Black does not harm him. After a violent final match, Harry catches the Snitch and Gryffindor win the Quidditch Cup for the first time, making Harry feel like "he could have produced the world's best Patronus."[12] Later, after a violent episode in the Shrieking Shack, Harry learns the truth about Sirius Black and feels like he has a family for the first time. In order to save himself and Sirius, he produces an exceptional Patronus.

THE GOBLET OF FIRE

Discussing ring composition in *Thinking in Circles*, Mary Douglas writes, "If the end is going to join the beginning[,] the composition will at some point need to make a turn toward the start. The convention draws an imaginary line between the middle and the beginning, which divides the work into two halves, the first, outgoing, the second, returning. In a long text it is important to accentuate the turn lest the hasty reader miss it, in which case the rest of the carefully balanced correspondences will also be missed."[13] *The Goblet of Fire* certainly does "accentuate the turn" of the series. Even the book itself is split into two halves: the Quidditch World Cup and the Triwizard Tournament, or Harry's last few weeks as a child and his first few months as an adult.

There is no Hogwarts Quidditch Cup in this book, so Harry never plays Quidditch at Hogwarts, only for fun at the Burrow. This scene where Harry is playing Quidditch purely for fun for the first time (not at training or in a match) sets the tone for the first half of the book through the Quidditch World Cup. For the first time since reentering the Wizarding world, Harry is acting like a child and a spectator rather than a player in the main event.

Back at Hogwarts after the Quidditch World Cup, although Harry wants to continue as a spectator during the Triwizard Tournament, he is thrust instead into the role of participant against his will—a theme throughout the series. Instead of a Quidditch season, which is often violent enough, in his fourth year Harry competes in a much more serious event—but one that still mirrors a Gryffindor season of Quidditch. Each year the order of the Quidditch matches is supposed to be the same. Gryffindor is supposed to always play Slytherin, then Hufflepuff, then Ravenclaw. In *Goblet of Fire*, the three Triwizard tasks are a symbolic season of Quidditch for Harry.

In the first task (or match) of the year, Harry faces a dragon and uses his broom to retrieve the golden egg. This is the Slytherin challenge, as Harry goes up against a serpent and uses his broom to retrieve the Snitch. He always catches the Snitch when playing against Slytherin, and he catches the metaphorical Snitch here as well.

In the second task of the year, Harry uses gillyweed to save Ron, Hermione, and Fleur's sister from the lake. This alludes to his match against Hufflepuff, as Harry uses a plant or Hufflepuff symbol, considering the association of gillyweed with Professor Sprout, to save (or capture) three people. Harry has no responsibility to retrieve two of these people, and by doing so, he exhibits Hufflepuff traits of being just, loyal, and true, based on the Sorting Hat's characterization of that house. In preparing for the task, Harry is also helped by Cedric, the Hufflepuff seeker and his rival first in Quidditch, then in the tournament.

In the third task of the year, Harry has to work his way through a maze, which includes answering a riddle, to get to the Triwizard Cup. In this task (or match) Harry has to use his cleverness to solve puzzles in order to win, just as Ravenclaws do for even such mundane tasks as entering their common room. More narrative mirroring occurs here when Harry thinks he has won, and the two Seekers—Harry and his old opponent, Cedric—have caught the Triwizard Cup together. They wind up in the graveyard where the Death Eaters assemble, just like at the Quidditch World Cup, albeit in a much more sinister fashion.'

10. Quidditch as Narrative Mirror

The absence of actual Quidditch matches for Harry and the replacement of school games with the more high-stakes games of the Triwizard Tournament that still mirror his typical Quidditch season are another step in Harry's journey from child to adult.

ORDER OF THE PHOENIX

In Harry's fifth year, Voldemort lives, and the Order of the Phoenix has come together again. In this book, Harry only plays in the first Quidditch match, Gryffindor versus Slytherin, as he, Fred, and George receive lifelong bans after the match. Angelina Johnson is made Quidditch captain, and with Ron as Keeper, there are new faces and positions on an old team, just as the Order of the Phoenix is resurrected with some new faces and positions. And just like the Order, the Gryffindor Quidditch team runs into a bit of trouble all year.

As soon as Dolores Umbridge interrupts Dumbledore's announcement about Quidditch tryouts, readers should know that she is going to get in the way of Harry playing. He subsequently gets detention after detention and even misses Keeper tryouts because of them. Umbridge punishes Harry by making him do lines, which end up scratched in the back of his hand, and the same injury happens during Harry's only match of the year as he tries to catch the Snitch and Malfoy scrabbles at the back of his hand. Umbridge separates Harry from normal student life and takes away everything he cares about, such as the Firebolt he received from Sirius in *Prisoner of Azkaban*. All of this is continued training to operate alone, withstand pain, and not confide in those in power, however sweetly they might ask.

Throughout *Order of the Phoenix*, the plight of Dumbledore's Army and the Gryffindor Quidditch team is almost exactly the same. Educational Decree Number Twenty-Four is created to keep the DA from meeting, but of course it extends to all student groups and therefore to Quidditch. Umbridge refuses to reinstate the Gryffindor team, so they can't practice to beat Slytherin, just as she refuses to teach them proper Defense Against the Dark Arts, so they can't practice defense against dark wizards. When the Gryffindor team is finally reinstated, the weather is so bad that they can't use the pitch at all, just as the DA wants to practice but can't figure out a space. When the Gryffindor team finally gets to practice for the first time, the Slytherins come out to make it as difficult as possible, just as the

Inquisitorial Squad interferes in the DA's practice. When Ron makes the Quidditch team, Angelina asks Harry to help him, just as Hermione asks Harry to help everyone with Defense Against the Dark Arts. On a positive note, Luna shows up in her life-size lion's-head hat and needlessly points out that she's supporting Gryffindor. Later, she's the only non-Gryffindor who goes to the Ministry to save Sirius.

The Gryffindor versus Hufflepuff match is the first Hogwarts match shown in which Harry does not play. This frustrates him, as do the facts that he is barred from joining the Order and that Dumbledore is ignoring him. After he is banned from Quidditch, he claims that the DA is the only thing that makes him want to be at Hogwarts. It's only when the Death Eaters break out of Azkaban and Harry begins to see the real gravity of the situation that Quidditch begins to move from being the most important thing to Harry to being maybe just a game, a marker of his maturation and a foreshadowing of the leading role he will assume in the fight against Voldemort.

Hearing about the breakout, he thinks of his fellow students: "There they all were, talking about homework and Quidditch and who knew what other rubbish, and outside these walls ten more Death Eaters had swollen Voldemort's ranks."[14] When he looks up at the staff table, he sees that the teachers have reacted to the news, but no students aside from him, Ron, and Hermione seem to be affected. This separation of the trio from other student "players" is mirrored in a game of Quidditch.

The main design of a Quidditch game is the two spheres of play. In one sphere, two Seekers go after the Snitch. In the other sphere, the Chasers face off against the Keeper, with the Beaters and Bludgers intersecting the two spheres. The trio has always operated separately from their peers, but the parallels between the narrative and the two spheres of play in a Quidditch match become even more obvious at this turning point, widening the gap between the trio and their peers.

Harry and Hermione miss the last match, Ravenclaw versus Gryffindor, to visit Grawp with Hagrid, and Gryffindor wins the match and the Quidditch Cup without Harry. Just as Harry has trained the DA to fight after he is gone, there are new members of the Quidditch team who can take his place, like Ginny, who has been practicing Quidditch on her own since age six and is showing that she is quite capable, given the chance.

10. Quidditch as Narrative Mirror

The Battle at the Ministry is the first time she has her own agency in the trio's activities against Voldemort. And of course, in the last match of the year, she catches the Snitch (and later, Harry himself) right out from under Cho's nose.

Before Harry's last school exam of the year, he thinks that the next day, he and Ron will "go down to the Quidditch pitch—he was going to have a fly on Ron's broom and savor their freedom from studying,"[15] but during that exam he has his vision of Voldemort torturing Sirius in the Ministry of Magic. His leisurely flight with Ron is canceled and replaced by a much more sinister one, on the back of a Thestral to the Ministry. Harry isn't allowed to fly for fun anymore. His childhood is a thing of the past.

Throughout *Order of the Phoenix*, Harry has visions of catching the prophecy, a small, round ball just like a Snitch. In these visions, capturing the prophecy is described just like Harry's Snitch catches in the series' descriptions of Quidditch matches. "He stretched out his hand. . . . His fingertips were inches from it."[16] Pursuit of the prophecy also casts Voldemort in the role of Seeker again, trying to "catch" the prophecy, but he should know better than to send his Death Eaters in place of himself, for they are less-than-worthy Seekers. As in *Sorcerer's Stone*, if Voldemort doesn't play Seeker himself, he is unsuccessful.

HALF-BLOOD PRINCE

In *Half-Blood Prince*, Harry is made captain of the Gryffindor Quidditch team at the start, while at the end he is made "captain" of the team fighting against Voldemort after Dumbledore's death. Right off the bat, Katie Bell warns Harry that "good teams have been ruined before now because Captains just kept playing the old faces, or letting in their friends."[17] Meanwhile, both Dumbledore and Voldemort have "let in their old friends." Here, readers are led to believe that Snape is the friend who has caused Dumbledore's downfall but find out in the very end that Snape was contributing to Voldemort's downfall. Of course Harry keeps Ron on the team, and Ron causes problems all year, both with Quidditch and with Harry's growing feelings for Ginny.

It is interesting to note that there are no chapters named for Quidditch in this book. In each book, Harry says Quidditch is the thing he misses most when he is away from Hogwarts, aside from Ron and Hermione, and that the sport is the only thing that has ever come easily to him. The absence of any chapters named for Quidditch when Harry has finally been made captain is a reflection of how preoccupied he is during his fifth year. His priorities have begun to shift, further reflecting his maturity. In fact, Harry "had never been less interested in Quidditch; he was rapidly becoming obsessed with Draco Malfoy."[18] He is so obsessed that he barely makes it to the match against Hufflepuff on time and even admits to Ron that he would consider missing a Quidditch match to follow Malfoy. When he finally confronts Draco and they fight, Harry's use of Sectumsempra lands him in detention, causing him to miss the last match of the season. He has made his choice; he has decided that figuring out what Malfoy is up to is more important than Quidditch.

The Quidditch mirroring between *Chamber of Secrets* and *Half-Blood Prince* is robust. Ron joins the Quidditch team, meaning he and Harry are working together without Hermione, just as they did in the chamber, although with her help in both cases; she figured out how the basilisk was moving through the school, and she got Ron onto the Quidditch team. In *Chamber of Secrets*, Harry is ready to put his life on the line for Quidditch as Oliver Wood requests, but by *Half-Blood Prince* he can hardly be bothered to show up to a match, which is a sort of anti-mirror. Because of his father, Draco gets a place on the Quidditch team in *Chamber of Secrets*, and because of Lucius Malfoy's mistakes, Voldemort chooses Draco to kill Dumbledore in *Half-Blood Prince*.

In the end, Harry misses the final match against Ravenclaw while doing detention with Snape, and Gryffindor still wins the match—and the Quidditch Cup—again anyway. At this point, Harry has moved completely beyond games and on to Horcruxes. The time has finally come for him to take his place in the war against Voldemort outside Hogwarts. And just as Gryffindor won the match and the Quidditch Cup without him, they will restart Dumbledore's Army and carry on the resistance with-out him.

THE DEATHLY HALLOWS

In *Sorcerer's Stone*, Wood tells Harry that "the Golden Snitch . . . is the most important ball of the lot" and "a game of Quidditch only ends when the Snitch is caught."[19] In *Deathly Hallows*, this advice no longer refers

10. Quidditch as Narrative Mirror

merely to a game. One Seeker has to beat—kill—the other. Life itself has become a Quidditch match, and Harry is both Seeker and Snitch.

At the Burrow, Harry, Hermione, and Ron are constantly trying to "practice" for their Horcrux hunt, and Molly gets in their way, mirroring the many ways in which Harry has been detained from Quidditch over the years, such as detention and being banned. The "game" begins when Kingsley arrives at the wedding and announces that Scrimgeour is dead, essentially blowing the whistle to start the match. The narrative immediately moves into the two spheres of play of a Quidditch game; the trio are playing Seeker, while the Order of the Phoenix and the Death Eaters are facing off separately. Just as in a Quidditch game, the two spheres intersect occasionally and often violently, such as when the trio encounters the Snatchers. Still, like a Seeker, the trio is mostly acting on their own with a different goal in mind. They set out on their search with little idea of where to look for the Horcruxes, just like a Seeker looking for a Snitch. Meanwhile, there was a Horcrux—Harry—right under the trio's noses, much as the sneaky little Snitch likes to hide in plain sight.

As Seeker, Harry is hunting the Horcruxes. But he is also hunted, making him a Snitch as well. The Snitch's job is to avoid getting caught, which is also Harry's struggle throughout each book. No matter what is happening in the game, everything ends when the Snitch is caught. In the game of Quidditch, the Snitch is the Chosen One. Again, in *Deathly Hallows*, Voldemort serves as Seeker, always searching for Harry the Snitch, but also going after the Elder Wand. Both Seekers are following multiple prizes. In many Quidditch games throughout the series, Harry gets distracted from his quest: by the dementors, by the Grim or Sirius, by Malfoy, Cho, and the weather. Once again, he is distracted. He should be singularly focused on Horcruxes, but he becomes fixated on the Hallows. Little does he know that he already possesses two of them—the cloak and the stone. Throughout the series, Harry often possesses tools he doesn't recognize or fully understand. There always seems to be a useful tool right under his nose.

When Harry the Snitch is out in the world, hunting Horcruxes, those at Hogwarts don't really know what's going on, but when Harry returns to Hogwarts, Voldemort knows he is there and so does everyone else, and the Battle of Hogwarts begins. With all eyes on Harry, it is like that moment in a game when the Seeker makes a sudden move, and then everyone can suddenly see the Snitch. And as with the tasks in the Triwizard Tournament, Harry destroys three of the last Horcruxes in the order of a Gryffindor season of Quidditch: Slytherin's locket, Hufflepuff's cup, and Ravenclaw's diadem.

At the end of the day, only the Seeker can end the game, so Harry leaves Ron and Hermione behind once more. As he heads toward the Forbidden Forest to meet Voldemort and his own death, he thinks, "The long game was ended, the Snitch had been caught, it was time to leave the air."[20] But, as he always does, the Boy Who Lived scrapes by, saves himself, and—"with the unerring skill of the Seeker"[21]—ends the game on his own terms.

The Harry Potter series is a masterful coming-of-age story (or really, life story, as it follows Harry's "birth" as a wizard to his death by magic in the Forbidden Forest), showcasing Harry's transition from student athlete to adult hero. Quidditch serves as both the actual training ground for Harry's heroic actions and the lens through which he sees himself and the world sees him: Chosen One, Seeker, the only one who can end both the game and the "game." From his discovery of both his hidden Quidditch and magical talents to his positions as both Seeker and hunter of Horcruxes, his role on the pitch mirrors his role in the Wizarding world's fight against Voldemort. As each broken bone, win, and loss plays out on and off the pitch and Harry matures to leave literal Quidditch behind, the reader gains a greater understanding of how childhood trials shape how we tackle adult tribulations. Just as Rowling "needed a sport"[22] to create a fuller Wizarding world, Harry needed a sport to ensure he had the stamina and skills to endure the "long game."[23]

NOTES

1. Furness, "Rowling Invented Quidditch."
2. Strand, "Second War," 120.
3. Granger, "Wizarding War."
4. Lee, "There and Back Again," 20.
5. Lee, 25.
6. Houghton, "English School Story."
7. Rowling, *Sorcerer's Stone*, 77. All Harry Potter book citations in this essay refer to the original Scholastic (US) editions.
8. Rowling, 107.
9. Rowling, 58.

10. Quidditch as Narrative Mirror

10. Rowling, 180.
11. Rowling, *Prisoner of Azkaban*, 393.
12. Rowling, 313.
13. Douglas, *Thinking in Circles*, 36.
14. Rowling, *Order of the Phoenix*, 545.
15. Rowling, 724.
16. Rowling, 384.
17. Rowling, *Half-Blood Prince*, 176.
18. Rowling, 409.
19. Rowling, *Sorcerer's Stone*, 169.
20. Rowling, *Deathly Hallows*, 698.
21. Rowling, 744.
22. Furness, "Rowling Invented Quidditch."
23. Rowling, *Deathly Hallows*, 698.

11. Eye Wonder?

Reflecting Harry in Animal Eyes

Catherine Olver

"HARRY IS THE eyes through which you see the world," remarked J. K. Rowling in a 2003 interview.[1] Many philosophers have considered sight the highest among the senses for the way it seems to present objects (including humans and nonhuman animals) at a distance from the viewing subject, a perspective supposedly inclining the viewer to more rational and perhaps even objective judgments.[2] Focalization in fiction, however, thrives on the fact that objectivity is an illusion, as Mieke Bal explains in *Narratology*: "Perception depends on so many factors that striving for objectivity is pointless. To mention only a few factors: one's position with respect to the perceived object, the fall of the light, the distance, previous knowledge, psychological attitude towards the object; all this and more affects the picture one forms."[3] Harry's position as the internal focalizer throughout the Harry Potter series gives descriptions a double function: they both sketch the magical world and reflect Harry's character, communicating his interests and attitudes.[4] In "Perspective, Memory, and Moral Authority," Karin Westman argues that Rowling uses internal focalization in a deliberate manner, influenced by her love of Jane Austen's *Emma*.[5] Just as Emma's flaws convey her character, the limited world-building and dismissive depictions of giggling girls in the early Potter books indicate Harry's ignorance and immaturity. "Rowling asks us to witness the process of Harry's education," contends Westman. "The narrative result marks the limitations of private vision while also evoking sympathy for others."[6] Inspired by Westman's argument that Harry's view of the magical world widens, this chapter assesses whether Harry's wide-eyed views of magical creatures become more complex.

Harry's acts of seeing remind readers that the text communicates his understanding of the world. Sight as a metaphor for knowledge permeates

11. Eye Wonder? Reflecting Harry in Animal Eyes

Western languages, as Martin Jay playfully demonstrates in *Downcast Eyes*:

> Depending, of course, on one's outlook or point of view, the prevalence of such metaphors will be accounted an obstacle or an aid to our knowledge of reality. It is, however, no idle speculation or figment of imagination to claim that if blinded to their importance, we will damage our ability to inspect the world outside and introspect the world within.[7]

The pervasive metaphor of sight informs both the term and the technique of focalization. Internally focalized visual descriptions may convey characters' development without explicit introspection, as they "inspect the world outside" and review their understanding of it.[8] The Harry Potter books are packed with references to seeing: the opening chapter of *Sorcerer's Stone*, for example, contains no fewer than sixty-four verbs and participles of seeing, plus eighteen mentions of eyes and glasses, and at least twenty-four references to colors and light. Those moments when Harry exchanges stares with nonhuman animals constitute only a segment of a larger topic, which importantly includes debates over the masculinity, queering, and whiteness of Harry's gaze.[9]

Animal gazes demand that Harry consider their subjectivities in the same way that Derrida's cat famously prompted him to philosophize "the animal": "It can allow itself to be looked at, no doubt, but also . . . it can look at me. It has its point of view regarding me."[10] Exchanging looks with animals also highlights Harry's embodied viewpoint. Animal gazes therefore doubly emphasize the human protagonist's entanglement in more-than-human relationships, repudiating the idea that sight holds viewers at a distance from the world. In the first four novels, Harry engages in "staring contests," which foreground his physical vulnerability at the cost of framing nonhumans as his opponents. He gains knowledge about magical creatures but, feeling threatened, can't help struggling to be the subject of the gaze rather than its object. In "Seeing Death," Harry's first visual encounter with the thestrals in *Order of the Phoenix* is a moment of wonder, which signals a change in how Harry conceptualizes the more-than-human world. In the later books, he often sees animals as fellow participants in the more-than-human mystery of death. Internally focalized descriptions powerfully convey Harry's changing attitude: animals that once represented conquerable peril later reflect Harry's own inevitable mortality.

STARING CONTESTS

Harry's first magic witnessed by readers takes place in a zoo, prompted by a human-animal visual encounter. In "Why Look at Animals?" John Berger regrets that zoo animals' apparent indifference to spectators is disappointing and prompts the question, "Why are these animals less than I believed?"[11] For Harry, however, the boa constrictor turns out to be *more* than he expected. The snake ignores Dudley, apparently asleep and radiating such indifference that Harry "wouldn't have been surprised if it had died of boredom."[12] Harry empathizes with the snake's captivity, relating its experiences of confinement and visitors rapping the glass to his similar embodied experiences of being woken in the cupboard under the stairs. After Harry has "looked intently" at it for a few moments, the snake opens its eyes[13]:

> Slowly, very slowly, it raised its head until its eyes were on a level with Harry's.
> *It winked.*
> Harry stared. Then he looked quickly around to see if anyone was watching. They weren't. He looked back at the snake and winked, too.[14]

Syntax and paragraphing mimic the snake's gradual movement and brief wink, helping to convey Harry's mesmerized and then surprised staring. That wink banishes what Berger calls the "abyss of non-comprehension" colored by "ignorance and fear" that supposedly separates humans from animals.[15] Suddenly, the snake's gaze is *not* as "uninterpretable, unreadable, undecidable, abyssal and secret" as the gaze of Derrida's cat, whom he feels is too "other . . . to call it my fellow, even less my brother."[16] The snake's wink positions Harry as a friend, or at least a coconspirator in a world where unequal social structures make captives of human children and nonhuman animals alike.

11. Eye Wonder? Reflecting Harry in Animal Eyes

Berger's comments on indifference and Derrida's insistence on radical Otherness imply that this episode is a hopelessly wishful trip to the zoo—but the wishful whimsy underscores the vital fact that Harry and the snake are two subjects caught by each other's eyes. Harry's ability to observe others is grounded in his body, and his wide-eyed encounters with nonhumans communicate the immersive experience of sight described by the phenomenologist Maurice Merleau-Ponty: "Immersed in the visible by his body, itself visible, the see-er does not appropriate what he sees; he merely approaches it by looking, he opens onto the world. . . . Visible and mobile, my body is a thing among things; it is one of them. It is caught in the fabric of the world."[17] Jim Kay's illustration beautifully captures the visual encounter, conveying the unexpected reciprocity of the look by reversing the expected viewpoint: the reader gazes along the snake's tongue to Harry's face pressed against the glass. Since, in the illustrated edition, this is the first picture within the story that shows Harry with his eyes open, it asserts his power as focalizer; however, the reader's act of looking with the snake intimates that the snake too is a seeing subject. The internally focalized text describes Harry seeing the animal Other, while Kay's illustration shows Harry "seen through the eyes of the other, in the seeing and not just the seen eyes of the other," as Derrida puts it.[18] The illustrated text thus positions humans as embodied animals who may respond to other animals. Furthermore, the vivid green of Harry's eyes matches the surrounding green vegetation. Captured in the act of looking, Harry's body does indeed appear "caught in the fabric of the world."[19] The textual and visual representations of this stare dramatize Harry's subjective gaze and simultaneously emphasize his embodied participation in more-than-human relationships.

Stories of talking with animals express a perennial desire for animal companionship "offered to the loneliness of man as a species," argues Berger.[20] Harry's conversation with the boa constrictor evidences that desire; an isolated boy sympathizes with a snake about its captivity. The snake confirms their friendship, hissing "Thanksss, amigo" when it slides past after Harry has unintentionally vanished the glass.[21] When Harry later reflects on the event, however, he remembers that "he set a boa constrictor on" Dudley in "revenge," and this reinterpretation challenges a reading that understands Harry's magic to have been sparked by cross-species empathy.[22] Was the boa constrictor Harry's friend? Or was his encounter with the snake more truthfully an instance of Harry using nonhuman bodies for his own ends? Responding to Dudley's punch by freeing the snake's fearsome body, Harry's experience of his body as "a thing among things" leads him to "appropriate what he sees" rather than to avoid appropriation.[23] In this instance, the animal appears to be on Harry's side of the fight. However, in most other encounters of the first four books, powerful animal gazes contribute to Harry's view of animals as threats to his body.

Moments when Harry stares at creatures wide-eyed signal a struggle for power between human and nonhuman. In *Sorcerer's Stone*, Harry, Ron, Hermione, and Neville find themselves "looking straight into the eyes of a monstrous dog . . . , standing quite still, all six eyes staring at them," and survive the encounter because "their sudden appearance had taken [Fluffy] by surprise" as much as Fluffy surprises them.[24] The second time, the children have the upper hand. Harry plays Hagrid's flute, and "from the first note the beast's eyes began to droop," allowing them to descend through the trapdoor Fluffy guards.[25] The defeat of the animal is described via the defeat of its gaze. The "mean little eyes" of the Halloween mountain troll are similarly dispatched to unconsciousness.[26] Jean-Paul Sartre has argued most prominently among twentieth-century thinkers that one is either the subject or the object of a gaze, and Berger's declaration that nonhuman "animals are held by the look. Man becomes aware of himself returning the look" implicitly raises humans above other animals due to our greater self-consciousness, reducing the power of animal gazes to make human bodies into objects rather than subjects.[27] Rowling's text stages this dichotomous power dynamic clearly during the Triwizard Tournament, when Harry defeats a dragon by outwitting her "fearsome yellow eyes" through a sudden reversal of the subject-object polarity.[28] Harry flies back and forth "to ensure she kept her eyes on him . . . watching him out of those vertical pupils," until finally she rears, and he dives toward her eggs before the dragon realizes "where he had disappeared to."[29] These references to the dragon's eyes characterize her as an intelligent and unpredictable subject while continuing to emphasize Harry's embodied vulnerability because her eyes are following his movements, his body the object of her gaze—until, moving her own body, she fails to hold Harry in her sight

11. Eye Wonder? Reflecting Harry in Animal Eyes

and he triumphs. Faced with nonhumans who function as intelligent obstacles, Harry aims to extinguish or perplex their subject-gazes.

The parallel between extinguishing the animal's gaze and defeating the animal is, of course, exemplified in the case of the Basilisk. Fawkes must puncture "both its great bulbous yellow eyes" before Harry can fight it.[30] As Philip Armstrong suggests in his historical overview of how humans have understood the animal gaze, a basilisk's eyes draw their symbolic strength from humans' fear of predatory animals. Gleaming animal eyes frighten humans because night-hunting predators (including big cats and wolves) have an area behind the retina in their eyes that enhances night vision by reflecting any available light back into the eye.[31] Pliny, medieval bestialists, and Renaissance natural historians took animals' gleaming eyes as evidence of the eye-beam theory of vision that held sway until the seventeenth century.[32] The theory persists in a bestiary of the Hogwarts library, which informs the protagonists that "the Basilisk has a murderous stare, and all who are fixed with the beam of its eye shall suffer instant death."[33] After such a perilous visual contest with the basilisk in *Chamber of Secrets*, Harry is understandably jumpy throughout *Prisoner of Azkaban* when he finds himself stalked by a creature with "wide, gleaming eyes."[34] His fear intensifies when he believes it is the Grim, which appears to people who will soon die. Symbolically, though, all predatory animals' gleaming eyes hold the threat of death. The books' many pairs of gleaming animal eyes fixed on Harry remind readers that our focalizer is corporal and therefore vulnerable to attack. Harry, too, is a magical creature whose gaze could be extinguished.

Harry's meeting with Buckbeak the hippogriff stands out as a rare moment when Harry resolves the physical threat of the nonhuman gaze through embodied respect rather than evasion or violence, using the eyes' dual function as sense organs and expressive features. When Harry first sees hippogriffs, a lengthy description details their body parts, focusing on their "cruel, steel-colored beaks," "deadly-looking" talons, and "large, brilliantly orange eyes."[35] Again, the brightness of the animal's eyes signals both its intelligent subjectivity and its predatory danger to Harry's body. Rather than extinguishing those eyes, Harry relates to the creature as Hagrid instructs: he overcomes his own discomfort at not blinking and allows himself to be held by the animal's gaze. When Harry bows, "exposing the back of his neck" to that beak, his body explicitly becomes the object of the hippogriff's gaze and so reverses the usual human-animal hierarchy.[36] Helen Ngo's study of the racializing gaze criticizes Sartre's insistence on an inevitable hierarchy of seeing subject and seen object for ignoring "the moments of ambiguity and ambivalence in the gaze relation."[37] Stares are often offensive, Ngo points out, but they may give time for ambiguities to develop and for the focalizer to consider how he is being seen.[38] For example, Harry's recognition that the hippogriff is "staring haughtily at him" may prompt the reader to wonder by what criteria the animal is evaluating him.[39] The ritualistic progression of staring, bowing, patting, and riding underscores the need to approach nonhuman others with the appropriate kinds of embodied respect—a respect that involves adapting one's embodied gaze to how the animal prefers to be seen while attending to its body language. "Ranging from the casual glance to the fixed glare, the eye can obey the conscious will of the viewer" and communicate emotions even as it receives information, leading Martin Jay to declare it "the most expressive of the sense organs."[40] Harry's meeting with Buckbeak demonstrates that interspecies sight (like sight among humans) is a relational skill: an embodied behavior that may convey or avert aggression.

Harry enters the magical world by vanishing a zoo's glass barrier between human viewers and an animal object of their gazes, poignantly promising more equal relationships between humans and animals in the magical world. In a world with no glass barrier, however, the viewing subject's body is under threat; the visual distance between viewer and viewed may collapse suddenly into violence. Harry's meeting with Buckbeak differs from other staring contests in the first four novels in that the stare they share negotiates intersubjective respect, and his climactic realization that he can "save more than one innocent life" by preventing Buckbeak's execution and freeing Sirius positions humans and animals together in more-than-human networks of injustice and mortality.[41] Although Harry continues to treat animals as opponents in *Goblet of Fire*, these human-animal encounters are staged as part of the Triwizard Tournament (in which Harry has been entered unwillingly) and so emphasize that humans are responsible for positioning animals as opponents. Having initially viewed magical animals as dangers to be defeated, Harry starts to see

11. Eye Wonder? Reflecting Harry in Animal Eyes

them as fellow participants in natural and political systems—vulnerable, like himself, to being killed.

SEEING DEATH

Harry encounters magical animals less frequently but more meaningfully in the last three books of the series. The thestrals in *Order of the Phoenix* open his eyes to a new way of seeing: their "pupil-less," "white and staring" eyes evoke the blindness of visionary prophets and the sightless eyes of the dead, challenging Harry to consider that great mystery in which human and nonhuman animals all participate.[42] As he processes Cedric's traumatic death, Harry's internally focalized view of the thestrals communicates his maturing perspective.

Harry's first sight of the thestrals is a powerful moment of wonder. Fantasy has a knack for defamiliarizing through wonder, "making the impossible seem familiar and the familiar new and strange," as Brian Attebery observes, and ecocritics have recently renewed interest in this emotion.[43] In *The Ecology of Wonder in Romantic and Postmodern Literature*, Louise Economides argues that we should distinguish the wide-eyed and open-ended aesthetic of wonder from the aesthetic of mastering the natural world that often attends the sublime.[44] Glenn Willmott's *Reading for Wonder: Ecology, Ethics, Enchantment* agrees, explaining that objects of wonder resist "mastery by the senses and knowledge alike" to challenge "cognitive schemes for understanding what we behold."[45] The thestrals certainly unseat Harry's expectations. Having "glanced quickly" at the "horseless stagecoaches," he does "a double-take" and looks again at the carriages, which are no longer horseless.[46] After calling attention to Harry as focalizer through his gaze movements, the text emphasizes his cognitive limits as Harry tries to categorize the thestrals: "If he had had to give them a name, he supposed he would have called them horses, though there was something reptilian about them too."[47] The thestrals unnerve Harry because they make him realize that his subjective understanding of the more-than-human world is limited by his previous experiences and by mortality itself.

Extrapolating from Aristotle's *Poetics*, Willmott identifies five features that constitute a poetics of wonder, all of which appear in Harry's first sight of the thestrals.[48] Three of these features defamiliarize the objects seen: shifting frames of reference for characters, shifting styles, and shifting concepts. Firstly, the thestrals are "personae," seen via comparisons rather than definitively identified; Harry thinks of them as horses, then as reptiles, but they have "dragonish" heads and the wings of "giant bats." Secondly, the text achieves a mixed style because the narrative voice pulls subtly against Harry's focalization. Delicate alliteration intimates the horses' eerie beauty, but it gives way to Harry's harsh judgment: "Wings sprouted from each wither. . . . Standing still and quiet in the gathering gloom, the creatures looked eerie and sinister." He settles on calling them "horrible horses," and the far-from-subtle sound effect serves now to convey Harry's revulsion. When Harry realizes that the thestrals could take them to London, their usefulness changes his opinion so completely that it is comic: "Harry stretched out his hand eagerly and patted the nearest one's shining neck; how could he ever have thought them ugly?"[49] The rhetorical question seems double-voiced, simultaneously an expression of Harry's thought and a pointed comment from the narrator. In this description of magical creatures visible only to certain people, the mixed style appropriately manifests in a momentary struggle over whose perception controls the narrative voice: Harry's or the narrator's? Harry's reversed opinion of the thestrals is also a moment of "semiotic disaccommodation," the third feature of Willmott's poetics of wonder, when characters and readers realize that they must adjust their understanding of a concept.[50] Moreover, Harry's first sight of the thestrals extends the revelation of the house-elves' servitude in the previous novel, prompting readers to wonder what other tasks at Hogwarts apparently performed by magic are actually done by magical creatures, invisibly. Presented via the poetics of wonder, these animals "watching [Harry] with empty white eyes" challenge the concept and mechanisms of sight itself.[51]

In order to elicit wonder rather than bafflement, such semiotic disaccommodation should help characters and readers recognize "an obscured system of meaning" (the fourth feature of Willmott's poetics).[52] The thestrals test Harry's assumption that what he sees is real. Like the visions that Harry struggles to interpret throughout this novel, thestrals defy the relational method that readers use to distinguish between perceptible and nonperceptible objects seen by a focalizing character, as Mieke Bal explains: "dreams, fantasies, thoughts, or feelings" are nonperceptible objects, and readers judge an object perceptible if there is "another character

11. Eye Wonder? Reflecting Harry in Animal Eyes

present that can also perceive the object."[53] Harry glimpses the thestrals "reflected in [Luna's] wide silvery eyes" as she explains that she can see them too, symbolically conveying how others' eyes confirm what we think we see, but Harry is "not altogether reassured" by Luna's statement that he is just as sane as she is.[54] As Peter Dendle argues, Luna and her father are problematically "unaware of the adaptable and impressionable nature of human cognitive perception."[55] Dendle persuasively demonstrates that Rowling's inclusion of paranormal and cryptozoological enthusiasts invites readers to reflect on the formation of truth by consensus, contributing to the series' investigations of power and authority. However, Dendle's position that "the world they inhabit is ultimately one in which objective reality is knowable" underplays the importance of what remains unknown in Rowling's world.[56]

The belief that reality is knowable but that knowledge raises further questions is precisely the dynamic of wonder.[57] Why can Harry see the thestrals when others cannot? Personae, mixed style, semiotic disaccommodation, and recognition combine to highlight the ecological and epistemic systems in which Harry positions the magical creatures. Drawing attention to systems is the final, encompassing feature of Willmott's poetics of wonder, which often involves the focalizer reflexively considering his position within the relevant systems. Harry learns he can see the thestrals because he has "seen death," but how has witnessing Cedric's death changed Harry (such that he can now see these skeletal horses) when witnessing his mother's death did not?[58] Questions about seeing and being seen by death become central when Harry realizes that his Invisibility Cloak is the Deathly Hallow that allows the wearer to evade death, but that to defeat Voldemort he needs to be seen as master by another Deathly Hallow, the Elder Wand—which has as its core a thestral tail hair.[59] Each fact about the thestrals generates questions about wandlore, sight, or mortality.

In the *Order of the Phoenix* chapter "The Eye of the Snake," Harry learns he can see thestrals because he has witnessed death, then suffers a vision in which he experiences the snake-Horcrux Nagini attacking Mr. Weasley, almost fatally. The moment stands out because Harry is not reflected in animal eyes but rather sees through the snake's eyes. There is therefore no staring contest in which Harry might try to master the animal's gaze; the description's repetition of "he" (e.g., "He was flat against the floor," "he was gliding," "he was turning his head," "he tasted") stresses that Harry is instead experiencing being a nonhuman animal subject.[60] His sense of sight is physically different: "It was dark, yet he could see objects around him shimmering in strange, vibrant colours," including the "gleaming" outline of Mr. Weasley under the Invisibility Cloak—perhaps a thermal image, as snakes can detect infrared radiation from their prey.[61] The snake is not straightforwardly a vicious killer; she manages to "master the impulse" to bite him and only strikes when Mr. Weasley awakens and attacks, defending herself from the "blurred outline towering above" and drawing a wand, a description that invites some empathy.[62] Overall, the scene hints at Harry and Nagini's joint embodied entanglement in Voldemort's mysterious attempts to evade death, as readers later learn that each carries a fragment of Voldemort's soul. In order to kill him, both must die.

Viewing animals as joint participants in mortality does not transform Harry into an animal lover. At Aragog's burial, Hagrid's characteristic refrain of "beau'iful" highlights his ability to see beauty in all creatures.[63] His aesthetic appreciation contrasts with Slughorn's money-motivated view of the spider's body as a resource, extracting its venom. Harry is present, fittingly, to find out about the measures Voldemort took to avoid death. Harry does not care for the spider, but his view of "the spider's head, where eight milky eyes stared blankly at the sky and two huge, curved pincers shone, motionless, in the moonlight" recognizes every animal's participation in the cosmic mystery of death, as the spider's eyes embody the Milky Way and its pincers crescent moons.[64] In its involvement of the dead body with the cosmos, the description foreshadows the death of a nonhuman whom Harry does love.

Dobby's gaze challenges Harry to wonder about the network of more-than-human relations. The appearance of his eyes in the Privet Drive hedge is another prominent moment of wonder in the series. They startle Harry out of his usual categories and into granting personhood to a nonhuman: "He had been staring absent-mindedly into the hedge—*and the hedge was staring back*. Two enormous green eyes had appeared among the leaves."[65] Jim Kay's illustration mimics the disturbance of categories by making the text seem part of his illustration, showing two large eyes that stare from the columns of text as if through the hedge. It is Dobby's turn to pause "in wonderment" at the novel's close, looking at Harry's "disgusting, slimy

11. Eye Wonder? Reflecting Harry in Animal Eyes

sock... as though it were a priceless treasure" after Harry uses it to manipulate the system of human-elf servitude and set Dobby free.[66] Once Lucius Malfoy has departed—"with a last, incensed stare at the pair of them" that reminds the reader of the more-than-human power hierarchies enacted through sight—Dobby gazes at Harry with "moonlight from the nearest window reflected in his orb-like eyes," exclaiming that "Harry Potter freed Dobby!"[67] Dobby becomes, literally, a starry-eyed reformer of more-than-human relationships.

Does Harry deserve the devotion Dobby shows him? Hardly. But the elf is free to show it, as he is free to speak Harry's name as his last words.[68] His subjectivity fades as he dies, and his eyes are reduced to objects, "nothing more than great, glassy orbs sprinkled with light from the stars they could not see."[69] The text dignifies and deepens Dobby's realization of his impending death by alluding to Greek tragedy: "He had stretched out his thin arms to Harry with a look of supplication," a formal gesture begging help from a god or authority figure. Harry is not a god and cannot save him from death, but he can honor Dobby's body with the work of his own, by burying the elf without magic.[70] Semiotic disaccommodation and recognition arise from the contrast with *Chamber of Secrets*, since Harry cannot free Dobby from death, but the events leading to that death affirm Dobby's freedom. These techniques are supported by mixed style and the use of personae (the gesture positions Harry and Dobby as characters from Greek tragedy), combining to produce a moment of wonder that makes Harry reconsider his destined role in the complex, obscure system of Dumbledore's plan to defeat Voldemort. He feels "slapped awake" from his "obsessive longing" to master death by possessing all three Hallows, and he renews his self-sacrificial quest to eliminate the Horcruxes.[71] The individual complexity of Dobby's existence "refuses to be conceptualized," as Derrida phrases it, leaving the words on his gravestone minimal: "Here Lies Dobby, a Free Elf."[72] For Derrida, the act of writing a name suggests an animal's "mortal existence, for from the moment that it has a name, its name survives it."[73] The gravestone's words gesture to both Dobby's objecthood and his subjectivity: to his animal mortality and the enduring significance of the choices he made.

Dobby's sacrifice mitigates the incomprehensibility of death by giving the moment meaning for those who continue living. At the start of *Deathly Hallows*, another well-loved nonhuman symbolizes death's horrifying meaninglessness. Like Cedric's, Hedwig's death is an accident that achieves nothing, her life vanishing so suddenly in a "burst of green light" that Harry "could not take it in."[74] By contrast, Nagini's death is marked by a moment of collective staring, as her decapitation "draw[s] every eye."[75] Voldemort's "scream of fury" emphasizes that her death is significant because it reduces him to mortality, but it may also express his grief for the snake herself. While Voldemort takes the form of a monstrous baby, "dear Nagini" is his surrogate mother, giving him her milk.[76] Others have observed that Nagini's relationship with Voldemort parallels Fawkes's relationship with Dumbledore symbolically.[77] Through their embodied actions also, both animals protect and help their masters, willingly risking death.[78] Eventually Harry himself dies to protect and help the people he loves, and he does so willingly. His death encourages readers' wonder as he reverses the pattern of previous books and allows Voldemort to kill him, revealing that the "master of Death" chooses a reason for dying.[79] All these interspecies relationships affirm animals' and humans' networked involvement in death, but Dobby's sacrificial death is particularly significant because the house-elf is so powerfully associated with freedom. Death itself remains a provocation to wonder, since no mortal can fully understand it, but Dobby's death asserts that nonhumans too have the subjectivity to make their deaths socially meaningful.

WIDER EYES

Harry stares at animals frequently, and these internally focalized moments both emphasize his embodied participation in the more-than-human world and reveal his changing attitude toward nonhumans. In the first four books he repeatedly views animals as threats; his staring is a struggle to be the subject of the gaze rather than its object, often sliding into violence. Saving Buckbeak helps Harry to see animals as potential allies (rather than opponents) and as fellow participants in the more-than-human mystery of mortality. This more mature view develops fully when

11. Eye Wonder? Reflecting Harry in Animal Eyes

he sees the thestrals, whose presentation through a textual poetics of wonder highlights what Harry's subjective gaze can never truly comprehend: death reduces humans to objects. Harry views nonhuman animals in the final books as symbols of mortality; importantly, taken together, these animals represent for Harry not death's inevitability but rather the more-than-human possibility of choosing a meaningful death. Rowling's use of internal focalization does, therefore, reveal development in Harry's view of animals as their many sets of eyes prompt him to position himself and nonhuman animals in ecological and epistemic systems.

This wider view remains Harry's subjective view, colored by his preoccupation with death. Nevertheless, Harry's encounter with a Gringotts dragon demonstrates how his awareness of shared ecological and epistemic systems improves his interactions with living animals. Gringotts dragons are mentioned as Harry enters the magical world; when he sees one in the final novel, Harry has indeed "been prepared" by many encounters with magical creatures, though the sight still brings him "to a halt."[80] The subsequent description conveys wonder mixed with pity, Harry's mature (if still problematic) emotional response to animals' unseeing eyes. Its "milkily pink" eyes neither gleam with the intelligence usual in a dragon nor meet Harry's stare directly, symbolizing that its subjectivity has been subdued.[81] Harry's escape plan does not seek to control it, instead relying on the dragon's own desire to be "free," and he patiently endures the "frightening" risks to his own body, letting the dragon fly where it wishes and starting to imagine the world through this animal's eyes: "He wondered whether it had divined the presence of fresh water by the flashes of reflected sunlight."[82] The verb *wonder* appears three times on a single page, underscoring Harry's improved ability to relate to animal Others despite their unknowable subjectivities, and Harry's guess about the dragon's sight beautifully illustrates Willmott's idea that "the cognitive aspect of wonder is always ecological because it reveals things acting in the environment for their own sakes according to their own logic" while also affecting the viewer.[83] Harry and his friends jump off the dragon's back and continue on their quest, but in a moment that seems to honor all the animals whose journeys have intersected theirs, "they paused in their preparations to watch [the dragon] climb higher and higher, now black against the rapidly darkening sky, until it vanished" from their sight.[84]

NOTES

1. Rowling, "Royal Albert Hall."
2. Daston and Galison, *Objectivity*; and Korsmeyer, *Making Sense of Taste*, 3, 11–37.
3. Bal, *Narratology*, 100.
4. Bal, 106.
5. Westman, "Perspective," 145–65; Austen, *Emma*.
6. Westman, 146.
7. Jay, *Downcast Eyes*, 1.
8. Jay, 100.
9. Camacci, "Multi-Gaze Perspective"; Cuntz-Leng, "Look . . . at . . . Me"; and Schuck, "Anti-Racist-White-Hero Premise."
10. Derrida, *Animal*, 11.
11. Berger, "Why Look?" 23.
12. Rowling, *Sorcerer's Stone*, 21. Citations for books 1–4 of the Harry Potter series in this essay refer to the illustrated Bloomsbury editions (2015–19); citations for books 5–7 refer to the original Bloomsbury editions (2003–7).
13. Rowling, 21.
14. Rowling, 23.
15. Berger, "Why Look?" 5.
16. Derrida, *Animal*, 12.
17. Merleau-Ponty, "Eye and Mind," 3.
18. Derrida, *Animal*, 12.
19. Merleau-Ponty, "Eye and Mind," 3.
20. Berger, "Why Look?" 6.
21. Rowling, *Sorcerer's Stone*, 23.
22. Rowling, 47.
23. Merleau-Ponty, "Eye and Mind," 3.
24. Rowling, *Sorcerer's Stone*, 132.
25. Rowling, 221.
26. Rowling, 143.
27. Jay, *Downcast Eyes*, 276–97; and Berger, "Why Look?" 5.
28. Rowling, *Goblet of Fire*, 227.
29. Rowling, 227, 230.
30. Rowling, *Chamber of Secrets*, 240.
31. Armstrong, "Gaze of Animals," 180.
32. Armstrong, 184.
33. Rowling, *Chamber of Secrets*, 220.
34. Rowling, *Prisoner of Azkaban*, 25.
35. Rowling, 84.
36. Rowling, 87.
37. Ngo, *Habits of Racism*, 195.
38. Ngo, 185.
39. Rowling, *Prisoner of Azkaban*, 88.
40. Jay, *Downcast Eyes*, 9, 10.

11. Eye Wonder? Reflecting Harry in Animal Eyes

41. Rowling, *Prisoner of Azkaban*, 297.
42. Rowling, *Order of the Phoenix*, 178.
43. Attebery, *Strategies of Fantasy*, 3.
44. Economides, *Ecology of Wonder*.
45. Willmott, *Wonder*, 29, 30.
46. Rowling, *Order of the Phoenix*, 178.
47. Rowling, 178.
48. Willmott, *Wonder*, 90–114.
49. Rowling, *Order of the Phoenix*, 672.
50. Willmott, *Wonder*, 98.
51. Rowling, *Order of the Phoenix*, 179.
52. Willmott, *Wonder*, 107.
53. Bal, *Narratology*, 109.
54. Rowling, *Order of the Phoenix*, 180.
55. Dendle, "Cryptozoology," 419.
56. Dendle, 411.
57. Willmott, *Wonder*, 30.
58. Rowling, *Order of the Phoenix*, 394.
59. Rowling, *Deathly Hallows*, 333, 595; and "Thestral Tail Hair," Harry Potter Wiki, accessed July 13, 2020, https://harrypotter.fandom.com/wiki/Thestral_tail_hair.
60. Rowling, *Order of the Phoenix*, 408.
61. Rowling, 408.
62. Rowling, 409.
63. Rowling, *Half-Blood Prince*, 453.
64. Rowling, 452–53.
65. Rowling, *Chamber of Secrets*, 6.
66. Rowling, 257.
67. Rowling, 258.
68. Rowling, *Deathly Hallows*, 385.
69. Rowling, 385.
70. Rowling, 387.
71. Rowling, 387.
72. Derrida, *Animal*, 9; and Rowling, *Deathly Hallows*, 389.
73. Derrida, 9.
74. Rowling, *Deathly Hallows*, 52.
75. Rowling, 587.
76. Rowling, *Goblet of Fire*, 5, 403.
77. Guanio-Uluru, *Ethics and Form*, 127.
78. Rowling, *Order of the Phoenix*, 719.
79. Rowling, *Deathly Hallows*, 333.
80. Rowling, *Sorcerer's Stone*, 54; and Rowling, *Deathly Hallows*, 432.
81. Rowling, *Deathly Hallows*, 432.
82. Rowling, 437, 439, 440.
83. Rowling, 440; Willmott, *Wonder*, 59.
84. Rowling, *Deathly Hallows*, 446.

12. The Otter and the Stag

Narration and Objectification in Harry Potter

Patrick McCauley

THE VIOLENCE THAT is so commonly inflicted upon women and girls in our own real world emerges as a central theme in J. K. Rowling's fictional world. The popular art and entertainments of our culture are filled with objectifying images of women and girls, and this cultural objectification and commodification of females tragically contributes to the violence suffered by existing females. However, objectification is at least partly an interior phenomenon that exists within the subjective assumptions and motivations of individual human beings. J. K. Rowling grants us access to the subjective realm through her carefully crafted use of both magic and narrative strategy, and in so doing, she offers her youthful readers a presentation of hope for authentic relationships that might escape the manipulations of these dehumanizing and dangerous indoctrinations.

How many of us have daydreamed about receiving a letter by owl inviting us to attend Hogwarts School of Witchcraft and Wizardry? J. K. Rowling's intricate use of fictional magic has proven for many to be one of the most endearing and engaging aspects of the Harry Potter series. By asking us to suspend our disbelief concerning the kind of magic Rowling presents in her series, these novels grant us admittance into a world within which our glasses can be mended, our horrid aunt inflated, and our enemies vanquished with a flick of the wrist and the pronouncement of an incantation. For children and young people forced to suffer authoritative, often arbitrary rules at school, at home, and among peers, such presentations are all the more alluring.

Magical power has been part of children's stories stretching back into the untraceable history of folktales carried by oral tradition and shared around the hearth during long winter nights. There can be little doubt of the draw of magical stories granting children the opportunity to imagine wielding the very power they lack in their real lives. However, once this

12. The Otter and the Stag

disbelief is suspended and the aesthetic reality of magic is granted, magical elements can also be put to uses beyond their initial ability to engage and entertain. Fictional magic handled well can be used as a literary device.

Consider the following example. In *Prisoner of Azkaban*, Professor Lupin offers a class on boggarts. Seamus Finnigan steps forward, and "*Crack!* Where the mummy had been was a woman with floor-length black hair and a skeletal, green-tinged face—a banshee. She opened her mouth wide and an unearthly sound filled the room, a long, wailing shriek that made the hair on Harry's head stand on end."[1] In this scene, all characters and all readers are invited to see what Seamus fears most. The boggart, as a fictional magical element, can be used to expose fears that people try to hide or deny. Through the boggart, what is usually internal and private is made external, evident, and public. Something similar occurs in *Order of the Phoenix*, when Molly Weasley confronts the boggart at 12 Grimmauld Place:

> Someone was cowering against the dark wall, her wand in her hand, her whole body shaking with sobs. Sprawled on the dusty old carpet in a patch of moonlight, clearly dead, was Ron.
>
> All the air seemed to vanish from Harry's lungs; he felt as though he were falling through the floor; his brain turned icy cold—Ron dead [. . .]
>
> "Mrs. Weasley?" Harry croaked.
>
> "R-r-riddikulus!" Mrs. Weasley sobbed, pointing her shaking wand at Ron's body.
>
> *Crack.*
>
> Ron's body turned into Bill's, spread-eagled on his back, his eyes wide open and empty. Mrs. Weasley sobbed harder than ever.
>
> "R-riddikulus!" she sobbed again.
>
> *Crack.*
>
> Mr. Weasley's body replaced Bill's, his glasses askew, a trickle of blood running down his face.
>
> "No!" Mrs. Weasley moaned. "No . . . *riddikulus! Riddikulus! RIDDIKULUS!*"
>
> *Crack.* Dead twins. *Crack.* Dead Percy. *Crack.* Dead Harry . . .[2]

We can see here the truth about Molly's fears. She is concerned above all else with the safety of her family. However, we might also note that Rowling takes advantage of this magical element to reveal Molly's true feelings for Harry. We see here that Molly considers Harry a family member. This is perhaps the profoundest expression of Molly's concern for Harry, and the use of the boggart allows for no doubt as to its veracity. The truth of her internal feelings is made evident and unmistakable. The Patronus Charm also functions as a magical revealer of internal, perhaps unrecognized truths even for the person wielding it. Harry's stag Patronus, a reflection perhaps of his father's Animagus form, implies a strong connection between father and son.

Narrative voice can also be considered a magical literary device capable of revealing purely internal truths and feelings. It is often perceived that much is lost when a book is transformed into a film. As Rowling's Harry Potter novels were translated into a film series, little of Rowling's delicate narration made it across the gap. Where a novel's narrator can easily grant us access to a character's interior thoughts and feelings, it is much more challenging to accomplish such a thing on film. Awkward cinema voice-overs stand as enduring testimony to this difficulty.

The great aesthetic power and potential of novels and of narrative voice have been demonstrated by the likes of Emily Bronte, Joseph Conrad, James Joyce, Toni Morrison, and Virginia Woolf, to name just a few. Those of us who are drawn to such novels often look first to narrative voice as we begin an encounter and analyze such works. Regarding Rowling's work in this regard, Lauren Camacci notes that *"Harry Potter*'s narrator is third-person limited, indicating an anonymous narrator who has omniscience only within one character (i.e., Harry)."[3] This can also be called a close third-person narrator. We might also think of this narrator as heterodiegetic, in that Rowling's narrator does not participate in the action of the story.

What is of particular concern here is the narrator's proximity to Harry Potter himself and the fact that Rowling's close narrator relates the story in strict accordance with Harry's own point of view. The narrator's omniscience extends (usually) to Harry's subjectivity alone. This pattern is, however, broken at least four times. The first occurs at the very opening of the series. On the first page of *Sorcerer's Stone*, we find that "Mr. and Mrs. Dursley, of number four, Privet Drive, were proud to say that they were

12. The Otter and the Stag

perfectly normal, thank you very much."[4] Rereaders of the series will know that at this moment Harry is a baby and not yet on Privet Drive. We hear about the Dursleys and about Professors McGonagall and Dumbledore, but Harry is not yet there. A similar point-of-view shift is employed at the outset of *Goblet of Fire*, where the narrator follows Frank Bryce, gardener, and his encounter with Tom Riddle, Barty Crouch Jr., and Peter Pettigrew.[5] Chapters 1 ("The Other Minister") and 2 ("Spinner's End") of *Half-Blood Prince* also offer narration without proximity to Harry, as does chapter 1 ("The Dark Lord Ascending") of *Deathly Hallows*.[6] The chapters bearing these narrative variations function something like prologues, occurring only at the beginning of the novels in which they appear. Sequestering these narrative shifts at the very beginning of the novels helps limit the jarring impact these variations might otherwise have.

However, aside from these brief forays into a broader, more omniscient form of third-person narration, not to mention the occasional report related by a character within the plot, such as Elphias Doge or Rita Skeeter, the story is revealed to the reader as strictly tethered to Harry's individual perspective and subjective reflection.[7] In July 2005, Rowling was interviewed by children on CBBC Newsround. Eun Ji An, reporting for Raincoast.com, Canada, asked Rowling about Harry and his glasses. In response she said that she herself had worn glasses through her childhood and was tired of the usual portrayals of such children in books. She said that she wanted to read about a hero who wore glasses. She then said, "It also has a symbolic function, Harry is the eyes on to the books in the sense that it is always Harry's point of view, so there was also that, you know, facet of him wearing glasses."[8]

We can see here that a narration closely attached to Harry's perspective is of central importance from Rowling's point of view. She seems to be saying Harry's glasses are symbolic of the point of view connecting to him; that as Harry sees his world through his glasses, we see his world through Harry. Harry is "the eyes on to the books."[9]

Any reader of magical stories knows that Rowling does not have to restrict the narration like this. We might also assume that to limit the narration in this way presents certain daunting challenges for the author. Veritaserum, the Sorting Hat, boggarts, and Legilimency, to name just a few, are magical devices Rowling employs for revealing interior thoughts and feelings that might have been more easily, if less entertainingly, disclosed through an omniscient narrator. So, why do it? Why is it so important to limit the narration, primarily, to Harry's point of view?

Part of the answer might be that this narrative technique solves a problem concerning exposition. In any work of fiction, the author must reveal the details of the work's setting so as to orient, to some degree, the reader within a fictional world. Realistic fiction, that is, fiction set in a world that closely resembles that of the reader, does not require a lot of detailed exposition, since details of the setting are shared, to some degree, by the presupposed reader. However, if a work of fiction invites a reader into a fantastical world, the rules of that world have to be revealed and explained. The more complex the fantastical world, the more onerous and cumbersome the exposition may be. Scriptwriters almost always find exposition the least enjoyable aspect of their profession, often referring to it disparagingly as "laying pipe."[10]

At the opening of the Harry Potter series, however, Harry is just as uninformed as to the nature of the Wizarding world as is the first-time reader. Tethering the narration to Harry's point of view allows the details of the Wizarding world to be delivered to the reader little by little as Harry himself discovers them, so that a complex fantastical world can be exposed less obtrusively as background for an unfolding plot. In this way exposition, often regarded as a resented drag on the page-turning excitement of a moving plot, can instead help enliven the story, having been reshaped into something like the unwrapping of a surprise drawn out over time.

This technique is crucial in that the creation of a detailed fantastical world requires an articulation of the copious rules and conditions of that world. By weaving the exposition into the plot across all seven novels as well as, perhaps, *The Tales of Beedle the Bard*, Rowling adds layer upon layer of intricacy and detail to the systematic conditions of Harry's world. We might suppose that the intensive immersion experienced by many of Rowling's readers owes something to this layered detail.

Even if we admit that this narrative technique solves an expositional challenge, this does not seem to address the narration issue at the level of "symbolic function." Camacci has well noted that "Harry is nearly James's doppelganger but with Lily's eyes [. . .]. Harry sees the world through his mother's eyes."[11] Harry sees his world through his glasses, and we see that world through Harry. However, Harry sees this world also through his mother's eyes. This fact is made poignantly clear in the moment Severus Snape dies while gazing into eyes that may be seen as either Harry's or Lily's.[12] Camacci makes much of the fact that Rowling's protagonist is male and, as such, bears something of Laura Mulvey's male gaze, that culturally conditioned gaze that exists as a presupposition in regard to the reception and production of almost all American popular culture. Mulvey's male gaze is that hegemonic tendency through which everything is seen and evaluated from the perspective of a heterosexual and objectifying male. Harry bears something of this gaze, this unconscious enforcement of cultural hierarchies, even while Harry's author/narrator is female.[13]

As I have argued elsewhere, violence against women is a foundational theme in the Harry Potter novels.[14] The violence inflicted on Ariana Dumbledore initiates Albus Dumbledore's plotline, the violence inflicted on Merope Gaunt initiates Tom Riddle's plotline, and the violence inflicted on Lily Potter initiates Harry Potter's plotline. We may also recall that the reason the Grey Lady haunts Hogwarts is the violence inflicted upon her by the Bloody Baron, and that Dolores Umbridge is assaulted by the centaurs. There are few who would doubt, I suspect, that the Harry Potter series brings with it something of the insight and perspective of a female author.

However, it may also be important to note that Rowling seems to have taken the age and developmental level of her youthful audience into consideration in her portrayal of violence against women, limiting the brutality of its representation. The degree of this limited portrayal and representation can be glimpsed when we compare the presentation of such violence in the Harry Potter series to that presented in *The Casual Vacancy*, Rowling's stand-alone novel published under the same pen name as and immediately following the Harry Potter series.[15] Readers of *The Casual Vacancy* can attest to the thoroughly unrestrained representation of violence against women and girls provided there.[16] In other words, the subtlety or understatedness of Rowling's thematic handling of violence perpetrated against women may reflect more her concern for the needs of her younger readers than anything else.

In fact, we might expect to see this subtle articulation play out at the level of narration. As we have said, narration, like the Patronus Charm or boggarts, has a near-magical ability to make interior subjective truths plain. This delivers us to a question. Why would a female author sincerely interested in a thematic representation of violence against women choose a male protagonist, and why choose a narration limited within the point of view of that male protagonist? Let us look a little more closely. Rowling has said that she envisions Harry's world through Harry's glasses, through Harry's eyes, just as her readers do. And yet she goes to great pains in the series to emphasize that these eyes are Lily's eyes, the eyes of a mother, the eyes, we might say, of a woman.

Violence against women in fiction and in the real world has much to do, one might suggest, with Mulvey's male gaze and the utter objectification of the female that is its common result. Objectifying a woman can make it easier to impose violence upon her. References to this can be seen throughout the series. Consider again the Muggle boys who abuse Ariana, the Gaunts' treatment of Merope, or the Bloody Baron's murder of Helena Ravenclaw.[17] Leaving Tom Riddle to the side for a moment, perhaps the most direct and blatant example of the treatment of subjects as objects rests with Fenrir Greyback:

> Blood trickled down his chin and he licked his lips slowly, obscenely.
> "But you know how much I like kids, Dumbledore."
> "Am I to take it that you are attacking even without the full moon now? This is most unusual. You have developed a taste for human flesh that cannot be satisfied once a month?"
> "That's right," said Greyback. "Shocks you that, does it, Dumbledore? Frightens you?"
> "Well, I cannot pretend it does not disgust me a little," said Dumbledore. [. . .]
> "I wouldn't want to miss a trip to Hogwarts, Dumbledore," rasped Greyback. "Not when there are throats to be ripped out . . . delicious, delicious."[18]

The omniscience of Rowling's narrator does not extend to the inner thoughts and true motivations of Fenrir Greyback, yet the passage cited above leaves us little doubt as to his reduction of human subjects to objects of his desire and discretion. It appears that for Greyback, the students of

12. The Otter and the Stag

Hogwarts are mere confections for consumption, means to his own ends. We may see in this a literal representation of the perhaps only slightly more figurative version imposed, according to Mulvey and others, upon females in popular film. How often are images of women and girls on film reduced to something like confections for consumption?

If, however, we are going to be serious with regard to the negative results of an objectifying gaze, we are also going to have to get serious about the nature of subjective motivation. The objectification of a person happens, or often happens, at the level of subjective presumption. In other words, a human being will, either consciously or unconsciously, regard another human being as either a subject, an object, or a strange mixture of the two. If one person walks across a room to ask another person on a date, with what subjective presumptions does the first person gaze upon the second? At the level of subjective presumption, how much does that first person's gaze share with that of Fenrir Greyback? This sort of introspection can be uncomfortable for many of us.

As Kierkegaard and others have emphasized, the motivational context of another person's decision can never be truly understood or grasped by an onlooker. In real life, another person's subjective interiority must always remain indefinite, even mysterious for us. This is not true, however, within the magical context of a novel wherein a narrator's omniscience can, in fact, stretch into a character's subjective interiority and motivational grounds. These otherwise elusive thoughts and emotions can, in fiction, become the subject matter of intense and direct analysis and investigation. No matter how much I may want to hide what scares me most, a boggart will reveal it for all to see. An omniscient narrator can do something quite similar if I find myself a character in a novel.

Let us also consider the idea that a close omniscient narration bears a significant resemblance to the stream-of consciousness narration made famous by the likes of Virginia Woolf and James Joyce. In both narrative forms, stream of consciousness and close omniscient, the narration is usually restricted within one subjectivity. During discussions on this topic, some of my students let me know that they never spontaneously noticed the uncommon closeness of the narration in the Harry Potter series. They encountered the narration as quite natural and unobtrusive. I suspect that this is in part as a result of the mimetic resemblance this kind of narration bears to our lived experience, in which consciousness and interiority is limited within a single subjectivity.

Let us assume for the time being that for an individual subject, empathy stands, to some degree at least, in opposition to objectification. Loris Vezzali and others have found empathy for those who are often exiled, Othered, or dismissed, a major theme in the Harry Potter novels.[19] Let us say that empathy, as we are discussing it here, can be understood as the deliberate and perhaps presumptive intention to regard and recognize the subjective human dignity of another subject as such. Empathy, in this interpretation, would resist or reject any Greyback tendency to reduce or objectify another for primarily personal ends. However, any such investigation would be impossible without reliable omniscient access to subjective interiority at the level of motivation and presumption.

Even more problematic is the idea that we are incapable of seriously and reliably accessing our own motivational grounds and presumptions as a result of unrecognized and unconscious drives and indoctrinations. In both a Freudian and a Postmodern sense, we may not even be positioned to offer an honest analysis of our own motives and presumptions. In fact, it may very well be the case that we unconsciously enforce the power hierarchy of our cultural context every time we gaze on ourselves or any other. We may be nothing more than the discursive enforcement of these cultural power hierarchies even as we masquerade as free-willed individuals.

Nonetheless, if we wish to resist, destabilize, or trouble a cultural context that results in the kind of violence grounded on objectification described above, how might we embark? What can be done, if anything, about unrecognized culturally imposed presumptions that coerce or privilege one subject to objectify another? Let us for the moment restrict this question to a fictional context within which a close omniscient narrator can reveal a character's subjective interiority as reliably as a boggart can.

As we have noted, Rowling does not resist presenting characters who objectify others. For the sake of our investigation, let us functionally define objectification as the tendency to deny, within (or at the level of) one's own subjective interiority, the subjective interiority of another. This tendency is particularly dangerous in regard to potentially romantic or sexual scenarios. The Bloody Baron stands as one example of this dangerous tendency. The Baron's perpetual ghostly presence at Hogwarts can give the reader

12. The Otter and the Stag

the impression of the everlasting nature of his guilt and responsibility for sexual violence born, we suspect, of coercive objectification. We should not miss that the Baron forever bears the blood and the Grey Lady the wound of a murder committed by a wizard with a penetrating knife, not a wand. Bellatrix Lestrange's murder of the free elf Dobby echoes this act (as does her utter disregard of Dobby's subjective dignity).

Being a school for teenagers, Hogwarts sees its share of romantic and sexual encounters. One such drama plays out for our protagonist in *Order of the Phoenix*. In chapter 21, Harry encounters Cho Chang under the mistletoe after the last meeting of Dumbledore's Army before Christmas break. Cho says "I really like you, Harry" and moves, presumably, closer to him. The narrator's recounting of the scene ends before they kiss. The story picks up in the common room less than an hour later with Hermione and Ron, who commence a discussion of the event. Ron and Hermione react differently.

> "HA!"
>
> Ron made a triumphant gesture with his fist and went into a raucous peal of laughter that made several timid-looking second years over beside the window jump. A reluctant grin spread over Harry's face as he watched Ron rolling around on the hearthrug. Hermione gave Ron a look of deep disgust.[20]

Readers of the series will know that Hermione then enters into a long discussion of all the conflicting emotions Cho must be experiencing. In between these two reactions, Harry is asked about the kiss itself. Rowling writes, "Harry considered for a moment. 'Wet,' he said truthfully."[21] All of this happens in a conversation involving the three of them. Later, however, the close omniscient narrator will take us into Harry's private reflections.

> Maybe next time . . . if there was a next time . . . she'd be a bit happier. He ought to have asked her out; she had probably been expecting it and was now really angry with him . . . or was she lying in bed, still crying about Cedric? He did not know what to think. Hermione's explanation had made it all seem more complicated rather than easier to understand.

That's what they should teach us here, he thought, turning over onto his side, *how girls' brains work.*[22]

Let us recall that this expression of the interior thoughts of a teenage boy (wondering about the interior thoughts of a teenage girl) was written by a woman. Harry may need help understanding how the brains of girls work, but Rowling presumably does not. Her understanding of the workings of at least one female brain is almost certainly among the reasons why Hermione's reaction seems so believable.

Immediately after this scene, readers follow Harry into a dream within which he is accused of luring Cho to the D.A. room under false pretenses. In this dream, Hermione suggests that he should sacrifice his Firebolt. Shortly thereafter, dream Harry becomes a snake who tries to murder his eventual father-in-law. We shall not linger here on the perhaps obvious Freudian implications of all of this. What is fascinating is Harry's odd response. When I read the Harry Potter series for the first time, Harry's first kiss caught me off guard. When he had been asked how the kiss was, I did not expect him to say "wet." I was a heterosexual teenage boy, and I was close friends with many others. I cannot imagine any of us answering the question the way Harry does.

This strange passage is particularly rich in regard to the level of subjective interiority that is revealed. In real life, we may not have trustable access to our own subjective reality at the level of motivation and presumption, but a novelist, as we have noted, has the option to offer clear, if fictional, articulation of just such subjective interiority. It may very well be the case that Harry himself will never remember the dream within which he is admonished by Hermione to relinquish his Firebolt to Cho, but we as readers can reflect as long as we like on the direct presentation of that dream. Rowling is allowing us the opportunity to really consider the motivational ground of a young man as he romantically/sexually approaches a young woman.

Harry's response was made all the stranger to me in my first reading in part, I suspect, because of how familiar Ron's fist-pumping response was. Ron's reaction bears something of the conquest imagery that so often accompanies the aesthetic representation of male heterosexual pursuit of desired females in popular literature, music, films, and television. In fact,

12. The Otter and the Stag

Ron's reaction called to my mind something of the stock "boys will be boys" presumptions that often accompany enforcements and acceptances of Mulvey's male gaze in both real life and aesthetic instances of predatory heterosexual male sexual pursuit.

Having grown up identifying as a heterosexual man in our culture, I have always found myself deeply troubled and perhaps insulted by the implications maintained within the "boys will be boys" presumption. Even as a young person, I always felt as if there was within that idea the assertion that men do not have a fully human level of self-control over their own instinctually sexual and romantic drives. The "boys will be boys" phrase and mentality seem to assert that these boys' choices in the matter of their inclinations and behavior are very limited or nonexistent. For me, the phrase and mentality have always held something of an imputation of the animalistic, regardless of how often it is so warmly embraced and perpetuated.

At the 2018 Southwest Popular/American Culture Association annual meeting in Albuquerque, I got the chance to sit down with Christopher Bell, PhD, Harry Potter scholar, and former plenary speaker at the annual Harry Potter Academic Conference held at Chestnut Hill College. Bell is a leading voice in the national academic conversation surrounding issues of race, identity, and gender within popular culture. Bell explained how powerful popular culture can be in regard to the representation of those who are often disenfranchised and oppressed within the hegemonic hierarchy. To paraphrase him, the more African American people, for example, we see on-screen, the less strange it becomes to encounter African Americans on-screen. As the popular audience grows ever more accustomed to seeing diverse faces on-screen, the actors who play these parts may very well find that they are increasingly offered less stereotypical, pigeonholing roles. Frequent presentations of minorities in popular culture may allow the audience to become more readily accepting of this expansion of roles in regards to race, religion, gender, orientation, identity, class, and so forth.

One of the most enduring and important contributions made by J. K. Rowling and her Harry Potter series is her presentation of the nonromantic relationship between Harry Potter and Hermione Granger. In *Deathly Hallows*, Harry and Hermione are abandoned in the forest by Ron. Ron leaves in part as a result of how apparently directionless and even hopeless their quest has come to seem. "They were three teenagers in a tent whose only achievement was not, yet, to be dead," the narrator notes.[23] If despair, in part, drives Ron away, the two remaining are all the more at risk of despondency having been thus abandoned. The narrator reveals that Harry is "staggered now to think of his own presumption in accepting his friends' offers to accompany him on this meandering, pointless journey. He knew nothing, had no ideas, and he was constantly, painfully on the alert for any indications that Hermione too was about to tell him that she had had enough, that she was leaving."[24] But Hermione does not leave. When Ron forces her to choose, she does. Looking "anguished," she says, " 'Yes—yes, I'm staying. Ron, we said we'd go with Harry, we said we'd help.' "[25] Harry stands by Hermione, and Hermione by Harry. Ron's betrayal makes the commitment of these two to each other and to the quest all the more apparent and impressive. Harry and Hermione do not devolve into lovers. They develop in paired heroic commitment to an overwhelming challenge of global magnitude.

While Hermione gained a reputation for "Books! And Cleverness!" earlier in the series, she has become much more than that by this late point in the story. With self-possessed courage and steely-eyed determination, Hermione takes the lead at both Godric's Hollow and the Lovegoods' home, saving the day by Disapparating in midair (with passengers) in both instances. Hermione is no sidekick, and Harry knows this better than anyone, telling her "You were trying to get us out of there alive, and you were incredible. I'd be dead if you hadn't been there."[26]

Popular culture is awash with instances of male/female partnerships that, in the final act, resolve in a heteronormatively romantic conclusion. Rowling refuses this resolution. Harry says, "She's like my sister [. . .] I love her like a sister and I reckon she feels the same way about me. It's always been like that."[27] We, the readers, know he is telling the truth, for the narrator has granted us omniscient access to Harry's interior subjectivity throughout the series. If he had had romantic feelings toward Hermione, even feelings he himself never acknowledged, the reader would have been informed. This is made poignantly clear in the scene on Christmas Eve in the churchyard at Godrick's Hollow: "Hermione had taken his hand again and was gripping it tightly, he could not look at her, but returned the pressure [. . .]. He put his arms around Hermione's shoulders, and she put hers around his waist, and they turned in silence and walked away through the snow, [. . .] back toward the dark church and the out-of-sight kissing gate."[28] For Harry and Hermione, the kissing gate is always out of sight. Harry will eventually marry Ginny, and Hermione will eventually marry Ron, and yet neither of them will swear a commitment to the betrothed that exceeds what Harry and Hermione swore to each other shoulder-to-shoulder in determined, unextinguishable, and unconditional opposition to Tom Riddle.

The Clothesline Project, among other organizations, works tirelessly to bring awareness to the scale of violence that is commonly and continually perpetrated against women in our culture on a daily, even hourly basis. There can be little doubt that the dominant cultural hegemony wherein we live and breathe continues to discursively enforce the diminishment of females through the ways in which we raise and narratively entertain both boys and girls. If we are to address violence born of objectification, it will have to be encountered at the level of motivation, presumption, and subjective interiority.

I think that Christopher Bell is right when he suggests that popular culture can be used to break dismissive and demeaning cultural assumptions and indoctrinations. Myth is translated through narrative, and narrative is at our disposal. We have spoken here about the violence that so often derives from the commodification of females in popular culture, but we must also consider all that is lost when a boy is raised to see nothing but a trinket where a human being of infinite complexity and significance actually stands. In his *Nicomachean Ethics*, Aristotle suggests that complete or character relationships (as opposed to those grounded on pleasure or utility) are based not only on trust and shared history but also on a mutual and profound regard of each person's developing drive toward a specific, individual, and subjectively envisioned excellence.[29] In a character relationship, each knows the other not merely as who they are but also as whatever each strives courageously and uniquely to become. Each knows the other at the level of their own creatively discovered and inspired calling. Each knows the other at the level of the determination, commitment, passion, and fortitude that both mean to continually bring to the project of realizing, incarnating their own personally defined character and virtue.

If Mulvey's male gaze leaves its objectifying fingerprints on certain types of violence and oppression, then it seems that we must endeavor subjectification. How much easier will it be for even a heterosexual boy who grew up reading the Harry Potter series to consider the possibility of a best friendship—untethered to romance or sexuality—with a girl? How much easier will it be for a girl who grew up reading this series to envision herself in such a relationship? How much easier will it be for each of them—and for the many other fans of the series—to bring characteristics of such a partnership into even romantic and sexual relationships? If we are ever to attempt a response to that particular violence born, at least in part, of the objectifying male gaze, the presumptions within those bearing that gaze will have to be addressed. In her 2008 speech at Harvard, Rowling famously said that we "can think [our]selves into other people's places [. . .] we have the power to imagine better."[30] Bellatrix Lestrange saw in the free elf Dobby nothing but a servant, a means merely, and the Bloody Baron saw in Rowena Ravenclaw nothing, we suspect, but a conquest. Let us not even ask what Fenrir Greyback saw in the students of Hogwarts. Readers of the series may find, however, that something quite different can be said about Harry's gaze upon Hermione or, most likely, of hers on him. Readers of the series can say this of Harry because they have been granted, through the specific nature of the narration, omniscient access to his subjective interiority throughout the entire story.

In the last novel of the series, Rowling describes Harry's and Hermione's synchronously conjured Patroni: " '*Expecto patronum!*' A silver otter burst from the end of Hermione's wand and swam gracefully through the air to join the stag."[31] Despite the fact that many fans have discussed the apparent suitability of Harry and Hermione romantically, I find myself moved by the symbolic power of the silvery image cited just above. Within the Harry Potter series, a corporeal Patronus always reveals something of the authentic individuality of the person who casts it. Seen in this way, these Patroni call to mind something of the dæmons from Philip Pullman's His Dark Materials series. It is a matter of no small importance that even at the level of their authentic selves (magically revealed), Harry and Hermione, the stag and the otter, stand together, mutually committed in the face of insurmountable odds.

J. K. Rowling uses both magical elements and narrative strategy to draw our attention to the reality of subjective motivation, its relation to dehumanization and objectification, and its usefulness for overcoming

12. The Otter and the Stag

both. Her decision to limit the narration of her Harry Potter series to Harry's perspective and subjectivity stands as a testimony to the idea that objectification and its accompanying violence must be addressed at the level of subjective presumption. Terry Doughty's *Locating Harry Potter in the "Boys' Book" Market* suggests that the Harry Potter series stands out as a beacon of hope in a sea of boys' books that assume a hard, violent, and gritty reality. Doughty concludes that by "celebrating male heroism at a moment when popular culture fears male violence, indeed when boys are seen as killers, Rowling has tapped into a kind of collective unconscious need to be reminded that boys have a path toward maturity to follow, and that they can indeed make it."[32] I agree with Doughty that the Harry Potter books represent a call to hope. The limited and focused narrative strategy of the Harry Potter series allows even young readers to come away assured that boys do not have to be boys in the culturally traditional and objectifying sense. It will be their choices, not their gender-based, culturally enforced predeterminations, that make the difference and determine who they really are.

NOTES

1. Rowling, *Prisoner of Azkaban*, 90. All Harry Potter book citations in this essay refer to the original Scholastic (US) editions.
2. Rowling, *Order of the Phoenix*, 175–76. My ellipses are bracketed throughout this essay.
3. Saunders, *Rhetorical Power*, 156.
4. Rowling, *Sorcerer's Stone*, 1.
5. Rowling, *Goblet of Fire*, 1–15.
6. Rowling, *Half-Blood Prince*, 1–37; and Rowling, *Deathly Hallows*, 1–12.
7. Rowling, *Deathly Hallows*, 16–20, 353–59.
8. Rowling, "Read the Full Rowling Interview."
9. For a deeper discussion of the significance of Harry's eyes, see Catherine Olver, "Eye Wonder? Reflecting Harry in Animal Eyes," chapter 11 of this volume.
10. Prady, "Fear the 'Bono's.'"
11. Saunders, *Rhetorical Power*, 156.
12. Rowling, *Deathly Hallows*, 658.
13. Saunders, *Rhetorical Power*, 150.
14. McCauley, *Into the Pensieve*.
15. Rowling, *Casual Vacancy*.
16. A discussion devoted exclusively to *The Casual Vacancy* can be found in M. Katherine Grimes, "Hopelessness and Hope in *The Casual Vacancy*: The Cost and Joy of Discipleship," chapter 15 of this volume.

17. Rowling, *Deathly Hallows*, 564, 616; and *Half-Blood Prince*, 204–5.
18. Rowling, *Half-Blood Prince*, 593–94.
19. Vezzali et al., "Greatest Magic," 105–21.
20. Rowling, *Order of the Phoenix*, 458.
21. Rowling, 458.
22. Rowling, 461–62.
23. Rowling, *Deathly Hallows*, 308.
24. Rowling, 313–14.
25. Rowling, 309.
26. Rowling, 352.
27. Rowling, 378.
28. Rowling, 329.
29. Aristotle, *Nicomachean Ethics*, 119–27.
30. Rowling, "Text of Rowling's Speech."
31. Rowling, *Deathly Hallows*, 263.
32. Doughty, "Locating Harry Potter," 256.

13. "Perfectly normal, thank you very much"

Exploitation of Hybridity in the Borderlands of Harry Potter

Molly L. Burt

GIVEN THE INTRICACY and depth of the Wizarding world that J. K. Rowling develops in the Harry Potter series, it's not surprising that many critics have turned their attention away from the main storyline to investigate structural institutions within the universe.[1] Some, for example, have thoroughly explored the social hierarchy of Harry Potter, in which wizards dominate and perpetuate injustices against nearly all other magical creatures, some almost human, some not, some in between. One critic, Jen Harrison, examines the expanding boundaries of humanity itself, asserting in her article "Posthuman Power: The Magic of Hybridity in the *Harry Potter* Series" that the posthuman hybridity Rowling presents through a variety of magical life forms actually indicates the limitations of a hierarchy with the "rational individual human being as the ultimate moral achievement."[2] She points out how Rowling melds people, animals, and even objects, until defining humanity becomes "at best problematic and at worst impossible," which, at first glance, supports the series' firm condemnation of aspirations of purity.[3] Furthermore, Harrison considers Voldemort as a hybrid who "not only blurs the boundaries of human ontology but also gives voice and power to the animals aligned with him,"[4] demonstrating how hybridity can function as a means of resistance against oppression. She ultimately argues that in Rowling's world, wizards' "control over the human/nonhuman divide is illusory, and it cannot be maintained . . . the hierarchy is shown to be not merely unethical but unviable as well."[5]

Despite Harrison's optimistic take on the implications of the concept of humanity being complicated throughout the series, and the series' explicit messages about the power of love, friendship, and community between wizards themselves as well as between wizards and magical creatures, wizards—claiming fully human status—still dominate and control other beings throughout the series. The resistant hybridity Harrison describes does little to actually change the system or help anyone except the wizards in control. Abuse of power extends past the figures of political injustice such as the Ministry of Magic, which is intentionally provided by Rowling as an opportunity to criticize systemic inequality. It is perpetuated by even the wisest and kindest protectors of Otherness, particularly Albus Dumbledore, ultimately undermining the series' critique of social injustice. Even as Rowling condemns the concept of purity with Muggleborns and other hybrids, she constructs heroes who use and abuse the hybrids to their own ends. Though she offers readers a position from which to experience and resist prejudice, her approach to hybridity remains hypocritical, and resistance to the oppressive faction consistently fails to outweigh the controlling forces of inequality.

A close examination of humans who are both wizard and Other—who belong to multiple communities, such as Muggleborns, Squibs, Animagi, and half-human wizards—through Gloria Anzaldúa's borderlands theory reveals that the original Harry Potter narrative[6] represents hybridity as dichotomous, and as a tool to be wielded by socially superior characters, rather than appreciating it as a valuable and fluid identity.

Though Harrison uses the word *hybridity* in a posthuman context, its roots in colonialism highlight asymmetrical power dynamics in Rowling's fantasy world that are reminiscent of real colonized spaces. Hybridity is essentially "the creation of new transcultural forms within the contact zone produced by colonization,"[7] so the hybrids discussed here are the most prominent examples of those "transcultural forms" in Harry Potter. Each of them signifies a meeting place of two or more cultures, an overlap usually formed by the Wizarding world's version of colonization, where the dominant humans conquer and oppress other magical beings. Several times throughout the series, Rowling mentions wizards having driven other races from their native environments into hiding, or even extinction. Umbridge tells the centaurs, "I would remind you that you live here only because the Ministry of Magic permits you certain areas of land,"[8] and Ron says of the giant population, "There aren't any left in Britain now,"[9] indicating at least two communities forced out by wizarding rule, which seems to operate much like European expansion. In this wizard-dominated hierarchy, some Other communities have more agency than others; goblins have become integral to wizarding society and gained respect after centuries of rebellion, while house-elves are actively enslaved, and Muggles live parallel to wizards in total obliviousness. Cultural hybridity, as opposed to posthuman hybridity, provides an opportunity to consider these power dynamics in the overlap, through hybrids who are of two communities, yet neither. Leading postcolonial theorist Homi K. Bhabha stresses the interdependence and imbalance of cultural forces in his theory of the third space of enunciation (the emergence of cultural identity in a contradictory and ambivalent space), which makes all hybrids unique and "the claim to a hierarchical 'purity' of cultures untenable."[10] Thus, "it is the 'in-between' space that carries the burden and meaning of culture, and that is what makes the notion of hybridity so important," according to Ashcroft, Griffiths, and Tiffin.[11]

Cultural hybridity has a complicated history as both a means of controlling colonized peoples and a way to resist colonial influences, with a variety of interpretations over time. African American artist Renée Green, quoted by Bhabha, describes "cultural difference as the production of minority identities that 'split'—are estranged unto themselves—in the act of being articulated into a collective body."[12] Bhabha references her work and furthers it in *The Location of Culture* by questioning how hybrids are "formed 'in-between' or in excess of the sum of the parts of difference (usually intoned as race/class/gender, etc.)," noting that "the borderline engagements of cultural difference may as often be consensual as conflictual."[13] Chon Noriega, meanwhile, leans toward the more conflictual stance, arguing that "the hybrid truth of cultural experience may lie not in a comfortable middle ground between two cultural experiences, but in the irreconcilable distance between."[14] Marwan M. Kraidy contributes consideration of how the experience can be exploited, explaining that "hybridizing processes have helped cultural traditions recruit new adherents, but cross-cultural conversion was successful only 'when favored by a powerful set of political, social, or economic incentives.' "[15] Additionally, Noriega notes that hybridity has also offered a means to resist the concept of singular identity in postcolonial culture, "demonstrating that stories of original, 'native,' prelapsarian cultures are produced by the conquerors to dehumanize the conquered," and warns against the use of hybridity as "simply another tool to dissolve difference, celebrate homogeneity, erase history."[16] Thus cultural hybridity, or the meeting place of two distinct identities often in conflict, has historically functioned as both a form of control and a path to resistance in postcolonial cultures. While Harrison addresses hybridity in the Harry Potter series as resistance to and deconstruction of the Wizarding world hierarchy, it simultaneously functions as a means of controlling the marginalized.

While general hybridity theory offers valuable insight into how hybridity functions in Rowling's series, one particular metaphor emerges as the most appropriate lens: borderlands. The concept of the borderlands originated with Gloria Anzaldúa's study of her experience on the American-Mexican border. However, she herself prefaces *Borderlands/La Frontera: The New Mestiza* by confirming the ubiquity of the concept: "The psychological borderlands, the sexual borderlands and the spiritual borderlands are not particular to the Southwest. In fact, the Borderlands are physically present wherever two or more cultures edge each other, where people of different races occupy the same territory."[17] The Wizarding world, as the intersection of countless races, human and otherwise, with a vast variety of hybrids in constant conflict, offers exactly the conditions Anzaldúa describes. Like the southwestern experience, Rowling's fictional world is "not a comfortable territory to live in, this place of contradictions. Hatred, anger and exploitation are the prominent features of this landscape."[18] Certainly many magical creatures, including goblins and centaurs, express dissatisfaction with their treatment by wizards, while wizards insist that they themselves are the victims of prejudice. Anzaldúa further emphasizes the violence and alienation of this crossroads in her poetry: "you are the battleground / where enemies are kin to each other; / you are at home, a stranger."[19] This divisive experience of hybridity takes many different shapes among wizardkind, such as Muggleborns, half-bloods, Squibs, Animagi, and creatures with half status, such as half-giants. Anzaldúa's theory works best across the scope of the Wizarding world because it takes into account the importance of community in cultural hybridity, as well as the strong sense of conflict/battle between different groups and identities.[20]

Hybridity in Rowling's series is not only a consistently painful and contradictory status; it is also perplexingly dichotomous. While some writers approach hybridity as a spectrum, wherein a character flows between two cultures and lines become blurred between the binary poles, characters within the Harry Potter narrative generally act as one cultural "side" of themselves or the other (sometimes the culture they identify with more, sometimes not). Many moments throughout the series suggest that no one—especially pureblood wizards—is all good or all bad. For example, Draco Malfoy refuses to identify a disguised Harry to Death Eaters, and Ron Weasley directs unwarranted bouts of cruelty toward Hermione. However, any differences demonstrated by hybrids are typically attributed to their Otherness, if only by implication. For example, the narration describes Peter Pettigrew's unpleasant traits in relation to his Animagus rat form. "Something of the rat," Harry notes, "lingered around his pointed nose and his very small, watery eyes."[21] Instead of speaking, he "squeaks," and his eyes often dart toward the door in search of escape, similar to rats and other rodents.[22] Peter is a coward and traitor regardless of his Animagus status, yet the text relates his flaws directly to the Other part of him, highlighting the dichotomy.

The depiction of hybridity allows for its weaponization by Dumbledore, especially, who has a long history of exploiting outcasts. Most notably, he polices resources and opportunities provided by "good" characters' experiential hybridity of light and dark, often to their own severe self-detriment. Within the magical community, dark wizards maintain a distinctly separate community and culture with exclusive spaces and experiences: Knockturn Alley, Slytherin House, Death Eater involvement, Dark Mark wearing and conjuring, and so on. Dumbledore is able to use wizards aligned with his cause who have history with or access to the dark community, which usually results in the hybrids' suffering. For example, Snape's past as a Death Eater allows the Order to use him as a spy, despite his extreme reluctance, and this personal sacrifice culminates in his death. Similarly, Dumbledore requests that Sirius, who was raised to be a dark wizard and Death Eater, share his access to his family's house, which leads to the last year of Sirius's life being steeped in misery and loneliness. Finally, Harry's partial identity as Voldemort's Horcrux allows him a mental connection that often saves lives and puts him a step ahead of Voldemort, but Dumbledore forces Harry into painful and humiliating Occlumency lessons with Snape rather than risk infiltration of the Order. If Dumbledore (and by extension, his wizard followers) can accept—or at the very least, ignore—the differences of hybrids, unlike other wizards, they gain access to the doors opened by Otherness, and have tools and resources that even the hybrids themselves aren't allowed to utilize alone in wizarding society.

Dichotomization of cultural hybridity allows those in power to distance the individual from their Other identity and offer the illusion of acceptance. This distancing begins with the Wizarding world's relationship with the Muggle world, which ultimately forces Muggleborns to fully integrate into the Wizarding world or risk ostracism, despite the valuable skills their Muggle experience provides. Not only is the Wizarding world physically separate from Muggle society—with Hogwarts, Hogsmeade, Diagon Alley, Platform Nine and Three-Quarters, the Ministry of Magic, St. Mungo's, and so on all intentionally gated and hidden from Muggles—but there is little to no overlap (though there are certainly similarities) between the two worlds in systems of government, law enforcement, medical treatment, journalism, sports, music, fashion, zoology, botany, and the like. While it's natural for distinct cultures to inspire immense variation in many fields, the magical and Muggle realms seem unnaturally divided at times. Why are nightgowns apparently only worn by Muggle women?[23] How is the Venomous Tentacula (or any magical wildlife, for that matter) restricted to wizard-occupied spaces? Why are no publications with moving pictures reporting about the Muggle world? It seems that for wizards to maintain their preferential perch atop the hierarchy, they must discourage fraternization and mixing of the two worlds, keeping to themselves the qualities that make them more powerful, with the excuse that "Everyone'd be wantin' magic solutions to their problems," according to Hagrid in *Sorcerer's Stone*.[24] The systematic separation of wizard and Muggle societies exacerbates the power divide inherent between those who have access to magic and those who don't. Again, despite Harrison's examples of hybridity disrupting social hierarchy, the dichotomy Rowling creates limits the potential for overlap, making resistance to oppression and exploitation by lower-status characters difficult.

Furthermore, the Weasley family, who are symbols of the middle class as well as Muggle sympathizers, indicate how crossing the wizard/Muggle border by showing interest in or interacting with Muggles is even more damning than appearing poor in the Wizarding world. Alyssa Hunziker points out in "The Embodiment of Collective Exclusion" that Arthur Weasley has a weak understanding of Muggles after years of study, suggesting that even he hasn't dug particularly deep,[25] and he cannot so much as pronounce *electric*, or remember a common word such as *telephone*.

Nevertheless, his interest is regularly derided by other purebloods for bringing him too close to Mugglehood.[26] In Lucius Malfoy's frequent digs at the Weasley family for being poor, it may initially seem as though Rowling is simply criticizing the upper class's disdain for the middle class. However, it quickly becomes apparent that Malfoy's real issue with them is their acceptance of Muggles. Twice in *Chamber of Secrets* alone, the Malfoys and Weasleys skirmish over the Granger family, when Lucius insults "the company [the Weasleys] keep." Draco also calls Hermione a "filthy little Mudblood"[27] and later disregards class entirely when he tells Harry and Ron, disguised as Crabbe and Goyle, "Arthur Weasley loves Muggles so much he should snap his wand in half and go and join them. . . . You'd never know the Weasleys were purebloods, the way they behave."[28] Thus, the emphasis is ultimately on difference of wizarding status rather than of social class. Class insults mainly become a thinly veiled criticism of hybrids who are relatively impoverished because of their hybridity. Lucius remarks about Hagrid's cabin, "D'you call this a house?"[29] and Draco comments on Lupin's patched robes, "He dresses like our old house-elf."[30] Both Hagrid and Lupin rely on Dumbledore for gainful employment, as they wouldn't be welcome nearly anywhere else due to prejudice originating in their hybridity.[31] The Malfoys only voice prejudices that are actually commonplace throughout the wizarding community. Differences such as class can be overlooked, but hybridity—at the root of the working class throughout the series—cannot.

As a result, the divide between the Muggle and Wizarding worlds runs so deep that only half-bloods like Harry and Mugglelborns like Hermione can penetrate both sides, though they will never feel as at home in either; instead, they exist in Anzaldúa's borderlands. Yet wizarding society consistently discourages any return to the Muggle world. Once trained as wizards, Muggleborns and half-bloods are expected to remain in the Wizarding world, to work, raise families, and participate in magical communities. These expectations constrain hybrids like Remus Lupin, for example, who is socially compelled to struggle, penniless and ostracized as a werewolf in the Wizarding world, rather than pursue a well-paying career among Muggles—where his condition would go undetected and couldn't limit his job opportunities—despite his being a half-blood, and likely well versed in Muggle culture. Similarly, entire groups of Muggleborns like Ted

13. "Perfectly normal, thank you very much"

Tonks and Dean Thomas (though he could potentially be a half-blood, not knowing both of his parents) go on the run in the second Wizarding War, living off scraps instead of hiding out comfortably among Muggles, and most are caught and killed. The series frequently implies that it is preferable to die a wizard than live like a Muggle.

It's worth considering whether wizards even have the ability to live as Muggles, given the separation of the two cultures. Not only are wizards consistently baffled by Muggle fashion, currency, technology, and transportation, as evidenced by the Quidditch World Cup and the Weasleys' confusion about telephones and trains, but they do not appear to learn math or language skills after they begin wizarding education at eleven, though it appears that most wizard children attend primary school beforehand. When fifth-years meet with their heads of house to discuss careers, only wizarding jobs are presented as options. The closest that their choices get to the Muggle world is "Muggle Relations," which Hermione implies is a lowly last resort, noting, "You don't seem to need many qualifications to liaise with Muggles. . . . All they want is an O.W.L. in Muggle Studies."[32] Wizards remain blind to their own shortcomings even as they limit their own chances at happy and comfortable lives. Squibs, who are even less equipped to live among wizards than Muggles, given their inability to develop their magic to a passable level, still occupy the lowest of menial labor jobs in the Wizarding world, Filch being a janitor, and Figg spending well over a decade babysitting Harry in a Muggle suburb. Even Harry, upon fearing he will be expelled, resorts to the hope that he can stay at Hogwarts as Hagrid's assistant.[33] The only known pureblood wizard to choose differently is Molly Weasley's second cousin, who works as an accountant and is apparently such a disgrace that Ron says the family doesn't talk about him.[34] Ultimately, the pervasive condescension toward the Muggle world, even by hybrid wizards themselves, supports a dichotomous reading of Muggle-wizard hybridity and indicates how susceptible hybrid wizards are to being taken advantage of because of their tenuous wizarding status.

A close look at Hermione illustrates the potential for exploitation. As the primary Muggleborn in the series, she reveals that wizards ridicule her Muggleness, yet have no qualms taking advantage of the useful qualities provided by her hybridity. Ron especially mocks Hermione's attempts to learn about and belong in the Wizarding world, calling her a know-it-all "at least twice a week,"[35] and "doing a cruel but accurate impression of Hermione jumping up and down in her seat every time Professor McGonagall asked a question."[36] Social expectations gradually distance Hermione from the Muggle world, so that she spends breaks with Harry and Ron instead of her parents, and by the end of the series she is fully integrated in the Wizarding community, her existence wiped from her parents' memories.[37] Conveniently, Hermione's upbringing allows her certain skills, such as critical reading, researching, and logic, that are rarely depicted among other wizards, and make her a valuable asset. Mary P. Freier writes that Hermione "interacts with texts critically and evaluates all of the information given rather than simply accepting or dismissing the publication," citing examples such as Hermione's subscription to the highly biased *Daily Prophet*.[38] Her experience living as a Muggle, with access to many more relevant news sources and more advanced information technology during childhood, allows her to develop not only reading abilities but also the creativity and open-mindedness of an advanced researcher. Freier points out that Hermione's willingness to dig through "flawed sources" like *Hogwarts: A History*, *The Life and Lies of Albus Dumbledore*, and *The Tales of Beedle the Bard* sets her apart and often leads the characters to the information they need to prevail.[39] Finally, Hermione herself identifies her key strength during the search for the Sorcerer's Stone: "A lot of the greatest wizards haven't got an ounce of logic."[40] Where purebloods and even half-bloods are often able to rely on magic to solve their problems from a young age, Hermione's Muggle childhood required her to develop common sense and logic to problem-solve, giving her an advantage over magic-dependent wizards. Similarly, Snape, who designed the logic-based obstacle for the stone, and Voldemort, who also thwarted it, are both half-bloods who were raised among Muggles, like Hermione. Clearly their Otherness is useful and even desired as a tool, but Hermione is never encouraged to identify with that Muggle side of herself, only to use it when necessary and pack it away again.[41]

Animagi continue the pattern of structural potential for exploitation without true acceptance of the Other. Wizards who can shift into an animal form automatically become hybrids, part of a secondary community culture as they gain the ability to communicate with other animals, as Peter Pettigrew does with fellow rats to find Voldemort in Albania, and as Sirius

Black does to convince Crookshanks to help him break into Gryffindor Tower.[42] While animals like rats and dogs are not in outright conflict with wizardkind, they are very much disdained,[43] and the Ministry of Magic strictly regulates wizards who wish to become Animagi, creating a constrictive borderland for wizard-animal hybrids that allows wizards to take advantage and retain control.

Animagi are consistently discouraged from leaning too far toward their animal halves, or even remaining in the shape for longer than necessary, and being a wizard is the socially preferred form, despite the great personal advantages of shape-shifting. In her cat form, Minerva McGonagall is able to stand guard and spy on Privet Drive; Rita Skeeter can infiltrate Hogwarts throughout the school year without detection in her insect form; and, of course, the Marauders kept a werewolf in check for years. Yet, significantly, only the most villainous Animagus in the series, Pettigrew, prefers the animal status to humanity enough to remain a rodent for more than brief periods of time, suggesting that good and reliable people do not need to hide among animals and therefore should not. Sirius Black even comments, "If you made a better rat than a human, it's not much to boast about,"[44] perpetuating that disdain for animalkind despite often becoming a dog to survive, which emphasizes how deeply the dislike of Otherness runs in wizarding culture. The disgust is certainly due in part to Pettigrew's nature manifesting in a less desirable animal than a stag or dog, but also implies that Pettigrew is no longer human enough.

Similarly, Sirius is strongly discouraged from using his Animagus form when it doesn't benefit the Order's cause, again indicating how wizards exploit hybrids and limit their agency. Sirius is reprimanded for using his hybridity to achieve a brief reprieve from his long and miserable house arrest and make up for lost time with Harry, whom he has very few opportunities to see, in *Order of the Phoenix*. Though Dumbledore claims that keeping Sirius locked up is for his own safety, the Death Eaters already know Sirius's affiliations and Animagus shape, so he is in no more danger from them in public than the rest of the Order. Even if the Ministry found out, Sirius could at that point commit to staying inside Grimmauld Place, and Kingsley's position leading the investigation could easily prevent them from capturing him. Regardless, the Order's refusal to let Sirius use his hybridity for his own goals and priorities continues the disturbing pattern of hybridity exploitation. His duality is only acceptable as an occasional tool for them, not for himself.

As with Muggleborns and Animagi, wizards who are part of Other magical communities are expected to use their Otherness for wizarding aims, but to otherwise adhere as closely to their wizard identity as possible, or else risk further shame and suffering. Rubeus Hagrid, for example, can get away with masquerading simply as a large wizard or a small giant, living in the borderlands between two races who despise each other and are quite literally at war. Wizards harbor a deep hatred for giants, blaming them for their own extinction at the Ministry's hands: "They were dying out anyway, and then loads got themselves killed by Aurors."[45] Thus Hagrid hides his hybridity until his exposure at the hands of Rita Skeeter in *Goblet of Fire*, when Ron, Maxime, parents, and total strangers judge and condemn him for his duality. Some wizards go so far as to suggest that suicide is preferable to his existence, though he is innocent of any wrongdoing.[46] Of course, as Michael Morris points out in a review of animal treatment at Hogwarts, even before his giant blood is revealed, Hagrid's giant-like inclinations, particularly his love for dangerous magical creatures (attributed to his inherent "brutal nature" by Rita Skeeter), are still widely disparaged, even by the main characters, in another instance of Otherness without usefulness going unappreciated.[47] His devotion to monstrous creatures seems sensible to other wizards only when those creatures can be used for security, like Fluffy, or entertainment, like the dragons and Blast-Ended Skrewts in the Triwizard Tournament. Furthermore, while he is an adequate Care of Magical Creatures teacher, his every absence reminds students and readers alike that there are more competent candidates. Yet Dumbledore keeps him on as an instructor, and seems to be Hagrid's one haven from the criticism of the Wizarding world, refusing to accept his resignation after the scandal of his exposure.[48] By the end of the school year, however, Dumbledore has taken advantage of the public revelation and enlisted both Hagrid and Maxime to cross the cultural border and live among giants as ambassadors at risk of a painful, lonely death. Despite good intentions for the rest of wizardkind, it's no coincidence that Dumbledore is simultaneously the creator of a safe harbor for Hagrid and also the one person who capitalizes on the giant half of his identity. He reveals a strategic undertone to his messages of tolerance and acceptance—that he embraces not just the cultural hybrids themselves but the opportunities they represent to gain an edge on opponents.

As with Hagrid's giantness, Remus Lupin's werewolfness makes him wizard yet constantly Other, in a borderland that allows for his exploitation. Though he is only physically wolf once in a moon cycle, that part of his nature is always with him, exhausting him around the full moon and giving him "wolfish characteristics," a phrase used in *Half-Blood Prince* to describe Bill's future tendencies.[49] Again similarly to Hagrid, Lupin is hated by most wizardkind with the exception of Dumbledore, under whose leadership he enjoys a brief year of peace and prosperity—the same year, conveniently, that his closest childhood friend, Sirius, poses a threat to Dumbledore's school—until his werewolf identity is exposed by Snape, and he is forced to flee the anger and rejection of the Wizarding world. He is unemployed and readily available, due to the exposure, two years later just when Dumbledore needs him for the wizarding cause. Harry notices how bitter Lupin sounds when he says, "Dumbledore wanted a spy and here I was . . . ready-made," emphasizing the pain of Lupin's exploitation.[50] Again, even accepting and generous wizards like Ron struggle to tolerate Lupin for what he is. Furthermore, werewolves are as suspicious of him as giants are of Hagrid, for their closeness with other wizards, as Lupin finds out while using his werewolf status to spy for the wizard-led Order of the Phoenix.[51] He tells Harry, "I bear the unmistakable signs of having tried to live among wizards, you see, whereas they have shunned normal society and live on the margins."[52] Thus, like Hagrid, Lupin demonstrates his and Hagrid's existence in a borderland, uneasy with both halves of his identity, leaving him wide open for exploitation by the man who promises to protect him.

Significantly, neither the giant nor the werewolf community sides with the Order of the Phoenix in the end, and the two populations only appear in the last novel to be fought and killed by Dumbledore's followers. Their final appearance furthers their Othering and impending extinction, implicitly justified by their joining the Death Eaters, who promise a future out of hiding and shame when Dumbledore cannot. The hybrids, then, are compelled by the privilege and discriminatory attitudes of the Wizarding world to aid in the destruction of one of their own communities, for the perceived betterment of the other. While it is true that neither Hagrid nor Lupin wishes to be involved with his Other community, their preference for wizardkind clearly stems, as demonstrated above, from the social, political, and economic power wizards have as the peak of the hierarchy. Lupin might be more willing to interact with and learn from other werewolves if they were afforded the same rights as wizards. Hagrid certainly would be more open about his heritage, not to mention his brother Grawp, were giants not so taboo. The recurring pattern of Otherness being weaponized in the case of hybrids who are given no promise of acceptance in either community, or the betterment of Others, is a troubling indication that Dumbledore's reputation for love and tolerance is inflated and influenced by opportunity for power against dark forces. Half-breeds like Hagrid and Lupin willingly lay down their lives to fight their own kind for the wizarding community yet receive only a fraction of the benefits victory offers for full wizards.

Fleur is the exception to the rampant use of Other for wizard goals, as her quarter-Veela status is never exploited by the Order, but she remains significant as a feminized version of disdained hybridity that many wizards refuse to tolerate. While her beauty and grace can be advantageous socially, many characters like Molly, Ginny, and Hermione—whose judgment readers learn to trust—make discriminatory assumptions about her character and firmly reject her from their community, showing a lack of tolerance even for Otherness that is not inherently dangerous (after all, while Veela can entice men to behave recklessly, so can anyone with a wand) when it cannot be co-opted. Fleur must emphatically reject Veela characteristics by demonstrating that she loves Bill for his courage instead of being motivated by vanity, as the Weasley women expect of a part-Veela, and she is finally accepted into the family at the end of *Half-Blood Prince* because she does not reject Bill when he acquires a hybrid status.[53] Again, her struggle shows the extremes hybrid characters must go to just to gain wizards' trust and be tolerated in their midst. Furthermore, while the contention between Molly and Fleur is clearly a commentary from Rowling on prejudice and overprotective motherhood, Fleur is accepted only as Bill's wife, not as the powerful individual she is demonstrated, as a Triwizard Tournament competitor, to be. Ultimately, wizards abuse hybridity when they can, and reject it when they cannot.

Rowling certainly succeeds at offering a valuable perspective from which to experience and criticize the injustices of the Wizarding world through

13. "Perfectly normal, thank you very much"

Harry, a half-blood wizard essentially adopted into a family of purebloods. Seeing the wizarding community through Harry's privileged eyes offers only a limited understanding of hybrid characters and Other communities, because he isn't privy to the entirety of the giant, werewolf, Veela, or Animagus experiences. His restricted view has to be accommodated in interpreting the nuances of hybridity in the series. For example, Harry lives in fairly self-contained bubbles—Hogwarts, the Burrow, and Grimmauld Place—and rarely interacts with the general public or even ideologies particularly disparate from his. He knows only one half-giant, one part-Veela, and one werewolf (not including enemy Fenrir Greyback), and only in environments that are friendly and relatively safe for them. However, Rowling manages to inspire empathy even with this limited view; though Harry is first filled with wonder at the privileges and joys of his newly discovered community, his rapid exposure to prejudice against loved ones encourages readers to survey their own world from a new perspective, even if they haven't experienced inequality personally.[54]

The series lays an effective foundation for recognizing and appreciating hybridity, with so many characters experiencing prejudice due to their hybrid identities, yet it misrepresents its heroes as champions of such characters, when really Dumbledore and the Order are exploitative and single-minded in the same ways they accuse Voldemort's followers of being. While Dumbledore and other wizards may be considered morally sound in prioritizing the many over the few, readers can't help but notice the lengths wizards go to in order to ensure their status as the "many" by exploiting the "few,"[55] and to control rather than resist. This very same concept is criticized through a letter from a power-hungry young Dumbledore to Grindelwald: "We seize control FOR THE GREATER GOOD."[56] Dumbledore's claim unsettles Harry and makes him doubt his mentor. Similarly, Harry's worst fear throughout *Order of the Phoenix* is that Voldemort will exploit their connection (Harry's Otherness) to gain power, yet Dumbledore and his supporters hypocritically take what they need from hybrid, marginalized characters under the guise of acceptance and love, while still failing to considerably improve those hybrid characters' quality of life by embracing their full identity or challenging others to do the same. Wizard hybrids consistently offer their services and sacrifice themselves and their Other communities for the wizarding war, while reaping only minimal benefits.

Full wizards can happily return home after the Battle of Hogwarts, start families, and enjoy lucrative careers. Meanwhile, Muggleborns, Squibs, shapeshifters, half-wizards, and other hybrids will continue to struggle under the restrictions the hierarchy places on them, their Other qualities no longer useful, with no prospects for equality on the horizon.[57] Though the realistic elements of Harry Potter prevent Rowling from solving all the problems and injustices of the world she's created—which in so many ways reflects our own, where there is no neat little bow—the ending seems to again prioritize privileged wizards over the hybrids who fought (and in some cases died) for their peace. Harry names his child Albus Severus, after Dumbledore and Snape, rather than naming him (or James Sirius, or Lily Luna) after Lupin, Hagrid, or Hermione—all hybrid characters who loved him unconditionally and never manipulated or used him. All the recognition and praise after their triumph goes to wizards who exploited the hybrids who suffered for their cause without any personal betterment. Thus Harry Potter promotes the weaponization of hybridity, but not the appreciation of it, or of its ability to resist the social hierarchy. Hybridity is instead limited to use by and for the controlling social group.

NOTES

1. Jackie C. Horne, Alyssa Hunziker, and Michael Morris, to name a few.
2. Harrison, "Posthuman Power," 326.
3. Harrison, 327.
4. Harrison, 330.
5. Harrison, 334.
6. Specifically, the original seven books in the Harry Potter canon.
7. Ashcroft, Griffiths, and Tiffin, *Postcolonial Studies*, 135.
8. Rowling, *Order of the Phoenix*, 754–55. All Harry Potter book citations in this essay refer to the original Scholastic (US) editions.
9. Rowling, *Goblet of Fire*, 430.
10. Ashcroft, Griffiths, and Tiffin, *Postcolonial Studies*, 136.
11. Ashcroft, Griffiths, and Tiffin, 136.
12. Bhabha, *Location of Culture*, 3.
13. Bhabha, 2.
14. Noriega, " 'Barricades,' " 250.
15. Kraidy, *Hybridity*, 3.
16. Noriega, "Barricades," 249 and 250.
17. Anzaldúa, *Borderlands*, 19.
18. Anzaldúa, 19.

13. "Perfectly normal, thank you very much"

19. Anzaldúa, 216.
20. While it's tempting to also consider magical creatures like centaurs and merpeople—who display external hybridity and exist in the Wizarding world—in this context, they belong wholly to their own distinct cultures, and therefore do not qualify as cultural hybrids like many wizards. Werewolves, though they have their own separate community, are still partially human wizards and can live among/pass as fully human wizards, having been turned after birth.
21. Rowling, *Prisoner of Azkaban*, 366.
22. Rowling, 367.
23. Rowling, *Goblet of Fire*, 83.
24. Rowling, *Sorcerer's Stone*, 65.
25. Hunziker, "Revealing Discrimination," 5.
26. Rowling, *Goblet of Fire*, 41.
27. Rowling, *Chamber of Secrets*, 62, 112.
28. Rowling, 222.
29. Rowling, 262.
30. Rowling, *Prisoner of Azkaban*, 141.
31. Rowling, 309.
32. Rowling, *Order of the Phoenix*, 657.
33. Rowling, *Sorcerer's Stone*, 150.
34. Rowling, 99.
35. Rowling, *Prisoner of Azkaban*, 172.
36. Rowling, *Half-Blood Prince*, 310.
37. Rowling, *Deathly Hallows*, 84.
38. Freier, "Librarian," 4. For further discussion of Hermione's critical thinking abilities, see Leslie Bickford's essay elsewhere in this volume.
39. Freier, 4.
40. Rowling, *Sorcerer's Stone*, 285.
41. The other central Muggleborn in Harry's year, Dean Thomas, maintains his love for soccer, a strictly Muggle sport, and it quickly becomes a point of contention between him and Ron in *Sorcerer's Stone*: "Ron couldn't see what was exciting about a game with only one ball where no one was allowed to fly. Harry had caught Ron prodding Dean's poster of West Ham soccer team, trying to make the players move." Again, Rowling's narrative establishes Muggle qualities and interests without use as nonsensical and impractical early on, while wizards take advantage of the useful qualities for their own gain.
42. Rowling, *Prisoner of Azkaban*, 364.
43. Morris, "Middle Earth," 348.
44. Rowling, *Prisoner of Azkaban*, 373.
45. Rowling, *Goblet of Fire*, 430
46. Rowling, 544.
47. Morris, "Middle Earth," 348.
48. Rowling, *Goblet of Fire*, 453.
49. Rowling, *Half-Blood Prince*, 613.

50. Rowling, 334.
51. Rowling, 334.
52. Rowling, 334.
53. Rowling, 623.
54. See Westman, "Perspective," for further discussion of this theme.
55. Given the dwindling numbers of pureblood human wizards, hybrids are hardly a minority.
56. Rowling, *Deathly Hallows*, 357.
57. Jackie Horne similarly points out the shortcomings of Rowling's approach to antiracism at the end of the series in "Harry and the Other."

SECTION 5

HARRY POTTER AND BEYOND

14. Literary Alchemy in "The Fountain of Fair Fortune" from *The Tales of Beedle the Bard*

Kris Swank

BEEDLE THE BARD's wizarding fairy tale "The Fountain of Fair Fortune" follows three witches and a Muggle knight attempting to reach a fountain at the heart of an enchanted garden. The setting of the tale is rich with the symbolism of the alchemical quest (the "Great Work") as it traces the steps of the process to transform base material into the philosopher's stone and unite warring opposites—the "white queen" and "red king"—into a perfect union. Likewise, the names of the four seekers encode information about the transformations that each will undergo in the course of the quest. Symbols on the fountain also represent the questers and the quest. None of this is accidental, for the author has stated that *The Tales of Beedle the Bard* are "really a distillation of the themes found in the Harry Potter books."[1] Thus "The Fountain of Fair Fortune" is not just a simple fairy tale but a hermetic text that invites readers to decipher hidden meanings and to reflect upon themes also embedded in the Harry Potter series.

LITERARY ALCHEMY: THE GREAT WORK

Alchemy is an ancient branch of learning in which the magnum opus, or Great Work, is to create a philosopher's stone. As Beatrice Groves explains, this is either "the literal (or 'exoteric') search for a real stone that will bring eternal life and endless gold, [or] the mystical (or 'esoteric') version of the quest, in which the stone and its elixir are metaphors for spiritual riches of the eternal life hereafter."[2] Lyndy Abraham, in *A Dictionary of Alchemical Imagery*, summarizes the literal alchemical process of transmuting base material into a perfected stone:

> The [raw] matter for the Stone must be dissolved and returned to its primal state before it can be recreated or coagulated into the new

pure form of the philosopher's stone. This cycle of *solve et coagula* or separation and union has to be reiterated many times throughout the opus. During this circulation, the elements earth, air, fire and water are separated by distillation and converted into each other to form the perfect unity, the fifth element.... The contrary qualities of the four elements are likened to quarrelling foes who must be reconciled and united in order for harmony to reign.[3]

As a device in art and literature, the mystical, or esoteric, alchemical quest has been used to describe the personal and spiritual transformation of the alchemist, known as a seeker. The seeker's path mimics the steps involved in distilling the philosopher's stone from raw material. Catherine Beyer writes, "This involves spiritual transformation, the shedding of impurities, the joining of opposites, and the refinement of materials. Exactly what the end result of this profound transformation is varies from author to author; it could be, self-realization, communion with divinity, fulfillment of purpose, etc."[4] Groves notes that such quests rely on symbols to represent complete concepts.[5] And Bernard Roger observes that fairy tales often "illustrate each stage of the Great Work and the alchemical iterations required to achieve them."[6] In fact, the fairy tales of wizards and Muggles alike frequently embody hermetic meaning.

Several scholars have analyzed the significant role of alchemy in the Harry Potter series.[7] John Granger is foremost among those who have argued for such a reading.[8] Priscilla Hobbs and Signe Cohen separately examine the Triwizard Tournament in *Harry Potter and the Goblet of Fire* as an alchemical quest.[9] And Groves illustrates the author's continued engagement with alchemical (and Masonic) symbolism in the Fantastic Beasts film franchise.[10] Both Granger and Audrey Spindler have blogged specifically on the alchemical symbolism of "The Fountain of Fair Fortune."[11] Granger focuses on Christian interpretations, while Spindler explores occult symbolism.

Several alchemical symbols related to the esoteric quest are at once evident in "The Fountain of Fair Fortune." According to the tale, each year a "single unfortunate" is given the opportunity to enter a walled garden, climb a hill at its center, bathe in its fountain, "and receive Fair Fortune for evermore."[12] According to Abraham, the enclosed garden "is the matrix in which the alchemical plant or tree grows, blossoms and comes to fruition."[13] The esoteric quest has been depicted in classic alchemical texts as a journey through just such a garden with a fountain at its center.[14] Blooming roses symbolize "attainment of wisdom or inner knowledge."[15] As Spindler observes, "The whole book of [Beedle's] tales is decorated with roses and the Fountain drawing itself is framed with roses."[16] Ascending a mountain also "means to rise in awareness."[17] Meanwhile, a fountain is symbolic of the final washing and purification of the philosopher's stone.[18] Nearly every element of the garden setting has some alchemical significance.

ONOMASTIC SYMBOLISM

Another source of symbolism comes from character names. Alchemical texts frequently use character names with allegorical or symbolic meaning. Onomastics (the study of names) reveals these specific meanings. Vanessa Compagnone and Marcel Danesi argue that the names in the Harry Potter novels "evoke ancient mystical concepts, such as the belief that a given name contains prophetic information about its bearer's destiny, personality, and outlook on life."[19] The author herself has indicated the importance of character names, saying in a 1999 radio interview that "names are really crucial to me . . . for some reason I just can't move on until I know I've called [characters] the right thing."[20]

In "The Fountain of Fair Fortune," all four character names are carefully chosen and, as suggested by Compagnone and Danesi, embedded with self-fulfilling prophecies, here reflecting the personal transformation that each character will undergo by the end of the quest. Hoping to be chosen to enter the garden are three witches who suffer from personal misfortune. Asha suffers from a mysterious illness; Altheda has been robbed of her wand (and thus her livelihood) by an evil sorcerer; and Amata has been jilted by a false lover. The three agree to unite their efforts to reach the Fountain of Fair Fortune. As dawn arrives, enchanted vines pull them into the garden along with a Muggle knight, Sir Luckless. Asha and Altheda complain that the knight's presence will make it more difficult to decide who will receive the honor of bathing in the fountain. Sir Luckless offers to withdraw, but Amata enjoins him to remain and aid them on their quest. The quartet faces three obstacles before reaching the fountain: a giant white worm,[21] a mysterious piece of earth, and an impassable stream. Working backward through the three obstacles, we will examine the names Amata, Altheda, and Asha.

Amata, the third witch, has been jilted by a false lover, and "hoped that the Fountain would relieve her of her grief and longing."[22] At the crest of the hill, an impassable stream blocks the quartet's way. A stone in the stream bears the words *"Pay me the treasure of your past."*[23] Amata uses her wand to extract her memories of the false lover and sends them down the stream. Amata's name is clearly derived from the Latin verb *amare*, "to love"; Granger and Spindler observe that *amata* is the past participle of the verb, as in *amâta est* ("she has been loved").[24] However, her previous relationship was a false love, and the same participle can also be used to say *amâta erit* ("she will have been loved"). In other words, once loved, Amata will be loved again. Her wish is granted, she is relieved of her grief and longing, and her heart is transformed, ready for true love.

Altheda, the second witch, has been robbed of her wand and gold by an evil sorcerer, and "hoped that the Fountain might relieve her of powerlessness and poverty."[25] Halfway up the hill at noon, with the sun overhead, the travelers find their way blocked by words cut into the ground: *"Pay me the fruit of your labours."*[26] Altheda works the hardest to move past the obstacle, and waters the earth with the sweat of her brow, clearing the words away and allowing the group to proceed. Later, when the ailing Asha collapses, Altheda gathers some herbs to mix a remedy. She realizes she can become a healer and "earn gold aplenty!" even without her wand.[27] Granger contends that the name Altheda is related to the name Alethea, from the Greek *alētheia* ("truth").[28] Spindler argues that the name is related to that of the medicinal marshmallow plant, *Althaea officinalis*, derived from the Greek *altho* ("to cure").[29] This is the more likely derivation, for Altheda, like Amata, has her wish granted: she is relieved of her powerlessness and poverty and transformed into a healer by her knowledge of herbology.

Asha, the first witch, suffering from an illness that no other healer can cure, hopes "that the Fountain would banish her symptoms and grant her a long and happy life."[30] At the bottom of the hill, a "monstrous white Worm" blocks their advance and says, *"Pay me the proof of your pain."*[31] Asha feeds the worm with tears of frustration, and the worm allows them to pass up the hill. Later, at the top, Asha is cured by Altheda's medicinal herbs. We are told that she (along with her companions) will lead a long and happy life following the completion of their quest, just as she'd hoped.[32] Granger and Spindler both associate Asha's name with its near homonym, "ashy."[33] Spindler argues that "ash . . . is what remains after calcination in alchemy," and she relates this to the rebirth of the phoenix from its own ashes.[34] Yet as with the pattern established by the names of the other two witches, readers might expect that Asha's name foreshadows her transformed state at the *end* of the quest rather than her raw state at the beginning. Considering Asha's hope to be cured of her illness and restored to life, her name is likely to be derived from the Sanskrit *asha* ("hope") and/or the Arabic name Aisha (*'āsha*: "alive, thriving").[35] No longer ill, unemployed, or heartbroken, the three witches are transformed by their efforts into living, healing, and loving women.

Granger and Spindler both additionally note that each of the witches' names begins and ends with the letter *a*—the first letter of the Greek alphabet, alpha—which represents beginnings.[36] Thus the witches also have embedded within each of their names new beginnings at the end of the quest. This becomes even clearer when the witches reach the fountain. The omega symbol on the fountain, representing the last letter of the Greek alphabet, can be paired with the witches's alpha names to represent the azoth in alchemy. Formed with the first and last letters of the English alphabet, *a* and *z*, the azoth represents completion, fulfilment, and the full circle.[37]

The fourth seeker in the party is unlike his companions in magical ability, gender, and style of name. Sir Luckless is a Muggle knight transported into the garden with the three witches. Observant readers will note that a "single unfortunate" is allowed the chance to bathe in the fountain each year and win "Fair Fortune for ever more."[38] The name Luckless is a clue that he will be that "single unfortunate," for now that the three witches have been transformed, they have no use for the fountain and invite Luckless to bathe. Unlike his fellow seekers, however, his name symbolizes his state at the *beginning* of the quest, rather than the end. And yet, like the witches, he also has embedded within his name a new beginning, because *luck* is found within *luckless* just as *fortunate* is found within *unfortunate*. When Luckless emerges from the fountain with rusted armor and a flushed face, he asks Amata to marry him. She realizes he is worthy of her true love and accepts his proposal. The tale concludes, "All four led long and happy lives, and none of them ever knew or suspected that the fountain's waters carried no enchantment at all."[39]

THE STAGES

Beyond the symbolism of the garden and its contents, and the onomastic symbolism of character names, the plot of "The Fountain of Fair Fortune" is itself symbolic of the alchemical quest, for each stage of the quartet's journey reflects a stage in the process of creating the philosopher's stone. Alchemists write about many different processes involved in the Great Work, and they often disagree on specifics and terms. Nevertheless, three main stages are generally acknowledged: the *nigredo*, the *albedo*, and the *rubedo*.

In the initial stage of the alchemical process, the impure raw material "or the old, outmoded state of being is killed, putrefied and dissolved" in the alchemist's alembic (that is, vessel), immolated by fire, calcinated, and reduced to dark ashes.[40] This is called the *nigredo*, or black stage. Asha, the first witch, is surrounded by images of blackness and death, including the black dress she wears, the cane she walks with, and the sword Sir Luckless wields in the author's original illustration of the four seekers available in some editions of *The Tales of Beedle the Bard*.[41] The white worm also signifies death; as Abraham writes, "the mercurial worm devours the old corrupt body" and reduces it to "dust or ashes."[42] Recall Granger's and Spindler's observations that Asha's name sounds like the black ashes left in the alembic.[43] The sound of Asha's name points to her corrupt body, while its Arabic meaning signals the new life she will experience at the completion of the quest.

The second stage of the alchemical transformation involves washing the burned matter in the alembic with mercurial waters, turning it a brilliant white.[44] For this reason it is called the *albedo*, or white stage. The *albedo* is also associated with the silver of mercury. Amata, the third witch, is surrounded by white and silver imagery, including her white gown in the author's illustration, the crystal waters of the fountain, the silver shield Sir Luckless attempts to float across the stream, and the stream's clear waters, where Amata casts her memories.

Distillation—purifying by heating and cooling—continues until the white matter in the alembic turns red, a process "sometimes likened to blushing . . . frequently likened to staining with blood."[45] For this reason, it is called the *rubedo*, or red stage. Sir Luckless is surrounded by red imagery, including a ruby sunset when they reach the fountain, rusty armor, and a flushed face.

There is a fourth character in the tale: Altheda, the witch who lost her wand. There is also a fourth stage of the alchemical process found especially in texts written before the fifteenth century: the *citrinitas*, or yellowing stage, which occurs between the *albedo* and *rubedo*.[46] This phase sees the transmutation of silver into gold. Metaphorically, it is said to represent the death of the lunar light and the dawning of the solar light.[47] While the moon only reflects the sun's light, the sun creates its own. Seekers in this stage learn to look for inner wisdom. Altheda, the second witch, is surrounded by golden imagery, including the bright sun at noon, the coin with which Sir Luckless attempts to buy their passage, the glittering drops of her sweat, and her later realization that she can earn "gold aplenty" with her knowledge of plants.

Here, the traditional order of the stages—*nigredo*, *albedo*, *citrinitas*, and *rubedo*—has been slightly altered: *nigredo* (Asha), *citrinitas* (Altheda), *albedo* (Amata), and *rubedo* (Sir Luckless). The author has used this idiosyncratic order before in the Triwizard Tournament in *Goblet of Fire*. As Hobbs observes, the tasks of the tournament correspond to the major stages of the alchemical process.[48] Yet there are not merely three tasks (dragons, lake, maze/graveyard); there are four, because the riddle of the golden egg must be solved before the task in the lake is revealed. The four steps of the Triwizard Tournament, then, consist of fiery dragon (*nigredo*), golden egg (*citrinitas*), watery lake (*albedo*), and maze/bloody graveyard (*rubedo*; see Table 1).

Placing the albedo stage directly before the rubedo highlights the "chemical wedding," which is a critical final step in the creation of the philosopher's stone, as it represents the reconciliation of two opposing elements in the transmutation process: white mercury (also known as quicksilver) and red sulfur. Mercury is related to the moon, coolness, and the feminine principle, while sulfur is related to the sun, heat, and the masculine principle. Alchemists believed that the successful chemical union of these opposites, represented by a "quarreling couple," could produce the philosopher's stone. Esoterically, the union represents the resolution of opposition

14. Literary Alchemy in "The Fountain of Fair Fortune"

Table 1. "Alchemical Stages"

Alchemical stages, traditional order	*nigredo* (black)	*albedo* (white)	*citrinitas* (yellow)	*rubedo* (red)
Order of trials in "The Fountain of Fair Fortune"	*nigredo* (Asha: black, death, worm)	*citrinitas* (Altheda: gold, coins, sun)	*albedo* (Amata: silver-white, stream)	*rubedo* (Sir Luckless: red, rust)
Order of tasks in the Triwizard Tournament, *Goblet of Fire*.	*nigredo* (fiery dragon)	*citrinitas* (golden egg)	*albedo* (watery lake)	*rubedo* (maze/ bloody graveyard)

within the seeker(s), symbolized by the marriage of a "red man" to a "white lady." Granger has discussed at length the chemical wedding of red-haired Bill Weasley and silver-haired Fleur Delacour.[49] Another example is the marriage of red-haired Ron Weasley to Hermione Granger, whose first name is derived from the Greek god Hermes, known in Roman mythology as Mercury. In "The Fountain of Fair Fortune" these roles are played by the white woman, Amata, and the red man, Sir Luckless, who become betrothed at the end of the tale.

Abraham also speaks of uniting and reconciling four "quarrelling foes"—the basic elements of fire, earth, air, and water—"in order for harmony to reign" and to produce a fifth perfect element, the quintessence: the philosopher's stone.[50] The quarreling quartet in this tale comprises the four seekers who initially view one another as competitors. Their trials, or obstacles, also represent the four elements: Asha's worm (fire), Altheda's earth (earth), Amata's memories (air), and Sir Luckless's fountain (water). When the tale ends, the four discover they have won more through cooperation than competition, and they "set off down the hill together, arm in arm."[51]

THE FOUNTAIN SYMBOLS

At the heart of the tale is the fountain itself, which, it should be no surprise, is also highly symbolic. The author's original illustration of the fountain consists of four basins ascending a central pillar in the shape of a dragon.[52]

Spindler notes that the dragon is an *ouroboros*, or serpent who eats its own tail. Water sprays from the dragon's mouth and trickles down through the basins to its tail. The water is then pumped back to the top to begin the cycle again.[53] The quest for perfection is never-ending.

Each basin is inscribed with two symbols: an astrological/alchemical symbol and a special symbol (see Table 2). These might be read, in keeping with the quest of climbing a hill, from the bottom to the top: the Deathly Hallows symbol beneath the symbol for Saturn (basin 1), an eye beneath Mercury (basin 2), an omega symbol beneath Jupiter (basin 3), and the moon and sun beneath the symbol for Mars (basin 4). As with the garden setting and the characters' names, the symbols also have alchemical meanings. And, like the characters' names, the symbols also contain encoded information about the quest and the questers.

The four astrological/alchemical symbols represent the four questers. Saturn, the alchemical symbol for lead, is also the symbol for death. Lead is dissolved and burned in the *nigredo*, or black stage, which "removes all the unhealthy matter."[54] Likewise, the mortally ill Asha is cleansed of her illness by the medicinal herbs. Mercury represents the element of mercury and the *albedo*, or white stage, of the alchemical process. As the blackened material is washed to whiteness, Amata's memories of her false love are washed away to purify her heart for true love. Jupiter represents the element of tin, considered "the most perfect of the imperfect metals . . . it takes only a little work to convert it into the perfect metal, gold."[55] In astrology, Jupiter is also associated with the intellect and good fortune. These aspects suggest the *citrinitas*, or yellow stage, and correspond to Altheda, who can earn "gold aplenty" through her knowledge of herbology. Mars, the "red planet," represents the element of iron and the *rubedo*, or red stage, of the alchemical process. Redness, a sword and shield, and rusty armor all point to Sir Luckless, whose status as a knight recalls Ares/Mars, the god of war. Interestingly, read from the bottom up, the astrological symbols represent the traditional order of the four stages of the alchemical process, rather than the author's idiosyncratic order: Saturn (*nigredo*, Asha), Mercury (*albedo*, Amata), Jupiter (*citrinitas*, Altheda), and Mars (*rubedo*, Sir Luckless). The author's original illustration of the fountain may, then, encode remnants of an earlier draft of the tale in which the order of the trials adhered to the traditional alchemical sequence which was later altered to place Amata's

14. Literary Alchemy in "The Fountain of Fair Fortune"

Table 2. "Fountain Symbols"

	Fountain Symbols (read in vertical order from the bottom up)	
Basin 4	Mars (iron, sulfur, sun, red man)	♂
	Moon & Sun / Electrum	☽ ☉
Basin 3	Jupiter (tin, good fortune)	♃
	Omega	Ω
Basin 2	Mercury (quicksilver, moon, white lady)	☿
	Eye	👁
Basin 1	Saturn (lead, death)	♄
	"Deathly Hallows"	⚰

trial (*albedo*) closer to Luckless's (*rubedo*) and their alchemical wedding (although this is merely speculation).

As the astrological symbols relate to each of the four questers, the four special symbols relate to the quest itself. Xenophilius Lovegood explains in *Deathly Hallows* that questers for the three Hallows (i.e. the Elder Wand, the Resurrection Stone, and the Cloak of Invisibility) seek to become masters of Death, similar to ancient alchemists who sought eternal life through their quest for the philosopher's stone.[56] Lovegood says the purpose of wearing the Hallows symbol is "to reveal oneself to other believers, in the hope that they might help one with the Quest."[57] The Hallows symbol on the fountain, then, urges seekers to help one another with their quests. The symbol of an eye perhaps refers to the Eye of Providence, the all-seeing eye of divine protection. As mentioned previously, the omega, the last letter of the Greek alphabet, signifies the fulfilment of the quest. When paired with the alphas in the witches' names, it creates the azoth and represents a cycle of beginnings and endings, like the dragon ouroboros embedded at the center of the fountain.[58] Like the circle, the search for enlightenment is never-ending. Finally, the moon-and-sun symbol on the topmost basin represents the alchemical symbol for electrum, an alloy of silver and gold. Here the symbol represents the union of silver and gold, or the "chemical wedding" which occurs on the summit of the hill between the white lady, Amata (the lover), and the red man, Sir Luckless (the warrior). Summarily, the four special symbols represent qualities needed to complete the quest successfully: cooperation, providence, perseverance, and unity.

DISTILLING MEANING

The author of *The Tales of Beedle the Bard* stated that the stories are "really a *distillation* of the themes found in the Harry Potter books."[59] The word "distillation" has a double meaning. In alchemy, it means "the action of purifying a liquid by a process of heating and cooling." Rhetorically, it means "the extraction of the essential meaning or most important aspects of something."[60] Beedle's "Fountain of Fair Fortune" employs both meanings. In the literal sense, the seekers are purified by their trials as they are heated by the sun and cooled by water (Asha's tears, Altheda's sweat, Amata's stream, and Luckless's fountain). In the rhetorical sense of distillation, this short tale indeed extracts essential meanings from the Harry Potter series.

In *Prisoner of Azkaban*, Harry learns it is not the light of his father's Patronus that guides him, but the light that shines from within himself. Likewise, readers learn that the fountain is not enchanted after all. Instead, each seeker discovers his or her own inner "solar" light, the key to each one's personal transformations. The witches' names, with their initial and final alphas, and the *ouroboros* in the fountain signify new beginnings from

14. Literary Alchemy in "The Fountain of Fair Fortune"

old endings. Illness gives way to thriving life. A knowledge of herbs leads to assurance of plenty. False love gives way to true.

A second lesson this tale shares with the Harry Potter series is that although we must seek answers within ourselves, we cannot succeed alone. Harry could not defeat Voldemort without the Order of the Phoenix, Dumbledore's Army, and so many others. Asha would not have been cured without Altheda's knowledge of herbs. Altheda would not have discovered a new career without Asha's illness. Amata and Luckless would not have found true love and courage without one another's support throughout the quest. It takes all the parts to create a whole: Asha (body), Altheda (mind), Amata (heart), and Luckless (spirit).

Table 3. "Alchemical Correspondences"

Character	Asha	Altheda	Amata	Sir Luckless
Trial / Obstacle	worm (dragon)	earth	stream (memories)	fountain
Element	fire	earth	air	water
Alchemical Stage	nigredo (black)	citrinitas (gold)	albedo (white)	rubedo (red)
Symbol	♄	♃	☿	♂
Planetary Symbolism	Saturn (lead, death)	Jupiter (tin, good fortune)	Mercury (quicksilver, moon, white lady)	Mars (iron, sulfur, sun, red man)
Aspect	body	mind	heart	spirit
Name Meaning	"to live"	"to cure"	"to love"	"unfortunate"

As Table 3 summarizes, "The Fountain of Fair Fortune" is much more than an entertaining fairy tale. It is a carefully constructed alchemical fable. According to Granger, "story, in whatever form, has an instructional or initiatory purpose."[61] This tale, steeped in the symbolism of alchemy and onomastics, tracing four interconnected journeys of personal transformation, is a meditation on several themes from the Harry Potter series: self-reliance and cooperation, providence and perseverance, health, and life and love. As such, "The Fountain of Fair Fortune" truly does serve to *distill* and *reflect* the same universal truths explored in the Harry Potter novels, and thus the tale reflexively deepens rereadings of the original series.

NOTES

1. Sotheby's, "Autograph Manuscript."
2. Groves, "Alchemical Symbolism."
3. Abraham, *Dictionary*, 137–38.
4. Beyer, "Magnum Opus."
5. Groves, "Alchemical Symbolism."
6. Roger, *Initiatory Path*, book jacket.
7. See, for example, Sweeney, "Cracking the Planetary Code"; Andréa, "Alchemy of Harry Potter"; and Geo Athena Trevarthen, *Seekers Guide*.
8. See, for example, Granger, *Unlocking Harry Potter*.
9. Hobbs, "Tri-Wizard Cup," 212–14; and Cohen, *Two Alchemists*, 214, 217.
10. Groves, "Alchemical Symbolism."
11. Granger, "'Fountain of Fair Fortune'"; and Spindler, "Tales."
12. Rowling, *Beedle the Bard*, 21–22.
13. Abraham, *Dictionary*, 84, 83.
14. See, for example, the 1610 frontispiece for François Béroalde de Verville, *L'Histoire Véritable, ou Le Voyage des Princes Fortunez*.
15. Abraham, *Dictionary*, 84.
16. Spindler, "Tales." Spindler is referring to the original edition of the *Tales* featuring the author's own illustrations.
17. Abraham, *Dictionary*, 132.
18. Abraham, 81.
19. Compagnone and Danesi, "Naming Strategies," 133.
20. Rowling, interview by Christopher Lydon.
21. The author is here using the term *worm* in the sense of the Old English *wyrm*, a serpent or a dragon. The Anglo-Saxon poem *Beowulf* refers to the dragon as both a *draca* and a *wyrm*.
22. Rowling, *Beedle the Bard*, 23.
23. Rowling, 30.
24. Granger, "Esoteric Meaning"; and Spindler, "Tales."
25. Rowling, *Beedle the Bard*, 23.
26. Rowling, 28.
27. Rowling, 33.
28. Granger, "Esoteric Meaning"; and Hanks, Hardcastle, and Hodges, *Dictionary*.
29. Spindler, "Tales."
30. Rowling, *Beedle the Bard*, 22.
31. Rowling, 27.
32. Rowling, 35.
33. Granger, "Esoteric Meaning"; and Spindler, "Tales."

14. Literary Alchemy in "The Fountain of Fair Fortune"

34. Spindler.
35. Hanks, Hardcastle, and Hodges, *Dictionary*. Ayesha is also the name of the immortal queen in H. Rider Haggard's *She: A History of Adventure*.
36. Granger, "Esoteric Meaning"; and Spindler, "Tales."
37. Spindler, "Tales."
38. Rowling, *Beedle the Bard*, 22.
39. Rowling, 34–35.
40. Abraham, *Dictionary*, 135.
41. Rowling, *Beedle the Bard*, 26.
42. Abraham, *Dictionary*, 220, s.v. "mercurial worm." The color white is associated with silver and mercury in alchemical symbolism.
43. Granger, "Esoteric Meaning"; and Spindler, "Tales."
44. Abraham, *Dictionary*, 4.
45. Abraham, 174.
46. Abraham, 42. After the fifteenth century, the *citrinitas* was usually merged with the *rubedo*.
47. Hamilton, *Alchemical Process*, 7.
48. Hobbs, "Tri-Wizard Cup."
49. Granger, *Unlocking Harry Potter*, 102–7.
50. Abraham, *Dictionary*, 138.
51. Rowling, *Beedle the Bard*, 34.
52. Rowling, 32.
53. Spindler, "Tales."
54. Abraham, *Dictionary*, 179.
55. Abraham, 110.
56. Rowling, *Deathly Hallows*, 409–10. All Harry Potter book citations in this essay refer to the original Scholastic (US) editions.
57. Rowling, 405.
58. Spindler, "Tales."
59. Sotheby's, "Autograph Manuscript." (emphasis mine).
60. "Distillation," Dictionary.com.
61. Granger, *Unlocking Harry Potter*, 58.

15. Hopelessness and Hope in *The Casual Vacancy*

The Cost and Joy of Discipleship

M. Katherine Grimes

ONE OF MY early fears was that I would be falsely accused of murder. As a teenager, I loved reruns of *Perry Mason*, a television show featuring an attorney who always saved innocent clients. Knowing that Perry Mason was as imaginary as Superman, I was afraid that, like the fictitious lawyer's clients, I would be falsely accused and executed, because in real life there is no Perry Mason.

J. K. Rowling's *The Casual Vacancy* also raises fears. No Harry Potter will save these characters. No Cormoran Strike will restore justice. No Newt Scamander or Albus Dumbledore will reveal the truth behind the myths. Although meetings often take place in a church, Jesus seems absent; and major characters who are Sikh do not seem to find Guru Nanak for most of the novel. The term *casual vacancy* refers to an unexpectedly empty local council seat, but in this novel it might refer to the empty chair where the hero should sit.

The man who should be the hero dies on page five. On Gustav Freytag's famous pyramid of dramatic tragedy, Barry Fairbrother's death is the inciting event. But the rising action for most of the novel is not tragedy but pathos, a Modern cast in a Postmodern world, a great lot of unhappy characters trying to win some game with no clear rules and no prize. What ensues in *The Casual Vacancy* is what might have happened if Voldemort had succeeded in killing one-year-old Harry Potter—no "boy who lived," no hero to fight Death Eaters, defeat evil, and restore order.

Published in 2012, five years after the last Harry Potter book, *The Casual Vacancy* must have shocked Rowling fans who hadn't read a description. Littered with vulgar language and even more vulgar behavior, the novel is definitely not for the *Sorcerer's* or *Philosopher's Stone* reader. It also has nearly as many characters as William Faulkner's Yoknapatawpha County

15. Hopelessness and Hope in *The Casual Vacancy*

or George Eliot's Middlemarch, characters it follows as they plot, struggle, suffer, and fall—or, occasionally, grow.

Set in the fictional English town of Pagford near the fictional city of Yarvil, the novel focuses on the Pagford parish council, those who want to join, and those affected by its decisions. Before the death of Barry Fairbrother, council members are divided. On one side are those who, like him, want to continue to support the Fields, a housing project whose residents struggle with poverty and sometimes addiction, and Bellchapel, an addiction recovery clinic. On the other side are those who want to turn the Fields over to Yarvil, arguing that the housing complex is almost as close to the city as to the town, and who want to end Bellchapel's building lease, forcing clients to take a bus into Pagford instead of walking to the nearby facility.

Barry Fairbrother is the best of both worlds. A product of the Fields, he has become a successful banker and an even more successful human being. When he dies, his squash-playing pal Gavin Hughes realizes "that Barry Fairbrother had been his best friend."[1] The paranoid Colin Wall, who "felt himself to be perpetually the outsider and the oddball, for whom life was a matter of daily struggle," thinks it "a small miracle" that he "had managed to forge a friendship with the cheerful, popular, and eternally optimistic Barry."[2] Fairbrother coached the girls' rowing team—sort of a Dumbledore's Army with oars—giving purpose and pleasure to Krystal Weedon, a Fields girl whose mother is a drug addict, and the child Sukhvinder Jawanda, whose physician mother and a bullying boy have made her so miserable that her greatest relief is cutting herself. As his widow, Mary, says, "Barry wasn't in [the council] for power. . . . He couldn't help himself. . . . He thought everyone was like him, that if you gave them a hand they'd start bettering themselves."[3]

Barry Fairbrother, then, is the moral center of Pagford and of the novel. But Barry Fairbrother is dead.

Those who live on seem to fall into four categories: those who loved Fairbrother and wish to carry on his mission; those who loved him and are devastated by his loss; those who are so self-absorbed that they hardly knew he existed; and those who opposed him.

Those who opposed him seem from the outside to be a self-satisfied lot. They are led by Howard and Shirley Mollison, opponents of the Fields and

Bellchapel Clinic and, consequently, of Fairbrother. Howard Mollison, chair of Pagford Parish Council, owns a delicatessen and a new café, both of which he runs with partner Maureen Lowe. Shirley Mollison manages the council website, albeit ineptly. When her fellow council member dies, she thinks that "she had hated Barry Fairbrother."[4] The casual vacancy provides the Mollisons the opportunity to encourage their son, Miles, to run for the seat.

Among those too self-absorbed to care about Barry Fairbrother or the council are three adults—Samantha Mollison, Simon Price, and Terri Weedon—and two teenagers—Stuart Wall and Andrew Price. Like the plowman in *Landscape with the Fall of Icarus*, attributed to Pieter Brueghel the Elder, they focus on their own quotidian affairs despite the tragedy that has transpired in their midst. Miles Mollison's wife, Samantha, whose boutique is failing, has tired of her husband and her life; her latest thrill is imagining an affair with a young member of a band her daughter likes. Simon Price works for and steals from a printing company, browbeats his wife, and physically and emotionally abuses his sons.[5] He decides to run for the vacant council seat, presuming that the position involves graft. Terri Weedon is a drug addict who vacillates between using heroin and going to Bellchapel Clinic for methadone so that she can keep her children, teenage Krystal and three-year-old Robbie. Stuart Wall, ironically called "Fats" because of his beanpole build, is the adopted son of school deputy headmaster Colin Wall and guidance teacher Tessa Wall. He prides himself on his authenticity, uses Krystal Weedon for sex, and torments Sukhvinder Jawanda on social media. Stuart's friend Andrew (Arf) Price is one of Simon Price's bullied sons, whose oppression is enabled by his mother, Ruth, out of misguided loyalty to her husband. Andrew is infatuated with Gaia Bawden, whose mother, Kay, has recently moved the two of them to Pagford because of Kay's affair with Gavin Hughes.

Those overcome by Barry Fairbrother's death include his widow, two rowing team members, and his friend Gavin Hughes. Mary Fairbrother, who was with her husband when he had a brain aneurism in a parking lot on their anniversary, seems to be a fragile woman, but she is also angry at her late husband, whose volunteer work took him away from her and their four children. Two girls from the rowing team that Barry Fairbrother coached have painful lives that are made even more unbearable by their mentor's death. Sukhvinder Jawanda knows that her parents have more

15. Hopelessness and Hope in *The Casual Vacancy*

pride in their other two children; her family sarcastically calls her "Jolly." As a consequence of her parents' rejection and Stuart Wall's cruelty, she privately cuts herself. Krystal Weedon assumes a great deal of responsibility for her little brother, Robbie. She also has no filter; she curses all the time, moons an opposing rowing team, and generally sparks awe among her less bold classmates. Gavin Hughes is focused on ending his relationship with Kay Bawden, as he wanted only a casual affair. Gavin admired Barry Fairbrother but is not motivated to take on civic responsibility by this friend's death.

Colin Wall, on the other hand, is motivated to run for the vacated seat, despite his constant paranoia that he will do something terrible, such as touch a child inappropriately. Like the physician Parminder Jawanda, who already serves on the parish council, he wants to carry on Barry Fairbrother's legacy. Parminder is motivated both by a genuine concern for the people she serves and by her love for the dead hero, feeling "Barry's absence like a ghost at the table."[6] Although she denies to others and even to herself that she loved the man, she finally concedes, but only to herself, like Mary Magdalene in *Jesus Christ, Superstar*, "Perhaps I did love him."[7]

Thus Rowling has given us the exposition, the inciting event, and now the beginning of the rising action: three entries into the campaign to fill the vacant seat. A further complication arises when Andrew Price hacks into the parish council website and, under the username "The_Ghost_of_Barry_Fairbrother," posts the truth about his father's thefts.[8] Although Shirley Mollison eventually removes the post, Simon is fired. He quits the race for the council seat and orders his sons to help him toss the stolen computer into the river. Andrew shares his knowledge of how to hack the council site with Stuart Wall, who uses it to expose his father's paranoia to get revenge for Colin's not having wanted to adopt him, although Colin's reluctance was related to his terror of harming a child. Sukhvinder Jawanda, as "Barry Fairbrother's Ghost," then exposes her mother's love for the late council member, and Andrew and Simon Price, in a strange act of conspiracy, expose Howard Mollison's affair with his business partner, Maureen Lowe.

Meanwhile Krystal's grandmother, Catherine Weedon, called Nana Cath, dies. In a comment on a *Hogwarts Professor* post by John Granger, Susan Raab points out that this death occurs at almost the exact midpoint of the novel and that Nana Cath's "death and funeral trigger the tragic series of consequences that lead to Krystal's rape and ultimate demise."[9] Thus perhaps Catherine Weedon's death is the novel's climax, the point after which Krystal cannot be saved. Nana Cath has been much more of a mother to Krystal than Terri, and the grief-stricken and angry Krystal blames her grandmother's physician, Parminder Jawanda, for the death. Krystal is also raped by her mother's heroin supplier, Oboo. Afraid that she will get pregnant from the rape and aware of Terri's uselessness in rearing Robbie, Krystal paradoxically decides to have unprotected sex with Stuart Wall, hoping to become pregnant with his child so that the council will provide housing for her and her brother separately from their mother.

Thus the novel's catastrophe arrives, a catastrophe in both dramatic and literal terms. Krystal and Stuart have sex beside the river, leaving three-year-old Robbie unattended. In a failed Good Samaritan[10] kind of story, three characters—like the priest and the Levite in Jesus's parable[11]—see Robbie on his own and leave him while they go about their dreary lives. Gavin Hughes has just declared his love to Mary Fairbrother and been rebuffed. Samantha Mollison is guiltily remembering kissing Andrew Price in the kitchen during a party the night before. Shirley Mollison—who, J. K. Rowling points out, is a foil to Barry Fairbrother because of her opposite trajectory from a painful childhood to a self-satisfied adult[12]—has just learned from "The Ghost of Barry Fairbrother" about her husband's affair and has contemplated using an EpiPen to cause Howard to have a heart attack so that she can be a pitiable widow like Mary Fairbrother. Thus when they see little Robbie walking around looking for a drink, Gavin, Samantha, and Shirley walk away.[13]

Predictably, Robbie drowns. Our Good Samaritan, Sukhvinder Jawanda, jumps into the river to try to save him, but the current prevents her from pulling him out in time. A man walking his dog pulls Robbie and Sukhvinder from the water but, despite a concerted effort, cannot save the boy. Left with nothing but grief and guilt, Krystal goes to her family's flat, finds her mother's heroin and syringe, and kills herself.[14]

With the tragedy of Robbie and Krystal Weedon and the heroism of Sukhvinder Jawanda, this novel that has been filled with pettiness and pathos changes course. The falling action certainly exudes a sense of the tragic.

15. Hopelessness and Hope in *The Casual Vacancy*

The haughty have been brought down. Council chair Howard Mollison has been exposed as an adulterer by his lesbian daughter, who, because the Mollisons overlook her partner, reveals that she discovered the affair at the age of twelve in a sort of Biff-and-Willy-Loman moment; at the end of the novel Mollison is in the hospital following a heart attack (not brought on by an EpiPen). Simon Price has tossed his stolen computer into the river and lost his job. And Stuart (Fats) Wall, who has thought that "true authenticity could not exist alongside guilt and obligation,"[15] must acknowledge his role in Robbie's death. Rowling writes, "He kept imagining the funeral. A tiny little coffin.... Would the weight of the dead child ever lift from him?"[16] Unlike Draco Malfoy, who is never redeemed, Stuart Wall shows that at least he can feel guilt, even if his concern about that guilt is its weight on his conscience.

The petty are less petty. The self-satisfied Shirley Mollison's awareness of her husband's affair spoils her view of her standing in the town, and she has faced her guilt over contemplating murder. Samantha Mollison has reached her nadir by kissing a teenager and has stopped fantasizing about twenty-year-olds while having sex with her husband. Gavin Hughes, who rejected Kay Bawden, has been rejected by Mary Fairbrother.

And many of the pitiful have become less pitiable. Sukhvinder's courage has saved her, the way Neville Longbottom's saves him. Andrew Price has avenged himself on his father and is no longer under Stuart Wall's influence. Mary Fairbrother has substituted anger for some of her grief at her husband's death.

Terri Weedon remains perhaps the most pitiful and pitiable of all. Rejected by her own family, she has avoided her own mother's funeral. A drug addict used by her supplier to store contraband, she has now lost her children primarily due to neglect. When the police inform her of Robbie's death, her neighbors form "a fascinated audience.... Nobody stepped forward to comfort or calm. Terri Weedon had no friends."[17] However, at the end of the funeral for Terri's children, "her family half carried Terri Weedon back down the royal blue carpet."[18]

So is *The Casual Vacancy* a Modern novel? Postmodern? A tragedy? A tragicomedy? With a dead hero on page five, the novel certainly has characteristics of the Modern novel: lack of authentic communication, presentation of characters' inner thoughts, and a sense of meaninglessness and despair. However, much of the book rejects the Modern novel's seriousness, giving it a Postmodern feel. It certainly has tragic events: Barry Fairbrother's death, Krystal Weedon's rape, and Krystal and Robbie's deaths. However, Fairbrother doesn't bring about his own death in the Aristotelian sense, due to some tragic flaw, and Krystal is not of sufficiently high status to qualify as a tragic heroine. At the same time, both Lev Grossman of *Time*[19] and Allison Pearson of the *Telegraph* describe *The Casual Vacancy* as, among many other adjectives, "funny"; Dan Kois of *Slate* writes that "Rowling remains one of the funniest writers in the English language"; and Malcolm Jones of the *Daily Beast* calls the novel "a comedy, but a comedy of the blackest sort"[20]; and after the horrors of the drowning and suicide, the final pages are more uplifting than the first six hundred or so. Perhaps *The Casual Vacancy* qualifies as a tragicomedy. J. K. Rowling herself called it a "comic tragedy."[21]

Ian Parker in the *New Yorker*, on the other hand, writes that Rowling's novel has "a kind of Thomas Hardy finale,"[22] and Rowling quotes Hardy in a lengthy discussion of the book.[23] If Tess Durbeyfield were projected a century into the future, she could be Krystal Weedon, victim of an absent father and a drug-addicted mother instead of alcoholic parents. Fanny Robin of *Far From the Madding Crowd* is also Krystal's literary ancestor, used for sex and deserted. All three women die; each loses a child. Although Tess and Fanny are humbler—more Sukhvinder than Krystal—all are victims of a society that sets them up for misery, then condemns them. In fact, almost all the characters in *The Casual Vacancy* are victims of society or their own weaknesses or pettiness, with free will limited by biology (Barry Fairbrother's aneurysm), economics (the Weedons' poverty), and environment (the provincial limitations of Pagford). Thus, despite being published almost a hundred years after the Naturalistic period of Western literature ended, *Vacancy* feels more like a Naturalistic novel than any other type.[24]

If *The Casual Vacancy* is Naturalistic, then a new question arises: can a Naturalistic novel have a true hero, or does it just have a victim who endures as long as possible, then dies, like Tess and Krystal? In Rowling's novel, it seems that almost everyone is a victim of something, but usually that is the person's own weaknesses and selfishness. The people of Pagford are left like the disciples after Jesus's death and the Hogwarts students just

15. Hopelessness and Hope in *The Casual Vacancy*

after Harry, Ron, and Hermione go on the quest to destroy Horcruxes in *Deathly Hallows*. Those left behind cannot find their way because they are not sure what the way is.

With no heroes—no epic Beowulf to kill Grendel, no tragic Oedipus to poke his eyes out, no fantastic Harry Potter to defeat Voldemort, no Moses to lead Pagford to the Promised Land, and no Jesus to forgive the council members who want to wash their hands of the Fields and the Bellchapel clients—we have instead all these Modern, misunderstood, misguided characters who, like J. Alfred Prufrock, keep hoping that the mermaids will sing to them but know they never will.

The characters are left like Flannery O'Connor's Misfit, who says while his henchmen are killing a family, "Jesus thown everything off balance. . . . If He did what He said, then it's nothing for you to do but thow away everything and follow Him, and if He didn't, then it's nothing for you to do but enjoy the few minutes you got left the best way you can. . . . I wisht I had of been there. . . . It ain't right I wasn't there because if I had of been there I would of known."[25]

However, the disciples become apostles, and Neville Longbottom revives Dumbeldore's Army. Sukhvinder Jawanda, too, was walking in misery, just like the others who saw Robbie. The night before, her friend Gaia kissed Stuart Wall, the bully who had tortured Sukhvinder on social media, posting photos of a woman with a beard and comments such as "the hairy man-woman" and "The Bearded Dumbbell" on her Facebook page.[26] Even though she fails to save Robbie, Sukhvinder's action saves herself. Rowling writes, "Just as Robbie had come out of the river purified and regretted by Pagford, so Sukhvinder Jawanda, who had risked her life to try and save the boy, had emerged a heroine."[27] Water is almost always transformational in literature. Sukhvinder is born again after her plunge into the river. Like Guru Nanak, the founder of the Sikh religion, she disappears into a river. While she is not under the water for three days, as legend says he was, she does emerge with wisdom and truth. Guru Nanak, the story goes, came out of the water saying, "There is no Hindu, there is no Muslim." Sukhvinder comes out of the water no longer the miserable victim but now, in another irony, the true Jolly. Her mother, who until this point has blatantly criticized her, now is "finding excuses to touch her."[28] Sukhvinder three weeks after her heroic action is no longer cutting herself; "her near drowning seemed to have purged her of the need."[29] The new Sukhvinder organizes the funeral for Robbie and Krystal, her former rowing teammate, and, with her mother's help, coordinates a fundraiser to pay for the children's coffins.

In the end, perhaps *The Casual Vacancy* is a religious book, or at least a moral one. In fact, in an interview with the *New Yorker*'s Ian Parker, J. K. Rowling said, "Mortality, morality, the two things I obsess about."[30] The connection with religion here is not to assert that Barry Fairbrother is Moses or Jesus or Guru Nanak. However, his effect on people, at least the right sort of people, is inspiring in the way that those religious leaders inspire: his death prompts his opponents to double down on their opposition to his goodness and his friends to work to fill the void he has left and carry on his mission.

Rowling's interest in morality is suggested in *The Casual Vacancy* by numerous references to churches. At least three Christian church buildings are mentioned: the empty, ruined abbey that stands between Pagford and the Fields; a "pretty Victorian church" where the council meets;[31] and a "mock-Gothic church" where Barry and Mary Fairbrother's daughters appear in *Joseph and the Amazing Technicolor Dreamcoat.*[32] In addition, Shirley and Howard Mollison live on Church Row, and the Jawandas live in the Old Vicarage. The funerals of both Barry Fairbrother and the Weedon children take place in St. Michael's Church, and all three are buried in the church graveyard.

However, church references do not necessarily endorse conventional religion. The abbey is a ruin. The "mock-Gothic" and "pretty Victorian" churches are not discussed in religious terms. The Mollisons are not noted for their Christian charity. The Jawandas are Sikh, although Vikram is not religious. And the Weedon children's funerals are somewhat empty; Sukhvinder, waiting in vain for the vicar to say something real about Krystal, reminisces about a time her late rowing teammate got the upper hand on a rowing team by mooning and insulting them. Christianity is not criticized directly, but we do not see it actively practiced.

We *do* see direct criticism of false religion or misplaced worship in Andrew Wall's thoughts about his family, who live in Hilltop House. Remembering his class on religion and philosophy, Andrew thinks about the "arbitrary wrath and violence" of "primitive gods" and "attempts of earlier civilizations to placate them."[33] He relates this scenario to the relationship between his parents, with "his father as a pagan god" and "his mother as the high priestess of the cult, who attempted to interpret and intercede, usually failing, yet still insisting . . . that there was an underlying magnanimity and reasonableness to her deity."[34] Considering the misery and undeserved suffering endured by some characters, one might wonder whether J. K. Rowling is writing here about adherents to all religions who try but fail to find magnanimity in their gods.

Religion, then, does not come in traditional Christian terms or from the church; in fact, the most traditionally religious character is Parminder Jawanda, who is Sikh.[35] Although we get part of the story of Guru Nanak from Sukhvinder (whose classmates express incredulity at the story of his returning after three days under water, even though presumably the Christians among them believe that Jesus rose from the dead after three days), it is her mother who practices her religion. Parminder Jawanda remembers telling Barry Fairbrother about Bhai Kanhaiya, a Sikh man who cared for men injured in battle, no matter what side they fought on, because "the light of God shone from every soul."[36] Parminder realizes that she has not followed that teaching, although Fairbrother did, and she is "ashamed."[37]

Parminder also adheres to the law, not moral obligation to human life, when she refuses to attend to Howard Mollison following his heart attack. When Miles begs her to help his father, she says that she cannot come, as she has been suspended from medical practice for breaking doctor-patient confidentiality. Like the priest and Levite in the story of the Good Samaritan and like Gavin Hughes, Samantha Mollison, and Shirley Mollison, she turns her back on someone in need, despite having almost certainly taken a Hippocratic Oath. Granted, the Mollisons have been instrumental in her suspension, but she still can be blamed for failing to help a person in mortal danger.

But Parminder responds differently when Sukhvinder decides to help with the Weedon children's funeral. Parminder has considered repeatedly that her daughter "might have died!"[38] and agrees to help her daughter, thinking "The light of God shines from every soul."[39] At this point Parminder truly seems to believe that quotation, which might very well be the theme of the novel.[40]

Three reasons might account for the emphasis J. K. Rowling places on Sikhism in *The Casual Vacancy*: universality, unity, and discipleship. In the *janam-sakhis*, or legends about Guru Nanak's life written half a century and more after his death, it is reported that when Guru Nanak emerges from his three days underwater, he says, "There is neither Hindu nor Muslim."[41] The first words of the Guru Granth Sahib, the holy book of the Sikh faith, are "Ek Onkar, God is One."[42] The book contains Muslim and Hindu poems as well as Sikh hymns. In fact, M. S. Kalsi, himself a Sikh, says that he knows Hindu families who designate one of their sons as Sikh, signifying the lack of exclusivity between those faiths.[43] As Harvard University's Pluralism Project explains in its entry on Sikhism, the religion does not divide people into believers and nonbelievers, and it proclaims "the kinship of all people," as well as "the equality of men and women."[44] Unlike many religions, including Orthodox Judaism, some branches of Evangelical Christianity, and Islam, in which often only men are educated in the faith, Sikhism educates both men and women, for Guru Nanak saw all people as equal, no matter their caste or gender. Kalsi points out that one of his sisters knows far more about the Granth Sahib than he does, because although they both studied the scriptures in school, she has continued to study on her own far more than he has.[45] Both Parminder and Vikram Jawanda are physicians; they are on a more equal level professionally than most couples in the novel. The emphasis on inclusivity and equality reflects the concepts of universality and unity.

It is the importance of discipleship in Sikhism, however, that seems most relevant to *The Casual Vacancy*; in fact, "Sikhs call their tradition of belief and practice the Sikh Panth, meaning the 'community of the disciples of the Guru.'"[46] Before Guru Nanak died, he appointed a successor. The succession of gurus continued for ten generations, ending with the book of scriptures, itself designated a guru. *Guru* means "teacher," just as in Hinduism, for Nanak was born into a Hindu family; *sikh* means "student" or "learner." Thus, the significance of discipleship is imbedded in two of the most important words of Sikhism.

Parminder Jawanda sees herself as a disciple of Sikhism, even as she realizes that she is a flawed disciple. But it is Sukhvinder who is the true disciple, both of Guru Nanak and of Barry Fairbrother. Fairbrother saw the light of God in the people of the Fields, Bellchapel Clinic clients, and

15. Hopelessness and Hope in *The Casual Vacancy*

girls on the rowing team, especially Krystal Weedon. Sukhvinder, too, sees the light of God in Krystal and in Krystal's brother, Robbie. It is the light of God in herself that she has trouble finding, until the end of the novel.

Discipleship is certainly not limited to Sikhism. In the book of Deuteronomy in the Torah, Moses appoints Joshua to succeed him as leader of the Hebrew people. In the book of Matthew in the Christian New Testament, Jesus says to Simon, "And I tell you, you are Peter, and on this rock I will build my church."[47] Jesus also instructs Peter, "Feed my sheep,"[48] and he disperses his twelve disciples to "proclaim the kingdom of God and to heal the sick."[49] Upon his death, Jesus's disciples take up his mission. Confucius claimed seventy-seven true disciples in his lifetime. Gautama Buddha's disciples traveled with him and continued to spread his teachings after his death.[50] Without disciples, every religion would die.

The teachings and example of Barry Fairbrother do not die. They surpass the pettiness and selfishness and foolishness of most characters in the novel. Those who cannot follow his example are defeated, but those who can follow usually prevail.

Even as she plans her suicide, Krystal Weedon remembers the three people who have loved her: her brother, Robbie; her grandmother, Nana Cath; and her mentor, Barry Fairbrother—the three people she sees as almost purely good. Thus she dies "in hope and without regret."[51] In a cryptic statement, Rowling points out that Krystal joins her brother in death. One can read belief in an afterlife into that statement or see it as meaning only that both are dead.

Andrew Price realizes that his mother sees the family's move, necessitated by his father's need for a new job, as a sacrifice. He perceives that she hopes "in her perennially optimistic way" that "they would be rewarded with a rebirth."[52] Andrew is the insightful teenager who realizes what other people are like, yet does not reject them.

And at the end of the novel, as a grieving Terri Weedon is being half dragged from the church, Sukhvinder Jawanda remembers not just Barry Fairbrother, whose name certainly echoes justice and community, but his disciple, Krystal Weedon, who "faced the world" in a way that protected the rowing team. Sukhvinder remembers Krystal carrying Robbie's picture as a good luck charm. And Sukhvinder remembers following Krystal into a tough rowing competition with both "faith and fear."[53]

We usually define a hero by what he does. But perhaps he should be defined by whom he inspires. In *The Casual Vacancy*, Barry Fairbrother inspires people who love and follow him to find the god within themselves and the light of God in every soul. Thus the hopelessness that his friends and loved ones feel at his death moves to hope as his disciples eventually step forward.

NOTES

1. Rowling, *Casual Vacancy*, 31.
2. Rowling, 179.
3. Rowling, 580.
4. Rowling, 18.
5. If Simon Price seems incredibly vile, compare him to Lt. Col. Wilbur "Bull" Meechum in South Carolina author Pat Conroy's 1976 novel *The Great Santini*; Conroy says in a 2002 *Fresh Air* interview with Terry Gross that the character is based on his own abusive father. See "Remembering 'Great Santini' Author Pat Conroy," NPR, March 11, 2016, https://www.npr.org/2016/03/11/469944762/remembering–great–santini–author–pat–conroy.
6. Rowling, *Casual Vacancy*, 371.
7. Rowling, 439.
8. Rowling, 309.
9. Susan Raab, comment on Granger, "Casual Vacancy 7."
10. In a *Hogwarts Professor* post, John Granger points out parallels between the failure of several characters in Robbie's death and Jesus's parables in the book of Luke, noting that others have commented on those connections. Granger, "Casual Vacancy 15."
11. Luke 10:25–37.
12. Brown, "How She Crafts."
13. The fact that three adults ignore a preschooler wandering alone seems unfathomable. Because I am white, if one of my Ethiopian children went to get a drink refill in a restaurant, African American adults would look around for black parents, then ask my son where his parents were, even when the boys were already in elementary school. Those adults would never have walked past a preschooler alone.
14. In the HBO three-part miniseries *The Casual Vacancy*, based on Rowling's novel, screenwriter Sarah Phelps changes many aspects of the book, but the most drastic—and I believe mistaken—change is the ending: Robbie is saved by Vikram Jawanda, husband of Parminder and father of Sukhvinder, who has been fairly insignificant throughout the rest of the series, and Krystal drowns trying to save Robbie instead of committing suicide. Sukhvinder Jawanda's role is greatly minimized. Thus the series misses much of both the tragedy and the heroism of the novel's ending. While the show has some lovely moments, it differs significantly from Rowling's book.
15. Rowling, *Casual Vacancy*, 548.

15. Hopelessness and Hope in *The Casual Vacancy*

16. Rowling, 606.
17. Rowling, 611.
18. Rowling, 639.
19. Grossman, "*Casual Vacancy.*"
20. Rowling, *Casual Vacancy*, front matter.
21. Trachtenberg and Sher, "Rowling's Personal Struggle."
22. Parker, "Mugglemarch."
23. Brown, "How She Crafts."
24. In her 2020 book *Murder, in Fact: Disillusionment and Death in the American True Crime Novel*, Lana A. Whited argues that Naturalism persisted at least through the publication of Truman Capote's 1965 book *In Cold Blood*.
25. O'Connor, "Good Man," 151.
26. Rowling, *Casual Vacancy,* 185.
27. Rowling, 629.
28. Rowling, 629.
29. Rowling, 629.
30. Parker, "Mugglemarch."
31. Rowling, *Casual Vacancy,* 65.
32. Rowling, 4. The story of Joseph and his brothers in Genesis has similarities to *The Casual Vacancy* in the conspiracy of one group—Mollison and other council members (Joseph's brothers)—against a far superior person, Barry Fairbrother (Joseph). Sukhvinder Jawanda, too, emerges like Joseph, rising above her tormenters.
33. Rowling, *Casual Vacancy,* 216.
34. Rowling, 216–17.
35. John Granger calls one of his *Hogwarts Professor* posts about *The Casual Vacancy* "Christian Hypocrites and Sympathetic Sikhs."
36. Rowling, *Casual Vacancy,* 437.
37. Rowling, 438.
38. Rowling, 602.
39. Rowling, 630.
40. Upon reading Parminder's quotation, certainly every American literature student hears the echo of Walt Whitman: "In the faces of men and women I see God, and in my own face in the glass."
41. Groves, "'Nagini Maledictus.'" Groves points out the similarity between the statement attributed to Guru Nanak and the declaration by Paul in the Christian New Testament: "There is neither Jew nor Greek, there is neither slave nor free, and there is neither male nor female, for you are all one in Christ Jesus." Galatians 3:28, New English Version.
42. Harvard University, "Sikhism."
43. Kalsi, interview.
44. Harvard University, "Sikhism."
45. Kalsi, interview.
46. Harvard University, "Sikhism."
47. Matthew 16:18 (New Revised Standard Version).

48. John 21:17 (NRSV).
49. Luke 9:2 (New International Version).
50. The question of whether Buddhism is a religion or a philosophy is not really relevant here, but I am aware that both sides of that question have advocates.
51. Rowling, *Casual Vacancy*, 612.
52. Rowling, 632.
53. Rowling, 638.

16. Parenting Models in the Potter Saga and *Cursed Child*

Human and Divine

Emily Strand

FROM *Sorcerer's Stone* to *Cursed Child*, Harry Potter is a story about parents and children. While the overarching narrative focuses on Harry's stand against Voldemort's bloody quest for immortality, one crucial way the narrative cultivates proper attitudes toward human mortality is through its depiction of various parent-child interactions. Some of the books' parent-child relationships are recognizable as caricatures of parenting models identified by modern psychology and as cautionary tales regarding those models' child outcomes. Four families in Potter represent the range of possibilities the text envisions: the Dursleys, the Malfoys, the Grangers, and the Weasleys. But the parent-child relationships idealized in the series are not necessarily practical. Rather they are constructed and symbolic, rooted in a Christian worldview that envisages humans in relationship with an earthly mother who bridges the magical and nonmagical worlds, providing an essential model of self-sacrifice, and a loving, numinous Father who mysteriously requires trust and obedience. Potter's conclusions about parenting are deeply influenced by Christian theology, especially in its affirmation of relationships that image the divine.

Moreover, parent-child relationships in the series are significant because they form the only viable path to immortality. This immortalizing understanding of parenting contextualizes both the centrality of parenting to the narrative and the emphasis on the next generation in the series' epilogue. But not just any style of parenting makes one immortal. The narrative sends a message in the parent-child relationships it depicts: one's method of parenting matters—and matters ultimately. *Cursed Child* supports and furthers this message, cautioning that even Harry, who himself benefited from the saga's ideal form of parenting, can find himself parenting his own son poorly, with potentially disastrous results.

16. Parenting Models in the Potter Saga and *Cursed Child*

POTTER'S PARENTS: FOUR [HUMAN] MODELS ON DISPLAY

Building on Diana Baumrind's groundbreaking work on parenting styles from the 1960s,[1] modern psychologists continue to identify distinct types or models of parenting constructed from dimensional scales of parental warmth and parental control.[2] These main types include authoritarian-autocratic (low warmth, high control), indulgent-permissive (high warmth, low control), indifferent-uninvolved (low warmth, low control), and authoritative-reciprocal (high warmth, high control).[3] Rowling seems at least superficially or observationally aware of these four styles of parenting, for she depicts all four among the parents who populate the pages of her Hogwarts saga. In her series, four sets of parents particularly embody the modern psychological construct.

"Mr. and Mrs. Dursley, of number four, Privet Drive, were proud to say that they were perfectly normal, thank you very much."[4] Rowling's introduction of the Dursleys flags them as typical, average people, but as the reader gets to know them in the book's early chapters, it becomes clear that they are not only the "worst sort of Muggles"[5] but also the worst sort of parents. In fact, this unfortunate couple is a devastating caricature of poor parenting in more ways than one. The variety of their poor parenting stems from their egregiously inequitable treatment of the two children under their care: their biological son, Dudley, to whom they are permissive and indulgent, and their nephew, Harry.

To Harry, the Dursleys are a brazen example of the authoritarian-autocratic pattern, in which "parents' demands on their children are not balanced by their acceptance of demands from their children."[6] These parents do not tolerate challenges to their authority, and when "children deviate from parental requirements, fairly severe punishment (often physical) is likely to be employed."[7] The authoritarian, abusive nature of the Dursleys' style of parenting Harry is well documented. Danielle M. Provenzano and Richard E. Heyman chart instances of the Dursleys' neglect and abuse, both emotional and physical, toward Harry, pointing up instances of Harry having frying pans thrown at his head, being choked, and generally subjected to a routine pattern of physical abuse: "long experience had taught [Harry] to remain out of arm's reach of his uncle whenever possible."[8]

Child outcomes for the authoritarian-autocratic pattern include unhappiness, social withdrawal, anger and defiance (especially in boys),[9] anxiety, and depression.[10] While these outcomes do not affect Harry to any significant degree,[11] they certainly affect Merope Gaunt, the abused daughter of Marvolo Gaunt, the other clearly authoritarian-autocratic parent depicted in the Potter saga, and Merope's treatment at the hands of both her father and her brother in the single scene in which she appears ("The House of Gaunt," in *Half-Blood Prince*) recalls Harry's treatment by the Dursleys. Unlike Harry, however, Merope exhibits the associated child outcomes of authoritarian-autocratic parenting. Harry describes her as the most "defeated-looking person" he has ever seen.[12] She appears anxious (facial blanching, shaking hands) and incapable of meaningful social interaction with Bob Ogden.[13] Merope also exhibits signs of depression, manifesting as magical and nonmagical incompetence (dropping pans, using incorrect spells), and *Half-Blood Prince* explicitly links depression to a decline in magical ability, especially in the romantic subplot regarding Tonks and Lupin.[14] Dumbledore confirms this association between Merope's abuse and her magical incompetence, suggesting that once her abusers were locked away in Azkaban, she would have been "able to give free rein to her abilities."[15]

As authoritarian-autocratic parents go, the Dursleys get far more narrative space than the Gaunts. Thus they demonstrate that authoritarian-autocratic parents emphasize control, consequently denying the child's independence and individuality.[16] Vernon and Petunia refer to the magical abilities that set Harry apart as his "ABNORMALITY"; Provenzano and Heyman identify this insult as a put-down of Harry's heritage, genetically and culturally.[17] Janet Seden and Sarah Fiona Winters both point out that the Dursleys' poor parenting of Harry throws the differences between Muggle and Wizarding worlds into sharp relief, with Seden suggesting that their weaknesses as parents may stem from their blanket disapproval of "imagination,"[18] a quality she says is essential to healthy, compassionate parenting[19] and which seems essential, in the narrative, to both accepting and participating in Harry's new world of magic.

But the Dursleys' parenting style points up another important disparity. When Albus Dumbledore confronts the Dursleys about their treatment of Harry at the beginning of *Half-Blood Prince*, he brings the great irony that characterizes their parenting to a head: "You have never treated Harry as a son. He has known nothing but neglect and often cruelty at your hands. The best that can be said is that he has at least escaped the appalling damage you have inflicted upon the unfortunate boy sitting between you."[20] Harry has been subjected to authoritarian, abusive parenting, while Dudley's has been indulgent and permissive, and between himself and Dudley, Harry's is the better lot. Winters sums up the overarching message of this ironic, saga-long motif: "because [Harry] still turns out a well-adjusted, intelligent child, the series suggests that children are not stunted by neglect, only by indulgence."[21]

As fascinating as the Dursleys prove, given the diverse forms of their disastrous parenting within the fourfold psychological scheme, it is the Malfoys who more consistently represent the indulgent-permissive pattern. Consider Draco Malfoy's most significant lines of dialogue on the occasion of his and Harry's first, anonymous meeting in Madam Malkin's: " 'My father's next door buying my books and Mother's up the street looking at wands,' said the boy. He had a bored, drawling voice. 'Then *I'm going to drag them off* to look at racing brooms. I don't see why first years can't have their own. *I think I'll bully Father* into getting me one and I'll smuggle it in somehow.' Harry was strongly reminded of Dudley."[22] Draco reminds Harry of Dudley because both Draco and Dudley are products of the indulgent-permissive pattern, in which parental warmth is high, but parental control is low. Maccoby and Martin describe permissive parents as those who "take a tolerant, accepting attitude toward the child's impulses, including sexual and aggressive impulses; who use little punishment, and avoid, whenever possible, asserting authority or imposing controls or restrictions; they make few demands for mature behavior (e.g., manners or carrying out tasks); they allow children to regulate their own behavior and make their own decisions when at all possible."[23]

While Harry and Draco appear to have much in common in the scene described above (two young boys of the same age, headed for the same school, left alone in a tailor's shop by their responsible adults), their disparate upbringings create a chasm between them. Harry is alone because Hagrid looked "a bit sick" and needed a "pick-me-up" after the wild Gringotts cart ride, so although he feels "nervous," Harry must cope.[24] Draco is alone because his parents act as his servants, running his school errands for him, allowing their son's impulses to set the agenda of their shopping trip—even, he claims, permitting themselves to be bullied into unwise purchases by their pampered only child. Although Mr. Malfoy can be critical of his son (as will be apparent), when the Malfoy parents appear throughout the series, indulgence and permissiveness dominate their interactions with Draco.

The Malfoys illustrate the indulgent-permissive pattern in terms of child outcomes as well. This pattern has been shown to produce "bossy, dependent, impulsive behavior in children, with low levels of self-control and achievement and a failure to learn persistence and emotional control."[25] Draco certainly seems to inhabit the "bossy" quality in the scene at Madam Malkin's, and in myriad others as well. Throughout the series, he makes at least seventeen conspicuous references to his father's authority or access to information in order to establish his own,[26] so we can check off "dependent" as a child outcome for Draco as well. Draco demonstrates his impulsivity when he decides to show off his flying skills despite Madam Hooch's express prohibition under threat of expulsion.[27] And although Draco seems an intelligent boy, his father laments his lack of academic achievement to Mr. Borgin in *Chamber of Secrets*: " 'I hope my son will amount to more than a thief or a plunderer, Borgin,' said Mr. Malfoy coldly. . . . 'Though if his grades don't pick up,' said Mr. Malfoy, more coldly still, 'that may indeed be all he is fit for.' "[28] Throughout the series, Draco's successes at Hogwarts fall more into the bureaucratic realm (prefect, Inquisitorial Squad member), and his hatred of Hermione Granger signals both his blood-purity ideology and his jealousy of her many academic achievements, which Draco himself lacks.

E. E. Maccoby and J. A. Martin describe the indulgent-permissive pattern as resulting not simply from an ideology of child freedom but in some instances "undoubtedly [reflecting] parental inattention and indifference,"[29] thus overlapping with another of the four patterns of parenting: the indifferent-uninvolved pattern. In contrast with the indulgent Malfoys, these parents exhibit low levels of both warmth and control, displaying "little interest in being a parent. Communication is limited, nurturance is low," and the child has an excess of freedom to negotiate.[30]

The best example of this style of parenting is the Grangers, Hermione's double-dentist Muggle mum and dad, who seem quite content to drop their daughter off at Hogwarts each fall, then to completely forget about her and (what must seem to them) her bizarre lifestyle. Seden says they are a touchstone for "hands off" parenting, doing just what is needed "with great consistency, but no magic."[31] They have no lines of dialogue throughout seven books (although they appear twice, once with descriptors of their behavior ranging from "nervous" to "shaking with fright.")[32] Rowling has said that she "deliberately kept Hermione's family in the background. You see so much of Ron's family so I thought that I would keep Hermione's family, by contrast, quite ordinary."[33] Their ordinariness contrasts sharply indeed with Ron's family, but even more sharply with their own daughter's unusual giftedness and noble pursuits, such as consistently acing her magical education and annually besting the darkest wizard who ever lived, while her parents care for Muggle teeth, occasionally sending her sugar-free snacks,[34] as if those will be helpful.

The Grangers' withdrawn style has a purposeful trajectory in the narrative, however. The *Harry Potter Lexicon* notes that Hermione becomes less and less involved with her Muggle parents the further she becomes involved in the magical community,[35] and her parents fade even further to the background as the series progresses. This fading foreshadows the moment when they will fade into total parenting oblivion at their daughter's own hand in *Deathly Hallows*; because she has confided dangerous information about Harry to them, she must modify their memories so they assume other identities, move abroad, and "don't know they've got a daughter."[36] The Grangers' apparently indifferent-uninvolved parental pattern is owing to the deep disparity between their mundane lives and the enchanted, dangerous life of their daughter, as opposed to any empirical lack of affection for or interest in such an exceptional daughter. This narrative rationale for the Grangers' aloofness also explains why Hermione exhibits next to none of the child outcomes associated with the indifferent-uninvolved pattern, which include behavioral problems, depression, hostility, attention problems, and homesickness.[37]

It may appear that no parents get parenting *right* in the Harry Potter books. To some extent, this is because, as Deborah Chan points out, "Rowling portrays families as they *are*, rather than how we'd like them to be."[38] But she also calls the Weasleys "good parents, raising children who know they are unconditionally loved, and for the most part they encourage their children's interests and careers."[39] The Weasley family, on the whole, achieves that balance of high parental warmth and control which fosters positive child outcomes: the authoritative-reciprocal pattern, one in which "children are required to be responsive to parental demands, and parents accept a reciprocal responsibility to be as responsive as possible to their children's reasonable demands and points of view."[40]

The Weasleys embody an imperfect give-and-take approach to parenting from the first moments they step into the narrative, as in *Chamber of Secrets*, when Fred, George, and Ron incur Mrs. Weasley's wrath for sneaking out to rescue Harry using Mr. Weasley's flying car. The punitive rant she inflicts upon them is dominated by her own admonitions, without much room for the boys' excuses (which are fairly honorable). Yet on some level she recognizes their point of view, because her tirade fades seamlessly to the provision of a scrumptious breakfast.[41] Her relenting, responsive parental nature does not, however, permit the boys' immediate return to sleep; chores are assigned as usual, because in the Weasley household, parental demands must be honored to at least the same degree as the children's. The boys finish their breakfast and commence their chores while "yawning and grumbling," but not to an extent significant enough for the reader (or likely their mother) to hear.[42]

But Molly doesn't parent alone. Seden notes that Arthur Weasley's character develops more slowly over the series, due to the time he spends on his career with the Ministry, in support of their large family.[43] But, she says, he is "developed into a genial, ordinary, active, authoritative father."[44] Certainly Arthur's moral example of defending Muggles and standing up to bullies such as the Dursleys and Malfoys speaks to his children as loudly as his (usually)[45] amiable demeanor.

Of course, the Weasleys have their family problems, which seem, at least in part, of Arthur and Molly's own making. Some toxic sibling rivalry exists among their offspring, causing the reader to wonder if the Weasleys' give-and-take parenting style might have been more evenly applied, with more consideration for and encouragement of each child's particular gifts. The Weasleys tend to hold all the children to their older, more conventionally gifted children's standard. Lana Whited posits that the children's efforts to distinguish themselves in their achievements exacerbate their sibling rivalry. While the two older boys, Bill and Charlie, distinguish themselves naturally with their impressive gifts and diverse career paths, "Percy flounders because he tries primarily to recreate himself in Bill's image (prefect, head boy, etc.), and, because he does not have a strong sense of identity, he is more preoccupied with the trappings of his achievements (his badge, for example) than with the achievements themselves."[46] His manufactured self-importance makes him a target for his jokester twin brothers, who do not wish to tread the same path as Percy. Their relentless stirring of that pot (cauldron?) pushes Percy's fragile ego too far. This teasing (by which the twins protest their parents' expectations) combines with Percy's differing ideological position regarding the war with Voldemort, creating a painful family rift.

The pressure to distinguish themselves felt among the children (with the possible exception of Ginny, who is distinguished naturally as the only girl)[47] proves particularly crushing to Ron, and his concern over it manifests as early as his initial meeting with Harry on the Hogwarts Express:

> I'm the sixth in our family to go to Hogwarts. *You could say I've got a lot to live up to.* Bill and Charlie have already left—Bill was head boy and Charlie was captain of Quidditch. Now Percy's a prefect. Fred and George mess around a lot, but they still get really good marks and everyone thinks they're really funny. *Everyone expects me to do as well as the others, but if I do, it's no big deal, because they did it first.* You never get anything new, either, with five brothers. I've got Bill's old robes, Charlie's old wand, and Percy's old rat.[48]

Ron's lack of confidence, based on his own comparisons to his brothers (and eventually to Harry), is the very character flaw he must overcome to succeed in the narrative.[49] Thus imperfect parenting serves a narrative purpose; while Arthur and Molly's parenting style should result in exceptionally mature children, Ron's maturation is a haphazard process, and this lends depth to the story. In the end, Ron makes good, rising above and beyond his family's expectations, and his progress and eventual success is deeply satisfying to mark. Chan's observation again seems apt: even when depicting ideal forms of parenting, families in Harry Potter are drawn from life, not from psychology textbooks, and the ups and downs of the Weasleys' family dynamics are one reason this fantasy story "rings true"[50] for real-life readers.

Despite these realistic family troubles, it is difficult to judge Arthur and Molly harshly as parents when all seven children so clearly (if, in Ron's case, eventually) exhibit those desirable child outcomes associated with the authoritative-reciprocal pattern, described by Mullins and Tashjian as "greater child competence, exceptional maturity, assertiveness, and self-control."[51] Whited points to the parents' willingness to include their children in the plans and workings of the Order of the Phoenix,[52] though this inclusion is particularly painful for Molly, whose name suggests a tendency to "mollycoddle" or overprotect. Still, this inclusion of the children in the Order is evidence of the Weasleys' successful negotiation "between providing children with security and granting them their freedom," which Winters says "forms the substance of popular debates over childhood."[53] Striking such a balance is not without cost for Molly and Arthur, even before the death of Fred Weasley in the Battle of Hogwarts. Molly, from the beginning of *Order of the Phoenix* onward, lives in constant fear and dread, admitting to Lupin that even without a boggart's assistance, she experiences premonitory visions and dreams of her husband and children's deaths "all the time."[54] This poignant admission reminds that while authoritative-reciprocal parenting like that of the Weasleys is desirable in so many ways, it is not without its burdens on the parents who practice it.

DIVINE PARENTING IN HARRY POTTER

Sometimes the fourfold psychological construct satisfyingly explains parent-child relationships and outcomes in Potter. In other instances, it does not, as in Harry's and Hermione's cases, in which the negative child outcomes that should accompany their parents' styles of rearing them are (mostly) absent. To say that parents in the series are not drawn from psychology texts is not to deny the influence of psychology on Rowling's characterization; it is simply to say that other arenas of insight also inform the text. One such arena is religious studies, especially Christianity, with its emphasis on divine models for parenting. This lens suggests, for instance, another reason the Dursleys influence Harry so little.[55] It suggests that they are not Harry's operative parents. Looking at the story with an eye to religious symbolism reveals that the more formative parents in Harry's life are his mother Lily and his headmaster Albus Dumbledore, despite her early death and his lack of blood connection. These characters act as Harry's true parental figures, embodying archetypal mother and father roles within the Christian narrative to which Harry's story alludes.

16. Parenting Models in the Potter Saga and *Cursed Child*

Although she dies when her son is but a baby, Lily Evans Potter has a lifelong and overwhelming motherly influence on Harry. First, she was Muggle-born, and this fact, as well as his friendship with Muggle-born Hermione Granger, shapes Harry's empathetic stance toward Muggles. Lily is hardly more than a girl when she gives birth to Harry. Her name symbolizes purity in the Victorian love language of flowers,[56] and her unsullied characterization throughout the series flags her as a wholesome, saintly figure whose memory hovers protectively over Harry as he grows. (James Potter's characterization is less wholesome.) Harry hears over and over that he has his mother's eyes,[57] and this detail points to her enduring influence over him. Harry sees the world as Lily did: with grace and purity. (This parallel in Harry's and Lily's seeing with the same eyes is discussed at length by Catherine Olver in "Eye Wonder? Reflecting Harry in Animal Eyes," chapter 11 of this volume.)

But more of Lily than her memory or perspective accompanies Harry throughout his childhood. Lily left her son a lasting gift through her sacrificial death: a protective charm upon his blood that not only blocked and rebounded Voldemort's killing curse but remains effective (ironically, through his association with her sister, Petunia Dursley) until his childhood is complete.[58] Winters notes this mother's-love protection is unique, unlike other forms of protection Harry receives, such as his father's Invisibility Cloak, which "can be forgotten or misplaced or deliberately set aside. The mother's love protects Harry all the time."[59]

The protection Lily imparts to her son derives from her self-emptying act of willingly intercepting the killing curse Voldemort intended for her child. Her protection is other-focused, standing in sharp contrast to Voldemort's murderous, ego-driven obsession with protecting himself through Horcruxes. And Lily sets the example for Harry's method of protecting those he loves. When Harry, in *Deathly Hallows*, freely chooses to sacrifice himself for the lives of the entire wizarding community, his act effects the same blood charm as his mother cast upon him, protecting his community en masse. Voldemort's charms and curses from that point on are "unable to hold" over the entire gathered crowd. "I've done what my mother did," Harry tells his nemesis. "They're protected from you. Haven't you noticed how none of the spells you put on them are binding?"[60] Voldemort, in his ignorant, series-long dismissal of Lily's protection, fails to anticipate such a turn of events.

Lily's sacrifice is the essential forerunner of her son's more important, more widely reaching sacrifice, and in this way she alludes to Mary, the Mother of Jesus. Christians believe that when the angel Gabriel announced to Mary God's plan of salvation in Christ, and her role in it as the one chosen to bear God's son, she had the freedom to choose her response, and she said yes. Western Catholics call this Mary's *fiat*, a Latin term that sums up her self-emptying response: "May it be done to me according to your word."[61] In so doing, an insignificant young girl from a marginalized group (the Jews) played an important role in the redemption of the world. Saint Irenaeus famously said that Mary, in her *fiat*, "became to herself and to the whole human race a cause of salvation."[62]

Lily alludes to Mary in a few other interesting ways. One is her name; assumedly because of the lily's associations with purity, it also became associated with Mary, who is often depicted holding lilies of white. Ferguson notes that *Lilium candidum*, the Madonna lily, is among the most recognized symbols of the Virgin mother in Christian art.[63] Another way Lily Potter alludes to Mary is through her youth and relative insignificance; she is Muggle-born, and thus marginal and vulnerable, as Mary's Judaism made her. But Lily's Muggle-born status alludes to Mary in yet another way, for while Harry's father James has a noble magical heritage,[64] Harry's mother Lily, like Mary, is of far humbler origins. Yet in her, magic bubbles forth unexpectedly and completely. Lily's Muggle-born status makes her only offspring, Harry, a meeting place between the magic and nonmagical worlds, just as Jesus, for Christians, is the *axis mundi*, the meeting place between heaven and earth.[65] While Lily, because of her early death, cannot mother Harry in conventional ways, her motherhood impacts Harry and the narrative on deeply symbolic levels that allude to the Christian story.

James's role in Harry's parenting is more limited. He is a figure who, like Saint Joseph, provides a noble lineage, which both roots and protects his son (for James, this protection extends through the bequeathed Invisibility Cloak).[66] Carmeli notes that Harry's learning to produce a Patronus Charm in the stag form of his father is "one of the highlights of the series, paternally speaking. Harry finally is able to come to terms with his dead father, introjecting his father's potency and thus resolving the Oedipus complex."[67] Psychologically satisfying as this moment may be, the series goes on through four more books, and in them James is eclipsed by another father figure far more complicated and influential to Harry: Albus Dumbledore.

Chan notes that Rowling populates her world with "found families with no blood ties" and "continually demonstrates that such family ties, based on propinquity, love, friendship and shared ideals" are just as strong as in traditional families,[68] making the case that in the Harry Potter series, "insistence on blood purity is a corrupted way of thinking about kinship and family."[69] Thus we can have no qualm suggesting that Albus Dumbledore is the operative father figure in Harry's life, imparting by installments in every book, as Seden notes, the fatherly advice that guides Harry morally[70] and admitting, in his "we fools who love" speech at the end of *Order of the Phoenix*, to a love for Harry that extends well beyond the teacher and student relationship, echoing, as Winters notes, the painful choices that face parents every day.[71]

Dumbledore is also a dubious figure in Harry's life. Christina Littlefield says that Dumbledore, especially in *Deathly Hallows*, "provides a beautiful metaphor about man's struggle with God," or the "shedding of a childlike, naïve trust and the rebuilding of a stronger, more complicated faith."[72] She provides a compelling reading of Harry's struggle in *Deathly Hallows* to believe in an increasingly dubious Dumbledore and the increasingly perilous mission he left Harry—Horcruxes, not Hallows. Littlefield shows how this struggle fits a biblical pattern of figures who, despite direct knowledge of God, "still doubted that God really knew what he was doing in their lives or in the world."[73] Like Harry, Littlefield notes, these biblical figures affirm their faith by bending their will to God's, which "always proves to be the best path."[74] Littlefield's analysis is particularly compelling in its resonance with other religious readings of the text, particularly those that read Harry as a Christ figure, who is asked by his "father" to sacrifice self for the sake of all. When he proves himself "obedient to death,"[75] his own self-emptying becomes his—and his entire community's—salvation. "Harry," greets Dumbledore in the (religiously referential) King's Cross Station of Harry's vision. "You wonderful boy. You brave, brave man."[76] Harry has indeed gone from boy to man in this moment, not just in age or maturity but also in faith development, learning to trust Dumbledore completely, suppressing his own will to enact his "father's" plan. Littlefield says this makes the Harry Potter books particularly resonant with modern, secular readers for whom, as C. S. Lewis said—and in contrast with the ancient world's relationship with the divine—God is on trial rather than humans.[77]

PARENTING TO LIVE FOREVER

Pointing to Harry's "divine image" parents—Lily and Dumbledore—helps explain his positive (world-saving!) child outcomes, despite the poor parenting he received on Privet Drive. But it doesn't explain the centrality of parenting in the Potter series, which many scholars have noted is a modern example of the school story genre, one typically characterized by the distinct *absence* of parents, rather than, as we see in Potter, a concern with parent-child relationships that borders on the obsessive. Hasn't Rowling said that the Potter books are centrally concerned with death and our human response to it?[78] Why the emphasis on parents in Potter?

Léonie Caldecott sheds light on this puzzle, noting that Voldemort's isn't the only immortality quest depicted in the series: "There is another kind of immortality, even for those who confine themselves to the material sphere: having children. In the Harry Potter books, the happiest family is of course the Weasleys, who have no worldly riches, but they do have as many children as Voldemort has horcruxes."[79] This observation points up the ambivalent depiction of questing after immortality in Harry's story—it is not necessarily a bad quest; it is in fact very human to wish for never-ending life. Harry's and Voldemort's wands have twin cores, after all, because the desire for life everlasting, symbolized by their phoenix feathers, is natural; but one must go about fulfilling the desire to live forever in the right way and not by Voldemort's method of murder and domination.[80] Parenthood, as Caldecott points out, is the vehicle given by the Creator, in the Christian worldview, which enables us to see ourselves and our legacies continue in a new generation, and (we might hope) in the generation after that, and perhaps even the one after that. Voldemort, of course, has no children in the main series, and this is an expression of his disregard for the power of love (which is the ideal if not always actual force behind parenthood)—a disregard Dumbledore frequently notes to Harry in the last pages of each novel and which ultimately leads to the Dark Lord's downfall.

16. Parenting Models in the Potter Saga and *Cursed Child*

Both the beginning and end of *Deathly Hallows* bring to a head this series-long message about parenting as a path to immortality. First, the epitaph from Aeschylus's *Libation Bearers* places hope against "the torment bred in the race, the grinding scream of death" in "the children,"[81] asking a blessing upon them. The "children" in this passage refer not only to the trio and to all the young people who fight against Voldemort but also to the unnamed next generation, who represent the hope of a continuing lineage despite present trials. At the end of *Deathly Hallows*, these "children" have names: James, Albus Severus, and Lily Potter (representing all three of Harry's "parents"),[82] Rose and Hugo Weasley, even Scorpius Malfoy. Tonks and Lupin, who perished in the fight against Voldemort, live on in a glimpse of their son Teddy, kissing his girlfriend on Platform Nine and Three-Quarters,[83] intimating that he too will marry and have children someday, immortalizing both himself and his brave parents in the process.

The diverse styles of parenting Rowling portrays in her series send a message, however, that not just any kind of parenting makes one immortal—the way one parents matters—and matters ultimately. The Dursleys' and Malfoys' parenting styles are riddled with implicit egotism; their authoritarian and indulgent styles are more about themselves than their children, who are but totems of their self-regard.[84] We may be tempted to think that Harry will go on to become the perfect father through the influence of his "divine image" parents, Lily and Dumbledore. He certainly takes an authoritative, responsive, child-centered approach in *Deathly Hallows'* epilogue, when his second son, Albus Severus, expresses anxiety. Harry even crouches down "so that Albus's face was slightly above his own,"[85] a posture promoted by child psychology experts for effective communication with young children.[86]

This expectation is disrupted, however, by the Rowling-sanctioned script for the play *Harry Potter and the Cursed Child*, penned by Jack Thorne.[87] In the play, Harry, despite an ostensibly happy home life, cannot connect with young Albus, whose personality is darker than his father's and who resents his father's fame. Harry is unable to "see" Albus for who he really is,[88] and unlike the approach he takes in the *Hallows* epilogue, Harry cannot focus on his son's needs in *Cursed Child*,[89] or allow the child to make his own choices. It is the very same temptation Dumbledore had to overcome in his "parenting" of Harry in the main saga: the temptation, born of love, to shield Harry from the painful, necessary truth.[90] Harry and Dumbledore (in portrait form) even talk through this aspect of Dumbledore's imperfect "parenting" in a scene toward the end of the play.[91] Winters says this essential lesson for parents is one the Potter saga seeks to convey: the necessity of letting children "die"—in figurative ways, usually—when this is what they need to learn and grow.[92] When Harry cannot allow this, cannot bend his son's will to his own, he asserts an authoritarian control over Albus that would've made Uncle Vernon proud,[93] prompting the boy to rebel to great consequence, nearly allowing an alternate, tragic timeline of life events to take hold, in which Lord Voldemort returns through an evil daughter to prevail over the Wizarding world.

Despite its subversion of our expectations (or perhaps our hopes) for Harry's parenting skills, the play strongly affirms the centrality of parent-child relationships to the Potter story. *Cursed Child*'s plot hinges on the premise that Voldemort had a hidden child, and this revelation, on one hand, reinforces Rowling's theme throughout the Potter series that parenting is a mode of immortality; Voldemort is nearly permitted to return to life and power through the actions of his daughter. Even the announcement of this daughter's unexpected existence, when revealed, ripples like a specter of the Dark Lord himself through the leadership of a wizarding society in which Voldemort has long been defeated.[94] On the other hand, *Cursed Child*'s central premise is out of keeping with Dumbledore's many assertions that Voldemort undervalues the power of love. While the play is mercifully light on the details of his evil daughter's conception, it cannot avoid the suggestion that Voldemort's relationship with the child's mother, Bellatrix Lestrange, possessed an intimacy at least bordering on love.

But the product of Voldemort's relationship with Bellatrix Lestrange—this eponymous "cursed child," variously known as Delphi or Delphini Diggory, the Augury—shows us, much as Tom Riddle did,[95] what sort of immortality is achieved through a union that lacks a true, selfless, loving relationship. Delphi is a liar who represents herself falsely to gain access to Amos Diggory, a manipulator (in general and in a vaguely sexual way of a much younger Albus),[96] and a murderer who kills Hogwarts student Craig Bowker Jr. simply because he is in the way.[97] The characters consider her "fierce"[98] and "a very powerful witch,"[99] but she is fairly easily brought down by the trio and friends in the end (Albus plays a starring role) and reveals herself as more a Voldemort fangirl than the Dark Lord's protégée; after all, she was not raised by either of her biological parents but by a Death Eater guardian who, she earlier claims, "didn't like me much," and "only took me in for the gold."[100] Delphi's deeply flawed character reinforces the notion in the Potter books of the relative insignificance of blood lineage. Rather, a loving, reciprocal relationship must be at the core of the parent-child dyad, instead of mere one-sided admiration or ambition to succeed in the line or image of a biological parent.

CONCLUSION

The strong emphasis on parenting in the Harry Potter series, unusual for a school story, serves a number of important functions in the narrative. Some parents in Potter provide humorous caricatures of psychological constructs, with cautions as to their child outcomes. Other parent relationships point to the religious symbolism that operates close to Potter's core, suggesting that parenting well is a godly trait. Most fundamentally, however, parenting in Potter—whether biological or circumstantial—is portrayed as the only viable and wholesome way of satisfying our human desire for immortality. The story cautions, however, that parents must provide love and care in ways that honor and respect their children as individuals if the "magic" of parenting is to achieve this immortalizing end.

NOTES

Special thanks to Louise M. Freeman, who pointed me both to the psychological construct on parenting and to other literature on parenting in Potter. Louise, along with Lana Whited, Kathryn N. McDaniel, Kris Swank, and Kristen Silver-Moore, also read and helpfully commented on drafts of this chapter; many heartfelt thanks to them all. This essay is dedicated to my own near-perfect parents.

1. Estlein, "Parenting Styles."
2. Mullins and Tashjian, "Parenting Styles."
3. Maccoby and Martin, "Socialization," 39–56. Maccoby and Martin expand Baumrind's taxonomy to include four distinct types of parenting style. This fourfold typology continues to inform studies of parenting styles. One 2022 study aimed to diversify this typology by studying and classifying styles within abnormal variations of parenting among culturally diverse parents; it found that while more specific constructs can be added to Baumrind, Maccoby, and Martin's taxonomy, these new constructs "resembled and ran in parallel" with the overarching constructs previously defined. See Louis, "Young Parenting Inventory."

4. Rowling, *Sorcerer's Stone*, 1. All Harry Potter book citations in this essay refer to the original Scholastic (US) editions.

5. Columbus, *Sorcerer's Stone*.

6. Maccoby and Martin, "Socialization," 39.

7. Maccoby and Martin, 40.

8. Provenzano and Heyman, "Resilience to Adversity," 107; and Rowling, *Half-Blood Prince*, 45. Louise M. Freeman notes that this line occurs in a scene in which Dumbledore is present, which shows how deep Harry's expectation of abuse from his uncle runs; his instincts are to avoid Vernon Dursley even when his greatest protector is present. Freeman, personal correspondence, November 3, 2019.

9. Maccoby and Martin, "Socialization in the Context of the Family," 40.

10. Mullins and Tashjian, "Parenting Styles."

11. The fact that the Dursleys' abuse of Harry does not affect him significantly has a simple in-universe explanation: the protective blood charm Lily casts over Harry by sacrificing her life for his protects him not only from Voldemort but also from her relatives' abuse. Freeman notes that Harry does have his moments of anger and defiance, especially faced with authoritarian, abusive figures such as Snape and Umbridge. Freeman, personal correspondence.

12. Rowling, *Half-Blood Prince*, 205.

13. Rowling, 205.

14. Rowling, 95. Although the cause of Tonks's depression is initially misattributed to Sirius's death, Hermione speculates (rightly) that her cousin's death affects her powers.

15. Rowling, 215.

16. Maccoby and Martin, "Socialization," 40.

17. Rowling, *Chamber of Secrets*, 2; and Provenzano and Heyman, "Resilience to Adversity," 107. For "abnormality," see also Rowling, *Prisoner of Azkaban*, 19.

18. Rowling, *Sorcerer's Stone*, 5.

19. Seden, "Parenting and the Potter Stories," 303.

20. Rowling, *Half-Blood Prince*, 55.

21. Winters, "Bubble-Wrapped Children," 219.

22. Rowling, *Sorcerer's Stone*, 77 (emphasis mine).

23. Maccoby and Martin, "Socialization," 44.

24. Rowling, *Sorcerer's Stone*, 76.

25. Mullins and Tashjian, "Parenting Styles."

26. Potterarchy documents the results of their search through the Potter ebooks for the phrase "my father," as uttered by Draco. Potterarchy, "How Many Times DID Draco's Father Hear about It?" Reddit, 2015, accessed November 1, 2015, https://www.reddit.com/r/harrypotter/comments/2orxcf/how_many_times_did_dracos_father_hear_about_it.

27. Rowling, *Sorcerer's Stone*, 147. One wonders also if Draco's later decision to be branded as a Death Eater with the agreement to assassinate Dumbledore wasn't a very impulsive decision on his part; it is certainly one he later regrets as having left him with no "options." Rowling, *Half-Blood Prince*, 591.

16. Parenting Models in the Potter Saga and *Cursed Child*

28. Rowling, *Chamber of Secrets*, 52.
29. Maccoby and Martin, "Socialization," 45.
30. Mullins and Tashjian, "Parenting Styles."
31. Seden, "Parenting," 301.
32. Rowling, *Chamber of Secrets*, 56, 63.
33. Rowling, "Edinburgh Book Festival."
34. Rowling, *Goblet of Fire*, 28.
35. Scott, "Hermione's Family."
36. Rowling, *Deathly Hallows*, 96–97.
37. Mullins and Tashjian, "Parenting Styles."
38. Chan, "Love," 11.
39. Chan, "Love," 11.
40. Maccoby and Martin, "Socialization," 46.
41. Rowling, *Chamber of Secrets*, 33. Whited avers that the only indulgences in the Weasley household are love and food. Whited, personal correspondence, March 4, 2020.
42. Rowling, *Chamber of Secrets*, 36.
43. Seden, "Parenting," 300.
44. Seden, 300.
45. Rowling, *Chamber of Secrets*, 62. Mr. Weasley appears to usher in the physical phase of his argument with Lucius Malfoy.
46. Whited, personal correspondence.
47. Whited.
48. Rowling, *Sorcerer's Stone*, 124 (emphasis mine).
49. Rowling, *Deathly Hallows*, 374–77.
50. Chan, "Love," 11.
51. Mullins and Tashjian, "Parenting Styles." Even when it comes to the twins and their pranks and hijinks, these are of the cleverest nature, exhibiting high competence in magic, and eventually lead the twins to great commercial success. Also, their pranks never hurt anyone, or at least anyone who didn't deserve it.
52. Well, all except Ginny. See Rowling, *Order of the Phoenix*, 87–96; and Whited, personal correspondence.
53. Winters, "Bubble-Wrapped Children," 221.
54. Rowling, *Order of the Phoenix*, 176.
55. For the primary, in-universe reason, see note 12, above.
56. Groves, " 'History of Magic.' "
57. Rowling, *Sorcerer's Stone*, 47, etc.
58. Rowling, *Order of the Phoenix*, 836.
59. Winters, "Bubble-Wrapped Children," 225.
60. Rowling, *Deathly Hallows*, 731.
61. Luke 1:38 (New American Bible Revised Edition).
62. Irenaeus, *Adversus Haereses*.
63. Ferguson, *Signs and Symbols*, 95.

64. That the Potters are descended from the Peverell family is inferred by James's possession of the Cloak Hallow and is confirmed in Rowling, "Potter Family."

65. Lily is not simply born of Muggles; she's born from the same Muggles who produced her sister, Petunia, whose name is also allusive. In some interpretations of Victorian floriography, the petunia invokes "anger and resentment" (Pottermore staff, "Lily"). One must admit that Petunia and her Dursley family are the most Mugglish Muggles we meet in the series, and this makes Lily's magical ability even more surprising. For more on magic in Potter as an extended metaphor for the Christian life of grace, see Strand, "Potter and the Sacramental Principle."

66. Saint Joseph's lineage is detailed in the first chapter of the Gospel of Matthew, and links Jesus (through his adopted father Joseph) to King David and even Abraham.

67. Carmeli, "Four Models," 19.

68. Chan, "Love," 18.

69. Chan, 23.

70. Seden, "Parenting," 302.

71. Winters, "Bubble-Wrapped Children," 223. For Dumbledore's speech, see Rowling, *Order of the Phoenix*, 838.

72. Littlefield, "Potter as a Metaphor," 125.

73. Littlefield, 132.

74. Littlefield, 133.

75. Philippians 2:8 (NABRE).

76. Rowling, *Deathly Hallows*, 707.

77. Littlefield, "Potter as a Metaphor," 140.

78. Rowling, interview by Geordie Greig.

79. Caldecott, "Cult or Culture?"

80. Another expression of the ambivalence of the immortality quest in Potter is found in vault 713, in which the immortalizing Philosopher's Stone is kept at Gringotts. Rowling, *Sorcerer's Stone*, 73. The number 7 is strongly associated with spirituality and the divine life, while 13 is deeply unlucky, even evil, in the popular imagination. This dichotomy indicates that immortality may be sought by the good (such as the Flamels) and the wicked (such as Voldemort) alike.

81. Aeschylus, *The Libation Bearers*, quoted in Rowling, *Deathly Hallows*, xi.

82. And among these children named for Harry's "parents" is one named in part for Severus Snape, who was less a parent figure to Harry than the others but rather a man who wished he'd been Harry's father. Groves points out the allusion here to Sydney Carton from Charles Dickens's *Tale of Two Cities*, whose final vision before his execution is of his beloved Lucie someday having a grandson who bears his name; this comforts Carton, even though he will not be the boy's biological ancestor. Albus Severus, is of course, Lily's grandson. Groves, *Literary Allusion*, 123.

83. Rowling, *Deathly Hallows*, 756.

84. Draco's mother is aptly named Narcissa, an allusion to Narcissus, the figure from Greek myth who fell in love with his own reflection.

16. Parenting Models in the Potter Saga and *Cursed Child*

85. Rowling, *Deathly Hallows*, 758.

86. For example, this posture of kneeling "just below your toddler's eye level" is recommended in Karp, *Happiest Toddler*, 75.

87. Although the play is advertised as "based on an original new story by J. K. Rowling, John Tiffany and Jack Thorne," many Potter readers (the present one included) consider *Cursed Child* to be deuterocanonical at best.

88. Thorne, *Cursed Child*, 242. This inability of Harry to "see" his son Albus forms a component of a prophecy that foretells the Dark Lord's return, placing the parent-child dyad at the center of the plot as well as at the center of the play's deeper themes and meanings.

89. Thorne, 39–40.

90. Rowling, *Order of the Phoenix*, 838.

91. Thorne, *Cursed Child*, 257–58. Harry laments, "I have proved as bad a father to [young Albus] as you were to me." Thorne, 257.

92. Winters, "Bubble-Wrapped Children," 221.

93. Thorne, *Cursed Child*, 116.

94. Thorne, 247–48.

95. Recall that Riddle was conceived, per Dumbledore's informed speculation, through his mother Merope Gaunt's use of a love potion on Tom Riddle Sr. Rowling, *Half-Blood Prince*, 213.

96. Thorne, *Cursed Child*, 100.

97. Thorne, 229.

98. Thorne, 255.

99. Thorne, 283.

100. Thorne, 219.

17. The Snake Woman in Harry Potter and *Fantastic Beasts*

Beatrice Groves

IN THE HARRY Potter books, Voldemort's ability to talk to snakes and his choice to possess them act as markers of his satanic nature.[1] The film *Fantastic Beasts: The Crimes of Grindelwald* reinscribes this satanic snake imagery in Gellert Grindelwald, who, prefiguring Voldemort's ophidian symbolism, transforms carriage reins into snakes and gives his follower a forked tongue. *Crimes of Grindelwald*, however, also opens up new and more nuanced serpentine symbolism in the character of Nagini. The revelation of Nagini's humanity caused disquiet in fandom, primarily over issues of appropriation and her portrayal by a Korean actress.[2] But it is also an example of Rowling's trademark ability to find empathy for characters who had seemed symbolically clear. *Crimes of Grindelwald* reaches beyond the habitually satanic Western associations with snakes, responding instead to the complex snake-woman mythology found in Indian, Chinese, and medieval French culture. This chapter explores this wider context to illustrate how Rowling uses these literary sources to deepen and nuance her own myth.

The revelation of Nagini as a woman also underlines the importance of the snake-woman myth within Harry Potter itself. Nagini's feminization forms part of her satanic representation in the novels, for the Edenic snake was habitually depicted as female.[3] Likewise her eerie possession of Bathilda's body made her, within Harry Potter, the embodiment of the traditionally malefic snake woman. When Nagini pours out of Bathilda's neck in *Deathly Hallows*, the moment recalls the uncanny horror when the mysterious stranger in snake-woman folktales reveals her true ophidian nature by extending her grotesquely long neck.[4]

Crimes of Grindelwald, however, explores the contrasting hinterlands of snake-woman mythology—from cursed temptress to fertility goddess—and rewrites Nagini's symbolism. The revelation of Nagini as a woman has revealed new sources for Rowling's exploration of the snake-woman myth, as has the more recent revelation of her political fairy tale *The Ickabog*. According to Cornucopian superstition the Ickabog, which is described as both snakelike and dragonish, embodies the classic characteristics of the ophidian monsters of Greek myth: it is marsh-dwelling (like the Hydra) and child-eating (like lamia). At the end of the fairy tale, of course, we discover that this "monster" is in fact nothing to be feared.[5] This essay argues that Rowling's similar revolution in her characterization of Nagini is influenced, in particular, by the medieval tale of Melusine and its modern retellings, above all John Keats's *Lamia* (1820), which grafts the beneficent fairy Melusine onto the lamia, a creature otherwise "almost universally considered malign."[6]

In ancient Greek mythology, the lamia was a terrifying creature who, once a beautiful woman, was punished by Hera so severely for her beauty that she degenerated into a child-eating monster. This bogey figure later metamorphosed into a sexually rapacious demon who devoured the men she seduced.[7] But, as this essay will argue, Keats counters this myth with the sympathetic reading of an entrapped snake woman embodied in the medieval French tale of Melusine. Rowling, like Keats, turns to myth as a crucial mode for exploring the potential of imaginative sympathy.[8] The refashioning of Nagini rethinks the taboo power of the Edenic snake, making her into the embodiment of Rowling's Fantastic Beasts franchise, which is centered on a hero who, as Rowling has said, "loves the purity of creatures that the world might call monsters."[9]

Rowling draws on a broad range of snake-woman stories—from the book of Genesis, Indian and Indonesian nagas, lamia folktales, the Chinese Madam White, and Keats's "Lamia" and its sources—to widen her conception of her world. Above all, the French tale of Melusine lies behind both Keats's and Rowling's newfound sympathy for the snake woman. Keats's Lamia, like the Melusine of French myth, longs to be human—a longing that Nagini shares. As Claudia Kim has argued, Nagini is "a wonderful and vulnerable woman who wants to live. She wants to stay a human being and I think that's a wonderful contrast to the character [of Nagini in the books]."[10] And Rowling has signposted the importance of Melusine in her filmscript. Within the stage directions and speech prefixes of the printed script of *Crimes of Grindelwald* the reader discovers a name that is not available to the viewing audience: Melusine. By giving this evocative name to one of the film's characters, Rowling (still a novelist at heart) has left a clue to a literary source for her story that is only available to the reader.

THE SATANIC SERPENT

Nagini's possession by Voldemort links her with the serpent in Eden, and the traditional feminization of that serpent means that Rowling's revelation of Nagini as a woman was not, in and of itself, a break with her satanic imagery. As Frederika Bain has noted, "a significant portion of the tempting snakes portrayed between the thirteenth and seventeenth centuries bear the head, and often the upper body, of a woman combined with their serpentine tail."[11] And with the name Maledictus, Rowling has even deepened the links between Nagini and the Edenic snake.

When Rowling revealed Nagini's true nature, she claimed that she had been holding on to this secret "for around twenty years,"[12] and it is true that the Harry Potter series hints that Nagini is a snake woman, rather than simply a snake. She takes the form of a woman in *Deathly Hallows* and has a disturbingly humanoid, even quasi-loving relationship with Voldemort. He calls her "my dear Nagini," and Dumbledore notes, "I think he is perhaps as fond of her as he can be of anything."[13] Her most explicitly feminine aspect within the Harry Potter books is when she performs a caricature of maternal nurture for Voldemort's grotesque parody of a baby, sustaining him with the "milk" of her venom. The implicit satanic parody of the Madonna and child created by this tableaux is supported by the satanic links to Nagini created within *Crimes of Grindelwald*,[14] particularly by using a new term for her: Maledictus.[15] Rowling has explained that "a Maledictus is someone who carries a blood curse that, over time, turns them into a beast. They can't stop it, they can't turn back. They will lose themselves . . . they will become the beast with everything that implies."[16] In Genesis 3:14, the serpent in Eden is cursed to go without legs: "So the LORD God said to the serpent, 'Because you have done this, cursed [in the Vulgate, *maledictus*] are you above all livestock and all wild animals! You will crawl on your belly and you will eat dust all the days of your life."

By calling Nagini a Maledictus—the Vulgate's word for the cursing of the Edenic serpent—Rowling in *Crimes of Grindelwald* maintains Harry Potter's Satanic snake links. However, even in her apparently innovative sympathy for Nagini, Rowling is also building on something germane to her presentation within Harry Potter: her name.

NAGA AND MADAM WHITE

The potential for a positive shift in the presentation of Nagini has always been latent within her august name. In Hindu mythology, "Nagini is the personification of a snake goddess, related to the male counterpart, *Naga* . . . a class of demigods, serpents in form, who dwell in the *Patala-loka* (nether regions). . . . The *Nagas* are depicted as serpents or as humans with the area below the navel forming the coils of a serpent. They are most often in conflict with the *Devas*, although somewhat favourable to man."[17] Although nagas can be depicted as a hybrid of human and serpent, in ancient statuary they are generally depicted in their human form, like Nagini in *Crimes of Grindelwald*.[18] Nagas are said to take their snake form "when asleep, [or] angry,"[19] just as Nagini changes into a snake when she sleeps and when she is angry. She is introduced in *Grindelwald* as being transformed when she sleeps—"Every night when she sleeps . . . she is forced to become [a snake]"—and at the climax of the film she transforms herself again in her fury, as she defends Credence from the attack of Yusuf Kama.[20]

When Rowling was challenged for perceived racial stereotyping in the casting of a Korean actor, Claudia Kim, as Nagini, she drew attention to the Asian source of the character's name: "The Naga are snake-like mythical creatures of Indonesian mythology, hence the name 'Nagini.' They are sometimes depicted as winged, sometimes as half-human, half-snake. Indonesia comprises a few hundred ethnic groups, including Javanese, Chinese and Betawi."[21] Skender, ringmaster of the Circus Arcanus, also explicitly notes in *Grindelwald* that Nagini comes from Indonesia, which is perhaps surprising, given that the naga originates in India.[22] But Rowling's choice to locate the naga in Indonesia, and to stress that country's Chinese population, may be an intentional redirection of attention away from the Indian source of the naga and toward a Chinese future for her franchise.

Crimes of Grindelwald introduced a new Chinese beast—the Zouwu—and *Secrets of Dumbledore* increased the importance of China, both in terms of mythology and setting, as it opened with the film's central beast, the Qilin, being born in the Tianzi Mountains of China. The plot of *Secrets of Dumbledore* revolves around the Qilin, one of the "Four Numinous

Animals" of Chinese mythology, and its righteous ability to see into the truth of the human heart forms the film's central conceit.[23] Given Rowling's desire to draw on local mythology in Fantastic Beasts, it seems suggestive that China, the initial setting of *Secrets of Dumbledore*, has its own snake-woman myth: Madam White, whose earliest written appearance is in "The Legend of the Three Pagodas of West Lake" (1550). Claudia Kim has said that Nagini "has powers that are yet to be explored,"[24] and it seems likely that the third film of the series, as originally planned, would have continued to tell her story, perhaps drawing on the stories of Madam White (who may herself have been influenced by the naga, arguably the common origin of sympathetic snake-woman readings[25]). The third film of the franchise, however, was extensively rewritten, and in the final film Nagini is never even mentioned. Now that the Fantastic Beasts film series appears to have been curtailed to three films of the projected five-film franchise, the ending of Nagini's story remains untold, and she may never transform from the entirely sympathetic snake woman of *Crimes of Grindelwald* into the satanic Horcrux of the Harry Potter books.

MELUSINE

The nagas are fertility deities, but in the Western tradition, as with the Chinese Madam White, the sexual aspect of snake women is fatally seductive. From lamia to Lilith, from mermaids to sirens, there is an ancient and widespread tradition of snaky or scaly seductresses who feed off the men who desire them.[26] The fairy Melusine, however, stands as a lone, honorable exception to this tradition.

Jean d'Arras's prose version of the myth, *Melusine* (c. 1393), circulated widely in both manuscript and print.[27] It tells of how Raymondin enters a forest and meets his fate there in the form of a fairy woman by a fountain.[28] This woman—Melusine—has "the ability to see into the future but also the ability to see into the heart"[29]—an ability the Qilin will share in *Secrets of Dumbledore*. When Raymondin takes her home, Melusine proves herself the perfect medieval bride: she builds an impregnable castle for her husband to live in and bears him ten sons. His conjugal bliss comes with only one proviso: he must never look at his wife in her bath on Saturdays. Suspecting Melusine of adultery, however, Raymondin fails to keep this prohibition. He forces his sword through the door to make a peephole to spy on her and discovers her secret: from the navel downward she is a snake. He says nothing, and she forgives him for his treachery, but finally—in an argument brought on by one of their sons murdering another—he flings out the insult "deceitful serpent" at her.[30] She lets out a great cry, transforms into a dragon, and flies from the window, leaving nothing but a footprint behind.

One aspect of the story has a particular resonance with Nagini's history, for Melusine's snake curse comes from her mother, just as Nagini's does. Rowling has written that "the Maledictus carries a blood curse from birth, which is passed down from mother to daughter."[31] And Melusine's mother, likewise, has cursed Melusine: "I proclaim that henceforth every Saturday you shall become a serpent from the navel down."[32] Melusine, therefore, like Nagini—but unlike any other snake woman—is doomed to become a snake due to a curse from her mother.

This story of the curse was d'Arras's peculiar, and important, innovation. By framing Melusine's periodic ophidian form as a curse rather than inherent part of her nature, he cleansed it from diabolical origins.[33] And it was a narrative change that enabled a major shift in attitude toward the protagonist. *Melusine* is the first Western example of a snake-woman tale in which, as in Indian myth, she is not malign. Melusine genuinely loves her husband and confers solid, and lasting, benefits on him. Melusine's sons become heads of many European noble and royal families, and "the Castle of Luzignan" that she built for Raymondin remains a stronghold that, centuries later, is "esteem'd impregnable."[34] This description comes from a seventeenth-century English text, and it marks something else oddly distinctive about the Melusine myth: it was never popular in England. Wynkyn de Worde published *Melusine, a Tale of the Serpent Fairy* (1510)—a text that now exists only in fragments—after which Melusine "virtually disappears from the English cultural imagination."[35] Almost without exception, all English references to Melusine—like the description above—are either translations from French authors or come in descriptions of France.[36]

Melusine, the progenitor of the famous Lusignan dynasty, is a quintessentially French myth with a "strong and continued connection with the physical and cultural geography of France."[37] A. S. Byatt, in its most famous modern retelling, even claims for the story of Melusine the status of *the* French myth. In Byatt's Booker Prize–winning novel *Possession* (1990),

Christabel muses that if "a truly French mythology" might be found, "the Fairy Mélusine was indisputably one of its eminences and bright stars."[38] It is possible that Rowling encountered Melusine during her undergraduate French studies (the seminal essay on the myth was published in 1971[39]), or from reading Byatt's novel, and Melusine's specifically Gallic nature makes her story a perfect myth to underlie the first French installment of Fantastic Beasts. (Indeed, the Gallic nature of the character Melusine in the film is underlined by having her accompanied by other specifically French mythical creatures, Matagots, spirit familiars that take the form of black cats).[40]

Rowling has noted how the Fantastic Beasts films' international aspect has enabled her to raid local mythology: "I'm fascinated by different mythologies and traditions, particularly when you're moving around the world . . . it just adds so much texture and colour." *Crimes of Grindelwald* is set in Paris because Rowling was "looking to move to a place where there would be a more fluid relationship between the magic and the mundane."[41] And such fluidity is central to Melusine's myth. Melusine's hybrid form as both woman and snake embodies the liminal aspects of her story: the intermarriage between human and fey, and her own status as the offspring of a mortal and a fairy.

Melusine's ophidian form is itself fluid—even within d'Arras's tale, she is at once snake, dragon, and something more piscine: "Here, combing her hair, was a woman who from the navel down took the form of a massive serpent's tail, extremely long and as thick as a herring keg, splashing the water so hard it splattered the vaulting of the chamber."[42] Melusine—at once water fairy, snake woman, dragon, and mermaid—is "slippery in her polycorporeality."[43] Her Gallic tale therefore reflects not only—as French myth—the French setting of *Crimes of Grindelwald* but also—in her own hybridity—the "fluid relationship between the magic and the mundane" that Rowling hoped to find in that setting.

The other reason Rowling has given for her choice of a French setting is that she has "ancestry from there."[44] Ancestry and hereditary are, of course, central to *Crimes of Grindelwald*. They are the motivation behind almost all the actions of Yusuf Kama, Credence, and Leta Lestrange, and the film's denouement is precipitated by the fact that all the main characters have followed a (literal) family tree to a family mausoleum. It is also the film's central topic in relation to Credence's "quest for his true identity"[45] and the final "reveal" of his true name. D'Arras's Melusine, likewise, is "a medium of a dynastic memory."[46] She is both the subject of an ancestral curse and the originary ancestor of many great French dynasties, her suffering and prestige intertwined; her mother tells her, even as she curses her, that "a very great and noble lineage shall descend from you."[47]

The link between Nagini's true nature and Melusine's myth fuses together the film's concerns with both liminal and ancestral identity.[48] The importance of ancestry in both d'Arras's and Rowling's myth-making means that Melusine is a perfect name for Rowling to use not only in *Crimes of Grindelwald* but, in particular, for the guardian of its family records. The script names the keeper of the Records Room as Melusine, and its stage directions emphasize her role in guarding ancient things: she is a "very old woman" who consults "an ancient book."[49] Most importantly, she is the guardian of the Lestrange family tree, hidden in a room that revives the arboreal etymologies of both *book* and *library*. The doors of the Records Room are "carved to resemble trees," and within the room "an extraordinary acre of shelves stretches away from them, all carved to look like trees, so that they seem to be on the edge of the forest."[50] The Records Room of the French Ministry of Magic in which Newt, Tina, and Leta meet Melusine is strangely reminiscent of Melusine's home in the forests of French romance.

KEATS'S LAMIA

Melusine all but disappeared from English literature in the early modern period, but she returned with the Romantics. Her most famous rewriting in English is as Keats's Lamia, a snake woman who likewise falls in love with a mortal, builds him a beautiful dwelling, and is forced back to her ophidian form when her husband calls her a "serpent." In Philostratus's *Life of Apollonius*, the ultimate source of Keats's "Lamia," the lamia is the cannibalistic monster familiar from folktales, intent on killing and eating the man she has seduced. The lush furnishings, gold, and servants she has provided all vanish when she is unmasked, and her lover is told, "You cherish a serpent."[51] Robert Burton, in whose *Anatomy of Melancholy* (1621) Keats found the story, takes this accusation literally, and imbues it with satanic overtones. Burton tells Philostratus's story as an illustration of the universal dominion of love; it proves that even the "devils of hell themselves . . . [are]

enamoured and dote."[52] Apollonius, attending the wedding of Lycius and a mysterious young woman "found her out to be a serpent, a lamia" and, when he names her as a snake "she, plate, house, and all that was it in, vanished in an instant."[53]

In Burton this lamia is a "devil of hell" and this context remains in Keats's *Lamia* in which satanic snake imagery is generated through echoes of Milton's serpent in *Paradise Lost*.[54] Keats, in his own copy of Milton, underlined the long description of the serpent in *Paradise Lost* (9.498–503) and he borrows the description of Lamia's ornate, sinuous beauty from this passage. Both serpents are crested, beautiful, and brilliant with variegated colour. Lamia's "gordian shape" closely echoes the "gordian twine" of Milton's serpent. Lamia's "Circean head," likewise, recalls the "Circean call" in Milton's poem.[55] This reference to the Homeric witch (and Chocolate Frog card favourite) puns on her name, for "Circe" derives from the Greek verb *kirkoô* meaning "to secure with rings" or "hoop around." In Circe's name this etymology refers to the binding power of magic, and Keats draws on the pun to highlight Lamia's snakey coils.

In *Paradise Lost*, however, it is actually Eve, not the snake, who is connected to Circe. Milton notes that Eve feels no alarm at the approach of the snake because every beast in Eden is "more duteous at her call, / Than at Circean call the herd disguised."[56] The description of Satan's "rising folds" and "tortuous train" that "curled many a wanton wreath"[57] directly precedes this line and activates the latent pun within Circe's name; for all Eve's confidence in her power, she is about to be caught in Satan's coils. But it also means that Keats's reuse of the Circe pun makes Lamia a type of Eve, not simply a serpent.

In fact, Milton's Eve is just as important as a poetic prototype for Lamia as is Milton's serpent, and when Keats describes Lamia weeping "as Proserpine still weeps for her Sicilian air," for example, he echoes Milton's most important mythic trope for Eve.[58] Keats's method of symbolically intertwining Satan and Eve in "Lamia" recalls the hybrid nature of Melusine, who, in Lynne Reid Banks's retelling of the story in her young adult novel *Melusine*, is both "a direct descendent of the serpent who tempted Eve in the Garden of Eden" and "a woman—Eve herself, perhaps."[59]

The fundamental transfer in sympathy in "Lamia" toward the snake woman is underlined by the way in which Keats shapes his poem around

Melusine's folktale trope of a transgressed prohibition; and indeed, in some versions the interdiction Melusine imposes on her husband is not the usual one about her Saturday bath but—just as in "Lamia"—a ban on guests.[60] This trope of an idiosyncratic taboo—or *geis*—is central to Melusine's myth.[61] By highlighting this aspect of the transgressed prohibition, both d'Arras and Keats create a reading of the story that links the snake woman with Eden in a very different way than her traditional identification with the satanic snake. For, as Helen Cooper notes, Melusine's supernatural prohibition has "something of the illogic, the quality of pure trial divorced from rationality, of the forbidden fruit of Genesis."[62]

In "Lamia," as in *Melusine*, it is the husband's transgression of this prohibition that leads to the revelation of the bride's serpentine nature, rather than, as in the traditional lamia story, the providential arrival of someone who can see through her. In "Lamia" the snake woman disappears, with a doleful cry, at the moment her husband calls her a serpent—a break with Keats's other sources, but a close link with *Melusine*.[63] And likewise, uniquely to "Lamia" and *Melusine*, the husband is appalled by what he has done: Raymondin is suicidal and stricken with remorse, while Lycius dies of grief that very night. This reshaping of the story around the husband's transgression is crucial to these sympathetic reworkings of the snake-woman myth, for both Melusine and Lamia genuinely love their husbands. Raymondin, for example, never grows mysteriously pale, as the husbands of (traditionally vampiric) snake women generally do.[64] "Lamia" takes this idea one step further, pointedly inverting the folktale motif of the male victim growing wan under the attentions of his succubus bride. In this poem Lycius is "sanguineous," and his ruddy hue is contrasted with Lamia's oft-mentioned pallor: it is she who grows pale under his unloving treatment.[65]

"Lamia" and *Melusine* share a radical rewriting that inscribes guilt onto the man who shames the heroine for her serpentine nature, rather than the woman afflicted by this curse. And both texts express this idea through the transfer of serpentine imagery from the snake woman onto the man who publicly shames her. Raymondin berates himself in starkly ophidian terms: "Alas, sweet beloved, I am the vile and cruel asp and you the precious unicorn! I have betrayed you with my wretched venom"; while in Keats's poem Apollonius's revelation of Lamia's true nature poetically transforms him into the snake: "Mark how, possessed, his lashless eyelids stretch / Around his demon eyes."[66]

Keats's poem draws on *Melusine* more than has been previously noted, and one reason for this seems to be not only a shared narrative empathy with the snake woman but also a shared aesthetic interest in her creativity. In both *Melusine* and "Lamia," uniquely, fairies aid the protagonist in building her bridal pavilion, and both texts (unlike Keats's other sources) luxuriate in the aesthetic and sensual pleasures of this bridal feast. The texts' own aesthetic aims are in sympathy with the imaginative power of fairy creation. Melusine and Lamia, like their eponymous texts, have created a pleasurable aesthetic space for the reader, as well for their guests. Melusine provides an "awe-inspiring pavilion adorned with gold and precious stones . . . the ornamentation of gold, embroidery, and pearls, exotically crafted . . . and censers of gold and silver were all as impressive as anyone might wish. . . . The rich variety of fine foods, excellent wines, delicate pastries, and the spiced wine hippocras all served so copiously, made the guests wonder greatly about the source of such abundance."[67] Lamia's wedding feast likewise takes place in a perfumed fairy-built house of splendor that, just like Melusine's, is rich with goblets of "heavy gold," silken couches, myrrh-filled censers, unending wine, and a banquet-room of such "wealthy lustre" that it similarly causes the guests to wonder who could have created it.[68] Keats, just like d'Arras, celebrates the aesthetic creativity that links the snake-woman bride and her creator.

LAMIA, MELUSINE, NAGINI, AND MADAM WHITE

She was the snake . . . or the snake was her . . . all along.
—*Deathly Hallows*

Snake women in folktales are really man-eating lamia, not women. Keats's Lamia and Melusine, by contrast, are not monsters in human form but humans trapped in ophidian form. This radical shift in perception of the snake woman—from a terrifying monster to a real entrapped woman—is likewise the shift that occurs in Nagini's story as she transforms from the terrifying monster taking on the form of a woman (in her possession of Bathilda's body in *Deathly Hallows*) to the revelation of her as a Maledictus—a woman trapped in an ophidian form—in *Crimes of Grindelwald*.

Keats's poem, in its rereading of the monstrous lamia through the sympathetic lens of the Melusine myth, prefigures Rowling's attempted redemption of Nagini in *Grindelwald*. Melusine, "Lamia," and *Grindelwald* all share a basic narrative (unique among snake-woman tales) in which the central character is not a demon taking on the specious appearance of beautiful women, but a woman whose terrible fate deserves our sympathy. All three likewise share a narrative teleology toward a final, forced metamorphosis. In *Melusine* and "Lamia," the heroine's catastrophe is precipitated when the man she loves transgresses his wife's prohibition and publicly repudiates her as a "serpent."

Two aspects of these snake-woman parallels are particularly suggestive for the putative direction of Nagini's story, as originally conceived. Firstly, the unique importance of betrayal and a transgressed prohibition for both Melusine and Lamia suggests that some future action by Credence (or another man Nagini grows to love) will be instrumental in her final transformation into a snake. Secondly, the existence of the Chinese snake woman, Madam White, resonates with the franchise's increasing interest in Chinese mythology. Madam White, like d'Arras's Melusine and Keats's Lamia, takes the folktale snake woman in a more sympathetic direction, but she retains more terrifying—and cannibalistic—aspects than either of them. She would therefore have served as a perfect intermediary, in the planned fifth film of the franchise, for the shift between the fully sympathetic Nagini presented in *Crimes of Grindelwald* and the cannibalistic snake she is destined to become.

The chronological movement of the snake woman in Western literature—from the terrifying, man-eating lamia of Greek literature to Keats's sympathetic treatment of a loving, suffering woman trapped in a snake's body—is mirrored by the chronological movement of Nagini's myth within Rowling's works. In *Goblet of Fire* (2000), Nagini is a horrifying man-eating snake, but in a script published in 2018 she has become a woman cruelly trapped in her ophidian form. In publishing Nagini's early history eighteen years after first presenting readers with her as a vast man-eating snake, however, Rowling not only echoes this chronological movement from Othering to empathy for the snake woman. She also performs a radical shift in the snake-woman narrative. In snake-woman folktales the hero (and the reader) always encounter the beautiful woman first; only later does the horrifying disclosure takes place. For Rowling's audience, this revelation is reversed: in viewing *Grindelwald*, they learn that the snake they know from the Harry Potter series is really a woman. As in Keats's poem (the only other snake-woman text in which the reader meets the snake woman first in her ophidian form), the traditional uncanny narrative has been overturned. The reveal occurs in the opposite direction—the snake you know is really a woman, rather than the woman you know is really a snake—transforming the response to this revelation from horror to empathy.

In the Harry Potter books Nagini's ophidian form is one aspect of the satanic imagery that surrounds Voldemort. But it was always Voldemort, not the snake, who was evil. The revelation of Nagini as a snake woman, cursed by her snake form, disentangles Nagini herself from Voldemort's satanic imagery. Voldemort—like Satan possessing the snake in Eden—possesses Nagini, placing a splinter of his soul within her. It is he, not she, who is evil. In *Crimes of Grindelwald*, Rowling meditates on the metaphorical aspect of her beasts. In this sequel, she has said, "the original hunt for escaped creatures will become a hunt for something much more elusive and difficult: a return to humanity."[69] In Nagini's story Rowling has performed this idea at a narrative level. By reaching beyond the habitual Western associations of snakes with Satan, and responding to the more nuanced snake-woman mythology common to Indian culture, Chinese tales, and medieval French romance, Rowling performs an empathetic revision of her own myth.

NOTES

1 Groves, *Literary Allusion*, 68–71.

2. See, for example, Kang, "Consider This"; Sandwell, "What's All the Fuss"; and Kim, "Claudia Kim's Nagini." .

3. See Groves, " 'Nagini Maledictus.' "

4. Ting, "Holy Man," 151–52.

5. As the story continues, the reader discovers that the Ickabog is not child-eating—it eats only mushrooms.

17. The Snake Woman in Harry Potter and *Fantastic Beasts*

6. Evert, *Aesthetic and Myth*, 272.

7. A seductive, snaky version appears, for example, in Herbert James Draper's painting *The Lamia* (1909) in a navy dress, with snakeskin patterning that may well have influenced Nagini's costuming in *Crimes of Grindelwald*.

8. Tate, "Keats."

9. Rowling, "Answers to Questions."

10. Claudia Kim quoted in Hibberd, "Kim Breaks Silence."

11. Bain, "Tail of Melusine," 28.

12. J. K. Rowling (@jk_rowling), "Only for about twenty years," Twitter, September 25, 2018., 9:29 a.m., https://twitter.com/jk_rowling/status/1044579634581401600.

13. Rowling, *Goblet of Fire*, 569; and Rowling, *Half-Blood Prince*, 473. All Harry Potter book citations in this chapter refer to the original Bloomsbury editions published in the UK.

14. For satanic parody within the Harry Potter books, see Groves, *Literary Allusion*, 67–79.

15. Rowling, *Crimes of Grindelwald*, 86.

16. Rowling, "Rowling Discusses Paris."

17. Bunce, *Encyclopaedia of Hindu Deities*, 1:362, 360. A plausible source for Rowling's initial encounter with this name is the cobra Nagaina in Kipling's *Jungle Book*. With thanks to David Llewellyn Dodds for this suggestion. See Groves, " 'Nagini Maledictus.' "

18. Haque, *Bengal Sculptures*, 286–95; Bunce, *Encyclopaedia of Hindu Deities*, vol. 3, plates 112–15.

19. Ting, "Holy Man," 149.

20. Rowling, *Crimes of Grindelwald*, 87.

21. J. K. Rowling (@jk_rowling). "The Naga are snake-like mythical creatures of Indonesian mythology," Twitter, September 26, 2018, 7:11 a.m., https://twitter.com/jk_rowling/status/1044907311058358273.

22. Rowling may also be influenced by an aspect of Indonesian culture that is comparatively well known in the West: shadow puppet theater, or *wayang kulit*, which dramatizes episodes from Hindu epic. The naga is one of the shadow puppets used in *wayang kulit*, and it is tempting to note that Rowling compares Nagini to a shadow: "He called the snake in Parseltongue and it slithered out to join him like a long shadow." Rowling, *Deathly Hallows*, 445.

23. Groves, "Phoenix and the Qilin."

24. Quoted in Hibberd, "Kim Breaks Silence."

25. Ting, "Holy Man," 189; Zhao, "Metamorphoses," 283.

26. For the link between Lilith and snakes, see Langdon, *Semitic Mythology*, 361–66.

27. It was printed at least twenty-two times: D'Arras, *Melusine*, 13.

28. In a touch that has noticeable resonances with Harry's first journey into the Forbidden Forest, Raymondin is likewise told of a terrible fate that can be read in the stars when he enters this forest: D'Arras, *Melusine*, 29.

29. Cooper, *English Romance*, 197. Nagini shares in Melusine's moral wisdom, and at times she appears to likewise share in her preternatural sense.

30. D'Arras, *Melusine*, 191.

31. J. K. Rowling (@jk_rowling), "They're different conditions. Maledictuses are always women, whereas werewolves can be either sex. The Maledictus carries a blood curse from birth, which is passed down from mother to daughter," Twitter, September 25, 2018, 9:47 a.m., https://twitter.com/jk_rowling/status/1044584072285052930

32. D'Arras, *Melusine*, 25.

33. Wade, *Fairies*, 125.

34. Lacrose, *Description of France*, 429.

35. Urban, "How the Dragon Ate the Woman." See also Urban, *Monstrous Women*, 43–82; and Cooper, *English Romance*, 175.

36. See, for example, Thevet, *New Found Vvorlde*, 132; Chevalier, *Ghosts*, 18; d'Urfe, *Astrea a Romance*, 101–2.

37. Bain, "Tail of Melusine," 32.

38. Byatt, *Possession*, 173.

39. Le Goff and Ladurie, "Mélusine."

40. The French nature of the Melusine myth also reflects back into *Harry Potter* itself, and its main French character. Fleur Delacour is part Veela, from a race of sprites who are introduced as Bulgarian mascots and whose name derives from the Slavic *vila*. See Barber, *Origins of the Vilylrusalki*, 6–47; Conrad, "Female Figures"; and Cica, "Vilenica and Vilenjak." But Fleur herself is emphatically French, and her nationality may be a clue to the way that Rowling has, in her strongly loyal character, rewritten the lamia-like *vila*/Veela along Melusine lines.

41. Rowling, "Rowling Discusses Paris." For a reading of this "raiding" as appropriation, see Sims, "Parseltongue," 105–18.

42. D'Arras, *Melusine*, 181.

43. Urban, *Monstrous Women*, 66.

44. Rowling, "Rowling Discusses Paris." Rowling has not only named her own French ancestry as a source for *Crimes of Grindelwald*'s setting but has even placed one of these ancestors—her great-great-grandmother Salomé Volant—within the Lestrange family tree. Leslie, "Lestrange Family," 6.

45. Rowling, "Rowling Discusses Paris."

46. Péporté, "Melusine and Luxembourg," 179.

47. D'Arras, *Melusine*, 25. For dynastic applications of the Melusine story, see Darwin, "On Mermaids"; Péporté, "Melusine and Luxembourg," 162–79; Delogu, "D'Arras Makes History."

48. The Melusine story centers on the liminal idea of a "fairy bride"—the possibilities and dangers of romantic connections between magical and mortal realms. Melusine attempts to resolve her curse through a loving marriage with a mortal that (had it persisted until death) would have won for her a fully human body and soul. Within the film this aspect of the myth is exemplified by the similarly loving but fraught relationship between Jacob and Queenie.

17. The Snake Woman in Harry Potter and *Fantastic Beasts*

49. Rowling, *Crimes of Grindelwald*, 206.
50. Rowling, 206, 208.
51. Philostratus, *Life of Apollonius*, 218. In Philostratus it is possible that the word *serpent* is metaphorical.
52. Burton, *Anatomy of Melancholy*, pt. 3, sec. 2, mem. 1, subsec. 1.
53. Burton, pt. 3, sec. 2, mem. 1, subsec. 1.
54. This link with Milton's Satan is likewise present in the snake references in the Harry Potter books. See Groves, *Literary Allusion*, 69–71.
55. Keats, "Lamia," 1.47; Milton, *Paradise Lost*, 4.348, 9.522.
56. Milton, *Paradise Lost*, 9.521–22.
57. Milton, 9.498, 516–17.
58. Keats, "Lamia," 1.63; and Milton, *Paradise Lost*, 4.269–71, 9.396, 432.
59. Banks, *Melusine*, 114.
60. Darwin, "On Mermaids," 131. For narrative sympathy in "Lamia," see Chambers, " 'For Love's Sake,' " 600.
61. Cooper, *English Romance*, 210.
62. Cooper, 215.
63. Keats, "Lamia," 2.305–306; d'Arras, *Melusine*, 194; and Burton, *Anatomy of Melancholy*, pt. 3, sec. 2, mem. 1, subsec. 1.
64. The lamia in Philostratus, for example, is vampiric: "It was her custom to feed on young and beautiful bodies, for the sake of the pure blood in them." *Life of Apollonius*, 219. See also Ting, "Holy Man," 152–53.
65. See Keats, "Lamia," 2.76, 2.69, 135, 250, 276.
66. D'Arras, *Melusine*, 181–82; and Keats, "Lamia," 2.288–89.
67. D'Arras, *Melusine*, 42–43.
68. Keats, "Lamia," 2.173–98.
69. Rowling, "Answers to Questions."

18. Politics of Suppression and Violence in *Fantastic Beasts*

Carsten Kullmann

INTRODUCTION

Fantastic Beasts and Where to Find Them, the first film of a series set in J. K. Rowling's Wizarding world and originally announced as having five installments, premiered on November 17, 2016. One week earlier, Rowling disclosed in an interview with the *Telegraph* that the series "was partly inspired by 'the rise of populism' around the world."[1] Presumably, she was referring to Donald Trump's victory in the American presidential elections merely two days before the interview took place and the United Kingdom's vote to leave the European Union that same year.[2] To counter political anxieties in an increasingly globalized world, both campaigns were run on a conservative, populist rhetoric, emphasizing hegemonial control, nationalism, and isolationism.[3] As academics have noted, contemporary politics is also reflected in representations of the Wizarding world, albeit, naturally, in an allegorical way. To name but a few, academic discussions in this regard encompass Anthony Gierzynski and Kathryn Eddy's study on the political tolerance of Harry Potter readers, Diana C. Mutz's thesis that the series' readers are more likely to oppose Donald Trump, and Björn Sundmark's analysis of reactions to the 2016 US presidential election in internet memes.[4] The original Harry Potter series lends itself perfectly to political commentary, for it is, among other things, concerned with Harry's fight against Voldemort's totalitarian ideology. Totalitarianism is understood here in the sense used by Hannah Arendt, who proposed to view fanatic mass movements that rally around one charismatic leader as the base of totalitarian power.[5]

J. K. Rowling continues to tell a political story in the second film in her Fantastic Beasts franchise, *Fantastic Beasts: The Crimes of Grindelwald*, a narrative that confronts us with three competing views on the social and political system of the magical world, all of which speak to contemporary developments in real-world politics. Firstly, ostensibly democratic institutions secure their hegemonial power by concentrating on short-term solutions and seek to avoid being revealed to the nonmagical world at all costs. Secondly, the series' villain, Gellert Grindelwald, pursues the radical overthrow of the existing social order and, ultimately, total world domination. In populist fashion, he manipulates his audience's anxieties and promotes wizard supremacy over the nonmagical population. Lastly, the films' hero, Newt Scamander, deconstructs both political authority and Grindelwald's supremacist ideology and therefore is presented as the exemplary modern citizen. Scamander's liminal position in the Wizarding world enables him to resist attempts of institutional control and simultaneously question the social order.

MAGICAL INSTITUTIONS: POLITICS OF SUPPRESSION

The primary focus of the series' political institutions is to ensure the concealment of the magical community and, therefore, to implement and maintain hegemonial control over their subjects by monitoring magical activity. The actions of these bureaucrats, however, often lack long-term consideration and are aimed at short-term problem-solving rather than sustainable solutions to crises, thus bordering on populist discourses. In addition, the obsession with remaining in control over any magical activity facilitates the institutions' exploitation by the totalitarian Grindelwald. In *Fantastic Beasts and Where to Find Them*, the institutional focus is on the Magical Congress of the United States of America (MACUSA), while in the second film, *Fantastic Beasts: The Crimes of Grindelwald*, the British Ministry of Magic is at the center of action. The third film in the series, *Fantastic Beasts: The Secrets of Dumbledore*, shifts the focus to the German Ministry of Magic and the role of its leader, Anton Vogel, at the international level. The subsequent analysis of these governing bodies' portrayal in these films will concentrate on their interaction with two of their subjects, each of whom poses a threat to the concealment of the magical community: Newt Scamander, the series' main protagonist, and the Obscurial Credence Barebone.[6]

In *Fantastic Beasts and Where to Find Them*, the democratic character of MACUSA is called into question by the organization's suppressive treatment of Scamander and Barebone. Driven by the fear of exposure, the American government puts the community's safety before the fate of the individuals. The Wizarding World website specifies that, conceptually, MACUSA is a democratic institution with elected representatives dedicated to the creation of "laws that both policed and protected American wizardkind."[7] The historically strenuous relationship between the magical and nonmagical communities in the United States has resulted in a rigorously segregationist stance that shapes American wizard/No-Maj relations. In order to secure the wizards' concealment, MACUSA approved Rappaport's Law in 1790, prohibiting "intermarriage and even friendship between wizards and No-Majs,"[8] and issued a ban on beast ownership.[9] In the film, the importance of concealment is visualized by a gigantic dial in MACUSA's lobby, which points to different levels of exposure and ensures that MACUSA is able to remain in control over magical life in the United States at all times.

The opening sequence of the first Fantastic Beasts film sets the tone for the entire series by featuring an onslaught of newspaper headlines that explicitly address issues of hegemonial control and anxieties. The headlines instruct readers not to forget obliviating No-Majs, inform about the Beast Ownership-Ban, and fuel fears about the threat that Gellert Grindelwald poses to magical communities worldwide by risking their exposure.[10] By bringing magical creatures into the United States and failing to obliviate a No-Maj eyewitness, Scamander infringes the Beast Ownership-Ban and breaks Rappaport's Law within the film's first ten minutes. His presence in the city is immediately connected to the havoc wreaked by the Obscurus, as after Scamander's arrival the film's very next scene shows a house his Obscurus has demolished. Thus, the film establishes Scamander and the Obscurus as objects of MACUSA's effort to control magical activity right at the beginning. Through the sequential arrangement of scenes, the film privileges MACUSA's point of view and lets viewers believe, as the authorities do, that only a beast can be responsible for the destruction. Shortly thereafter, Scamander's Niffler escapes, causing mayhem at the city bank, and Scamander fails to obliviate the No-Maj Jacob Kowalski after using magic on him. Therefore, ex-Auror Tina Goldstein, who witnesses the incident, feels called upon to exercise executive power as a representative of the authorities and arrests Scamander for the violation of American law. When Scamander and Goldstein reach MACUSA headquarters, the dial in the atrium points to SEVERE: UNEXPLAINED ACTIVITY, which refers to both the Obscurus's activity and Scamander's fantastic beasts' presence in the city.[11] As MACUSA is unaware of the Obscurus' existence at that moment, Scamander constitutes the primary person of interest, because he is seen to have violated several American wizarding laws. However, since Goldstein fails to provide her superiors with evidence for Scamander's transgressions, he is temporarily let off. With more Obscurus attacks invariably attributed to beastly aggression by MACUSA over the course of the film, Scamander's search for his escaped beasts becomes more pressing if he is to protect both himself and Goldstein from being captured by the authorities in their attempt to regain control over magical activity.

The legal seriousness of Scamander's crimes is constantly emphasized by MACUSA's treatment of him. After Goldstein hands him over to the authorities, MACUSA refuses to listen to his claim that an Obscurus and not one of his beasts is responsible for the disruptions. Upon arresting him, MACUSA president Madam Picquery asserts her own hegemonial position by claiming that she and her colleagues will "be the judges"[12] of whether or not the content of his suitcase poses a threat to the American magical community. Subsequently, Scamander is imprisoned, questioned, and tried by the head of Magical Law Enforcement, Percival Graves, who is actually the international fugitive Grindelwald in disguise.[13] The fact that Grindelwald is able to infiltrate MACUSA's ranks effortlessly emphasizes the Congress's problematic stance toward power, which echoes his subsequent "for the greater good" doctrine. When Graves discovers another Obscurus in Scamander's suitcase, he sentences him to death for allegedly bringing "this Obscurus into the city of New York in the hope of causing mass disruption, breaking the Statute of Secrecy and revealing the magical world."[14] Goldstein, who is accused of having "aided and abetted"[15] Scamander, receives the same sentence. The judgment against them concentrates executive and judicative power in the hands of Graves and denies both Scamander and Goldstein the right to a fair trial or even an unbiased hearing; thus this action is utterly disconcerting and significantly delegitimizes MACUSA's status as a democratic institution.

The destruction in New York attributed to Scamander's beasts, however, is in fact caused by Credence Barebone's Obscurus. The havoc is wreaked by the "unstable, uncontrollable dark force that bursts out . . . attacks and then vanishes," alerting the nonmagical community and threatening to expose American wizardkind.[16] Initially, though, MACUSA mistakes the Obscurus for one of Scamander's beasts, and the Briton is falsely accused of being responsible for the magical community's imminent exposure until the authorities realize their error. When, at the film's climactic scene, the Obscurus is again loose in the city, Madam Picquery anxiously instructs her Aurors to "contain this."[17] Her idea of "containment" involves sending out MACUSA's Aurors, who eventually corner Barebone and fire spells at him until the Obscurus seems to disintegrate.[18] Thus, control over the Obscurus is represented as being vital to the American magical community's security and is achieved eventually by enforcing institutional hegemonic power, putting the community's concealment over the lives of Scamander and Barebone.

Only when Madam Picquery realizes at the end of the film that she has been played by Graves does she apologize to Scamander for erroneously arresting him. Picquery's apology prompts him to help MACUSA obliviate New York's nonmagical community, which has been alerted to the presence of magic by the final confrontation between Graves, Scamander, and the Obscurus. Yet Picquery remains adamant about obliviating Kowalski, even though she acknowledges his role in preventing Graves's scheme to fully come to play: "There can be no exceptions. I'm sorry—but even one witness . . . *you* know the law."[19] In the end, MACUSA's hegemonial control over magic in America is restored, if only with the help of the film's protagonist, who was mistaken for the villain. Meanwhile the real villain, Gellert Grindelwald, is able to hide within the magical authorities' ranks until Scamander discovers his true identity, and Grindelwald exploits the system's proclivity for control for his own nefarious purposes. Institutions like MACUSA, the film hence suggests, only attempt to uphold and regain control but cannot eliminate the actual causes of crises.

As the plot refocuses from America to Europe in *Crimes of Grindelwald*, the focus on magical authorities shifts from MACUSA to the British Ministry of Magic, which is the central institutional agent in the second installment. Like their American counterpart, the British Ministry of Magic is represented as being interested only in controlling its magical subjects by employing "policies of suppression and violence."[20] At the center of the Ministry's attention are, once more, Scamander and Barebone, as well as Albus Dumbledore, who is working together with Scamander.

18. Politics of Suppression and Violence in *Fantastic Beasts*

Facing Grindelwald's escape from custody in the beginning of the film and news of Barebone's survival, the Ministry requests Scamander's collaboration to search for Credence in Paris in order to gain control over him before Grindelwald does. In return, Scamander is offered the lifting of the ban on his international travel, which was implemented after the events in *Fantastic Beasts and Where to Find Them*. The presence of such a ban in the first place illustrates the Ministry's repressive policy, as Scamander was exonerated by MACUSA from having committed any crime in the United States, and the ban is used only as leverage against him. Still, Ministry officials hold him accountable for destroying "half of New York," perceive his position on the subject as "uncooperative and evasive," and admit to being "frustrated" with his behavior.[21] When Scamander eventually declines the Ministry's offer, the ban is upheld and his subsequent activities in the film are, again, technically criminal. In this case, the Ministry is depicted as resorting to undemocratic methods, for its policies appear arbitrary and extortive.

When Scamander nonetheless travels to Paris and tries to gather intelligence about Credence's whereabouts, the Ministry rightly suspects that he is acting on Albus Dumbledore's orders. Dumbledore is working together with Scamander to protect Barebone from both Grindelwald's manipulative intentions and the magical authorities' objective of killing him. The Ministry's head of Magical Law Enforcement, Torquil Travers, confronts Dumbledore at Hogwarts to increase the Ministry's pressure on him, and their encounter is framed by precisely the question of who controls the situation.[22] Travers attempts to implement his own authoritative position by bursting into Dumbledore's classroom, affirming that as the head of Magical Law Enforcement, he has "the right to go wherever [he] please[s]."[23] However, when he orders the students to leave, they all turn their heads to Dumbledore and only heed the command after their teacher asks them, much more politely, to obey.[24] Dumbledore's authority is not based entirely on the position he holds but more clearly on the respectful way he treats other people, whereas Travers has to rely on the respect for his office. In the ensuing conversation, Travers appears adamant that Dumbledore, just like Scamander, choose sides between the Ministry and Grindelwald, revealing once more the political institutions' binary black-and-white thinking, which seems incongruous with democratic principles. Dumbledore, however, insists that they want "the same thing. The defeat of Grindelwald."[25] Moreover, he warns Travers that his "policies of suppression and violence are pushing followers into [Grindelwald's] arms."[26] Travers's persistence in making Dumbledore officially side with the Ministry and his open disregard for the latter's warnings make him appear unsympathetic, egoistic, and inflexible as a representative of the British magical government. Upon Dumbledore's final statement that he cannot fight Grindelwald, Travers remarks, "Well, then you have chosen your side"; he then casts magical tags on Dumbledore's wrists to monitor his magical activity, doubles the watch on him, and bans him from further teaching Defense Against the Dark Arts.[27] As in populist discourse, it seems, the Ministry engages in a strict friend-or-foe-policy, and it reacts to resistance with undemocratic, restrictive measures such as surveillance and interference in education. Just as Scamander is denied documentation and forbidden international travel for refusing to work with the authorities, Dumbledore is removed from his teaching position in an attempt to make him comply with the Ministry's request. Overall, the Ministry is clearly exploiting its hegemonial position in a manner that seems more fitting for an oppressive government than a democratic institution.

Furthermore, the British Ministry of Magic also conducts intelligence operations on foreign terrain to remain in control and remove threats to their hegemonial position. After Scamander refuses the Ministry's offer, they send bounty hunter Gunnar Grimmson to the French capital to hunt down Barebone and, later, dispatch their Auror task force to Paris to capture Grindelwald. Grimmson, who is secretly working for Grindelwald, is already present at Scamander's hearing, hence suggesting that the Ministry did not even trust him to take the deal they offered. In this scene there is also the implication that the Ministry is unable to recognize the traitor, Grimmson, which is an indictment of their competence. Grimmson explains his objective to Scamander as "taking on a job that you're too soft to do"—that is, assassinating Barebone. His unconcealed delight in the assignment illustrates the Ministry's problematic handling of the threat they perceive Barebone to pose. As with the treatment of Dumbledore, their approach to any problem seems to be to remove it immediately without giving second thoughts to ethical ramifications or the consequences of their actions.

18. Politics of Suppression and Violence in *Fantastic Beasts*

In a similar manner, the Ministry tackles the threat posed by Grindelwald. When the British government learns of Grindelwald's rally at the Cimetière du Père-Lachaise in Paris, Scamander's brother Theseus leads a group of Aurors from the French and British Ministries to arrest Grindelwald. Previously warned by Dumbledore, Theseus is anxious to act only within the legal framework and advises the Aurors to "use minimum force on the crowd" as it "isn't illegal to listen to [Grindelwald]."[28] He is clearly worried that excessive use of force might prove Grindelwald right in claiming that "the old ways serve us no longer."[29] In contrast to Travers, his superior, Theseus shows more regard for the intricacies of politics as he warns that the Aurors "mustn't be who [Grindelwald] says [they] are."[30] Grindelwald openly acknowledges the presence of Aurors at the rally and likewise instructs his followers to "remain calm and contain [their] emotions."[31] He then describes provocatively how many of his followers have been killed by the authorities "for the simple crime of seeking the truth, for wanting freedom"[32] and how he himself has been confined and tortured in New York. Despite Theseus's attempts to restrain his Aurors, Grindelwald successfully provokes one of them into killing a young witch. He immediately makes the girl a martyr and instructs his followers to Disapparate and "spread the word [that] it is not we [Grindelwald's followers] who are violent."[33] In the ensuing skirmish, an unknown number of Aurors are killed and Grindelwald manages to escape. The Ministries' intelligence operation at the Père-Lachaise cemetery is a total disaster, not only costing the lives of government employees but also driving more followers to Grindelwald's cause as he successfully demonstrates the international governments' brutality in trying to stop him and to regain control over magical activity worldwide.

In the third installment, *Secrets of Dumbledore*, the series continues its critique of ostensibly democratic institutions. For a significant part of the film, the plot moves to Germany in the 1930s. Perhaps unsurprisingly, the German Ministry of Magic is housed in a towering brutalist building that would not look out of place in Albert Speer's sketchbook. Inside, the German magical government continues the questionable practices viewers have seen from their American, British, and French counterparts. Anton Vogel, German minister of magic and current president of the International Confederation of Wizards (ICW), lets Grindelwald run as his successor after Grindelwald has been acquitted of all criminal charges. Vogel's argument that "when he [Grindelwald] loses, the people will have spoken"[34] resonates gruesomely with the attitude of German politicians around Franz von Papen shortly before Adolf Hitler seized power in 1933. In so doing, Rowling again swiftly uses the parallel between fact and fiction as a storytelling device for suggesting evil. It fits the picture of an oppressive government that, when the group tried to prevent Grindelwald's candidature earlier in the film, Theseus Scamander has been arrested and imprisoned by the Germans without the benefit of a trial, like his brother Newt and Tina Goldstein in the first instalment. Viewers learn that the German Ministry has been undermined by Grindelwald's acolytes, and this fact echoes the plot of the first film when Grindelwald himself poses as American head of law enforcement and rather adds to the depiction of institutions as untrustworthy.

In summary, all principal magical governing bodies are portrayed unfavorably in the films as inflexible, unsympathetic institutions that are willing to literally go over dead bodies to maintain their hegemonial positions. While MACUSA adamantly retains the rigid segregation of magical and nonmagical life in the United States, the British Ministry of Magic undertakes restrictive actions against its own citizens to blackmail them into compliance, employs a bounty hunter to kill a young man, and conducts ineffective and lethal intelligence operations on foreign soil. Even though their actions are directed against a totalitarian criminal attempting to rise to power, their treatment of individuals and their methods make the political institutions appear less democratic than they are supposed to be. Short-term problem-solving and defining only certain groups as inclusive have been identified by Francis Fukuyama as hallmarks of populist discourse, and the efforts to maintain control at all times is presented as paving the way for rather than preventing Grindelwald's eventual success. While the German Ministry of Magic is not depicted as being as outrightly harmful as the American and British, its inability to prevent infiltration by Grindelwald and the visual and political parallel to the National Socialists in the 1930s fit the series' overall portrayal of political institutions and their practices. The films negotiate such repressive politics through individual characters and their respective narrative functions. The villain Gellert Grindelwald upholds the segregationist classification of humans into "magical" and "nonmagical" categories, and even promotes the racist ideal of magical supremacy. In sharp contrast, the films' hero figure, Newt Scamander, resists the neat categorization that authorities try to impose, hence deconstructing these seemingly stable categories altogether through his own liminal position in the magical community.

GELLERT GRINDELWALD: POLITICS OF VIOLENCE

Grindelwald seeks to overthrow the existing social order to assume dominance over the magical and nonmagical world and strives to establish his own hegemonial system, rigorously structured by a hierarchy of power and the wizards' "birthright to rule."[35] The films portray Grindelwald as a social and political "symptom" who, first, is able to exploit the political system and draw his power from an already repressive society, and second, proposes the radicalization of the social order to appease his audience's anxieties, taking the existing segregation between different human communities one step further and presenting his vision as "the greater good."[36]

In *Fantastic Beasts and Where to Find Them*, Grindelwald assumes the identity of Percival Graves, head of magical law enforcement in America, and exploits MACUSA's hegemonial position for his own agenda. Trying to expose the magical community in the United States in order to provoke war with the nonmagical community, Grindelwald seeks to uncover the identity of the Obscurus's host and gain control over that host. He deliberately attributes the havoc wreaked by the Obscurus in New York to the activity of a beast or beasts to cloak his secret plans and maintain cover in MACUSA's ranks. Until the end of the film, MACUSA president Madam Picquery is unaware of the breach of security in her own institution, and it takes the film's hero, Newt Scamander, to uncover Graves's true identity as Grindelwald. Only moments before he is finally apprehended, Grindelwald provides an insight into his ideology. Challenging the necessity for concealing the magical community, he argues that Rappaport's Law "has us [wizards] scuttling like rats in the gutter! A law that demands that we conceal our true nature! A law that directs those under its dominion to cower in fear lest we risk discovery. I ask you, Madam President—I ask all of you. Who does this law protect? Us? Or them?"[37] Grindelwald's binary division into us and them is exemplary of populist discourse and attempts to create communion among one group while directing members' fears and anxieties toward a common enemy. The decisive criteria for inclusion being magic, he even unveils his ideology's racist undertones.

Grindelwald's totalitarian social and political vision is expanded in *Crimes of Grindelwald*. Most noteworthy in this regard are Grindelwald's lesson in propaganda for Vinda Rosier, his speech at the Père-Lachaise cemetery rally, and his (apparent) persuasion of Queenie Goldstein to join his cause. As Grindelwald takes up residence in Paris, he has his acolytes casually murder the nonmagical owners of his future residence. Vinda Rosier, one of his followers, happily envisions that "when we've won, they'll flee cities in the millions. They've had their time."[38] Grindelwald immediately reprimands her—"We don't say such things out loud. We want only freedom. Freedom to be ourselves"[39]—but Rosier nonetheless continues the thought: "To annihilate non-wizards."[40] "Not all of them," Grindelwald replies, "not all. We're not merciless. The beast of burden will always be necessary."[41] Here Grindelwald clearly deploys the racist rhetoric indicative of totalitarian regimes by dehumanizing and Othering the nonmagical population as "beast[s] of burden" and suggesting ethnic cleansing.

Secondly, Grindelwald's speech at the rally bears typical hallmarks of totalitarianism. He suggests communion with his followers, continues the rhetoric of Othering, and speaks directly to the fears of his audience by drawing on war images, which he depicts as the immediate future he seeks to prevent. Grindelwald addresses his fellowship with words that draw on family imagery, calling them "my brothers, my sisters, my friends."[42] He further points to the discontent with current institutions and the social order and proclaims his antiestablishment position by presuming that he and his audience are united by "a craving and the knowledge that the old ways serve us no longer. You came today because you crave something new. Something different."[43] In classic populist fashion, Grindelwald swiftly moves from the subliminal feeling of antiestablishment discontent to presenting an Othered scapegoat as he outlines his political ideology:

> It is said that I hate the Non-Magique, the Muggles, the No-Majs, the Can't-Spells. I do not hate them. I do not. . . . I say the Muggles are not lesser but other. Not worthless but of other value. Not disposable but of a different disposition. Magic blooms only in rare souls. It is granted to those who live for higher things. Oh, what a world we

would make for all of humanity, we who live for freedom, for truth, and for love. The moment has come to share my vision of the future that awaits if we do not rise up and take our rightful place in the world.[44]

Grindelwald frames his rhetoric with positively connoted values like freedom, truth, and love. He ends the first part of his speech on the note that his audience has been denied its "rightful place in the world"[45] and moves on to appeal to the listeners' emotions. Bypassing any logical thought, Grindelwald presents emotive images of a future war, which the viewers immediately recognize as referring to World War II. Eight years after the end of World War I, which in the Wizarding universe also saw many members of the international magical communities fighting, these images horrify the audience present at the rally. "That is what we are fighting," Grindelwald claims, "that is the enemy. Their arrogance, their power lust, their barbarity. How long will it take before they turn their weapons on us?"[46] He uses his audience's heightened emotions and redirects their anxieties toward a common enemy: the nonmagical community. Grindelwald's tactics—using language that bears on family relations, presenting a homogenized, dehumanized other as a scapegoat, and manipulating anxiety and fear in order to direct negative emotions toward the scapegoated Other—all testify to Grindelwald's manipulative abilities and mark him as a totalitarian.

Lastly, Grindelwald's manipulative power is evident in his persuasion of Queenie Goldstein, who represents people susceptible to populist rhetoric in general, to join his cause. Goldstein is emotionally vulnerable, as she is torn between her love for Jacob Kowalski and her place in a repressive society that does not allow her to be with him. Logically, Grindelwald's strife for world domination by wizardry will probably not include permitting wizard-Muggle relationships, but his appeal to her emotional desperation bypasses Goldstein's logical thinking. While Kowalski, alarmed as he is as World War I veteran by the war imagery, remains immune to Grindelwald's manipulative deceits, Goldstein does not pause to reflect on the lack of logical coherence in Grindelwald's line of argument. She does not think critically and thus misses the fact that pureblood supremacy entails annihilating nonwizards, not being allowed to marry them. She only hears

Grindelwald's appeal to wizard freedom, the freedom to love. Seeing her wishes fulfilled in siding with him, she succumbs to the populist message. By the end of *Secrets of Dumbledore*, however, Goldstein has recognized Grindelwald's politics of suppression and violence for what they are and "returned" to the side of the hero. She thus, albeit belatedly, displays the same deconstructive ability to think logically that so characterizes Newt Scamander.

NEWT SCAMANDER: DECONSTRUCTING POLITICS

In contrast with the villainous Grindelwald, the franchise's hero, Newt Scamander, is presented as a model for the modern citizen. Though unequivocally a wizard, he occupies a marginalized position in the magical community, due to his love for allegedly dangerous creatures and his social ineptitude. This liminal status enables him to resist the attempts of authorities to restrict or control him and to refuse categorically to partake in the rigorous segregation of the magical community. Whereas Grindelwald seeks to overturn the existing order to create an even more hierarchical and repressive society, Scamander deconstructs and questions the social fabric and the conduct of politics. Grindelwald is a radical, while Scamander represents transformation. He "is not a great follower of orders,"[47] as Dumbledore puts it, and therefore disregards international laws, which he deems "rather backwards" and "mildly absurd."[48] Indeed, Dumbledore admires as one of Scamander's central characteristics that he does not "seek power or popularity, [he] simply ask[s] 'Is the thing right in itself?' "[49] When Scamander enters the United States at the beginning of *Fantastic Beasts and Where to Find Them* with his suitcase full of magical creatures, he is well aware that he is violating American law. Nonetheless, he regards his mission to return Frank the Thunderbird to his natural habitat as morally superseding the Beast Ownership-Ban. The violation of the law is justified through the law's inherent injustice, at least from Scamander's perspective. He claims that none of his beasts are dangerous,[50] and when Kowalski accidentally frees several of them in New York, Scamander is more concerned about the safety of the beasts, which are, in his opinion, "currently in alien terrain, surrounded by millions of the most vicious creatures on the planet. Humans."[51] The film emphasizes Scamander's morally superior position visually by coloring New York, the "alien terrain,"[52] in cold and desaturated colors, while the cryptozoological world inside his suitcase is bathed in a warm and comforting light that suggests notions of home and protection.

In addition to disregarding the Beast Ownership-Ban, Scamander also breaks Rappaport's Law unashamedly by befriending Jacob Kowalski. Haley Herfurth and Clair McLafferty have already pointed out how the law suggests that "wizards consider themselves superior to the No-Majs, believing it fine to wield control over the memories of the inferior group,"[53] and Scamander makes his own stance on the matter very clear to Tina Goldstein when he indicates that the American magical community has "rather backwards laws about relations with non-magical people."[54] Accordingly, he invites Kowalski into the Wizarding world without a second thought and treats him on equal terms. Pointedly, this invitation is visualized by Scamander's hand beckoning Kowalski to follow him into the suitcase. Thus Scamander's suitcase, rather than any place in New York, is presented as the gateway into the Wizarding world. Moreover, Scamander's egalitarian approach to wizard–No-Maj relations extends to his immediate social surroundings. Subsequently, Kowalski is regarded as "one of us"[55] also by Queenie and Tina Goldstein, and by the end of the film Scamander admits to him: "I like you. . . . You're my friend."[56] Even though Scamander has to surrender to MACUSA's hegemonial power eventually and obliviate Kowalski, the final scene of the first film suggests that Scamander's influence on the No-Maj has left traces that even magic cannot erase. Kowalski, who is able to found a bakery with a little financial help from Scamander, models his pastries after the images of the fantastic beasts that he has encountered and which have evidently remained in his subconscious. Although Scamander's overall narrative role consists in obtaining the political status quo in the face of greater evil—that is, Grindelwald—these small moments of change point to the character's subversive potential.

Not only Scamander's unusual profession as magizoologist and his professed love for allegedly dangerous creatures but also his occasional social ineptitude render him an outsider among his fellow wizards. Yet it is exactly this marginalized position in the magical community and his ability to see beyond surfaces that enable him to forsake traditional modes of making sense of the world and to question authorities who vigorously try to maintain the status quo and are unwilling to reflect on alternatives. Valerie Estelle Frankel has observed that Eddie Redmayne's performance and the overall characterization of Scamander point to Asperger's.[57] He has trouble making friends, or even holding eye contact, and unconcernedly admits to Kowalski that he "annoy[s] people."[58] However, his general uneasiness in social situations allows Scamander to see past the categorizations enforced by authorities and to interact with people simply on the basis of whether he likes or dislikes them. In summary, his liminality is reinforced by the implied social disorder and enables him to relate to all three communities—the magical, the nonmagical, and the beastly. The combination of Scamander's marginalized position in the magical community and his repudiating stance toward authority allows him to question and deconstruct regulations rather than blindly following and reiterating them. As Dumbledore rightly observes, Scamander is guided by critical thinking and his moral compass—which, conveniently, serves him excellently. As he functions within the narrative as the protagonist and hero figure, Newt provides a role model for the audience and can be read as the exemplary modern citizen.

CONCLUSION

The three Fantastic Beasts films tell the story of a liminal, deconstructionist protagonist struggling against ostensibly democratic but ultimately repressive political institutions and the attempts of a totalitarian populist to exploit these institutions' weaknesses to seize power. The new series thus roughly continues the plot pattern of the original Harry Potter books, but the city environment and the historical period place further emphasis on the franchise's political undertones. Already in the original Harry Potter films, the city of London was exclusively the place of politics, but the plot centered more on Hogwarts. In addition to the Fantastic Beasts franchise's setting in politicized cities, the historical period of the late 1920s is known in our world for its economic and political turmoil. Among other factors, it eventually gave rise to totalitarian regimes in Europe in the 1930s and 1940s. The inclusion of Germany as a setting location as well as its narrative function confirm the series' continued use of the intersection of fact and fiction as a device to quickly signal good and evil.

The writing and production of the Fantastic Beasts series began at a time that saw neo-nationalist and populist right-wing movements gain popularity in both Europe and the United States. As Rowling has confirmed, these

18. Politics of Suppression and Violence in *Fantastic Beasts*

political developments have at least partly inspired the series and find an expression in the negative portrayal of political institutions and, of course, in Gellert Grindelwald's character. And even though the films remain as clear-cut and simplistic as the Harry Potter books in their categorization of good and evil, the story encourages viewers to be more like Scamander by suggesting that questioning authority and deconstructing political narratives is a good way to challenge populism and to solve problems in our nonmagical world that cannot be magicked away. Queenie Goldstein's role, as I interpret it, is of particular interest, as she does not represent the easily identifiable and unquestionably "bad" villain but stands in for people "on the other side" who are, for very personal reasons, unable to readily deconstruct the lies and deceits of populist discourses and neo-nationalist ideologies. On the one hand, it might have been interesting to see how the rest of the Fantastic Beasts films engaged with topical political issues had Warner Bros. not put a stop to the series. On the other hand, the increasing demonstration of Rowling's political and social ideas since 2019 leads us to suspect that the continued use of oppressive politics in her stories as a shortcut to evil—be they as obvious as Voldemort's and Grindelwald's borrowings from fascism or more subtle, like the ostensibly democratic practices I have examined in this article—rather serves to legitimate her own conservative agenda.

NOTES

This article was written and submitted for publication in early 2019. In the time that has passed since then, Warner Bros. has ended the Fantastic Beasts film series after the release of the third installment, *The Secrets of Dumbledore* (2022), which had already been pushed back from 2020 due to the COVID-19 pandemic. I have tried to include references to *Secrets* where possible without altering the original article too much. Although the reasons for the decision to cancel the remaining two films in the franchise remain subject to speculation, three explanations spring to mind. First, the films have performed increasingly poorly at the box offices, especially in comparison to the original Harry Potter series. Second, the decision to replace Johnny Depp with Mads Mikkelsen for the third film in the wake of the *Depp v. Heard* trial, which ruled on allegations of defamation based on domestic abuse, has surrounded the series with controversy. Rowling had previously endorsed Depp, writing on her website that "conscience isn't governable by committee," and that "the filmmakers and I are not only comfortable sticking with our original casting, but genuinely happy to have Johnny playing a major character in the movies." Rowling, "Grindelwald Casting." Depp was eventually exonerated from the domestic abuse allegations but lost a separate defamation lawsuit in the UK against News Group Newspapers, whose reporter Dan Wootton ran an article in the *Sun* criticizing Depp's casting for the Fantastic Beasts series on the basis of the allegations. And third, J. K. Rowling has publicly voiced controversial views on sex and gender on Twitter and in the media since the end of 2019, displaying not only an antiquated understanding of gender identity but also quite overt transphobia on her part. Her statements divided fans, and the controversy led to boycotts of the film series. Actors Daniel Radcliffe and Eddie Redmayne have officially spoken out against Rowling despite continuing their professional relationship with her. For a detailed discussion of this issue, please see Lana A. Whited's introduction to this volume. As a literary and cultural scholar, I personally find the appeal of the frequently invoked "death of the author" concept greatly diminished when the author in question is vociferously campaigning against transgender people on social media while routinely practicing world-building through the same outlets, and especially if that author prides herself and her works on preaching love, tolerance, and the rejection of bigotry of any kind. Nonetheless, *Secrets*'s poor box office performance is likely a combination of the second and third issue I have listed above, as well as the Fantastic Beasts films' overall convoluted plot structure.

1. *Telegraph* reporters, "Rowling in 'Bleak Mode.' "
2. The reference to the rise of populism in the UK and the US should not be taken as an indication of my own Anglocentrism, but rather as the most likely frame of reference for J. K. Rowling's statement. I acknowledge that there was and is an increasing appeal to populist discourses and leaders on all continents. Jair Bolsonaro's election victory in Brazil in 2018 may be cited as a case in point, even though he has been voted out of office again in 2022.
3. Fukuyama, "Populism," 10–11; and Forgacs, *Gramsci Reader*, 422. Fukuyama distinguishes three characteristics of populism: the pursuit of popular short-term but unsustainable long-term politics; the exclusion of parts of the population; and the development of a personality cult, often coupled with antiestablishment rhetoric and the implementation of a direct relationship with "the people" in order to channel their hopes and anxieties into immediate action. Moreover, I use the concept of hegemony in its Gramscian meaning here as the directing rather than dominating leadership of some social groups over others. In contrast to totalitarian authority, hegemonial power is established consensually, although this does not mean that hegemons cannot exploit their position of power.
4. Gierzynski, *Millennials*, 6; Mutz, "Deathly Donald," 722; and Sundmark, "Memes and Muggles," 164. Gierzynski and Eddy claim in their study on the Harry Potter books' impact on the so-called millennial generation that the series' fans tend "to be more politically tolerant . . . [and] more liberal," and Mutz demonstrates "the relevance of Harry Potter consumption to oppositional attitudes toward Donald Trump and his worldview." Sundmark analyzes how internet memes reinterpreted specific "plot elements, topics, and themes from the novels . . . in political terms" to relate to the presidential elections in the United States.
5. Hannah Arendt, *Origins of Totalitarianism*. Arendt further claims that the movement's political activity is fueled by ideological premises and aims at the individual's

18. Politics of Suppression and Violence in *Fantastic Beasts*

total absorption in the movement. These ideological premises are often articulated through populist and demagogic propaganda to draw support to the movement, which also applies to Grindelwald, as we will see.

6. An Obscurus is a parasitical dark force developed by children who try to suppress and fail to harness their magical powers. An Obscurus's host is called an Obscurial. Significantly, an Obscurial cannot be killed while in their Obscurus form. Although Credence Barebone is later revealed to be Aurelius Dumbledore, I will keep referring to this character as Barebone in keeping with the films' denomination.

7. Rowling, "MACUSA."
8. Rowling.
9. Rowling, "1920s Wizarding America."
10. Yates, *Fantastic Beasts*, 00:00:52–00:01:43.
11. Yates, 00:14:57.
12. Yates, 01:03:17–01:03:18.
13. In keeping with the film's denomination, I will continue to refer to this character as Graves in the analysis of the first installment. It must be acknowledged, however, that Grindelwald's purposes underlie the character's actions.
14. Yates, *Fantastic Beasts*, 01:08:35–01:08:41.
15. Yates, 01:08:48–01:08:49.
16. Yates, 01:04:32–01:04:40.
17. Yates, 01:39:49.
18. Yates, 01:46:51–01:47:07.
19. Yates, 01:55:12–01:55:20.
20. Yates, *Crimes of Grindelwald*, 01:03:55–01:04:00.
21. Yates, 00:10:49–00:11:11.
22. With the benefit of knowing already what will happen in the Wizarding world in the 1990s, the name Travers should ring a bell with audiences. The family appears in the *Pure-Blood Directory* as one of the Sacred Twenty-Eight—that is, one of the last British families with entirely magical ancestry—and one of Torquil Travers's descendants will later join Lord Voldemort.
23. Yates, *Crimes of Grindelwald*, 01:02:24–01:02:25.
24. Yates, 01:02:28–01:02:35.
25. Yates, 01:03:40–01:03:49.
26. Yates, 01:03:55–01:04:00.
27. Yates, 01:05:11–01:05:12.
28. Yates, 01:47:20–01:47:24.
29. Yates, 01:45:44–01:45:47.
30. Yates, 01:47:27.
31. Yates, 01:47:15-01:49:10.
32. Yates, 01:50:18–01:50:23.
33. Yates, 01:51:24–01:51:29.
34. Yates, 01:01:28–01:01:31.
35. Yates, 00:12:00.
36. Yates, 00:55:58–00:56:00.

37. Yates, *Fantastic Beasts*, 01:47:55–01:48:24.
38. Yates, *Crimes of Grindelwald*, 00:15:33–00:15:38.
39. Yates, 00:15:38–00:15:44.
40. Yates, 00:15:45–00:15:47.
41. Yates, 00:15:48–00:15:56.
42. Yates, 01:45:22–01:45:26.
43. Yates, 01:45:39–01:45:58.
44. Yates, 01:46:01–01:47:50.
45. Yates, 01:47:48–01:48:50.
46. Yates, 01:48:42–01:49:04.
47. Yates, 01:03:03–01:03:05.
48. Yates, *Fantastic Beasts*, 00:24:32–00:24:39.
49. Yates, *Crimes of Grindelwald*, 00:20:33–00:20:45.
50. Yates, *Fantastic Beasts*, 01:03:23–01:03:30.
51. Yates, 00:45:25–00:45:32.
52. Yates, 00:45:26.
53. Herfurth and McLafferty, "Fantastic Non-Wizard Entities," 122.
54. Yates, *Fantastic Beasts*, 00:24:32–00:24:34.
55. Yates, 01:11:02–01:11:03.
56. Yates, 01:56:09–01:56:15.
57. Frankel, " 'Witches Live among Us!' " 105.
58. Yates, *Fantastic Beasts*, 00:48:21.

19. The Story Turn

Parallels in the Pivotal Texts of Harry Potter and Cormoran Strike

John Granger

TEN DAYS AFTER the June 2014 publication of the second Cormoran Strike novel, *The Silkworm*, I advanced the idea that "Rowling is writing this seven-book series in parallel with her previous seven-book series."[1] Subsequent installments *Career of Evil* (2016) and *Lethal White* (2018) have only confirmed that Rowling is intentionally echoing, even commenting on, her *Potter* novels in the parallel volumes of the Strike adventures. To see this requires an understanding of three premises about Rowling as a writer. In brief, Rowling is a "ring writer," and any serious reader should apprehend the centrality of the chiastic structure in her narrative method. These three premises undergird the parallel series theory: (1) the Harry Potter novels are individual ring compositions; (2) the Harry Potter saga is a seven-volume ring composition overall; and (3) each of the Cormoran Strike books is also a ring, with evidence available through four installments suggesting strongly that the first seven books of the Strike series will also be a ring.[2] Each of these ideas deserves and has received extensive discussion elsewhere,[3] but all the ideas are the foundation for the series-in-parallel argument.

In *Thinking in Circles: An Essay on Ring Composition*, anthropologist Mary Douglas writes that chiastic writing is the nearly universal way of human storytelling across millennia, cultures, and genres. She gives seven indicators by which to recognize ring parallelism, but these boil down to the existence of a story latch wherein features of the beginning and end resolve, a story turn that echoes the start and foreshadows the finish, and chapters in parallel before and after the turn in reverse sequence.[4] If a chiastic story has nine chapters, its structure will resemble figure 1. The traditional structure is often referred to as a "turtle-back." The defining or exotic characteristic of this structure, to a modern reader unfamiliar with chiasmus, is the sets of parallel lines across the story axis that reflect

19. The Story Turn

correspondences of scene, dialogue, and characters between these chapters. This interior echoing, a more or less precise there-and-back-again sequence, seems a remarkable conceit.

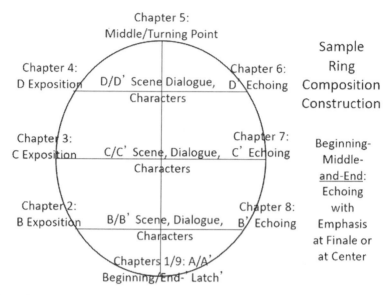

Figure 1.

Ring composition is Rowling's default way of writing. All of her work—novels, screenplays, even her longer Twitter threads—are written as turtle-backs.[5] The pattern is so integral to her writing that no less an artist than Lin-Manuel Miranda has called her the "maestro" of reprise.[6] Again, space prohibits more than a cursory look at this mirroring story structure, but as one instance, figure 2 illustrates the breakdown of *Philosopher's Stone*. Note the reappearance of characters and subjects from "front chapters" (those before the turn) in the "back chapters" (those after), in reverse order. In *Stone*, my favorite reprise is Ron and Harry's meeting on the Hogwarts Express and sharing their predicaments as new students—Ron, too much family; Harry, not enough—and their meeting at Christmas in front of the Mirror of Erised, in which each sees his heart's desire: Harry, his family; Ron, his individual glory. The place of mirrors in these chiastic stories provides an apt metaphor for this reflective structure.

As the Potter novels get longer, as you'd expect, the parallels within each become more pronounced and complicated, but the underlying structure,

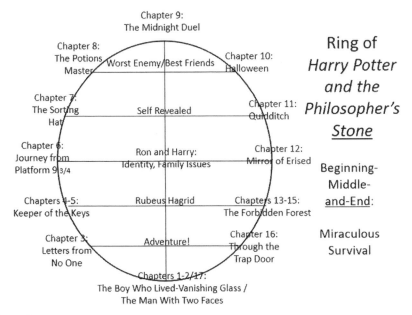

Figure 2.

once acknowledged, is hard to miss. The structure is present not only in each individual book but within the seven-book series as well. Many readers are already aware of the latch of beginning and end, *Stone* and *Hallows*, because of the many echoes of the first book in the seventh.[7] *Goblet* is, as Rowling said in 2000, the "crucial" book of the series,[8] and it shares essential and distinguishing features with *Stone* and *Hallows*: all three story turns feature Harry out after midnight under the Invisibility Cloak; two big plans and a final gauntlet-running (gauntlets including a magical plant, broomstick flight, mythological creatures, a logic test, and rescue by friends); and revelations about the right relationship with salvific blood. Furthermore, Harry's parents appear only in these three books, and the important scenes in these three alone involve Dumbledore and a mirror.[9] Briefly, the turtle-back lines of the series ring are best reduced to *Chamber* and *Prince* both being the books in which Harry learns the backstory of Tom Riddle Jr., and *Prisoner* and *Phoenix* being the novels that feature the advent and departure of Harry's godfather, Sirius Black.[10]

The third premise of the argument that Rowling is writing a series-in-parallel with the Cormoran Strike novels as well is that these mysteries,

19. The Story Turn

like the Hogwarts stories, are written as rings, both individually and as a series (fig. 3). The run is not yet done, be it seven books or the longer series Rowling has suggested,[11] but the four books in print as of 2019 conform to the ring rules evident in the Potter novels and series.

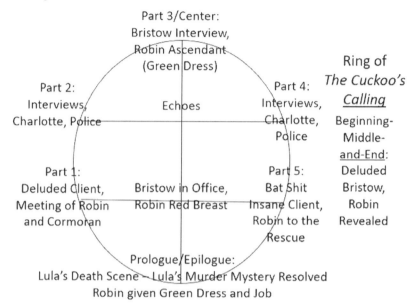

Figure 3.

Cuckoo's Calling, the first Galbraith mystery, is written in five parts with a prologue and epilogue. The opening and closing are the introduction of Lula Landry's seeming death by suicide and the resolution of that mystery. The stories' five parts feature scenes, characters, and self-referencing dialogues in mirror, with the third and central part highlighting a critical character from the first and fifth sections.[12] *Silkworm, Career of Evil*, and *Lethal White* also adhere to Rowling's practice of ring writing.[13]

It Is impossible to say definitively that the series will be a ring as well, but the first and fourth books, *Cuckoo's Calling* and *Lethal White*, have at least thirty correspondences, an astonishing number.[14] Some echoes are blatant; both, for example, involve faked suicides, with Strike hired by family members to find the killer, who turns out to be a family member. There are funny repetitions, including Polish cleaning women, tomato-red-haired ladies, and Cormoran's behavior when drunk in jealous grief. There are also subtleties requiring more reflection. For example, the murderers in the first and fourth books commit their crimes largely because of unresolved oedipal issues with an older, long-dead brother; the "mothering instinct" gone wrong afflicts Yvette Bristow and Della Winn; and both books present African students in the United Kingdom. Finally, both depict haunted portraits of young women: Charlotte Campbell in *Cuckoo* and Rhiannon Winn in *Lethal White*. Each turns out to be an important clue for Strike.

Perhaps the oddest echo in the first and fourth Strike novels is the story turn in *Lethal White*. The murder in this narrative does not happen until chapter 35 in a sixty-nine-chapter work. Rowling marks the story pivot unambiguously and with uncharacteristic clarity with a page that is blank except for the words "Part Two" before the beginning of chapter 36. What is queer here is that there is no "Part One" before chapter 1 of the book. Immediately after this break, however, Strike is approached by a grieving relative of the deceased, convinced that the death was not a suicide. Cormoran defers, saying that the dead relation was such a celebrity that the scrupulous Metropolitan Police would conduct an investigation that he, as a private investigator, could not improve on. He eventually relents on the condition of unqualified cooperation by his new client, whom he had known years earlier.

This same action happens in Strike's office at the opening of *Cuckoo's Calling*. Substitute John Bristow for Isabella "Izzy" Chiswell and Lula Landry for Jaspar Chiswell and the beginning of part 2 is the mirror image of part 1, the beginning of book 1 in the series. This Mystery of the Missing Page has become something of a touchstone for Serious Strikers who believe (as I do) that Rowling is writing a seven-book set, open-ended or not, with its turn in *Lethal White* in much the same way as "The Hungarian Horntail" chapter in *Goblet of Fire* is the pivot not only in that book's ring but also in the overall ring cycle.[15]

The three structure points shared by the Harry Potter and Cormoran Strike novels are the foundation for the hypothesis that *Rowling as Robert Galbraith is writing inside the Cormoran Strike mysteries a playful, intertextual revisiting of Harry's adventures in the Hogwarts saga*. The three structural points work as premises because they demonstrate the one condition that must be true of an author attempting such a design: a madness for parallelism and story correspondences. Every chapter in the Harry Potter novels

19. The Story Turn

has its echo in that same book. Every book in the series stands as a mirrored image to one or more books in the seven-book ring cycle. Each of the Cormoran Strike novels, too, is a ring, and based on the correspondences between *Cuckoo's Calling* and *Lethal White*, Strikes 1 and 4 respectively, these novels reflect a ring cycle as well. The Part 2 page at the center of *Lethal White* only adds credence to the theory.

As noted earlier, the possibility that Rowling was writing Cormoran Strike as a series of novels in parallel to the corresponding Harry Potter volumes—*Philosopher's Stone* paralleling *Cuckoo's Calling*, and so on—occurred to me after my first readings of *The Silkworm*, a book that turns, like *Chamber*, on the mystery of a book within a book. Since that time, other Serious Strikers at *Hogwarts Professor* have laid out the parallels and story echoes in the Potter–Strike book pairings.[16] In a nutshell, *Cuckoo's Calling* à la *Philosopher's Stone* is about Cormoran Strike's coming into his own, "becoming a name," and his escape from a relationship and living situation that was more a prison than a home. Louise Freeman summarizes the next three installments: "Book 2 centered on the havoc wreaked by a mysterious autobiographical book; Book 3, on a notorious escaped criminal stalking the protagonist; and Book 4 on patricide of a government minister, set against the backdrop of a major sporting event."[17]

A close comparison of *Goblet of Fire* and *Lethal White* as story pivots of their respective series is an excellent test of the theory that Rowling is writing a second series in parallel with her first. What follows assumes that the reader knows the plot lines and details of both novels.

The most important parallel is the mysterious murder in both books: the death of Barty Crouch Sr. in *Goblet* and the seeming suicide of Jasper Chiswell in *White*. Each man is killed by his son, what Louise Freeman calls "good old-fashioned unrepentant patricide."[18] Both fathers are horribly negligent, and both are government ministers in conflict with their respective government's minister for sport: Barty Crouch Sr. with Ludo Bagman and Jasper Chiswell with Della Winn and her husband, Geraint. Both sons have been previously investigated by a one-legged detective; Strike looked into the death of Chiswell's oldest boy in Iraq, and Mad-Eye Moody sent Barty Crouch Jr. to Azkaban as a Death Eater. Evan Willis describes the starkness of this parallel:

Frankly, I am miserable at determining the correct solution to mystery novels while reading them . . . . [but even] I noticed the Crouch/Bagman parallel while reading Strike's first meeting with Chiswell at the club. At that point I knew, by assuming the existence of a parallel with *Goblet of Fire*, that Chiswell would be murdered, and by Raphael. I was utterly unable to predict much of anything from intratextual reference, but [it] was enough that I was actually able to predict the result. Assuming parallelism to *Goblet of Fire* proved predictively powerful.[19]

That connection is the most important, the one that should strike (ahem) the attentive reader. There are, however, a host of others.

THE 2012 LONDON OLYMPIC GAMES—QUIDDITCH WORLD CUP

Louise Freeman was first to suggest that Strike 4 would have a natural *Goblet* correspondence because it could take place in 2012, the year of the London Olympic Games. For a while, this was taken so seriously as to be offered as evidence for the series-in-parallel theory. And then Rowling said that Strike 4 would begin at the wedding, right where *Career of Evil* left off. It seemed that had to mean the fourth book would be set in 2011 and not 2012. Instead, the prologue of *Lethal* covers the wedding, and the book proper begins "One Year Later." It is set in a London crowded with international visitors, where the Metropolitan Police are distracted by terrorist concerns and threats, and features regular references to the Games, with special emphasis on the opening and closing ceremonies, the ticket lottery, and a few famous athletes. Rowling was in the Olympics' opening ceremony and no doubt shared Strike's prayer, "Let it not be shit," with everyone in the United Kingdom that night. There is, then, a *Goblet–Lethal* match between the Quidditch World Cup and the London Olympic Games, especially with Strike's hobnobbing with "Ministry officials," watching their Death Eater and pureblood behaviors, and becoming more famous in the process, just as Harry does in his fourth year.

CORE—S.P.E.W.

A major subplot of *Goblet* is Hermione's adolescent idealism and her simultaneously heroic and pathetic "Society for the Promotion of Elvish Welfare."

The Muggle-born witch is clueless about what house-elves themselves want and deaf to anyone pointing out that the issue is more complex than "oppressor and oppressed." *Lethal White* features plenty of attacks both subtle and obvious on UK conservatives and aristocrats. But Rowling seems to reserve special comic and pointed ire for "progressives" who wear anti-Semitic and terrorist clothing, come from privileged backgrounds, and live in an ideological fog removed from any political reality. CORE is a clear correspondent with S.P.E.W.; check out the argument between a Marxist and a feminist at a party in *White* and ask yourself if the author doesn't want you to laugh or at least roll your eyes at their self-important cluelessness.[20]

THE EYES

There's a much stronger parallel between *Goblet of Fire* and *Lethal White* than white horses and Madame Maxime's herd of firewhisky-drinking uber Clydesdales (or the number of white horses in Henrik Ibsen's play *Rosmersholm*, source of every *Lethal White* chapter epigraph). Though Billy Knight thinks of the Uffington White Horse as a dragon (it is on "Dragon Hill"), the primary symbol set that *Goblet of Fire* and *Lethal White* have in common is the eyes of major characters.

Lethal White includes at least two correspondences with Mad-Eye Moody. The first is the blind minister of questionable virtue, Della Winn, who was born without eyeballs and usually wears dark shades, but on state occasions inserts artificial eyes. Her loyalties are questionable throughout the book, and she is credited with mythic status, not unlike Mad-Eye Moody, the Hephaestus of Harry Potter. But Robin is the story's more potent Mad-Eye stand-in. As an undercover agent, she is constantly playing a role to deceive others, and the key aspect of her disguise is change to her eyes. This feature is at least as important a connection with Moody as the PTSD status mentioned throughout the book.

THE BUGGING

A key part of the mystery in *Goblet of Fire* is how Rita Skeeter gets information from inside Hogwarts that she publishes in the *Daily Prophet*. Skeeter turns out to be an unregistered animagus whom Hermione outs and captures after overhearing the word *bug* used as a synonym for electronic surveillance. Skeeter is breaking the law to get an inside story. In

Lethal White, Robin takes on Rita's role. Her "bugging" of Geraint Winn's offices is patently illegal (and dangerous), but the end justifies the means, as the Strike partners benefit mightily from the recordings.

THE ROMANCE

Goblet has a lot in common, perhaps, with *The Casual Vacancy*, about which Rowling joked that there was plenty of sex, but none of the characters enjoyed it. The snogging and pairing-off in *Goblet* is painful to characters and readers alike as the adolescents long for but struggle with relationships, breaking off or continuing in awkward, unlikely matches. It gets worse (and funnier) in *Phoenix* and *Prince*, but Harry's feelings for Cho Chang and the Ron and Hermione (and Viktor!) problems around the Yule Ball occupy much of the large central book of the Hogwarts saga. *Lethal White* is very much about Robin and her failing marriage to Matt as well as Cormoran's meetings with Charlotte, his exploitative relationship with girlfriend Lorelei (he uses her, as she puts it, like a "restaurant and brothel" he can visit for free), and his growing understanding of his feelings for his partner. Readers get next to nothing of the overarching backstory, Leda Strike's death, because Galbraith went all in on the series' romance element.

The matches and alleged matches in both books are the subject of exaggerated tabloid-style gossip, speculation whose publication is used as strategy or threat. In *Goblet*, the *Daily Prophet* publishes Rita Skeeter's allegations about a relationship between Hermione and Harry, a rumor that results in Hermione's being buried in owls the next day with Howlers and bubotuber pus. Posing as Matthew in *Lethal White*, Raphael threatens to plant a story about Cormoran and Robin, and the newspapers do carry the gossip about Charlotte Campbell-Ross's meeting with Strike at a restaurant. After Skeeter's article, Viktor Krum confronts Harry about his feelings for Hermione, and the word at the end of *Lethal White* is that Jago Ross went ballistic about his wife sitting down with her ex-lover (she does wind up in the hospital).

THE GRAVEYARD SCENE

If there's one scene in *Goblet* that readers cannot forget, it may be Harry's one-on-one battle with Lord Voldemort, newly risen from a cauldron in a whole body, in the Little Hangleton graveyard. No corresponding meeting

19. The Story Turn

with a series villain equivalent to Voldemort ends *Lethal White*, but readers may recall the resurrection scene when Barclay, Strike, and Robin dig late at night in the dell of the Chiswell Estate for the body Billy says he saw buried there. When Robin pleads, "*God, let there be nothing there,*" I would guess almost every serious Potter reader remembers Harry thinking, as Wormtail adds ingredients to the Black Mass cauldron, "Please . . . *please let it be dead.*"[21] That it is a horse's head, in proximity to the Uffington White Horse and in relation (at least in Billy's mind) with a sacrifice made at its eye, seals the correspondence, especially in context of the *Rosmersholm* epigrams and Ibsen's use of white-horse imagery to represent ghosts of the dead.

THE BIG SAVE

In chapter 35 of *Goblet of Fire*, Albus Dumbledore saves Harry Potter from Barty Crouch Jr., who has been living as Alastair Moody via Polyjuice Potion throughout the school year. Dumbledore makes quite the dramatic entrance: "'*Stupefy*!' There was a blinding flash of red light, and with a great splintering and crashing, the door of Moody's office was blasted apart."[22] Harry had been secreted away by Crouch, pretending to be Moody, and the headmaster's quick thinking and decisive action saves his life.

In *Lethal White* a recently released convict, paroled early due to his aristocratic family's influence, has been playing the repentant bastard son. He lures the Gothic heroine to his "office" on a houseboat by pretending to be someone Robin trusts, despite conflicting feelings—namely, her soon-to-be-ex-husband. Enter Strike, through another wooden door, to save the day: "With a great splintering of wood, the door crashed open. Raphael spun around, pointing a gun at the large figure that had just fallen inside."[23] Just as Harry pleads with faux Moody about all that has happened in hopes of rescue, so Robin and Raphael review the whole case in her wild hope that she will be saved. The murderer's fear of returning to prison, the "great splintering" of the door, and the ideal rescuer's arrival are all together a direct pointer to *Goblet*'s parallel climax.

Those are seven connections that hit me on my first reading of *Lethal White*. Repeated readings as well as a review of Harry's traumas during and after the Triwizard Tournament also suggest the following correspondences.

Robin's panic attacks throughout *Lethal White* echo Harry's rising anxiety before each Triwizard task. Harry's angst about the Horntail in the first task is described as a "panic attack," and the interior conversation that helps him get through it resembles Robin's cognitive behavioral therapy (CBT) training. (See also Harry's monologue while under the influence of the maze's golden mist.) In the dragon task, his decision to summon his broom derives from Moody's earlier advice, "Play to your strengths" and from Harry's subsequent practice of the Summoning Charm.[24] Harry's instinct to "play to [his] strengths" resembles Robin's repeating "You're perfectly safe" to herself to hold off and work through a panic attack. Faux-Moody's coaching session would parallel Robin's final meeting with her counselor in *Lethal White*. When questioned about their emotional states, Robin and Harry always give the same stoic reply: "I'm fine." And it is always a lie, as each lives in a state of anxiety close to panic (and often spilling over).

The government gets involved in both books to suppress the reporting of information unfavorable to the offices of several ministers. Minister of Magic Cornelius Fudge forces the *Daily Prophet* to keep quiet about Diggory's death and Voldemort's return; Minister of Sport Della Winn's super-injunction about the background of Jasper Chiswell's death stops news coverage of the blackmail directed by her own husband against the late minister for culture.

A personal assistant parallel exists in the government offices of Barty Crouch Sr. and Jasper Chiswell, with Percy and Izzy playing that role, respectively. Izzy Chiswell, though, is really much more like Winky. The house-elf protects the secrets of the Crouches, a confidence that prevents faux Moody's exposure and indirectly leads to the deaths of the father and Cedric Diggory. Izzy, too, keeps the father's and the son's family secrets about the gallows and the strangling of Raphael "up by the horse," a discretion that keeps Strike and Robin from the answers before Izzy's father is set up as a suicide.

Both Barty Crouch Sr. and Jasper Chiswell suffer career setbacks because of the scandalous, even murderous, behavior of their only surviving sons. Each disowns his child publicly, but both move discreetly to get the boy released from a nightmarish prison before completion of his allotted sentence. The great love of each man's wife for this child causes the father's murder. Sirius fills in the trio on the nightmare of Azkaban, while Raphael shares with Robin (in their private conversation on the barge) what he

19. The Story Turn

experienced in prison, the ugliness and animal environment that he would rather die than return to.

Harry plays the part of the one-legged hero in the third task after being injured in his match with the giant spider. He limps thereafter until Fawkes cures his injury with phoenix tears. As if that weren't enough, Harry picks up a serious scar on the arm in the Little Hangleton graveyard thanks to Wormtail's collection of Black Mass potions ingredients. Strike, of course, is missing a leg and has a scar on the arm from his tussle with John Bristow in *Cuckoo's Calling*; Robin walks well, but the scar on her arm from the Shackleton Ripper attack aches during her wedding and is prominent throughout *Lethal White*.

The books also share a contraband theme. At the time of the Quidditch World Cup, Percy Weasley is assisting Barty Crouch Sr. with violations of a flying carpet embargo. Crouch defends his own grandfather's possession of a flying carpet by declaring that he owned it "before carpets were banned, of course."[25] In *Lethal White*, the Chiswell family's export of gallows to Africa has occurred before the European Union's ban on the export of execution and torture equipment.

A blackmail subplot also exists in both books, flat-out in *Lethal White* with Chiswell being threatened with exposure by both Jimmy Knight and Geraint Winn. In *Goblet of Fire*, the blackmail is under the radar, with Ludo Bagman receiving letters from the Weasley twins just on the edge of extortion, reminding him that it is time to pay up.

One aspect of the turtle-back structure is that some characters appear only in parallel books. In the Harry Potter series, readers see wandmaker Garrick Ollivander and Harry's parents only in the first, fourth, and seventh books. Charlotte and Spanner (the computer whiz) make their first appearances in the first and fourth Strike novels, so readers should also expect to see them in the seventh volume.

And the finish? Robin and Harry have traumatic stress in spades: the Boy Who Lived in escaping the Dark Lord and Death Eaters, Robin in surviving capture and interrogation at gunpoint by Raphael. The hostages' reward for eluding near-certain death at the hands of dedicated psychopaths is that both have to postpone rest and recovery in order to report their nightmare experiences: Robin to New Scotland Yard and Harry Potter to Sirius and Dumbledore.

Even before her ill treatment by Raphael, Robin Ellacott-Cunliffe is suffering from PTSD. Louise Freeman has established that Alastair Moody shows all the symptoms of this condition as well.[26] Moody's nickname is "Mad-Eye" because of the magical prosthetic eyepiece he wears; Robin in *Lethal White* wears colored lenses in her eyes to become Venetia Hall (something like Clark Kent's glasses disguising his Superman identity from the clueless public). That's an especially fun link because the Moody with the false eye in *Goblet* is impersonating someone else.

Review of all these parallels leaves the Potterphile and Serious Striker with the question, "So what?" Why would Rowling be playing a game of this intricacy and complexity, one that very few readers will discern without prompting?

For one thing, this game of playful parallel storytelling is the best explanation yet for why Rowling chose to write under a pseudonym. She has said she wanted to see if the books would sell to a publisher without her name on the manuscript, but her straight-faced denials before being outed as a mystery author led readers to believe she is happy to deceive readers when she chooses. An intelligent, self-confident, and powerful writer claims that her personal insecurities prompt her to write undercover? Given the evidence above that she is having fun creating murder mysteries laden with story points and character correspondences from her first series of fantasy novels, it seems at least as likely that she chose not to write under her first pseudonym lest she be outed promptly as a horribly self-involved Gilderoy Lockhart.

As to her motivation for this game of inter- and intratextual three-dimensional chess, is she not doing exactly what all of Harry Potter fandom asked her to do post–*Deathly Hallows*? "Write another seven-book series of novels like the Hogwarts saga!" She is answering, tongue in cheek, the prayers of millions of readers, and wondering how long it will be before anyone joins her in the game of "Find that Story Echo!"

The Dean of Harry Potter Scholars is more than a little frustrated by the greatest mystery of all regarding the Cormoran Strike novels; namely, why are so few of Rowling's Harry Potter readers enjoying the latest efforts of their favorite author? I have explored that question at some length elsewhere without having come to a definitive answer.[27] My thinking is that

19. The Story Turn

Rowling's series-in-parallel that few are reading may simultaneously be the best reason for Potter junkies to jump in—once they perceive the game—and a marker that they may never have completely understood what she is about as an author.

More than anything else, Rowling writes about writing and the experience of reading. Harry Potter and Cormoran Strike are characters struggling to decipher the narratives given them in order to get at the truth each conceals. Each hero, in brief, is a reader of texts whose journey of discovery mirrors the experience of the reader looking over his shoulder. The larger mysteries of their lives are the backdrop to their serial adventures unfolding in sequential, shorter narratives as the series progresses, an evolution or growing awareness reflecting the transformative effect that Rowling hopes the discerning reader will experience by joining her in the games she plays with literary allusion, genre-mixing and adaptation, and other exercises in what the Russian formalists called *ostrananie,* usually translated as "defamiliarization" or "estrangement." Reading Rowling is meant to be an experience in being constantly jarred out of mental ruts and biases, and into a greater awareness of our passive, uncritical acceptance of the stories and ideas that shape our thinking and lives.

And what about readers not equal to the task or declining to join Harry and Cormoran on their odysseys of reawakening or imaginative pilgrimages? No hard feelings. This game is only open to those able to find it on repeated readings, reflection, and in conversation with like-minded friends. If that, dear reader, describes you, please join the Serious Strikers in the play of reading Cormoran Strike in light of Harry Potter for the delight and wonder to be found in Rowling's chiastic artistry and parallelist narrative gymnastics.

NOTES

1. Granger, "Silkworm 2."
2. The first revelations that Rowling was writing under the Galbraith pseudonym suggested that the Strike novels would be a seven-book series, but Rowling and her publishers promptly denied that it would be limited to seven books. See "About Robert Galbraith":

Question: It's been widely reported you have seven Cormoran Strike novels planned. Is this correct?

Answer: It's not, there are actually more than that. The beauty of writing these types of novels is that they each have their own discrete story, so the series is pretty open ended. It will run for as long as I have stories to tell.

3. For example, see Granger, *Ring Composition*; and Lee, "There and Back Again."
4. Douglas, *Thinking in Circles*, 33.
5. For many posts on this subject, see "Ring Composition," *Hogwarts Professor* (blog), http://www.hogwartsprofessor.com/ring-composition/.
6. Lin-Manuel Miranda (@Lin_Manuel), "HBP is my favorite PRECISELY because of this reprise of Dumbledore's 'You are with me' at the beginning. You're deadly w a reprise, maestro," *Twitter*, December 8, 2016, 10:28 a.m., https://twitter.com/lin_manuel/status/806883036612726784.
7. See Granger, *Deathly Hallows Lectures*, 265–67, for a list of twenty-five of the most obvious ones.
8. Rowling, "Book Four."
9. Granger, *Harry Potter*, 49–52, 105–11. There are more than twenty-five links connecting books 1, 4, and 7 in the Hogwarts saga that are represented in a chart on these pages.
10. Granger, "On Turtle-Back Tales," 37–82. The series structure is complicated by the many parallels between 3 and 7 as well as 1 and 5, which are discussed at length in this article and in Granger, *Ring Composition*, 31–66.
11. See note 2.
12. A topos of chiastic writing is that the "meaning is in the middle." See Douglas, *Thinking in Circles*, 34–35. Thus far, each of the Strike novels has had the murderer highlighted in its central chapter or section.
13. For the ring diagrams of the first three Strike novels and discussion, see Granger, " 'Career of Evil.' "
14. These are detailed in Granger, " 'Cuckoo's Calling' Retold?"; "Seven Cuckoo's Echoes"; and "25+ *Lethal White* Finds."
15. See Granger, "Missing Page Mystery" and "Missing Page Mystery (2)," for more on this subject.
16. For *Chamber* and *Silkworm*, see Patrick Barker and Kenny Idan Rub, comments on Granger, "Silkworm 2," July 14, 2014 and May 16, 2016.
17. Freeman, "Creosote-Colored Tea Leaves."
18. Louise Freeman, comment on Granger, "Does Lethal White," September 20, 2018.
19. Evan Willis, comment on Granger, "Does Lethal White," September 21, 2018.
20. Rowling, *Lethal White*, 444.
21. Rowling, 571; Rowling, *Goblet of Fire*, 643.
22. Rowling, *Goblet of Fire*, 679.
23. Rowling, *Lethal White*, 633.
24. Rowling, *Goblet of Fire*, 344.
25. Rowling, 81.
26. See, for example, Freeman, "Potter and the Diagnostic and Statistical Manual."
27. Granger, "Five Reasons."

20. *The Ickabog*, Monsters, and Monstrosity

Lana A. Whited

> "We can't expect to find even an imaginary monster in the dark," pointed out Spittleworth.
>
> —J. K. Rowling, *The Ickabog*

AS THE COVID-19 pandemic sent students home from schools in the spring of 2020, J. K. Rowling rolled out new entertainments, feeling that the lockdown was "very hard on children, in particular."[1] On May 5 she announced the launch of *Harry Potter at Home*, a new section of the Wizarding World website featuring a free audio version of *Harry Potter and the Philosopher's Stone* and activities designed to help young readers endure social distancing. In late May, Rowling released a story called *The Ickabog*, to be serialized online over a seven-week period. She claimed to have composed *The Ickabog* as a bedtime story for her two youngest children and shelved it after the Harry Potter series concluded, when she turned to publishing novels for adults.[2] Rowling had referred to *The Ickabog* previously, though not by name, calling it a "political fairytale," intended for children ages seven to nine.[3] The tale's theme, she said, would concern "truth and the abuse of power"—a theme that, in a political context, may sound better suited to adult readers than to children.[4] Indeed, although Rowling claims to have written *The Ickabog* over a decade earlier, adult readers in 2020 commonly saw parallels between the buffoonish King Fred and Boris Johnson, then British prime minister, or Donald Trump, who was completing his term as US president.[5] But such stories of a political nature have always helped child readers adapt and acclimate to their culture. For example, Hans Christian Andersen's "The Emperor's New Clothes"—a potential source for King Fred of *The Ickabog*—introduces some young readers to the notion

20. *The Ickabog*, Monsters, and Monstrosity

of a ruler overly concerned with appearances and susceptible to nefarious influences.

In depicting these political themes, Rowling summons a standard trope of fantasy literature: the alignment of evil with monstrous creatures. This trope is used in all of Rowling's fantasy writing. The Harry Potter saga is brimming with creatures both charming and chilling, and the primary villain has assigned a portion of his soul to a giant snake whose demise signals the villain's death. In a veiled hint as early as chapter 3 of *Sorcerer's Stone*, Rowling introduces the human "beast" of the Fantastic Beasts series, Gellert Grindelwald. Grindelwald may seem innocuous when mentioned on Albus Dumbledore's Chocolate Frog card, but by the second film, he is exhaling a fiery weapon, dragon-like, and suggesting an ethnic cleansing campaign. *The Ickabog* features a title creature whose bestial qualities prove secondary to the depravity of the human villain, a political usurper.

In all these works, Rowling explores why humans—children in particular—need evil personified, why we sometimes make monsters of others as a projection of our fears, how monstrosity can be ameliorated, and why those who are purely evil may be beyond remedy.

THE MYTHIC MONSTER

Until chapter 51 of a sixty-four-chapter book, the Ickabog itself is a creature of imagination and hearsay bestowed, like the Big Bad Wolf, by one generation onto the next. It is described inconsistently by those claiming to have seen it but generally as reptilian: "Some made it snakelike, others dragonish or wolf-like. Some said it roared, others that it hissed, and still others . . . that it drifted as silently as the mists that descended on the marsh without warning."[6]

Confidence in the Ickabog's existence also varies within Rowling's tale. Some view events having other potential explanations as evidence of the creature's existence; this is the case with the shepherd who visits the king to seek assistance in recovering his dog, which he believes the creature has taken. Others laugh in the shepherd's face and view the king's resolve to visit the Marshlands as a royal snipe hunt. Later, five-year-old Bert Beamish accepts Spittleworth's story that the monster killed his father because, as a child, he lacks both skepticism and guile. Like his name source, the "beamish boy" of Lewis Carroll's poem "Jabberwocky," Bert believes it is his duty to slay the beast.

In launching *The Ickabog*, Rowling claimed to be telling a story about "truth and the abuse of power."[7] Her commentary on truth seems to be that it exists but may not be readily apparent, that people view it differently, and that discovering it requires effort and firsthand experience. Adrienne Rich's speaker in the poem "Diving into the Wreck" descends into the ocean's depths to see "the wreck and not the story of the wreck / the thing itself, and not the myth."[8] Daisy Dovetail, Bert Beamish, and Roderick Roach have grown up with the myth of the Ickabog, and their sense of it is dramatically altered when they encounter it directly.

The true monster in Rowling's fairy tale is the scariest sort of political creature: the truth-transforming monster whose power is predicated on maintaining his deception, whatever or whoever the cost. The self-appointed chief advisor, Spittleworth, bears a name suggesting a value roughly equal to spit, or perhaps that he is a "lickspittle," a person who behaves deferentially to those in power in the expectation of reward.[9] A Machiavellian villain, Spittleworth embodies Lord Acton's famous comment, "Power tends to corrupt and absolute power corrupts absolutely."[10] Like Voldemort, he has christened himself "Lord." He is perhaps a fairy-tale version of Grindelwald, and no reader would be surprised if he turned out to be Dolores Umbridge's brother in another narrative realm.

Many duplicitous acts, even whole webs of deceit, originate in a moment of accident, when someone sees that accident as personally advantageous. Such misfortune precipitates Spittleworth's deception of Cornucopians. Lord Flapoon fires a bullet into the foggy marsh in unlucky chapter 13, striking Major Beamish in the heart. The narrator immediately exposes Flapoon's mistake: the clouds roll back; the shepherd's lost dog is exposed, tangled in brambles; and Major Beamish lies "stone-dead."[11] At this point, the proper response will be clear to the youngest reader: when you hurt someone, you express regret and try to make amends—except that doing so requires thinking of others' feelings and needs.

Illustrating Albus Dumbledore's philosophy that we expose our true character in our choices,[12] Spittleworth immediately begins plotting a cover-up. As soon as Flapoon reacts to shooting Major Beamish, Spittleworth shushes him with one whispered word—"Quiet!" Rowling

20. *The Ickabog*, Monsters, and Monstrosity

writes, "He was thinking harder and faster than he'd thought in the whole of his crafty, conniving life."[13] He surveys the scene, then performs his only act of kindness in the entire story, freeing the shepherd's dog, albeit with a kick to speed it home. The dog caught in the brambles serves as an apt metaphor for the deception that will eventually ensnare its designer.

After a moment's calculation, Spittleworth turns to his men to launch his plan, into which Roderick Roach's father conveniently walks. Roach, like Flapoon, is immediately ordered to listen, while Spittleworth spins the account of Beamish's death that will be told in Chouxville: Major Beamish was killed by the Ickabog, which Flapoon frightened away by firing his weapon. Major Roach pursued the creature to retrieve the king's valuable sword protruding from its hide, but the Ickabog escaped. Roach's complicity is evident in his response: "Could you remind me what the Ickabog looked like, Lord Spittleworth? . . . For the three of us saw it together and will, of course, have received identical impressions."[14] Roach's collusion is rewarded with an immediate promotion and the gift of King Fred's sword.

After the group returns to Cornucopia, evidence of Spittleworth's monstrosity proliferates: he imposes and repeatedly raises taxes that lead many Cornucopians to lose their homes, their children, and sometimes their lives. Anyone whose skepticism threatens his plan is sent to the palace dungeons. He imprisons Lady Eslanda in his own home (her hardship ameliorated by being locked in the library). He bullies others into consent by threatening their families. He is a stock villain of Victorian melodrama, right down to his thin mustaches, and Rowling gives readers no explanation or backstory to account for or mitigate his monstrosity.

Not so in the case of the "monster" designated by the title. Even before the expedition headed by Daisy Dovetail reaches the Marshlands, there is reason to affirm the Ickabog's existence. The first clue comes just before Major Beamish's death, when King Fred "the Fearless" bursts out of the foggy marsh, claiming to have seen the creature and declaring, "The m-monster is real!"[15] Fred's description of the creature is consistent with other reports of it: "Tall as two horses . . . with eyes like huge lamps."[16] The consistency of this description is a clue that these eyewitness accounts are not imagined and that the Royal Guard's skepticism is based more on their perception of Fred as "soft" than on actual evidence. Significantly, Spittleworth repeats the king's words verbatim when Roach requests a description; thus, the king's perception is a kernel of truth shaping the official story.

The other important guide for the reader concerning the creature's existence is Martha, Daisy Dovetail's orphanage friend, with her repeated reminders that for Marshlanders, the Ickabog is a fact of life. Martha serves as a perspective-corrector in the story. After Daisy has told Lord Spittleworth that things were much better for Cornucopians before the Ickabog tax, Martha privately corrects her: "It isn't true that everyone was well fed and happy in the old days. My family never had enough in the Marshlands [because] the Ickabog kept stealing our sheep."[17] When Martha reminds Bert and Roderick that "there is an Ickabog, though," Bert treats her "gently," as if she were an overimaginative child, and Daisy is silent, but Roderick significantly does not laugh, indicating that the tide of uncertainty is turning.[18]

By the time she hears Martha's claims that the Ickabog is real, Daisy has already learned that confronting a creature labeled a monster by others is easier than fighting a corrupt government. In other words, monstrosity combined with power brings true evil. When Martha describes the Ickabog's sheep-stealing, Daisy "wished that she too believed in a monster in the marsh, rather than in the human wickedness she'd seen staring out of Lord Spittleworth's eyes."[19] Myth may be preferable to the harshness of truth.

Once the teens reach the Marshlands and find an actual Ickabog, Daisy's wish proves wise. The Ickabog's description is laden from the start with nurture imagery: it lifts the sleeping teens from the soldiers' wagon and, "as easily as if they were babies, . . . *bore them* away across the marsh."[20] As Louise Freeman has suggested, the snowy landscape reflects the albedo stage of the alchemical process, marking the start of transformation or purification.[21] And what is about to be transformed is the young people's—and subsequently all of Cornucopia's—perception of the Ickabog. Soon Daisy wakes in the womb-like cave, warm and smelling hot food, unable to remember being so "cosy" since childhood in her family home, convinced that she is either dreaming or in heaven.[22] Shortly after they eat, the Ickabog also sings a soothing lullaby.

Daisy's first look at the creature emphasizes the distortion of legends and hearsay: "Even though the old stories said the creature looked like a dragon, or a serpent, or a drifting ghoul, Daisy knew at once that this was the real thing."[23] Martha adds the coda: "I told you there was an Ickabog."[24] The myth busted, other illusions quickly fall: when Roderick notices the creature's pictograph of the encounter with King Fred on the cave wall, he reveals what he knows from his father about Spittleworth's cover-up. The truth is out.

Soon a more reliable story of the Ickabog emerges, one characterizing the creature as, in John Granger's words, "a much maligned and misunderstood survivor."[25] Just as she does with the Hogwarts Sorting Hat, Rowling presents the Ickabog's story through song, in a translation (from Ickerish) elicited by Daisy, who believes that their sympathetic listening can prevent the group from being eaten. The Ickabog's song is a creation story, beginning "at the dawn of time," a prelapsarian period when the world was "heaven's bright reflection" and Ickabogs were alone and without enemies.[26] But when an Ickabog experienced its "Bornding" far from home and in "darkness," its "Ickaboggle" emerged hateful, with an "evil eye" and an instinct for vengeance.[27] From this hatred, man was born, and armed conflict began: "In hundreds, Ickabogs were slain / [Their] blood poured on the land like rain."[28] An Ickabog diaspora followed, with the creatures moving to cold, wet, and foggy places, until the race declined to only one. As the verses progress, the singer's advice to new Ickaboggles shifts from "come Bornding back," then "be Bornded wise," and "be Bornded kind," to "be Bornded brave," and finally to "now kill the men."[29] The Ickabog explains to Daisy that its offspring must be born in kindness to show kindness, which seems unlikely, given the Ickabog's demonization in the kingdom.

A successful aspect of this tale is Rowling's depiction of a creature both recognizable and defying monster stereotypes. Like the "Wild Things" of Maurice Sendak's famous picture book, the Ickabog is a hodgepodge of leftover monster parts: it is "tall as two horses" and "roughly shaped like a person," with an enormous belly, arms, and feet, all of it covered with a "tangle of long, coarse greenish hair," with "large, mournful eyes" and "a low, booming voice."[30] It is strong enough to move a large boulder back and forth across its cave's opening. The "old stories" about the creature have categorized it as "a dragon, or a serpent, or a drifting ghoul," but encountering it, "Daisy knew at once that this was the real thing."[31] The

Ickabog is a *genuine* monster; like Sendak's Wild Things, it looks "like nothing ever seen in a children's book."[32]

THE CREATURE'S CHARACTER AND THE POSSIBILITY OF TRANSFORMATION

The creature's demeanor may seem more familiar to readers of Welsh and Celtic giant legends such as the Mabinogion, the earliest cycle of Welsh prose stories, than to others, as a reader called "Bonni" explains in a *Hogwarts Professor* thread: "giants are pretty much always nasty in English mythology, whereas in the [M]abinogion, giants are just part of the population of [W]ales, they're often helpful, but in any case[,] they have personalities and broader roles than marauding brutes." The likeliest source may be "Gogmagog" or "Goëgmagot," a giant chieftain hurled off a cliff by the Trojan warrior Corineus, according to Geoffrey of Monmouth's *Historia regum Britanniae*. One Dover cliff is still called "Giant's Leap."[33] The twin giants traditionally said to guard the city of London, Gog and Magog, are descended from this legend.[34] These giants' effigies appeared during Queen Elizabeth I's coronation and are still carried by Lord Mayors of London in an annual procession.[35]

Rowling allows her creature the full emotional range, with variations determined by the demeanor of its (apparently gender-fluid) parent or "Icker" as "Ickaboggles" enter the world. When Daisy asks the current Ickabog how many people it has eaten, it replies, "None so far. Ickabogs like mushrooms."[36] Apparently, this Ickabog had a felicitous Bornding, and Daisy connects with the creature on the level of emotional experiences, much the same way Harry finally wins over the house-elf Kreacher in their "I know what it's like to live in a cupboard" scene in *Deathly Hallows*. Soon the entire party is marching back to Chouxville, with the creature petting dogs and handing out flowers. (Even at this point, however, the creature claims that it will eat the four children when its Bornding time comes.)

Like the Ickabog, Roderick Roach is also swayed by Daisy Dovetail's goodness, particularly by Martha's accounts of Daisy's selflessness in Ma Grunter's orphanage. Early in the story, Roderick seems a Slytherin of Draco Malfoy's ilk: a boy from a prominent family, his father being a major in the Royal Guard (and, like Lucius Malfoy, a corruptible one).

20. *The Ickabog*, Monsters, and Monstrosity

Roderick has no experience with someone who puts others' needs first, so he imagines that Daisy is making friends with the Ickabog to try to save herself. Rowling writes that he had "been taught by his father to expect the worst of everybody he met and that the one way to get on in life was to be the biggest, the strongest, and the meanest in every group."[37] As a boy, he bullies Bert Beamish, urging him to fight back when Daisy slaps him for an insensitive comment about her dead mother, and he is so cruel as to mock Bert for wearing his dead father's medal, causing Bert to conceal it under his shirt. Children who would bully others about dead parents seem almost irredeemably mean, and Roderick first warms to Bert only because he feels "very proud to have the son of an Ickabog victim as a friend."[38]

But walking toward Chouxville, still fearing for his life in the Ickabog's company, Roderick realizes that "with his father dead, and his mother and brothers doubtless in prison," Daisy, Martha, and Bert are all the friends he's got.[39] When Martha rebukes him for presuming that Daisy's motives are selfish, he mutters an apology. Several pages later, he apologizes to Bert for not having told him the truth about Major Beamish's death. Roderick's conversion has begun, and by the time he arrives in Chouxville, this son of the Chief Advisor's conspirator is in full-fledged resistance, bearing a sign that reads, "Lord Spittleworth has lied to you."[40] Martha's later willingness to marry Roderick is confirmation that his transformation is genuine. But Roderick Roach is a young man just emerging from his family's influence, so he is more open to change than the story's older villains.

THE TRANSFORMATION OF MONSTROSITY

Flapoon is Spittleworth's buffoon of a henchman, a robust, toady companion with no ideas of his own and an overfondness for discharging his "blunderbuss," an implement whose very name highlights incompetence. Whereas Spittleworth gives advice that King Fred heeds, Flapoon offers only inane platitudes such as "A disloyal seamstress is no reason to spoil a sunny day."[41] Perhaps the most flattering thing the narrator says of him is that he is "not as clever as Spittleworth, [but] still far sharper than the king."[42] As the Ickabog's party approaches Chouxville in the story's climax, Flapoon turns to the Chief Advisor to ask, as a total sidekick cliché, "What do we do?"[43] Although he initially fires the shot that enables Spittleworth's deception, he does so accidentally, intending to shoot a monster instead. Flapoon is an unintentional villain, drawn along by weaknesses, especially his appetite. He'll do practically anything for someone who feeds him well. His primary function, besides setting the deception in motion, is to exchange looks with Spittleworth behind the king's back.

In addition, the physical contrast between Flapoon and Spittleworth reinforces the pair's identity as stock characters in fairy tales and folktales. Flapoon is the Sancho Panza to Spittleworth's Don Quixote, the Cogsworth to his Lumière, providing comic relief for the more serious man. His description as "so enormous that it required six men to heave him onto his massive chestnut horse" continues an unfortunate trend in Rowling's work of bestowing a weight problem on dislikable characters. (Think of Vernon and Dudley Dursley.)[44]

The reader has no opportunity to know whether Flapoon has regrets for his role in the Cornucopians' suffering, because he does not survive the monarchy's downfall. Instead, in an illustration of the principle that "what goes around comes around," he is immediately killed by the first-Bornded Ickaboggle, whose emergence Flapoon has corrupted by again firing his weapon. Flapoon's only expressed regrets are getting his clothes dirty and missing a few palace meals.

Flapoon and Spittleworth echo the trope of swindlers in fairy tales coming in pairs, as they also do in "The Emperor's New Clothes," wherein two weavers dupe a vain ruler into believing they can weave him a suit that can reveal the character of others by their reactions to his clothing. Such a suit would have been perfect for King Fred had it enabled him "to discover which men in [his] empire are unfit for their posts."[45] The king, who christened himself "the Fearless" based mostly on an affinity for alliteration, is cut from the same cloth as Andersen's Emperor. He is popular because he smiles and waves at his subjects; "King Fred the Friendly" would have been an apter name. The first details a reader learns of him are that he is good-looking and stylish, having "lovely yellow curls [and] fine sweeping moustaches and look[ing] magnificent in the tight breeches, velvet doublets, and ruffled shirts that rich men wore at the time."[46] He is a "clothes horse" so intent on getting a new suit for a state visit that he

20. *The Ickabog*, Monsters, and Monstrosity

disregards the illness of his head seamstress, Dora Dovetail. Her subsequent death, the narrator claims, is "the beginning of all the troubles that were to engulf that happy little kingdom."[47]

Fred's responsibility for Dora Dovetail's death might be described as tangential—removed from the actual causes. But his disregard concerning her illness reflects the lack of vigilance that permits Cornucopia to decline. Fred's are sins of omission; he is not a monster but a sort of distracted fool who places too much emphasis on appearance, and who expresses only superficial concern for his subjects. He holds audiences for them to encourage the perception that he is benevolent, not because he cares about their welfare. One suspects that he could venture down the street in no clothes, as long as someone was praising him. He does not seem to notice Lady Eslanda's lengthy absence from the Court after Spittleworth kidnaps her, just as he does not recognize the suffering that his Chief Advisor imposes on the kingdom. As long as Bertha Beamish continues to send Fred perfect pastries, how would he know whether the ordinary citizens of Chouxville have food? King Fred the Oblivious might be the aptest moniker of all.

Because of all he fails to do, Fred must also endure punishment after the monarchy falls. As king, he is responsible for his subjects' welfare, a duty that he shirks through superficiality and distractedness. Fred, however, like Roderick Roach, is both redeemable and aware of redemption's value. In the end, he can identify with the first-Bornded Ickaboggle because both the creature and the king need redeeming. So Fred becomes the agent of the Ickaboggle's rehabilitation. After a year in the dungeon alone with his despair and shame, a time spent "crying his eyes out," Fred accepts his culpability for the country's near-ruin, and in a "very unexpected" act of atonement, he volunteers to be caretaker of the "savage" creature.[48] Day after day, Fred nourishes the Ickabog with mushrooms and talks with it "about the terrible mistakes he'd made, and how you could learn to be a better, kinder person, if you really wanted to become one."[49] Still a prisoner of both the new prime minister and his own guilt, Fred advocates for the release of his charge "to a nice field instead of a cage," and, as if to demonstrate its capacity for reform, the Ickabog thanks him, albeit "gruffly."[50] More than anyone else except Daisy Dovetail, Fred is responsible for the survival of Ickabogs in their peaceable form, and when the first-Bornded Ickaboggle dies, the former king "mourned [it] as if it had been his brother"—an image of fraternity tying Fred and the creature to the theme of transforming a beastly nature.[51]

WHY SOME MONSTERS CANNOT BE REDEEMED

On first reaching the Marshlands in search of the Ickabog, Spittleworth declares, "We can't expect to find even an imaginary monster in the dark."[52] Of course, his comment is absurd; to locate the real monster, Spittleworth need not concern himself about visibility or, for that matter, travel to the Marshlands at all. Wherever he is, there the monster is also.

Following the downfall of the monarchy, Spittleworth is trapped, like the old shepherd's dog caught in brambles; he is remorseless, plotting to kill some civilians and ordering soldiers to kill others. He has three regrets: lying to the king (because it led Spittleworth to make mistakes), letting Bertha Beamish have knives in the dungeons, and "not hiring more spies."[53] Considering that he has covered up a death, impoverished citizens, and separated children and their parents, his "regrets" list seems sparse. The reader could feel more satisfied with Spittleworth's punishment only if an actual monster had eaten him, underscoring metaphorically that he is swallowed by monstrosity.

Spittleworth is the most recent in a series of unredeemed monsters in Rowling's published fantasy works. As a prisoner in the dungeons, he is unrepentant and, according to the narrator, would have preferred death.[54] In the Harry Potter series, Tom Riddle is incapable of reversing his transformation to Lord Voldemort, even when Harry encourages him to "try for some remorse."[55] Instead, Riddle attempts the killing curse and is disarmed by Harry's signature *Expelliarmus* spell. Even before the start of the Fantastic Beasts film series,[56] Harry Potter readers know that Grindelwald is headed toward a fate like Spittleworth's: imprisonment at Nurmengard. But only in the case of Spittleworth does Rowling decline to offer a shred of backstory to explain the monstrosity's pathology.

Rowling's most heroic characters are all savvy about monsters because confronting depravity in human nature is always confronting a beast. Harry's success in this regard is prefigured by his respect for creatures such as Aragog and Buckbeak and by his proficiency in speaking to snakes. But because Voldemort is not capable of rehabilitation, he must ultimately

20. *The Ickabog*, Monsters, and Monstrosity

be destroyed—and by the Hogwarts student initially least likely to be a chivalric hero, Neville Longbottom, who lops off Nagini's head. Newt Scamander, another unlikely hero, is the man for the job of subduing the draconian Grindelwald in the Fantastic Beasts film series because Scamander knows creatures better than anyone else does. And despite Leta Lestrange's claim that Newt "never met a monster [he] couldn't love," Grindelwald stretches Newt's tolerance.[57]

In *The Ickabog*, the task of confronting two monsters—one real, one formed by the imagination of a fearful citizenry—falls to Daisy Dovetail, who is transformed in the tale's final chapter into a nascent Newt Scamander: "Daisy became the world's foremost authority on Ickabogs. She wrote many books about their fascinating behavior, and it is due to Daisy that Ickabogs became protected and beloved by the people of Cornucopia."[58] For Rowling, then, expertise in confronting monsters always signifies insight into the beastlier aspects of human nature. And those with the most expertise and empathy for these creatures, who have learned enough to write books about them—those heroes will find routes out of the dark marshes of ignorance and thus provide the means of saving an Ickabog, and its species, and maybe an entire kingdom.

WHY FAIRY TALES NEED MONSTERS

In addition to Rowling's claims for *The Ickabog* as a "political fairy tale," the work is also part of a long tradition in fantasy literature of representing humans' vilest tendencies in the form of terrifying monsters. Rowling's use of this trope includes a Postmodern twist, a variation that the author underscores during her young heroes' first encounter with the Ickabog: leaving the cave, "as though a sudden thought had struck it, the Ickabog turns back to them and says, 'Roar.' " To emphasize the Ickabog as enacting a role, Rowling writes the word *Roar* on a separate text line, adding a stage direction: "It didn't actually roar. It simply said the word."[59] The creature thus underscores itself as not merely a monster but an iteration of a *literary* monster trope.

Thus, Rowling's monster signifies its awareness that the veneer of monstrosity has been bestowed upon it by humans. Indeed, the tale stipulates that any ferocity in the creature was cultivated by its interaction with monstrous humans, who are more dangerous by far than nonhuman monsters. Aragog may allow his descendants to eat Ron Weasley or Harry Potter for nutritional purposes, and Nagini may attack Arthur Weasley if directed by her master, but nonhuman creatures in these works lack the sadistic, calculated, and predatory hunger for power that characterize Voldemort, Grindelwald, and Spittleworth.

The alignment of humankind's darkest tendencies with frightening monsters is as old as storytelling, although some have always failed to appreciate the trope. Early critics of *Beowulf* faulted the poet for incorporating monsters into the narrative, finding Grendel's propensity for bone-crunching too lowbrow. No less a champion than J. R. R. Tolkien defended the monsters as not "an inexplicable blunder of taste . . . [but] essential, fundamentally allied to the underlying ideas of the poem."[60] In his defense, Tolkien draws on mythologist Joseph Campbell's contention that monsters are necessary to fantasy literature because there are "powers too vast for the normal forms of life to contain them."[61]

For adult readers, the monster trope intersects with the tale's political ramifications, especially when those adults have experienced a regime of Spittleworthian proportions. But the association of evil with monsters also facilitates the story's meaning for readers in Rowling's target demographic: young readers.

In his groundbreaking 1976 work *The Uses of Enchantment*, psychologist Bruno Bettelheim[62] argues that monsters are indispensable to "folk fairy tales," which Bettelheim declares the ideal literary form for character-building in childhood. The German title of his seminal work is *Kinder brauchen Märchen* (*Children Need Fairy Tales*). Bettelheim's insight is particularly relevant to *The Ickabog*, as Rowling declared her story "suitable for 7–9 year olds [sic] to read to themselves."[63] For Bettelheim, monstrosity in such stories aligns neatly with "the monster a child knows best and is most concerned with: the monster he feels or fears himself to be."[64] If children are allowed to read literature with only friendly monsters, Bettelheim says, they will be prevented from exercising their worst anxieties, which "the giants and ogres of the fairy tale" give "form and body."[65] In overcoming the monsters, the hero (or heroine) provides a model for mastery of the traits exaggerated in the monster but also present in the child reader. Through this process, fairy tales provide the child with the raw material from which he or she eventually forms the adult self.

Vandana Saxena maintains that the encounter with the monster plays an important role not only in identity formation but also in the process of socialization. "The abnormality of the monster," Saxena says, "becomes an essential feature against which the parameters of normality are instituted. . . . Abnormality takes on further connotations of immorality and evil, hence cementing the boundaries between 'us' and 'them,' those who are included in the legitimate structures of society and those excluded from them."[66] This is the conflict of Mary Shelley's *Frankenstein*, Saxena argues, represented in the question of whether "it is the monster who is fearsome and threatening or [whether] the threat emanate[s] from the vulnerabilities of humankind's conceptions of self and the other."[67] Or, as Jeffrey Jerome Cohen puts it, "The monster is the abjected fragment that enables the formation of all kinds of identities—personal, national, cultural, economic, sexual, psychological, universal, particular."[68]

With the two potential outcomes stemming from the nature of its Bornding, the Ickabog is an ideal emblem of the conflict between the monstrous and gentler instincts in human nature. The struggle with this duality is the oldest theme in literature. Human depravity generally begins in self-centeredness, in one person's failure to recognize that what he or she wants encroaches on others. Adam and Eve violate God's prohibition on eating from the tree of knowledge of good and evil because *they want this knowledge for themselves*. Gilgamesh sets out to search for a means of immortality because he covets it himself. He is only capable of reform after he recognizes that his aim is selfish.

Rowling's creature also lends itself to a psychoanalytic interpretation due to its association with water—the Marshlands. As Joseph Campbell explains regarding the psychoanalytic dimension of the Watcher in the Water from Tolkien's *Fellowship of the* Ring, "Metaphorically, water is the unconscious, and the creature in the water is the life or energy of the unconscious, which has overwhelmed the conscious personality and must be disempowered, overcome, and controlled."[69] By the association of the Ickabog with a pool of water, Rowling creates what Allison Harl calls a "psychospiritual landscape" reflecting the range of human behavior. As

Harl argues, monstrosity is always amplified by uncertainty; when the Fellowship of the Ring sense that their way into the Mountains of Moriah is blocked by the Watcher in the Water, Frodo's terror is worse because he senses the threat rather than seeing it directly.[70]

Similarly, the Royal Guard merely senses the Ickabog's presence in the marsh. Perhaps King Fred sees the actual creature, or perhaps he merely sees the shepherd's dog caught in briars. The night is dark, and the marsh is foggy. In both cases, uncertainty compounds the fear. Harl writes, "To see a thing is, in a sense, to have a measure of control over it, to have some power to resist it."[71] Merely sensing this "thing," by contrast, is an experience of vulnerability.

The initial expedition to see the monster goes horribly wrong in both the literal cloud of fog that obscures Major Beamish's death and the figurative one that obscures any truth about the "monster." The adolescent Chouxvillians who were as children the perfect age for the tale of a king-killing monster and who grew up watching a true monster tyrannize their families and their city then undertake their own expedition, and the fog of uncertainty begins to lift when they have seen the creature for themselves. For young readers, there are two lessons here: one concerns the importance of forming impressions firsthand rather than from others' reports, and the other is about the importance of introspection, of willingness to atone and change when our own actions bring misery to others.

Young readers will vary in their ability to fully empathize with the plight of characters such as Hansel and Gretel, whose own father put the stepmother's desires before his children's. Youngsters who have experienced emotional or literal separation from family will recognize the dark woods where the siblings wander lost as a perilous realm in which children must rely on themselves and the witch as a threat to self-preservation. All young readers, regardless of experience, will realize that the father's relief upon their reunion affirms that the fundamental error was his, not the children's. Such tales serve a purpose in the healthy psychological development of all children, helping them to process negative feelings they may otherwise be expected to eliminate or suppress. As James Heisig explains, "Using the psychoanalytic model of the psyche, fairy tales can be seen to communicate to the child an understanding of universal human problems in such a

20. *The Ickabog*, Monsters, and Monstrosity

way as to encourage the development of his budding ego, give expression to id pressures, and suggest ways to relieve them in line with the requirements of the superego."[72]

Child readers who have fortunately not encountered human monsters, political or otherwise, may not view Spittleworth through the lens of monstrosity. But the myth of a monster "tall as two horses" helps to align the monstrosity trope with the plot. Young readers *will* sense the marsh as a fearful place and recognize the purported sheep-stealing monster as a predator, even if they do not yet see Spittleworth's imprisonment of Bertha Beamish and Dan Dovetail as predation of a different sort. As the young readers age and learn more about the world (and, of course, varying with their own experiences), the shrewdest will see symbolic implications in nonmonstrous creatures: the sheep disappearing from the Marshlanders' pastures are equally the Cornucopians led astray by Spittleworth's deceptions or preyed upon by his decrees.

The fairy tale or folktale, like the parables of Jesus, takes a symbolic approach to problems of good and evil in human existence. Its universality is reinforced by its commencing in some indeterminate "Once upon a time" and occurring in a realm removed from (but resembling) our own. And although its narrator always assures us in the end that everyone "lived happily ever after," readers know that even after the final page is turned, some wounds have not healed, and some monsters have only been imprisoned, not eradicated or transformed. The Ickaboggle Bornded during the second firing of Flapoon's blunderbuss will always require watching. In this sense, authors of such tales are concerned less with the redemption of human nature than with its inherent redeemability.

Those same youngsters who read (or hear) the saga of Spittleworth's atrocities merely as a fairy tale will, one hopes, grow up to recognize its symbolic dimensions and to understand that the monster imagined—made myth—is far scarier than a monster one actually confronts. They will learn, through encounters in both literature and life, that Spittleworth is a *real* monster, who values his own power and luxury more than others' lives, and who is incapable of change. Villains like him can only be defeated, while others are monstrous only by reputation and can be transformed through courage, patience, and empathy. This maturer reading is what C. S. Lewis had in mind when he advised the child reader in the preface to *The Lion, the Witch, and the Wardrobe*, "Some day you will be old enough to start reading fairy tales again."[73]

NOTES

1. Rowling, "Meet the Ickabog."
2. Rowling.
3. Rowling.
4. Rowling, "Introduces *The Ickabog*."
5. Bundel, "Rowling's 'Ickabog' Story."
6. Rowling, *Ickabog*, 7.
7. Rowling, "Introduces *The Ickabog*."
8. Rich, "Diving into the Wreck," lines 62–63.
9. Thanks to M. Katherine Grimes for this insight regarding Spittleworth's name.
10. Dahlberg-Acton, "Letter to Creighton."
11. Rowling, *Ickabog*, 56.
12. Rowling, *Chamber of Secrets*, 333. Dumbledore's words are: "It is our choices, Harry, that show what we truly are, far more than our abilities."
13. Rowling, *Ickabog*, 56.
14. Rowling, 57.
15. Rowling, 51.
16. Rowling, 51.
17. Rowling, 161.
18. Rowling, 205.
19. Rowling, 161.
20. Rowling, 210 (emphasis mine).
21. Louise Freeman, "So . . . let's talk alchemy," comment on Granger, "Ickabog Structure," 7:09 p.m.
22. Rowling, *Ickabog*, 212.
23. Rowling, 212.
24. Rowling, 213.
25. Granger, "Ickabog Structure."
26. Rowling, *Ickabog*, 222.
27. Rowling, 223.
28. Rowling, 224.
29. Rowling, 223–24.
30. Rowling, 62, 229.
31. Rowling, 210, 213–14.
32. White, "Monsters Ink."
33. Bonni, comment on Granger, "Ickabog Structure."

34. The author is grateful to Valerie Estelle Frankel for a helpful exchange of email concerning giants in Welsh mythology. "Corineus," *Encyclopedia Britannica*. See also Noble, "Gog and Magog."
35. Gregory, "London's Giants."
36. Rowling, *Ickabog*, 225.
37. Rowling, 236.
38. Rowling, 106.
39. Rowling, 236.
40. Rowling, 242.
41. Rowling, 13.
42. Rowling, 2.
43. Rowling, 256.
44. Rowling, 2.
45. Andersen, "The Emperor's New Clothes." I am grateful to my colleague Tina L. Hanlon of Ferrum College for helping me to appreciate the parallels between *The Ickabog* and this Andersen tale.
46. Rowling, *Ickabog*, 1.
47. Rowling, 11. John Granger has repeatedly noted that nearly all of Rowling's plots are launched when something devastating happens to a woman. See Granger, "Violence against Women."
48. Rowling, *Ickabog*, 273–74.
49. Rowling, 274.
50. Rowling, 274.
51. Rowling, 274.
52. Rowling, 48.
53. Rowling, 255.
54. Rowling, 269.
55. Rowling, *Deathly Hallows*, 741.
56. On October 14, 2016, Rowling announced that the Fantastic Beasts series would run to seven films.
57. Rowling, *Crimes of Grindelwald*, 236.
58. Rowling, *Ickabog*, 272.
59. Rowling, 214.
60. Tolkien, "*Beowulf*," 19.
61. Campbell, *Power of Myth*, 278.
62. It is vital to acknowledge that Bruno Bettelheim's legacy is tainted by reports from some of his patients and colleagues characterizing Bettelheim "as a megalomaniacal tyrant who systematically abused children, undermined their self-confidence, and publicly humiliated and beat them. The angry charges, made by former patients and at least one former counselor at the school, question not only Bettelheim's judgment but his honesty." Bettelheim committed suicide in 1990. The following year, an article by Allen Dundes detailed allegations of shallow scholarship and plagiarism in Bettleheim's seminal work. Dundes, "Bettelheim's Uses of Enchantment." However, the allegations against Bettelheim do not invalidate the significance of his work in

bringing the psychoanalytic dimensions of fairy tales to public attention, a point acknowledged even by his detractors, such as Dundes. See Bernstein, "Accusations of Abuse."

63. Rowling, "Introduces *The Ickabog*."
64. Bettelheim, *Uses of Enchantment*, 120.
65. Bettelheim, 120–21.
66. Saxena, "Subversive Harry Potter," 137.
67. Saxena, 136.
68. Cohen, *Monster Theory*, 20.
69. Quoted in Harl, "Monstrosity of the Gaze," 62.
70. Harl, 62.
71. Harl, 62.
72. Heisig, "Bettelheim and the Fairy Tales," 95.
73. Lewis, *Lion*.

SECTION 6

THE FANDOM, 25 YEARS ON

21. "Accio Jo!"

Woke Wizards and Generational Potter Fandom

Rebecca Sutherland Borah

MY HUSBAND, TEENAGE sons, and I sit at home watching our digital purchase of *Fantastic Beasts: The Crimes of Grindelwald*, the first Harry Potter–related film we have not seen in a theater. I'm an "acafan" (academic + fan), and my two sons had no choice about being Harry Potter fans. I loved Jo Rowling's Harry Potter series before the boys were born, dragged them to book and film events, and read to them in the car on family vacations. Their bedroom has a mural of the Hogwarts Castle and grounds, the Hogwarts Express, Hagrid's hut, and the Forbidden Forest. Harry on his Nimbus 2000 soars above Hermione, Ron, Hagrid, and Crookshanks. The ceiling glows with constellations, waiting for Firenze to decipher the future. A trio of sculpted rag dolls sits atop a dresser, gathering dust. Reference books, knickknacks, and wands rest on my office shelves. Sometimes I forget the Quidditch mobile gently turning above my desk. Many calendars and posters have graced the walls to mark the passage of time.

Twenty-one years after the first Ivory Tower volume and sixteen after *Deathly Hallows*, Harry Potter and J. K. Rowling's world are still a commercial success. As headlines once proclaimed, Harry Potter touched a global generation of readers who embraced the stories and Rowling's worldview. It sounds like a perfect tale—but that's not how culture works. The fandom felt like a party that I mostly left after the final film in July 2011. Since then, Potter-related news stories have told of some fan community behaviors that gave me pride (fundraisers for disasters and LGBTQIA+ awareness) and some that made me despair (racially intolerant casting rants). Growing pains can be messy; generally, fandoms either find core values and hold tight or fracture and fly apart. Therefore, I was apprehensive about returning to the fan world.

Over the last two decades, powerful fandoms similar to Harry Potter's have seen tumultuous incidents. The conclusion of HBO's *Game of Thrones*

21. "Accio Jo!" Woke Wizards and Generational Potter Fandom

caused such uproar that creators David Benioff and D. B. Weiss withdrew from a three-film Star Wars deal with Disney because of concerns about toxic fans.[1] Cultural critic Rea McNamara explains, "In the past decade, fandom has emerged as an unparalleled force in mainstream culture.... Fans are no longer on the sidelines, but full-fledged participants in the ways studios and labels are packaging and distributing their media products."[2] Henry Jenkins's term "participatory culture" describes the intersections of identity, empowerment, and consumerism. This didn't sound like the mostly affirming experiences I remembered from the 2003 Harry Potter community. What happened to the multigenerational group who loved the books when they first came out? Now that the Harry Potter novels and films are finished, and Rowling and her new works disappoint many readers, how do fans keep fandom alive? Or do they?

To answer those questions, I looked online and talked to friends who had been fans. I soon learned that many fan activities had shifted to online communities. Facebook and Twitter emerged in 2004 and 2006, and Rowling joined Twitter in 2009. Young people who had grown up with the series quickly adopted interactive social media platforms and other forms of new media, due in part to MuggleNet, The Leaky Cauldron, Harry Potter Lexicon, Sugar Quill, and forums on platforms such as LiveJournal. The parallel rise of new media and HP fandom made it easier for fans across the globe to share discussions and creative works. Traditional forms of fan interaction such as book clubs, conventions, and fanzines still exist, but new media have become the gathering place of choice for the majority (53 percent) of active Potter fans I surveyed.

Henry Jenkins, whose examination of fan culture *Textual Poachers: Television Fans and Participatory Culture* helped frame my first study of Harry Potter fan culture, noted this adoption of technology among fandoms in his book *Convergence Culture: Where Old and New Media Collide*. "Fans have always been early adapters of new media technologies; [they] are the most active segment of the media audience, one that ... insists on the right to become full participants. None of this is new. What has shifted is the visibility of fan culture. The Web provides a powerful new distribution channel for amateur cultural production."[3] The number of webpages and volume of data on online fan sites are staggering. For example, eighty-eight Facebook group pages alone have "Harry Potter" as part of their title.

Because Harry Potter fandom is too large for exhaustive analysis, in this study I focused primarily on fans with online connections, using an online survey[4] and observing and interacting with fans through websites, primarily social media platforms. I also collected data through interviews and discussions with colleagues, students, and other fans. Almost all the 1,217 people who responded (99 percent) were college age and older, with 64.7 percent in the millennial category (ages 29–43).

My first dip back into Harry Potter fandom research was on the Quora platform, which hosts 300 million members and experts who post and answer questions. When I searched "J. K. Rowling" (240.1 million followers) and the "Harry Potter Creative Franchise" (1.2 million followers), the number of topics I found was astounding, ranging from "What if" plot scenarios to "headcanons" in opposition to Rowling's creative decisions. The topic with the most followers, at 131 million, was "Why is the Harry Potter fandom starting to turn against JK Rowling?" posted anonymously on May 9, 2018.[5] As of mid-April 2023, there are 129 posted answers.

The most popular answer, posted June 1, 2018 (updated November 23, 2019), with 495.7K views, 6,076 upvotes, and 359 comments to date, belongs to writer, journalist, and HP fan Amber Goldsmith. In her 6,135-word illustrated and well-documented response, "J. K. Rowling vs. the Internet," Goldsmith covers the parallel rise of the Harry Potter fandom and the internet as well as Rowling's discomfort with new technology and eventual adoption of Twitter. Goldsmith catalogues the numerous disputes between the author and fans, concluding that "the primary dispute, in regards to the Harry Potter books themselves, is thus: 'Who 'owns' the legacy of Harry Potter, as a franchise, and its future direction? J. K. Rowling, the original author who wrote the series, and continues to write content . . . or the Harry Potter fans, who support the franchise with their money?' "[6] Goldsmith points out the generational and political gap between Rowling and her millennial fans, identifying technology as the primary cause of this rift, "specifically, the rise of the Internet and social media in modern society. As opposed to the time Rowling grew up in, millennial Harry Potter fans are now much greater in number and vocal ability, thanks to growing up using (and forming communities on) the Internet."[7]

Goldsmith's post shows that fans have a story to tell. In the early 2000s Rowling was perceived as down-to-earth, fan-friendly, and even nurturing.

21. "Accio Jo!" Woke Wizards and Generational Potter Fandom

However, trouble was brewing. As Jenkins notes in *Textual Poachers*, "Fans recognize that their relationship to the text remains a tentative one, that their pleasures often exist on the margins of the original text and in the face of the producer's own efforts to regulate its meanings."[8]

Most Potterheads remember when Rowling revealed in October 2007 that Dumbledore is gay.[9] Fan responses included both joy at the revelation and frustration with Rowling for not stating it sooner or making it explicit in canon. Conservative critics shook their fingers. With the *Deathly Hallows* book and *Order of the Phoenix* film in release, Rowling's announcement that a major character was gay was fairly bold, especially for someone regarded primarily (at that point in her career) as a children's author. As a Gen-X adult, I was pleased with the pronouncement, as the books were always unrealistically "het heavy."

Rowling might have changed with the times, but commercial entities have long been involved with HP phenomena. Marketing expert Susan Gunelius describes the reversal in the early standoff over copyright between young webmasters and Warner Brothers as both a victory for fans and a move that became marketing strategy. Whereas Rowling's legal representatives had earlier discouraged young enthusiasts from launching online fan sites, Rowling, Warner Brothers, and Scholastic began steering the same group into official activities to build HP brand loyalty. Warner Brothers granted a few webmasters access to film sets, interviews, and pictures; the resulting posts created free marketing. "By embracing fan sites and communities," Gunelius writes, "listening to the fan buzz, communicating with online influencers and joining the conversation, the team behind Harry Potter carved a path for future word-of-mouth marketing campaigns to follow."[10]

This stratagem seemed to solve problems for everyone. Fans became more content; the harassing lawsuits went away; and the publishers, Warner Brothers, and Rowling made a Gringotts vault worth of money while reinforcing fans' loyalty to the HP franchise. Ironically, Rowling opposed product placement in the films, yet Harry Potter became a product itself. This symbiotic relationship with fans worked at the time, but the cozy fan-author-corporation triad would not flourish forever.

The long list of lawsuits by and against the HP franchise ranges from band names to unsuccessful plagiarism cases to fake versions of the films and books sold internationally.[11] The best-known case was filed in 2007 against RDR Books, which sought to publish a print version of Steve Vander Ark's online reference guide, the *Harry Potter Lexicon*. Vander Ark's project had been lauded by Rowling, who, like many fans, said she found the site useful, as none of her novels has an index. The case established a precedent in regard to intellectual property and its relationship to fan works, especially nonfiction. Rowling won, but Judge Robert P. Patterson used the case to establish guidelines for fan researchers. Fair-use expert Anthony Falzone noted, "The Court recognized that as a general matter authors do not have the right to stop publication of reference guides and companion books about literary works, and issued an important explanation of why reference guides are not derivative works."[12] According to the court, Falzone explained, the proposed print version of the *Lexicon* was not protected as fair use only because it contained too much of Rowling's original material.[13]

Vander Ark himself commented on Goldsmith's Quora post. On July 14, 2019, in a thread discussing the case and Rowling's failure to create a promised encyclopedia herself, he clarified, "The lawsuit against the publisher (not against me, I was only a witness) was actually about who gets to write readers' guides about an author's work. Rowling and her folks wanted that right to be given to the author [so] that she . . . could control who wrote about the series. This question had never been litigated. . . . The lawsuit sought to resolve that gray area."[14] The case helped establish parameters for scholarly works and fair use; however, as a well-known Big Name Fan (BNF) and academic, Vander Ark's apparent fall from Rowling's favor sent a message to other fans: censure could happen again. Although the Warner Brothers cease-and-desist letters are now a badge of honor, it was clear that Rowling would not tolerate fans making money if they infringed on her intellectual property rights. The initial Ivory Tower volume (not a "companion book" but an anthology of literary criticism) received similar legal correspondence from Rowling's publisher. (See the introduction to that book for details.)

By contrast, Rowling welcomed fans who used official Warner Brothers, Sony, or Rowling-owned websites like Pottermore and the Wizarding World. Fans who posted on approved (though not official) fan sites—The Leaky Cauldron or MuggleNet, for example—were also generally safe from censure. Favorite fans received invitations to premieres and scoops on

21. "Accio Jo!" Woke Wizards and Generational Potter Fandom

Rowling and the films' actors. Many young writers and web publishers went on to use skills honed in the fan community in successful careers. Notably, creators such as John and Hank Green, Rainbow Rowell, Victoria Lee, Laura Lam, Judith Lewis, Renae McBrain, Darren Criss, and A. J. Holmes have moved from producing Harry Potter fanfiction, musical dramas, and fan videos to becoming successful writers, entertainers, and YouTube stars. Notably, Ebony Elizabeth Thomas has blazed a path from fandom to academia, writing two award-winning volumes on children's literature and fan culture that deal with race and Othering. Thomas was a fifth-grade teacher in Detroit when she read her first Harry Potter novel.[15] She subsequently became involved in early Harry Potter conferences before earning graduate degrees in children's literature and is a leading expert on how people of color are represented in literature for children and young adults.

As long as underage fans are protected from sexually explicit content, Rowling has taken a hands-off approach to most fans' creative endeavors, allowing Harry Potter fanfiction to flourish. Although "fic" is found on all platforms that fans frequent, including the official HP sites, the two largest are FanFiction.Net, with over 12 million registered users, founded in 1998, and Archive of Our Own (AO3), with 5.48 million members, founded in 2009. As of this writing, FanFiction.Net has 8,975 Harry Potter communities and over 845,000 posted HP-tagged works, easily topping all fandoms and other areas.[16] AO3 numbers "Harry Potter—J. K. Rowling" individual works at 435,755, which places first in "Books & Literature" and third to "Marvel" and "Marvel Cinematic Universe" in "Movies."[17]

Of the fans I surveyed, 43.22 percent said they had read HP-related fanfiction, 40.92 percent said they had not, and 15.86 percent gave no response. Most fanfiction readers were enthusiasts, some noting they had read every work available. Many cited romantic relationships or "ships" as their favorite stories. These ships included canon and noncanon pairings from "fluff" (innocent handholding) to "slash" (same-sex romantic to explicit pairing) as well as Character x Reader inserts (second-person stories that include the reader). Favorite ships or One True Pairs (OTPs) mentioned most often included Harmony (Harry x Hermione), Dramione (Draco x Hermione), Drarry (Draco x Harry), Henny (Harry x Ginny), Jily (James x Lily), Remadora (Remus Lupin x Nymphadora Tonks), and Wolfstar (Remus x Sirius Black). Marauders-era, Next Generation/Post-Battle of

Hogwarts, and Alternate Universe (AU) were often identified as favorite time periods or backgrounds.

In his 2006 essay "Confronting the Challenges of Participatory Culture: Media Education for the 21st Century," Jenkins describes a healthy fandom as one in which "not every member must contribute, but all must believe they are free to contribute when ready and that what they contribute will be appropriately valued. . . . Many will only dabble, some will dig deeper, and still others will master the skills that are most valued within the community."[18] When survey participants were asked if they had written Harry Potter fanfiction themselves, 11.34 percent reported they'd written at least one piece, although some noted they had been too shy to post it or had shared only with friends. Others said that they had written numerous works, from Drabbles to multi-chapter, novel-length pieces:

> I wrote a lot in high school as a way of processing the things going on in my life. (Bethany)

> I finally published two of my stories. I have loved it! I get a few kudos almost every day and occasionally really sweet comments that encourage me to keep writing. I think fanfics go on to continue the best of what the HP story does. (Erin)

> I've done a lot of role play based character writing. A few years ago, it was a very active community of writers and fans. (Lauren)[19]

Most fans who reported writing HP fiction described similarly positive experiences. From the cathartic nature of writing to interacting with readers, many fan writers felt a strong sense of comradery and accomplishment. One anonymous writer described the AO3 HP community as "an absolute godsend. I will defend until my dying breath and I donate to [AO3] when I can." Unlike the fractiousness in some parts of HP fandom, members agreed (at the time of the survey) that the fanfiction community had largely stayed positive. Many said that they remained avid readers of fanfiction and still enjoyed writing. Millennial fans reported they had gone on to become corporate writers, journalists, editors, librarians, lawyers, performers, researchers, and teachers.

21. "Accio Jo!" Woke Wizards and Generational Potter Fandom

Although Rowling has often encouraged her readers to be creative, not all fan activities have received her praise. Draco-centric and Harry/Draco stories began to push boundaries. Judith Lewis, under the pseudonym Cassandra Claire (later Clare), wrote the now notorious Draco Trilogy of fan novels, which established a fanon (fan canon) of its own concerning Harry's bullying nemesis, Draco Malfoy. Scholar Cait Coker describes Lewis's version of the character as "a sympathetically-written and redeemed Draco Malfoy, who is revealed to be less loathsome than Rowling has presented him largely through being a victim of abuse and control by Lucius Malfoy." Coker further notes, "This was not an unusual characterization of Draco: in fact, far from it. Fan renderings of Draco Malfoy during [1998–2006] frequently took this approach."[20]

Although popular among fans, romances and shipping in fanfiction often shift from children's fare into young adult or explicitly adult territory, which for Rowling crosses a line. She clarified her views about Draco Malfoy on Pottermore in October 2015, "pouring cold common sense on ardent readers' daydreams as I told them, rather severely, that Draco was not concealing a heart of gold under all that sneering and prejudice and that no, he and Harry were not destined to end up best friends."[21] Draco fans did not take this chastisement well. Similarly, fans who gravitated toward Severus Snape often found themselves at odds with other fans. Rowling explained on Twitter that she views him as ambiguous: "Snape is all grey. You can't make him a saint: he was vindictive & bullying. You can't make him a devil: he died to save the Wizarding world,"[22] she wrote; and "Snape was a bully who loved the goodness he sensed in Lily without being able to emulate her. That was his tragedy."[23] Thanks to the late Alan Rickman's iconic performances, Snape will likely always inspire both admiration and scorn.

When fans identified controversies in the HP fan community, those surrounding Snape were mentioned second most often at 12.84 percent. This placed it just ahead of the play *The Cursed Child* (12.27 percent), which appeared in book form on July 31, 2016. In the survey, 62.9 percent of fans had read the play, and eighteen individuals reported that they had seen it performed live in London, New York, or Melbourne and generally enjoyed it. The play sold out during its New York run from March 25, 2018, to March 8, 2020, grossing over $174 million and selling over 1.3 million tickets before closing due to the pandemic.[24] The book also sold well, with Scholastic reporting that it initially kept pace with *Deathly Hallows* sales.[25] Fans' main complaints concerned jarring interpretations of characters, time travel that didn't follow rules in the books, a contrived villain, gratuitous cameos, and the genre shift from boarding school mystery to adventure caper. Some complained that it was marketed as a sequel to the books, although Rowling hadn't written it herself, and that it contradicted details in the *Deathly Hallows* epilogue. Fan complaints came mainly from readers who had not seen the play performed. Unfortunately, most fans will not be able to attend a live performance and judge for themselves, at least for the time being.

Perhaps the thorniest issue raised about *Cursed Child* was the casting of a black woman to play an adult Hermione. Many fans applauded the decision as a step toward diversity, which they saw as lacking in the books and films. One survey responder, Shelly, who had seen the play in New York professed, "Noma Dumezweni was absolutely amazing as Hermione in Cursed Child. Honestly, it's just strange to me that so many fans get so angry about those kinds of conversations, as if one person's interpretation of a character could somehow steal something from their own interpretation." At the time the casting was announced, some fans insisted that a black Hermione wasn't "canon" and was inconsistent with the casting of Emma Watson (who is white) in the films. In response, Rowling tweeted, "Canon: brown eyes, frizzy hair and very clever. White skin was never specified. Rowling loves black Hermione," with a kissy-face emoji, on December 21, 2015.[26] In interviews, Rowling called discontented fans "idiots" and "racists,"[27] while some fans argued that one black Hermione did not make up for the lack of diversity in the books and films.

This valid complaint is echoed by scholars such as Ebony Elizabeth Thomas in her 2019 work *The Dark Fantastic: Race and the Imagination from Harry Potter to the Hunger Games*. In her award-winning study, Thomas describes the Othering process that occurs as fans of color seek out spaces in popular narratives. She illuminates how writers, publishers, and fans relegate Black characters into supporting roles that end once a character's usefulness to the white protagonist is finished. Furthermore, when Black characters are absent from the narrative's center, the resulting void forces Black readers and audiences to identify with a story's Othered characters, who most often fulfill the function of monster. Thomas theorizes a Dark Fantastic Cycle—spectacle, hesitation, violence, haunting, and emancipation—that entraps characters of color, specifically Black women. She ends her study on a hopeful note, observing the HP fan community's embrace of Black Hermione through fan fiction, art, and other speculative works that emancipate the character from the role of Dark Other in the cycle.[28]

The model franchise's fracture that began with *The Cursed Child* continued with the Newt Scamander films, *Fantastic Beasts and Where to Find Them* (2016) and *Fantastic Beasts: The Crimes of Grindelwald* (2018). Columnist Mason Segall suggests that Rowling "laid waste to the 'Harry Potter' continuity" for very little payoff.[29] Despite the Fantastic Beasts films making around $814 million, $655 million, and $407 million respectively, they pale compared to *Deathly Hallows, Part 2*'s record-breaking $1.3 billion.[30] Survey participants mentioned issues ranging from the casting of Johnny Depp (accused of domestic violence) to continuity problems (McGonagall at the wrong age, for example) to the portrayal of Nagini as an enslaved Asian woman to failing to acknowledge Dumbledore and Grindelwald's homosexual relationship in the first two films. The Ilvermorny webpage created as a lead-in for the first film set in North America also received participants' criticism. Anthropologist Emma Louise Backe observes, "The creatures named as Ilvermorny houses are separated from their particular native context, treating Native mythology as a singular corpus shared across all tribes and indigenous communities across the country, which simply wasn't and isn't the case."[31]

Over the past decade, Rowling kept posting and tweeting, to some fans' delight, others' ire, and much head-scratching. Many people found the woman who had created a magical and nurturing place less than perfect. Given Ron's balance between connection and independence, Hermione's intelligence and compassion, and Harry's stance for principles despite the odds, it is unsurprising that millennial fans value those qualities, applying what they learned from the texts and the fan community to their own lives. Cue John Williams's theme music, and most fans would answer Fawkes's call.

On December 19, 2019, Rowling sparked her biggest controversy so far when she tweeted, "Dress however you please. Call yourself whatever you like. Sleep with any consenting adult who'll have you. Live your best life in peace and security. But force women out of their jobs for stating that sex is real? #IStandWithMaya #ThisIsNotADrill."[32] Rowling was responding to a court case involving Maya Forstater, an economist who, according to the BBC, was not reappointed to her job after accusations of making transphobic comments to coworkers and creating a hostile work environment. Forstater sued her employer and lost.[33] Human Rights Campaign and GLAAD called out Rowling's tweet as both factually inaccurate and hurtful to transgendered people. In the past, Rowling had liked other tweets considered by some to be transphobic as well.[34]

My survey was posted for a two-month period starting in mid-November 2019, so it was partially contemporaneous with the fallout. Respondents identified Rowling's December tweet (which they called "tone-deaf" and "unconscionable") as the leading controversy in the fandom, with 13.4 percent of participants describing it as a serious problem. Asked if Harry Potter had a positive or negative impact on her life, one responder, Jennifer, described it as a mixed experience because Rowling's "support of TERF (trans-exclusionary radical feminist) accounts on Twitter, her rejection of Scottish independence, her imperfect allyship to the lgbtqia+ community, and her tendencies toward non-intersectional feminist behavior [are] concerning in the best lights." Having come of age during the AIDS crisis and the fight for marriage equality, many millennial-aged fans grew up with empathy for vulnerable populations. The transgender community's status as a vulnerable population is well established,[35] so many fans with politically and socially aware attitudes were offended when Rowling made a statement perceived as hostile toward trans women. The irony, of course, is that researchers such as Jack Gierzynski and Loris Vezzali have established that these same ideologies derive in part from exposure to the Harry Potter novels.[36]

Then came Rowling's tweet on June 6, 2020, in reaction to an essay on the Devex news site entitled "Opinion: Creating a More Equal Post-COVID-19 World for People Who Menstruate." Rowling posted: " 'People who menstruate.' I'm sure there used to be a word for those people. Someone help me out. Wumben? Wimpund? Woomud?"[37] The blowback on Twitter was swift. Rowling posted three more tweets over the next couple of hours. In her last tweet, she wrote, "I respect every trans person's right to live any

21. "Accio Jo!" Woke Wizards and Generational Potter Fandom

way that feels authentic and comfortable to them. I'd march with you if you were discriminated against on the basis of being trans. At the same time, my life has been shaped by being female. I do not believe it's hateful to say so."[38] Medical doctors and health-care professionals responded, as did LGTBQIA+ advocates. Charlotte Clymer, a transgender woman who works for the Equal Rights Campaign, pointed out, "The vast consensus of medical and other scientific experts validate trans people and urge affirmation of us. Your own country's medical organizations have said as much."[39] Feminist author Naomi Wolf reached out to Rowling on Twitter: "@jk_rowling you're a cherished part of my kids' lives. That said, this thread baffles me. 'My life has been shaped by being female.' That's 100% true for trans women as well."[40] There were 95.3K retweets and 231.9K likes for Wolf's response two weeks after Rowling's original post.[41]

Four days later, Rowling posted on her website an expanded response, "J. K. Rowling Writes about Her Reasons for Speaking out on Sex and Gender Issues." In her 3,669-word essay, the author lays out her concerns about "the new trans activism" and her fears that "women's rights" are under attack. She states, "It would be so much easier to tweet the approved hashtags—because of course trans rights are human rights and of course trans lives matter—scoop up the woke cookies and bask in a virtue-signalling afterglow."[42] Rowling reveals that she is a survivor of sexual assault and domestic abuse from her first marriage. She states that she believes most trans people deserve protection; she then argues that allowing trans women to use women's restrooms or changing rooms will "open the door to any and all men who wish to come inside."[43] Rowling concludes that she is writing not to garner sympathy but to gain understanding for women who feel as she does.

Rowling makes some reasonable points—she wants to protect "women and girls" from abuse and predation. However, her definition of who qualifies as female seems limited to those born biologically female, which excludes trans women. In her essay "How JK Rowling Betrayed the World She Created," trans writer Gabrielle Bellot expresses her hurt as a Potter fan. Rowling's opinion, Bellot feels, "is a mainstream anti-trans view, arguing that people like me are dangerous and unfit to be in certain spaces."[44] If Rowling were just another Twitter user, her statements would be only one individual's opinion. However, as of this writing, Rowling has 14.5 million

Twitter followers; she has clout by virtue of her creations' commercial success and her millions of fans.[45]

All three corporate entities who have valuable properties on the line—Scholastic, Warner Brothers, and Universal Studios, owner of the Wizarding World theme parks—attempted to strike a balance between not alienating Rowling and supporting the LGBTQIA+ community, including their own employees and customers.[46] The films' millennial-age stars—Daniel Radcliffe, Emma Watson, Rupert Grint, Bonnie Wright, Katie Leung, and Eddie Redmayne—expressed their support for the trans community. Radcliffe wrote a post for the Trevor Project, a nonprofit organization dedicated to suicide prevention among LGBTQIA+ youth. After affirming support for the trans community, he addressed HP fans: "To all the people who now feel that their experience of the books has been tarnished or diminished, I am deeply sorry for the pain [Rowling's] comments have caused you. . . . If you found anything in these stories that resonated with you and helped you at any time in your life—then that is between you and the book that you read, and it is sacred."[47]

In response to the survey, graduate student Abbey Flentje noted the impact of Rowling's tweets and other questionable choices: "J. K. Rowling's Twitter has definitely affected my view of her rather than of her series. She has supported and retweets/follows many trans exclusionary radical feminists (TERFs) on the platform, which just says that a lot of her feminist leanings are more in the vein of white feminism than anything else." Although 17.99 percent of fans surveyed said they knew of no controversies in the fandom, 6.3 percent reported they had left the fandom because of anger over Rowling's views and other controversies. Flentje concludes, "Rowling herself has not diminished my enjoyment of Harry Potter or the fandom." It's a distinction fans in other fandoms have made when creators have fallen from grace. For example, filmmakers Roman Polanski and Woody Allen, both accused of having sex with teenage girls, are often regarded through a dualistic lens for their professional successes and personal behaviors.

In the 1967 essay "Death of the Author," Roland Barthes writes, "The reader has never been the concern of classical criticism; for it, there is no other man in literature but the one who writes. We . . . now . . . know that to restore to writing its future, we must reverse its myth: the birth of the reader must be ransomed by the death of the Author."[48] Similar to New Critics who isolate texts from outside influences (including the author), Barthes sees the relationship between reader and text as more important than that between writer and text. Divorcing the text from its creator certainly presents its own problems, but separating the books, films, and characters fans love from a creator with problematic views or behaviors is attractive for some aggrieved Potter fans.

Separating Rowling from her works might be a feat only a wizard can manage, partly because she has been intensely involved with the fan community. Nevertheless, fans have brought their own analytical skills to bear on what they deem problematic in her works. Flentje described this process happening during a college course. "I took a course on race, class, and gender roles in the original novels, which I believe gave me a fresher critical perspective to the books and also revealed to me how white and heteronormative the series is. Hermione is an excellent character, but she ends up being one of the only progressive women in the series" (Flentje). Other fans I surveyed noted that they found echoes of anti-Semitic tropes in descriptions of the Goblins. Several mentioned repeated fat shaming, usually applied to villainous characters such as the male Dursleys, Aunt Marge, Dolores Umbridge, and Crabbe and Goyle. With the exception of Hagrid, characters who are overweight are often depicted by Rowling as being mean, lazy, and stupid. A few responders observed how disturbing the enslavement of house-elves was despite Hermione's efforts with S.P.E.W. to liberate them; the subplot was unresolved in the books and omitted from the films. Unfortunately, once flaws are exposed, whether in the works or the author's behavior, not every fan can reconcile the incongruities. When fans believe an author has failed them, many turn to the fandom itself for consolation.

I wish I could take a wizard photograph of the current Harry Potter fandom and compare it to ten and twenty years ago. Some of us are middle-aged or older now, but most fans are young and willing to explore new content. Just over two decades into the twenty-first century, fans have seen angry fractures and self-inflicted wounds. Some fans say they have felt milked, gouged, trolled, and disappointed at some point with Rowling, the works, the franchise, or the fandom. Nevertheless, there is still more holding the fan community together than pulling it apart. A "whomping"

82 percent of survey responders came to the fandom through the books, not the films, and 93.5 percent identified themselves as "big fans who still participated in the community" or "huge fans who are very engaged with the community." Again and again, fans shared how the books and the HP community had gotten them through real-life struggles. They consoled us after losing loved ones, helped us survive illnesses and breakups, stood in for a friend or a mentor, offered comfort after a disaster, supported us when we stood alone, cheered us on down days, inspired us to do our best, gave us a laugh or a good cry, kept us sane, introduced us to friends and life partners, or brought us closer to our own little witches and wizards. We have written papers, poetry, songs, folk music, spell books, parodies, meta, and tons of fanfiction. We painted, drew, colored, composed, played, sang, critiqued, reimagined, speculated, commented, video blogged, TikToked, tweeted, and made podcasts. We have gone on studio tours, film location hikes, Wizarding World trips, scavenger hunts, pub crawls, and trivia-game dates. We have attended Harry Potter–themed birthday parties, speed dating sessions, engagement parties, weddings, baby showers, dinner parties, escape rooms, and conferences and conventions. We have made robes, wands, butterbeer, and pumpkin juice; created spell books; LARPed; and played Quidditch. We have bought T-shirts, jewelry, costumes, wands, Sorting Hats, socks, stuffed toys, FunkoPops!, action figures, brooms, board games, candy, Lego sets, video games, holiday ornaments, calendars, backpacks, pencils, bedsheets, scarves, house ties, key rings, phone cases, backgrounds, ringtones, Blu-Rays, posters, soundtracks, and face masks. People generously and joyously shared their experiences and assistance. Accio, indeed!

Before I began this project, I feared what I might find. Some of it turned out to be unpleasant, but as a maturing community, Harry Potter fans have held on to core values of loyalty, friendship, and cooperation, even if they had to stand up to authority or friends. The community has not imploded. Some have left because they lost interest or became disillusioned. Some have rejected the commodification of a special part of their childhoods. However, as I predicted more than twenty years ago, the development of social media alongside the fandom has helped keep members together. Along the way, something a bit magical happened: the community became more than the books, the films, more even than Rowling herself, transforming us

21. "Accio Jo!" Woke Wizards and Generational Potter Fandom

through our connections and our creativity. That shared experience cannot be taken away or sold—it can only be expanded in charm-like fashion to include those we love.

NOTES

1. Harrison, "Game of Thrones."
2. McNamara, "Fandom Turned Toxic."
3. Jenkins, *Convergence Culture*, 131.
4. As part of my primary research, I composed an original survey of twenty-three questions using Google Forms, titled "Harry Potter Inventory Survey," and asked fans about their experiences as individuals and as fans within the HP fan community, using both closed and open-ended questions. I asked friends via Facebook, Tumblr, and Twitter to forward the link to their friends in the fandom, and they shared my solicitation, most notably, on the My Favorite Avada Kedavra and Potterhead Running Club Facebook pages, which quickly garnered hundreds of detailed replies. I accepted answers from November 12, 2019, to January 15, 2020, and received 1,217 total responses.
5. "Why Is the Harry Potter Fandom?"
6. Amber Goldsmith, "J. K. Rowling vs. the Internet," answer to "Why Is the Harry Potter Fandom Starting to Turn against JK Rowling?" Quora, May 9, 2018, accessed June 17, 2020, https://www.quora.com/Why-is-the-Harry-Potter-fandom-starting-to-turn-against-JK-Rowling.
7. Goldsmith.
8. Jenkins, *Textual Poachers*, 24.
9. Reuters staff, "Dumbledore Is Gay."
10. Gunelius, *Harry Potter*, 34.
11. Griffin, "10 Disenchanting Lawsuits."
12. Anthony Falzone wrote the statement for Stanford University's Center for Internet and Society, which helped defend RDR Books against Rowling et al.'s plagiarism lawsuit.
13. Falzone, "Avada Kedavra."
14. Vander Ark, comment on Goldsmith, "Rowling vs. the Internet."
15. Dahlen and Thomas, *Potter and the Other*, 3.
16. *FanFiction*.
17. Archive of Our Own home page, accessed June 20, 2020. https://archiveofourown.org.
18. Jenkins, "Confronting the Challenges."
19. I have used responders' full names, first names, nicknames, or identified them anonymously, according to their preferences.
20. Coker, "Problematic Fan-Girl," 105–6.
21. Rowling, "Draco Malfoy."
22. J. K. Rowling (@jk_rowling), "Snape is all grey. You can't make him a saint: he was vindictive & bullying. You can't make him a devil: he died to save

the wizarding world," Twitter, November 27, 2015, 4:43 a.m., https://twitter.com/jk_rowling/status/670176159561326592.

23. J. K. Rowling (@jk_rowling), "Snape was a bully who loved the goodness he sensed in Lily without being able to emulate her. That was his tragedy," Twitter, November 27, 2015, 12:29 p.m., https://twitter.com/jk_rowling/status/670278271171457024.

24. Broadway World, "Potter and the Cursed Child."

25. Scholastic, "Announces Sales."

26. J. K. Rowling (@jk_rowling), "Canon: brown eyes, frizzy hair and very clever. White skin was never specified. Rowling loves black Hermione," Twitter, December 21, 2015, 5:41 a.m., https://twitter.com/jk_rowling/status/678888094339366914.

27. Robinson, "Rowling Addresses 'Racist' Critics."

28. Thomas, Dark Fantastic.

29. Segall, "15 Worst Retcons."

30. "Fantastic Beasts and Where to Find Them"; "Fantastic Beasts: The Crimes of Grindelwald"; "Fantastic Beasts: The Secrets of Dumbledore"; "Harry Potter and the Deathly Hallows, Part 2" (all from *Box Office Mojo*).

31. Backe, "Magical Maladies."

32. J. K. Rowling (@jk_rowling), "Dress however you please. Call yourself whatever you like. Sleep with any consenting adult who'll have you. Live your best life in peace and security. But force women out of their jobs for stating that sex is real?" Twitter, December 19, 2019, 7:57 a.m., https://twitter.com/jk_rowling/status/1207646162813100033.

33. Faulkner, "Maya Forstater."

34. Faulkner.

35. National Center for Transgender Equality, Discrimination Survey.

36. Gierzynski, *Millennials*; Vezzali et al., "Greatest Magic."

37. J. K. Rowling (@jk_rowling), "'People who menstruate.' I'm sure there used to be a word for those people. Someone help me out. Wumben? Wimpund? Woomud?" Twitter, June 6, 2020, 5:35 p.m., https://twitter.com/jk_rowling/status/1269382518362509313.

38. J. K. Rowling (@jk_rowling), "I respect every trans person's right to live any way that feels authentic and comfortable to them. I'd march with you if you were discriminated against on the basis of being trans. At the same time, my life has been shaped by being female. I do not believe it's hateful to say so," Twitter, June 6, 2020, 7:16 p.m., https://twitter.com/jk_rowling/status/1269407862234775552.

39. Charlotte Clymer (@cmclymer), "The vast consensus of medical and other scientific experts validate trans people and urge affirmation of us. Your own country's medical organizations have said as much," Twitter, June 6, 2020, 6:29 p.m., https://twitter.com/cmclymer/status/1269396116421988352.

40. Naomi Wolf (@naomirwolf), "@jk_rowling you're a cherished part of my kids' lives. That said, this thread baffles me. 'My life has been shaped by being female.' That's 100% true for trans women as well," Twitter, June 10, 2020, 6:23 p.m., https://twitter.com/naomirwolf/status/1270844071960031232.

41. Rowling, "I respect every trans person's right."

21. "Accio Jo!" Woke Wizards and Generational Potter Fandom

42. Rowling, "Sex and Gender Issues."
43. Rowling.
44. Bellot, "How Rowling Betrayed."
45. As of August 30, 2023, Rowling had 13.9 million followers on her Twitter page, a decline of 0.6 percent since the original tweet. J. K. Rowling, Twitter home page, https://twitter.com/jk_rowling.
46. Siegel and Abramovitch, "Universal Parks Responds."
47. Radcliffe, "Radcliffe Responds."
48. Barthes, "Death of the Author," 54–55.

Bibliography

"About Robert Galbraith." Robert Galbraith: The Cormoran Strike Novels. Accessed April 29, 2023. https://robert-galbraith.com/about/.

Abraham, Lyndy. *A Dictionary of Alchemical Imagery*. Cambridge: Cambridge University Press, 2001.

Ackerman, Alan L., Jr. "A Spirit of Giving in *A Midsummer Night's Dream*." In Banford and Knowles, *Shakespeare's Comedies*, 110–25.

Adams, Danny. "The Once and Future Wizard: Arthurian (and Anti-Arthurian) Themes in the Harry Potter Series." In *Critical Insights*, Whited and Grimes, 82–99.

Adney, Karley. "The Influence of Gender on Harry Potter's Heroic (Trans)Formation." In Berndt and Steveker, *Heroism*, 177–92.

"Agapanthus." *Harry Potter Lexicon*. Accessed April 29, 2023. https://www.hp-lexicon.org/thing/agapanthus/.

Aghtan, Kamillea. "Anticipating Exceptionalism: Institutionalised Silence and the State of Exception in Harry Potter and the Order of the Phoenix." In *Magic Is Might 2012: Proceedings of the International Conference*, edited by Luigina Ciolfi and Gráinne O'Brien, 49–58. Sheffield, UK: Sheffield Hallam University, 2013.

Alberti, John, and P. Andrew Miller, eds. *Transforming Harry: The Adaption of Harry Potter in The Transmedia Age*. Detroit: Wayne State University Press, 2018.

Anatol, Giselle Liza, ed. *Reading Harry Potter*. Santa Barbara, CA: Praeger, 2003.

———, ed. *Reading Harry Potter Again*. Santa Barbara, CA: Praeger, 2009.

Andersen, Hans Christian. "The Emperor's New Clothes." Translated by Jean Hersholt. The Hans Christian Andersen Centre, University of Southern Denmark. https://andersen.sdu.dk/vaerk/hersholt/TheEmperorsNewClothes_e.html.

Andréa, Hans. "The Alchemy of Harry Potter." *Harry Potter for Seekers*, 2009. Accessed October 25, 2019. http://www.harrypotterforseekers.com/articles/thealchemyofhpalchemyconf2009.php.

Anzaldúa, Gloria. *Borderlands / La Frontera: The New Mestiza*. San Francisco: Aunt Lute, 2007.

Apter, Michael J. "Developing Reversal Theory: Some Suggestions for Future Research." *Journal of Motivation, Emotion, and Personality* 1, no. 1 (2013): 1–8. doi.org/10.12689/jmep.2013.101.

Apter, Michael J., and Mitzi Desselles. "Disclosure Humor and Distortion Humor: A Reversal Theory Analysis." *Humor* 25, no. 4 (2012): 417–35. doi.org/10.1515/humor-2012-0021.

Bibliography

Arden, Heather, and Kathryn Lorenz. "The Harry Potter Stories and French Arthurian Romance." *Arthuriana* 13, no. 2 (2003): 54–68. https://www.jstor.org/stable/27870516.

Arendt, Hannah. *The Origins of Totalitarianism*. Cleveland: Meridian, 1962.

Aristotle. *Nicomachean Ethics*. Translated by Terence Irwin. Indianapolis: Hackett, 2007.

Armstrong, Philip. "The Gaze of Animals." In *Theorizing Animals: Re-thinking Humanimal Relations*, edited by Nik Taylor and Tania Signal, 175–99. Leiden: Brill, 2011. doi.org/10.1163/ej.9789004202429.i-294.43.

d'Arras, Jean. *Melusine; or, The Noble History of Lusignan*. Translated and edited by Donald Maddox and Sara Sturm-Maddox. University Park: Pennsylvania State University Press, 2012.

Ashcroft, Bill, Gareth Griffiths, and Helen Tiffin. *Postcolonial Studies: The Key Concepts*. New York: Routledge, 2013.

Attebery, Brian. *Strategies of Fantasy*. Bloomington: Indiana University Press, 1992.

Austen, Jane. *Emma*. 1816. Reprint, New York: Oxford, 1990.

Backe, Emma Louise. "Magical Maladies and Injuries: Cultural Appropriation in J. K. Rowling's Ilvermorny." *Geek Anthropologist*, July 8, 2016. https://thegeekanthropologist.com/2016/07/08/magical-maladies-and-injuries-cultural-appropriation-in-j-k-rowlings-ilvermorny/.

Bain, Frederika. "The Tail of Melusine: Hybridity, Mutability, and the Accessible Other." In Urban, Kemmis, and Elmes, *Melusine's Footprint*, 17–35.

Bal, Mieke. *Narratology: Introduction to the Theory of Narrative*. Toronto: University of Toronto Press, 1988.

Banford, Karen, and Richard Paul Knowles, eds. *Shakespeare's Comedies of Love: Essays in Honor of Alexander Leggatt*. Toronto: University of Toronto Press, 2008.

Banks, Lynne Reid. *Melusine*. 1988. Reprint, London: Puffin, 1994.

Barber, E. J. W. *On the Origins of the Vilylrusalki*. Washington, DC: Institute for the Study of Man, 1997.

Barratt, Bethany. *The Politics of Harry Potter*, New York: Palgrave Macmillan, 2012.

Barthes, Roland. "Death of the Author." In *The Rustle of Language*, translated by Richard Howard, 49–55. New York: Hill & Wang, 1986.

Barton, Benjamin H. "Harry Potter and the Half-Crazed Bureaucracy." *Michigan Law Review* 104, no. 6 (May 2006): 1523–38. https://repository.law.umich.edu/cgi/viewcontent.cgi?article=1524&context=mlr.

———. "The Harry Potter Books Critique Bureaucracy." In *Political Issues in J. K. Rowling's Harry Potter Series*, edited by Dedria Bryfonski, 46–58. New York: Greenhaven Press, 2009.

Bates, Catherine. "Love and Courtship." In Leggatt, *Cambridge Companion*, 102–22.

Baudiš, Josef. "Mabinogion." *Folklore* 27, no. 1 (1916): 31–68. http://www.jstor.org/stable/1254884.

Bausman, Cassandra. " 'Elder' and Wiser: The Filmic *Harry Potter* and the Rejection of Power." In Alberti and Miller, *Transforming Harry*, 38–70.

BBC. "Central Park Five: The True Story Behind *When They See Us*." *BBC News*, June 12, 2019. https://www.bbc.com/news/newsbeat-48609693.

Bibliography

Behr, Kate. " 'Same-as-Difference': Narrative Transformations and Intersecting Cultures in Harry Potter." *Journal of Narrative Theory* 35, no. 1 (Winter 2005): 112–32. doi.org/10.1353/jnt.2005.0009.

Bell, Christopher, ed. *From Here to Hogwarts*. Jefferson, NC: McFarland, 2016.

———, ed. *Transmedia Harry Potter*. Jefferson, NC: McFarland, 2019.

———, ed. *Wizards vs. Muggles: Essays on Identity and The Harry Potter Universe*. Jefferson, NC: McFarland, 2016.

Bellot, Gabrielle. "How JK Rowling Betrayed the World She Created." LitHub, June 10, 2020. https://lithub.com/how-jk-rowling-betrayed-the-world-she-created/.

Berger, John. "Why Look at Animals?" In *About Looking*, 3–28. New York: Vintage International, 1991.

Berndt, Katrin. "Hermione Granger; or, A Vindication of the Rights of Girl." In Berndt and Steveker, *Heroism*, 159–76.

Berndt, Katrin, and Lena Steveker, eds. *Heroism in the Harry Potter Series*. Burlington, VT: Ashgate, 2011.

Bernstein, Richard. "Accusations of Abuse Haunt the Legacy of Dr. Bruno Bettelheim." *New York Times*, November 4, 1990. https://www.nytimes.com/1990/11/04/weekinreview/ideas-trends-accusations-of-abuse-haunt-the-legacy-of-dr-bruno-bettelheim.html.

Béroalde de Verville, François. *L'Histoire véritable, ou le voyage des Princes Fortunez*. Paris: C. de La Tour, 1610. Reprinted in the Catalogue Général de Bibliothèque Nationale de France. http://ark.bnf.fr/ark:/12148/cb30092739p.public.

Bettelheim, Bruno. *The Uses of Enchantment: The Meaning and Importance of Fairy Tales*. New York: Vintage, 2010.

Bevington, David. "Love's Labour's Lost and Won." In Banford and Knowles, *Shakespeare's Comedies*, 80–97.

Beyer, Catherine. "Magnum Opus: The Great Work." *Learn Religions*, July 24, 2018. https://www.learnreligions.com/the-great-work-or-magnum-opus-95943.

Bhabha, Homi K. *The Location of Culture*. London: Routledge, 1994.

Bishop, Caroline. "Harry Potter and the Undead Author: Self-Interpretation from Rome to J. K. Rowling." *Eidolon*, June 28, 2017. https://eidolon.pub/harry-potter-and-the-undead-author-6cb8cab767202017.

Bloom, Harold. "Can 35 Million Book Buyers Be Wrong? Yes." *Wall Street Journal*, July 11, 2000.

Breimeier, Russ. "Redeeming Harry Potter." *Christianity Today*, 2005. http://www.christianitytoday.com/ct/2005/novemberweb-only/redeemingharrypotter.html.

Broadway World. "Harry Potter and the Cursed Child, Parts One and Two: Grosses." *Broadway World*. Accessed June 17, 2020. https://www.broadwayworld.com/grosses/HARRY-POTTER-AND-THE-CURSED-CHILDPARTS-ONE-AND-TWO.

Brown, Jake. "Scraping the Bottom of the Pensieve: Reflections from 'Generation Hex.' " Unpublished manuscript, 2021.

Brown, Patrick. "Exclusive: J. K. Rowling on How She Crafts Gritty, Realistic Characters." Goodreads, July 25, 2013. https://www.goodreads.com/blog/show/426-exclusive-j-k-rowling-on-how-she-crafts-gritty-realistic-characters.

Bibliography

Bunce, Fredrick W. *An Encyclopaedia of Hindu Deities, Demi-Gods, Godlings, Demons and Heroes with Special Focus on Iconographic Attributes.* 3 vols. New Delhi: D. K. Printworld, 2000.

Bundel, Ani. "J. K. Rowling's 'Ickabog' Story Is a Return to the 'Harry Potter' Sensibilities that Made Her Famous." *NBC News: Think*, May 26, 2020. https://www.nbcnews.com/think/opinion/j-k-rowing-s-ickabog-story-return-harry-potter-sensibilities-ncna1215091.

———. "The MACUSA's Salem Witchcraft Memorial." Wizards and Whatnot. Accessed November 3, 2019. https://wizardsandwhatnot.com/2016/04/26/the-macusas-salem-witch-trial-memorial/.

Burton, Robert. *The Anatomy of Melancholy.* Edited by Holbrook Jackson. New York: Vintage Books, 1977.

Burton, Tara Isabella. "How the 'Harry Potter' Books Are Replacing the Bible as Millennials' Foundational Text." *Religion News Service*, April 25, 2019. https://religionnews.com/2019/04/25/how-the-harry-potter-books-are-replacing-the-bible-as-millennials-foundational-text/.

Butler, Catherine, and Kimberley Reynolds, ed. *Modern Children's Literature: An Introduction.* 2nd ed. London: Palgrave, 2014.

Butler, Charles. *Four British Fantasists.* Lanham, MD: Scarecrow Press, 2006.

Byatt, A. S. *Possession.* 1990. Reprint, London: Vintage, 1990.

Caldecott, Leonie. "Cult or Culture? Some Reflections on Rowling, Pullman and the Contemporary Fantasy Scene." *Culture & Libri* 156–57 (2006): n.p. https://archive.secondspring.co.uk/articles/Leonie%20Caldecott%20on%20Fantasy.pdf.

Camacci, Lauren. "The Multi-Gaze Perspective of Harry Potter." In Saunders, *Rhetorical Power*, 149–72.

Campbell, Joseph. *The Hero with a Thousand Faces.* 1949. 3rd ed. Novato, CA: New World Library, 2008.

———. *The Power of Myth with Bill Moyers.* Edited by Betty Sue Flowers. New York: Anchor Books, 1988.

Cann, Arnie, and Chantal Collette. "Sense of Humor, Stable Affect, and Psychological Well-being." *Europe's Journal of Psychology* 10, no. 3 (2014): 464–79. doi.org/10.5964/ejop.v10i3.746.

Cannadine, David. *Ornamentalism: How the British Saw Their Empire.* Oxford: Oxford University Press, 2002.

Cantrell, Sarah K. " 'I Solemnly Swear I Am Up to No Good': Foucault's Heterotopias and Deleuze's Any-Spaces-Whatever in J. K. Rowling's Harry Potter Series." *Children's Literature* 39, no. 1 (2011): 195–212. doi:10.1353/chl.2011.0012.

Carey, Brycchan. "Hermione and the House-Elves: The Literary and Historical Contexts of J. K. Rowling's Antislavery Campaign." In Anatol, *Reading Harry Potter*, 103–15.

———. "Hermione and the House-Elves Revisited: J. K. Rowling, Antislavery Campaigning, and the Politics of Potter." In Anatol, *Reading Harry Potter Again*, 159–74.

Carmeli, Ronnie. "Four Models of Fatherhood: Paternal Contributors to Harry Potter's Psychological Development." In *Harry Potter's Worldwide Influence*, edited

by Diana Patterson, 11–33. Newcastle upon Tyne, UK: Cambridge Scholars, 2009.
Casciani, Dominic. "Analysis." *BBC News*, June 10, 2021. www.bbc.com/news/uk-57426579.
Castro, Adam-Troy. "From Azkaban to Abu Ghraib." In *Mapping the World of the Sorcerer's Apprentice*, edited by Mercedes Lackey, 119–32. Dallas: Benbella Books, 2005.
Cecire, Maria Sachiko, Hannah Field, Kavita Mudan Finn, and Malini Roy. *Space and Place in Children's Literature, 1789 to the Present*. Ashgate Studies in Childhood, 1700 to the Present. Farnham, UK: Ashgate, 2015.
Chambers, Jane. " 'For Love's Sake': Lamia and Burton's Love Melancholy." *Studies in English Literature 1500–1900* 22, no. 4 (1983): 583–600.
Chambers, Robert. *The Popular Rhymes of Scotland, with Illustrations*. London: W. & R. Chambers, 1870. https://books.google.co.uk/books/about/Popular_Rhymes_of_Scotland.html?id=99xZAAAAMAAJ.
Chan, Deborah. "Love Is the Strongest Family Tie." In McDaniel and Prinzi, *Potter for Nerds II*, 9–26.
Cherry, Katie E., Laura Sampson, Sandro Galea, Loren D. Marks, Katie E. Stanko, Pamela F. Nezat, and Kayla H. Baudoin. "Spirituality, Humor, and Resilience after Natural and Technological Disasters." *Journal of Nursing Scholarship* 50, no. 5 (2018): 492–501. doi.org/10.1111/jnu.12400.
Chevalier, Guillaume de. *The Ghosts of the Deceased Sieurs, de Villemor, and de Fontaines*. Translated by Thomas Heigham. Cambridge: Cantrell Legge, 1624.
Chism, Christine. " 'Ain't Gonna Study War No More': Geoffrey of Monmouth's *Historia Regum Britanniae* and *Vita Merlini*." *Chaucer Review* 48, no. 4 (2014): 458–79. doi.org/10.5325/chaucerrev.48.4.0458.
Chrétien de Troyes. *Arthurian Romances*. Translated by William W. Kibler and Carleton W. Carroll. London: Penguin, 1991.
Cica, Zoran. "Vilenica and Vilenjak: Bearers of an Extinct Fairy Cult." *Narodna Umjetnost: Croatian Journal of Ethnology and Folklore Research* 39, no.1 (2002): 31–63. https://www.academia.edu/11880412/Vilenica_and_Vilenjak_Bearers_of_an_Extinct_Fairy_Cult.
Classen, Albrecht, ed. *Violence in Medieval Courtly Literature*. Medieval Casebooks. London: Routledge, 2004.
———. "Introduction: Violence in the Shadows of the Court." In Classen, *Violence*, 1–36.
"Cockney." *Oxford Companion to the English Language*. Edited by Tom McArthur, Jacqueline Lam-McArthur, and Lise Fontaine. 2nd ed. Oxford: Oxford University Press, 2018.
Cockrell, Amanda. "Harry Potter and the Secret Password: Finding Our Way in the Magical Genre." In Whited, *Ivory Tower*, 15–26.
Cohen, Jeffrey Jerome. *Monster Theory: Reading Culture*. Minneapolis: University of Minnesota Press, 1996.

Bibliography

Cohen, Signe. "The Two Alchemists in Harry Potter: Voldemort, Harry, and Their Quests for Immortality." *Journal of Religion and Popular Culture* 30, no. 3 (Fall 2018): 206–19. doi.org/10.3138/jrpc.2017-0038.

Coker, Cait. "The Problematic Fan-Girl: Cassandra Clare's Gendered Revisions in the *Mortal Instruments Series*." In *Gender Warriors: Reading Contemporary Urban Fantasy*, edited by U. Melissa Anyiwo and Amanda Hobson, 97–109. Boston: Brill, 2018.

Columbus, Christopher, dir. *Harry Potter and the Sorcerer's Stone*. Burbank, CA: Warner Brothers, 2001.

Compagnone, Vanessa, and Marcel Danesi. "Mythic and Occultist Naming Strategies in *Harry Potter*." *Names* 60, no. 3 (2012), 127–34. doi.org/10.1179/002777 3812Z.00000000018.

Cooper, Helen. *The English Romance in Time: Transforming Motifs from Geoffrey of Monmouth to Shakespeare*. Oxford: Oxford University Press, 2004.

"Corineus." *Encyclopedia Britannica*. Accessed June 11, 2021. https://www.britannica.com/topic/Corineus#ref175839.

Cuntz-Leng, Vera. "Look . . . at . . . Me . . . : Gaze Politics and Male Objectification in the *Harry Potter* Movies." In Alberti and Miller, *Transforming Harry*, 81–100.

Dahlberg-Acton, John (Lord Acton). "Letter to Bishop Mandell Creighton," April 5, 1887. In *Lectures on Modern History*, edited by John Neville Figgis and Reginald Vere Laurence. London: Macmillan, 1906. https://oll.libertyfund.org/titles/acton-acton-creighton-correspondence#lf1524_label_010.

Dahlen, Sarah Park, and Ebony Elizabeth Thomas. *Harry Potter and the Other: Race, Justice, and Difference in the Wizarding World*. Jackson: University Press of Mississippi, 2022.

D'Arcens, Louise, ed. *The Cambridge Companion to Medievalism*. Cambridge Companions to Culture. Cambridge: Cambridge University Press, 2016.

———. Introduction. In D'Arcens, *Cambridge Companion to Medievalism*, 1–13.

Darwin, Gregory. "On Mermaids, Meroveus, and Mélusine: Reading the Irish Seal Woman and Mélusine as Origin Legend." *Folklore* 126, no. 2 (2015): 123–41.

Daston, Lorraine, and Peter Galison. *Objectivity*. New York: Zone Books, 2007.

Davis, Natalie Zemon. *Fiction in the Archives*. Stanford, CA: Stanford University Press, 1990.

Davis, Owen. *Witchcraft, Magic, and Culture, 1736–1951*. Manchester, UK: Manchester University Press, 1999.

Delogu, Daisy. "Jean d'Arras Makes History: Political Legitimacy and the Roman de Mélusine." *Dalhousie French Studies* 80 (2007): 15–28.

Dendle, Peter. "Cryptozoology and the Paranormal in Harry Potter: Truth and Belief at the Borders of Consensus." *Children's Literature Association Quarterly* 36, no. 4 (Winter 2011): 410–25. doi.org/10.1353/chq.2011.0048.

Derrida, Jacques. *The Animal That Therefore I Am*. Edited by Marie-Louise Mallet, translated by David Wills. New York: Fordham University Press, 2008.

"Distillation." Dictionary.com, 2019. https://www.dictionary.com/browse/distillation.

Bibliography

Doughty, Terri. "Locating Harry Potter in the 'Boy's Book' Market." In Whited, *Ivory Tower*, 243–57.

Douglas, Mary. *Thinking in Circles: An Essay on Ring Composition*. Terry Lecture Series. New Haven: Yale University Press, 2007.

Draper, Ronald P. *Shakespeare: The Comedies*. New York: St. Martin's Press, 2000.

Duckworth, George E. "The Architecture of the *Aeneid*." *American Journal of Philology* 75, no. 1 (1954): 1–15. doi.org/10.2307/291902.

Duggan, Jennifer. "Transformative Readings: Harry Potter Fan Fiction, Trans/Queer Reader Response, and J. K. Rowling." *Children's Literature in Education* 53 (2022): 147–68. https://doi.org/10.1007/s10583-021-09446-9.

Dundes, Alan. "Bruno Bettelheim's Uses of Enchantment and Abuses of Scholarship." *Journal of American Folklore* 104, no. 411 (1991): 74–83. Accessed July 18, 2021. doi:10.2307/541135.

Dunlap, David W. "A Memorial Inscription's Grim Origins." *New York Times*, April 2, 2014. https://www.nytimes.com/2014/04/03/nyregion/an-inscription-taken-out-of-poetic-context-and-placed-on-a-9-11-memorial.html.

Economides, Louise. *The Ecology of Wonder in Romantic and Postmodern Literature*. New York: Palgrave Macmillan, 2016. doi.org/10.1057/978-1-137-47750-7.

Eliot, T. S. "What Is a Classic?" In *Selected Prose of T. S. Eliot*, edited by Frank Kermode, 115–31. New York: Farrar, Straus and Giroux, 1975.

Estlein, Roi. "Parenting Styles." In *The Wiley Blackwell Encyclopedia of Family Studies*, edited by Constance L. Shehan. Hoboken, NJ: John Wiley & Sons, 2016. doi.org/10.1002/9781119085621.wbefs030.

Evert, Walter. *Aesthetic and Myth in the Poetry of Keats*. Princeton: Princeton University Press, 1965.

Fallon, Claire. "What J. K. Rowling's New Story Can Teach Us about Cultural Appropriation." *Huffington Post*, March 18, 2016. http://www.huffingtonpost.com/.

Falzone, Anthony. "Avada Kedavra—The Harry Potter Lexicon Disappears." Center for Internet and Society, Stanford Law School, Stanford University, September 8, 2008. http://cyberlaw.stanford.edu/blog/2008/09/avada-kedavra-harry-potter-lexicon-disappears.

"Fantastic Beasts and Where to Find Them (2016)." *Box Office Mojo*. Accessed April 27, 2023. https://www.boxofficemojo.com/title/tt3183660/.

"Fantastic Beasts: The Crimes of Grindelwald (2018)." *Box Office Mojo*. Accessed April 27, 2023. https://www.boxofficemojo.com/title/tt4123430/.

"Fantastic Beasts: The Secrets of Dumbledore (2022)." *Box Office Mojo*. Accessed April 27, 2023. https://www.boxofficemojo.com/title/tt4123432/.

Farnel, Megan. "Magical Econ 101: Wealth, Labor, and Inequality in Harry Potter." In Bell, *From Here to Hogwarts*, 28–53.

Farrell, Joseph. "*Aeneid* 5: Poetry and Parenthood." In Perkell, *Reading Vergil's Aeneid*, 96–110.

———. *Juno's Aeneid: A Battle for Heroic Identity*. Princeton: Princeton University Press, 2021.

Bibliography

Faulkner, Doug. "Maya Forstater: Woman Loses Tribunal over Transgender Tweets." *BBC News*, June 10, 2021. http://www.bbc.com/news/uk-57426579.

Ferguson, George. *Signs and Symbols in Christian Art*. New York: Oxford University Press, 1961.

"500 Million Harry Potter Books Have Now Been Sold Worldwide." Wizarding World, February 1, 2018. www.wizardingworld.com/news/500-million-harry-potter-books-have-now-been-sold-worldwide.

Flaherty, Colleen. "'TERF' War." *Inside Higher Education*, August 28, 2018. https://www.insidehighered.com/news/2018/08/29/philosophers-object-journals-publication-terf-reference-some-feminists-it-really.

Forstater, Maya. "Joss Stone, Maya Forstater." Interview by Emma Barnett. *BBC Woman's Hour*, March 9, 2022, 57:22. http://www.bbc.co.uk/sounds/play/m00154ct.

Forgacs, David. *The Gramsci Reader: Selected Writings 1916–1935*. New York: New York University Press, 2000.

Frankel, Valerie Estelle. "'Witches Live among Us!' The Minorities Battle Prejudice in *Fantastic Beasts*." In Firestone and Clark, *Harry Potter and Convergence Culture*, 101–13.

Freeman, Louise. "Creosote-Colored Tea Leaves: Louise's First Musings for Cormoran Strike 5." *Hogwarts Professor*, March 18, 2019. http://www.hogwartsprofessor.com/creosote-colored-tea-leaves-louises-first-musings-for-cormoran-strike-5/#more-18967.

———. "Harry Potter and the Diagnostic and Statistical Manual: Muggle Disorders in the Wizarding World." *Study and Scrutiny: Research on Young Adult Literature* 1, no. 1 (2015): 156–214. doi.org/10.15763/issn.2376-5275.2015.1.1.156-214.

———. "Monuments in *The Ickabog*: Commentary on Today's News?" *Hogwarts Professor*, July 13, 2020. https://www.hogwartsprofessor.com/monuments-in-the-ickabog-commentary-on-todays-headlines/.

Freier, Mary P. "The Librarian in Rowling's *Harry Potter* Series." *CLCWeb: Comparative Literature and Culture* 16, no. 3 (2014).

Friedman, Leslee. "Militant Literacy: Hermione Granger, Rita Skeeter, Dolores Umbridge, and the (Mis)use of Text." In Anatol, *Reading Harry Potter Again*, 191–205.

Furness, Hannah. "J. K. Rowling Invented Quidditch after a Row with Her Boyfriend." *Telegraph*, May 18, 2013. https://www.telegraph.co.uk/culture/books/10065868/JK-Rowling-invented-Quidditch-after-a-row-with-her-boyfriend.html.

Fukuyama, Francis. "What Is Populism?" *Atlantik-Brücke* 8 (2017): 10–18. https://www.atlantik-bruecke.org/en/19230-2/.

Galbraith, Robert (J. K. Rowling). *Cuckoo's Calling*. New York: Mulholland Books, 2013.

———. *Lethal White*. New York: Mulholland Books, 2018.

Garrett, Greg. *One Fine Potion: The Literary Magic of Harry Potter*. Waco, TX: Baylor University Press, 2010.

Geoffrey of Monmouth. *The History of the Kings of Britain*. Translated by Lewis Thorpe. London: Penguin, 1966.

Bibliography

———. *The Vita Merlini*. Translated by John Jay Parry. University of Illinois Studies in Language and Literature 10.3. Urbana: University of Illinois Press, 1925.

Gibbs, Nancy. "*Time*'s Person of the Year 2007, Runners Up: J. K. Rowling." *Time*, December 19, 2007. https://content.time.com/time/specials/2007/personofthe-year/article/0,28804,1690753_1695388_1695436,00.html.

Gierzynski, Anthony. *Harry Potter and the Millennials: Research Methods and the Politics of the Muggle Generation*. With Kathryn Eddy. Baltimore: Johns Hopkins University Press, 2013.

Granger, John. "Casual Vacancy 7: The Seven Part Ring Composition." *Hogwarts Professor* (blog), October 2, 2012. https://www.hogwartsprofessor.com/casual-vacancy-7-the-seven-part-ring-composition/.

———. "Casual Vacancy 11: Christian Hypocrites and Sympathetic Sikhs." *Hogwarts Professor* (blog), October 2, 2012. https://www.hogwartsprofessor.com/casual-vacancy-11-christian-hypocrites-and-sympathetic-sikhs/.

———. "Casual Vacancy 15: A Telling Re-Take on 'The Good Samaritan.'" *Hogwarts Professor* (blog), November 4, 2021. https://www.hogwartsprofessor.com/casual-vacancy-15-a-telling-re-take-on-the-good-samaritan/.

———. "*Cuckoo's Calling*: 25+ Lethal White Finds." *Hogwarts Professor*, November 20, 2018. http://www.hogwartsprofessor.com/cuckoos-calling-25-lethal-white-finds/.

———. *The Deathly Hallows Lectures: The Hogwarts Professor Explains Harry's Final Adventure*. Oklahoma City: Unlocking Press, 2008.

———. "Does Lethal White Echo Goblet of Fire?" *Hogwarts Professor*, September 20, 2018. http://www.hogwartsprofessor.com/does-lethal-white-echo-goblet-of-fire/.

———. "The Esoteric Meaning of 'Fountain of Fair Fortune.'" *Hogwarts Professor*, December 14, 2008. http://www.hogwartsprofessor.com/the-esoteric-meaning-of-fountain-of-fair-fortune/#more-550.

———. "Five Reasons Harry Potter Fandom Isn't Excited about Cormoran Strike—Yet." *Hogwarts Professor* (blog), March 7, 2017. http://www.hogwartsprofessor.com/five-reasons-harry-potter-fandom-isnt-excited-about-cormoran-strike-yet/.

———. *Harry Potter as Ring Composition and Ring Cycle: The Magical Structure and Transcendent Meaning of the Hogwarts Saga*. Oklahoma City: Unlocking Press, 2010.

———. *Harry Potter's Bookshelf: The Great Books behind the Hogwarts Adventures*. New York: Berkley Books, 2009.

———. "The Ickabog Structure: Three Notes." *Hogwarts Professor*, June 27, 2020. https://www.hogwartsprofessor.com/the-ickabog-structure-three-notes/.

———. "*Lethal White*: Add Seven Cuckoo's Echoes." *Hogwarts Professor*, November 7, 2018. http://www.hogwartsprofessor.com/lethal-white-add-seven-cuckoo-echoes.

———. "*Lethal White*: *Cuckoo's Calling* Retold?" *Hogwarts Professor*, September, 20, 2018. http://www.hogwartsprofessor.com/lethal-white-cuckoos-calling-retold.

———. "*Lethal White*: The Ring Structure." *Hogwarts Professor*, November 6, 2018, http://www.hogwartsprofessor.com/lethal-white-the-ring-structure/.

———. "The Missing Page Mystery." *Hogwarts Professor*, November 30, 2018. http://www.hogwartsprofessor.com/lethal-white-the-missing-page-mystery/.

Bibliography

———. "The Missing Page Mystery (2)." *Hogwarts Professor*, May 6, 2019. http://www.hogwartsprofessor.com/lethal-white-missing-page-mystery-2/.

———. "On Turtle-Back Tales and Asterisks." In Prinzi, *Potter for Nerds*, 37–82.

———. *Harry Potter as Ring Composition and Ring Cycle*. Self-published, 2010.

———. "Rowling Says 'Career of Evil' is Her 'Best Planned Book' ——— Is It a Ring?" *Hogwarts Professor*, October 23, 2015, https://www.hogwartsprofessor.com/rowling-says-career-of-evil-is-her-best-planned-book-is-it-a-ring/.

———. "Russian Formalism." Unpublished manuscript, November 3, 2019.

———. "The Silkworm 2: Shades of and Keys to The Hogwarts Saga?" *Hogwarts Professor*, June 29, 2014. https://www.hogwartsprofessor.com/the-silkworm-2-shades-of-and-keys-to-the-hogwarts-saga/.

———. "The Tweet Heard Round the World, Part 2." *Hogwarts Professor*, June 11, 2021. https://www.hogwartsprofessor.com/the-tweet-heard-round-the-world-part-2/.

———. *Unlocking Harry Potter: Five Keys for the Serious Reader*. Cleveland: Unlocking Press, 2007.

———. "Violence against Women [in] Harry Potter." With Patrick McCauley. *MuggleNet Academia*, lesson 36, September 26, 2015. Podcast, MP3 audio, 1:27:42. https://mugglenetacademia.libsyn.com/mugglenet-academia-lesson-36-violence-against-women-harry-potter.

———. "The Wizarding War Was Won on the Quidditch Pitch of Hogwarts." With Emily Strand. *MuggleNet Academia*, lesson 40, December 22, 2015. Podcast, MP3 audio, 1:22:06. https://mugglenetacademia.libsyn.com/mugglenet-academia-lesson-40-the-wizarding-war-was-won-on-the-quidditch-pitch-of-hogwarts.

Gregory, Alden. "London's Giants." *Historic Royal Palaces*, October 14, 2016. https://blog.hrp.org.uk/curators/londons-giants/.

Griffin, Simon. "10 Disenchanting Lawsuits Involving 'Harry Potter.' " *Listverse*, March 1, 2018. https://listverse.com/2018/03/01/10-disenchanting-lawsuits-involving-harry-potter/.

Grimes, M. Katherine. "Harry Potter: Fairy Tale Prince, Real Boy, and Archetypal Hero." In Whited, *Ivory Tower*, 89–122.

Grossman, Lev. "J. K. Rowling's *The Casual Vacancy*: We've Read It, Here's What We Think." *Time*, September 27, 2012. https://time.com/4132710/j-k-rowlings-the-casual-vacancy-weve-read-it-heres-what-we-think/.

Groves, Beatrice. "The Alchemical Symbolism of the Deathly Hallows in 'Crimes of Grindelwald.' " MuggleNet, November 18, 2018, http://www.mugglenet.com/2018/11/the-alchemical-symbolism-of-the-deathly-hallows-in-the-crimes-of-grindelwald.

———. " 'Harry Potter: A History of Magic' and Plant Lore, Part 4: 'We Can Talk, if there Is Anyone Worth Talking To': The Language of Flowers." *Leaky Cauldron* (blog), October 18, 2018. http://www.the-leaky-cauldron.org/2018/10/18/harry-potter-a-history-of-magic-and-plant-lore-part-4-we-can-talk-if-there-is-anyone-worth-talking-to-the-language-of-flowers/.

———. *Literary Allusion in Harry Potter*. London: Routledge, 2017.

———. " 'Nagini Maledictus' Literary Allusion in Fantastic Beasts."

Bibliography

Hogwarts Professor, December 1, 2017. http://www.hogwartsprofessor.com/beatrice-groves-nagini-maledictus-literary-allusion-in-fantastic-beasts/.

———. "The Phoenix and the Qilin in 'Secrets of Dumbledore': Fantastic Bestiaries and Where to Find Them." MuggleNet, April 7, 2022. https://www.mugglenet.com/2022/04/the-phoenix-and-the-qilin-in-secrets-of-dumbledore-fantastic-bestiaries-and-where-to-find-them-part-3/.

Guanio-Uluru, Lykke. *Ethics and Form in Fantasy Literature: Tolkien, Rowling and Meyer*. London: Palgrave Macmillan, 2015. doi.org/10.1057/9781137469694.

Gunelius, Susan. *Harry Potter: The Story of a Global Business Phenomenon*. London: Palgrave Macmillan, 2008.

Gupta, Suman. *Re-Reading Harry Potter*. London: Palgrave Macmillan, 2009.

Haggard, H. Rider. *She: A History of Adventure*. London: Longmans, 1887.

Hallett, Cynthia J., and Peggy J. Huey, eds. *J. K. Rowling: Harry Potter*. New York: Palgrave Macmillan, 2012.

Hamilton, Nigel. *The Alchemical Process of Transformation*. PDF, 1985, 7. Accessed October 31, 2019. https://www.sufismus.ch/assets/files/omega_dream/alchemy_e.pdf.

Hanks, Patrick, Kate Hardcastle, and Flavia Hodges. *A Dictionary of First Names*. 2nd ed. Oxford: Oxford University Press, 2006.

Haque, Enamul. *Bengal Sculptures: Hindu Iconography up to c.1250 A.D.* Dhaka: Bangladesh National Museum, 1992.

Hardie, Philip. *The Epic Successors of Virgil: A Study in the Dynamics of a Tradition*. Cambridge: Cambridge University Press, 1993.

———. *The Last Trojan Hero: A Cultural History of Virgil's Aeneid*. London: I. B. Tauris, 2014.

Hardy, Elizabeth Baird. "Pack Your Bags! Newt Scamander's Fantastic Beast-y Suitcase, Hermione's Handbag, and Their Literary Relatives." *Hogwarts Professor*, November 17, 2018. http://www.hogwartsprofessor.com/pack-your-bags-newts-fantastic-beast-y-suitcase-hermiones-handbag-and-their-literary-relatives/.

Harl, Allison. "The Monstrosity of the Gaze: Critical Problems with a Film Adaptation of *The Lord of the* Rings." *Mythlore* 25, nos. 3/4 (2007): 61–69. doi:10.2307/26814608.

Harrison, Jen. "Posthuman Power: The Magic of Hybridity in the *Harry Potter* Series." *Children's Literature Association Quarterly* 43, no. 3 (2018). muse.jhu.edu/article/701317.

Harrison, Mark. "Game of Thrones, Star Wars and the Showrunner Backlash." Den of Geek, November 1, 2019. https://www.denofgeek.com/movies/game-of-thrones-star-wars-and-the-showrunner-backlash/.

"Harry Potter and the Deathly Hallows, Part 2." *Box Office Mojo*. Accessed June 20, 2020. https://www.boxofficemojo.com/title/tt4123430/.

Harvard University. "Introduction to Sikhism." Pluralism Project. Accessed July 21, 2021. https://pluralism.org/introduction-to-sikhism.

Heisig, James. "Bruno Bettelheim and the Fairy Tales." *Children's Literature* 6 (1977): 93–114. doi.org/10.1353/chl.0.0380.

Bibliography

Henderson, Ben. "18% of Americans Veritable Potter-Maniacs, 61% Seen at Least One Movie." YouGovAmerica, July 18, 2022. https://today.yougov.com/topics/lifestyle/articles-reports/2011/07/18/18-americans-veritable-potter-maniacs-76-seen-leas.

Henderson, Tolonda. "A Coda: She-Who-Must-Not-Be-Named." In Konchar Farr, *Open at the Close*, 223–25.

Herfurth, Haley, and Clair McLafferty. "Fantastic Non-Wizard Entities and How to Other Them: Representations of the Other in *Fantastic Beasts*." In Firestone and Clark, *Harry Potter and Convergence Culture*, 114–24.

"Hestia: Greek Goddess of the Hearth." *Greek Mythology*. Accessed May 1, 2023. https://www.greekmythology.com/Olympians/Hestia/hestia.html.

Hibberd, James. "Fantastic Beasts Actress Claudia Kim Breaks Silence on Playing Nagini." *Entertainment Weekly*, September 25, 2018. https://ew.com/movies/2018/09/25/fantastic-beasts-claudia-kim-nagini/.

Hinds, Stephen. *Allusion and Intertext: Dynamics of Appropriation in Roman Poetry*. Cambridge: Cambridge University Press, 1998.

Hobbs, Priscilla. "The Tri-Wizard Cup: Alchemy and Transformation in Harry Potter." *Mythological Studies Journal* 1, no. 1 (2010). Accessed October 31, 2019. http://journals.sfu.ca/pgi/index.php/pacificamyth/article/view/10/55.

Hopkins, Lisa. "Harry and His Peers: Rowling's Web of Allusions." In Berndt and Steveker, *Heroism*, 55–66.

Horne, Jackie C. "Harry and the Other: Answering the Race Question in J. K. Rowling's *Harry Potter*." *Lion and the Unicorn* 34, no. 1 (2010): 76–104. doi.org/10.1353/uni.0.0488.

———. "Harry and the Other: Multicultural and Social Justice Anti-Racism in J. K. Rowling's *Harry Potter* Series." In Dahlen and Thomas, *Harry Potter and the Other*, 17–50.

Houghton, Patti L. "Harry Potter and the English School Story." *Dartmouth College Library Bulletin*. April 2000. https://www.dartmouth.edu/~library/Library_Bulletin/Apr2000/Houghton.html.

Hudson, David, Jr. "Counterspeech Doctrine." *First Amendment Encyclopedia*. Updated December 17, 2017. https://www.mtsu.edu/first-amendment/article/940/counterspeech-doctrine#.

Hunziker, Alyssa. "Revealing Discrimination: Social Hierarchy and the Exclusion/Enslavement of the Other in the *Harry Potter* Novels." *disClosure* 22, no. 1 (2013). https://www.academia.edu/83476368/Signs_of_Exclusion_Monsters_from_Classical_Mythology_in_Children_s_and_Young_Adult_Culture.

Ide, Todd. "The Dark Lord and the Prince: Machiavellian Elements in Harry Potter." In Whited and Grimes, *Critical Insights*, 108–207.

Irenaeus. *Adversus Haereses*, 22.4, 180 A.D. Quoted in Michael S. O'Carroll, "Mary, Mother of God," in *New Dictionary of Theology*, edited by Joseph A. Komonchak, Mary Collins, and Dermot A. Lane, 637–43. Collegeville, MN: Liturgical Press, 1987.

Jackson, Rosemary. *Fantasy: The Literature of Subversion*. New Accents. London: Methuen, 1981.

Bibliography

James, Edward. "Tolkien, Lewis and the Explosion of Genre Fantasy." In James and Mendlesohn, *Cambridge Companion to Fantasy Literature*, 62–78.

James, Edward, and Farah Mendlesohn, eds. *The Cambridge Companion to Fantasy Literature*. Cambridge Companions to Literature. Cambridge: Cambridge University Press, 2012.

Jaques, Zoe. *Children's Literature and the Posthuman*. New York: Routledge, 2015.

Jay, Martin. *Downcast Eyes: The Denigration of Vision in French Twentieth-Century Thought*. Berkeley: University of California Press, 1993.

Jenkins, Henry. "Confronting the Challenges of Participatory Culture: Media Education for the 21st Century." Pop Junctions, October 19, 2006. http://henryjenkins.org/blog/2006/10/confronting_the_challenges_of.html.

———. *Convergence Culture: Where Old and New Media Collide*. New York: New York University Press, 2006.

———. *Textual Poachers: Television Fans and Participatory Culture*. Philadelphia: Routledge, 1992.

Jost, Jean E. "Why Is Middle English Romance So Violent? The Literary and Aesthetic Purposes of Violence." In Classen, *Violence*, 241–67.

Kalsi, M. S. (Sikh). Interview by author, July 22, 2021, Conover, NC.

Kang, Biba. "If You Think the Controversy Surrounding J. K. Rowling's Nagini Casting in Fantastic Beasts is Unfair, Consider This." *Independent*, September 28, 2018. https://www.independent.co.uk/voices/jk-rowling-nagini-fantastic-beasts-asian-actor-racism-snake-a8559581.html.

Karp, Harvey, MD. *The Happiest Toddler on the Block*. New York: Bantam Dell, 2008.

Keats, John. "Lamia." In *The Poems of John Keats*, edited by Miriam Allott. London: Longman, 1970.

Kelch, Dean G. "Consider the Lilies." *Fremontia* 30, no. 2 (2002): 23–29. https://cnps.org/wp-content/uploads/2018/03/Fremontia_Vol30-No2.pdf.

Kempner, Brandon. *Discworld and Philosophy: Reality Is Not What It Seems*. Edited by Nicolas Michaud. Chicago: Open Court, 2016.

Kendi, Ibram X. *How to Be an Antiracist*. New York: One World, 2019.

———. *Stamped from the Beginning: The Definitive History of Racist Ideas in America*. New York: Nation Books, 2016.

Kellner, Rivka Temima. "J. K. Rowling's Ambivalence toward Feminism: House Elves—Women in Disguise—in the 'Harry Potter' Books." *Midwest Quarterly* 51, no. 4 (2010): 367–85. ResearchGate, https://www.researchgate.net/publication/294692249_JK_Rowling's_Ambivalence_Towards_Feminism_House_Elves_-_Women_in_Disguise_-_in_the_Harry_Potter_Books.

Kim, Lorrie. "Claudia Kim's Nagini: A Korean Woman in Potterverse." Mugglenet, May 23, 2021. https://www.mugglenet.com/2021/05/claudia-kims-nagini-a-korean-woman-in-potterverse/.

Klinger, Barbara. "The Art Film, Affect and the Female Viewer: *The Piano* Revisited." *Screen* 47, no. 1 (Spring 2006): 19.

Konchar Farr, Cecilia, ed. *Open at the Close*. Jackson: University of Mississippi Press, 2022.

Bibliography

Korsmeyer, Carolyn. *Making Sense of Taste: Food and Philosophy.* New York: Cornell University Press, 1999. doi.org/10.7591/9780801471339.

Kraidy, Marwan M. *Hybridity, or the Cultural Logic of Globalization.* Philadelphia: Viking Press, 1958.

Lacrose, J. de. *An Historical and Geographical Description of France, Extracted from the Best Authors, Both Ancient and Modern.* London: T. Salusbury, 1694.

Lamb, Hannah. "The Wizard, the Muggle, and the Other: Postcolonialism in Harry Potter." In *A Wizard of Their Age*, edited by Cecilia Konchar Farr, 57–73. Albany: State University of New York.

Langdon, Stephen. *Semitic Mythology.* New York: Cooper Square, 1964.

Larrington, Carolyne. *King Arthur's Enchantresses: Morgan and Her Sisters in Arthurian Tradition.* London: I. B. Tauris, 2006.

Lee, J. Steve. "There and Back Again: The Chiastic Structure of J. K. Rowling's *Harry Potter* Novels." In Prinzi, *Potter for Nerds*, 17–35.

Leggatt, Alexander, ed. *The Cambridge Companion to Shakespearean Comedy.* Cambridge: Cambridge University Press, 2002.

Le Goff, Jacques, and Emmanuel Le Roy Ladurie. "Mélusine Maternelle et Défricheuse." *Annales* 26, nos. 3/4 (1971): 587–622. https://www.jstor.org/stable/i27566738.

Lerer, Seth. *Children's Literature: A Reader's History, from Aesop to Harry Potter.* Chicago: University of Chicago Press, 2008.

Leslie, Calum. "The Lestrange Family." *Rowling Library Magazine* 31 (2019): 4–7. https://www.therowlinglibrary.com/magazines.

Levy, Michael, and Farah Mendlesohn. *Children's Fantasy Literature: An Introduction.* Cambridge: Cambridge University Press, 2016.

Lewis, C. S. *The Last Battle.* 1956. Reprint, New York: Scholastic, 1988.

———. *The Lion, the Witch and the Wardrobe.* 1950. New York: Scholastic, 1988.

Lewis, Timothy. "An English Serjeanty in a Welsh Setting." *History* 31, no. 114 (1946): 85–99. http://www.jstor.org/stable/24402602.

Littlefield, Christina. "Harry Potter as a Metaphor for Struggling with God." In *Harry Potter's Worldwide Influence*, edited by Diana Patterson, 125–43. Newcastle upon Tyne, UK: Cambridge Scholars, 2009.

Long, David. "Quidditch, Imperialism, and the Sport-War Intertext." In *Harry Potter and International Relations*, edited by Daniel H. Nexon and Iver B. Neumann, 127–54. Lanham, MD: Rowan and Littlefield, 2006.

Louis, John Philip. "The Young Parenting Inventory (YPI-R3) and the Baumrind, Maccoby and Martin Parenting Model: Finding Common Ground." *Children* 9, no. 159 (2022): 1–14. doi.org/10.3390/children9020159.

Lovatt, Helen. "Harry Potter and the Metamorphoses of Classics." In *Classical Reception and Children's Literature: Greece, Rome and Childhood Transformation*, edited by Owen Hodkinson and Helen Lovatt, 16–24. London: I. B. Tauris, 2018.

Lynch, Andrew. *Malory's Book of Arms: The Narrative of Combat in Le Morte Darthur.* Arthurian Studies. Cambridge: D. S. Brewer, 1997.

———. "Medievalism and the Ideology of War." In D'Arcens, *Cambridge Companion*, 135–50.

Bibliography

Lyne, R. O. A. M. *Further Voices in Vergil's Aeneid*. Oxford: Clarendon Press, 1987.

Maccoby, E. E., and J. A. Martin. "Socialization in the Context of the Family: Parent-Child Interaction." In *Socialization, Personality, and Social Development*, edited by E. Mavis Hetherington, vol. 4 of *Handbook of Child Psychology*, edited by Paul H. Mussen, 39–56. New York: John Wiley & Sons, 1983.

Malory, Thomas. *Le Morte Darthur: The Winchester Manuscript*. Edited by Helen Cooper. Oxford World's Classics. Oxford: Oxford University Press, 2008.

Mangan, Michael. *A Preface to Shakespeare's Comedies: 1594–1603*. London: Longman, 1996.

Martin, David M. "Why So Old-Fashioned? A Note of J. K. Rowling's World Building." Paper presented at the Harry Potter Academic Conference at Chestnut Hill College, Philadelphia, Pennsylvania, October 2018.

"Maya Forstater: Woman Loses Tribunal over Transgender Tweets." BBC, December 19, 2019, https://www.bbc.com/news/uk-50858919.

McCauley, Patrick. *Into the Pensieve: The Philosophy and Mythology of Harry Potter*. Schiffer Publishing Ltd, 2015.

McDaniel, Kathryn N., host. "The Ickabog: Thoughts in Progress." With John Granger, John Patrick Padziore, and Lana A. Whited. *Reading, Writing, Rowling*, episode 44, July 20, 2020. Podcast audio, 1:04. https://www.mugglenet.com/2020/07/reading-writing-rowling-episode-44-the-ickabog-thoughts-in-progress/.

———. "Quidditch and Cultural Imperialism." Paper presented at the Harry Potter Academic Conference at Chestnut Hill College, Philadelphia, Pennsylvania, October 2018.

———. "The 'Real House-Elves' of J. K. Rowling." In McDaniel and Prinzi, *Potter for Nerds II*, 63–92.

McDaniel, Kathryn N., and Travis Prinzi, eds. *Harry Potter for Nerds II: Essays for Fans, Academics, and Lit Geeks*. Oklahoma City: Unlocking Press, 2015.

McEvoy-Levy, Siobhan. "Reading War and Peace in *Harry Potter*." In *Peace and Resistance in Youth Cultures*, 121–42. Rethinking Peace and Conflict Studies. London: Palgrave Macmillan, 2018.

McGraw, Peter A., and Caleb Warren. "Benign Violations: Making Immoral Behavior Funny." *Psychological Science* 21, no. 8 (2010): 1141–49. doi.org/10.1177/0956797610376073.

McLeod, Madison. "Critical Survey: Literary Criticism on J. K. Rowling." Unpublished critical survey, master's level. King's College London, 2017.

McNamara, Rea. "Was 2019 the Year Fandom Turned Toxic?" *Now Toronto*, December 20, 2019. https://nowtoronto.com/music/features/toxic-fandom/.

Mendlesohn, Farah. "Crowning the King: Harry Potter and the Construction of Authority." In Whited, *Ivory Tower*, 159–81.

Merleau-Ponty, Maurice. "Eye and Mind." In *The Merleau-Ponty Aesthetics Reader: Philosophy and Painting*, edited by Galen A. Johnson, translated by Carleton Dallery, 3–17. Evanston, IL: Northwestern University Press, 1993.

Milton, John. *Paradise Lost*. Edited by Alastair Fowler. 2nd ed. London: Longman, 2007.

Moline, Nicholas. "Introduction to Wizarding Law." *Justia Law Blog*, November 18, 2010. https://lawblog.justia.com/2010/11/18/introduction-to-wizarding-law/.

Bibliography

Morris, Michael C. "Middle Earth, Narnia, Hogwarts, and Animals: A Review of the Treatment of Nonhuman Animals and Other Sentient Beings in Christian-Based Fantasy Fiction." *Society and Animals* 17, no. 1 (2009): 343–56. https://www.animalsandsociety.org/wp-content/uploads/2015/11/morris.pdf.

Mullins, Jordan L., and Sarah M. Tashjian. "Parenting Styles and Child Behavior." *Psychology in Action* (blog), May 16, 2018. https://www.psychologyinaction.org/?s=Jordan+Mullins+and+Sarah+M.+Tashjian.

Munson, James. "Christmas in Austria." *Contemporary Review* 263, no. 1535 (December 1993): 313.

Mutz, Diana C. "Harry Potter and the Deathly Donald." In "Elections in Focus," special issue, *PS: Political Science & Politics* 49, no. 4 (October 2016): 722–29. doi:10.1017/S1049096516001633.

National Center for Transgender Equality. *National Transgender Discrimination Survey: Full Report*, September 11, 2012. https://transequality.org/issues/resources/national-transgender-discrimination-survey-full-report.

Nexon, Dan. "Terror, Counter-Terror, and Insurgency, or Why Harry Won." *Duck of Minerva*, July 21, 2011. https://www.duckofminerva.com/2011/07/terror-counter-terror-and-insurgency-in.html.

Ngo, Helen. *The Habits of Racism: A Phenomenology of Racism and Racialized Embodiment*. Lanham, MD: Lexington Books, 2017.

Noble, Will. "Gog And Magog: Who Are They and What Have They Got to Do with London?" *Londonist*. Updated Jan. 4, 2016. https://londonist.com/2016/01/gog-and-magog-who-are-they-and-what-do-they-have-to-do-with-london.

Noriega, Chon A. " 'Barricades of Ideas': Latino Culture, Site-Specific Installation, and the U.S. Art Museum." In *Performing Hybridity*, edited by May Joseph and Jennifer Natalya Fink, 182–96. Minneapolis: University of Minnesota Press, 1999.

Nosich, Gerald. *Learning to Think Things Through: A Guide to Critical Thinking across the Curriculum*. 4th ed. Boston: Pearson, 2012.

Oakes, Margaret J. "Secret Domination or Civic Duty: The Source and Purpose of Magical Power in Harry Potter." In Anatol, ed., *Reading Harry Potter Again*, 143–57.

O'Connor, Flannery. "A Good Man Is Hard to Find." *The Avon Book of Modern Writing*, 1953. Rpt. *Flannery O'Connor: Collected* Works. New York: Library of America, 1988.

Odell, Joyce. "Second Guessing." Red Hen, 2005. http://www.redhen-publications.com/2ndGuessing.html. Reprinted in Granger, *Ring Composition*, 115–19, 123–24.

Pandey, Nandini B. "Sowing the Seeds of War: *The Aeneid*'s Prehistory of Interpretive Contestation and Appropriation." Classical World 111, no. 1 (Fall 2017): 7–25. https://doi.org/10.1353/clw.2017.0062.

Panoussi, Vassiliki. "Harry's Underworld Journey: Reading *Harry Potter and the Deathly Hallows* through Vergil's *Aeneid*." *Lion and the Unicorn* 43, no. 1 (January 2019): 42–68. doi.org/10.1353/uni.2019.0003.

Bibliography

Parker, Ian. "Mugglemarch: J. K. Rowling Writes a Realist Novel for Adults." *New Yorker*, September 24, 2012. https://www.newyorker.com/magazine/2012/10/01/mugglemarch.

Péporté, Pit. "Melusine and Luxembourg: A Double Memory." In Urban, Kemmis, and Elmes, *Melusine's Footprint*, 162–79.

Peppers-Bates, Susan, and Joshua Rust. "The House-Elves, Hogwarts, and Friendship: Casting Away the Institutions Which Made Voldemort's Rise Possible." *Reason Papers* 34, no. 1 (2012): 109–24. https://reasonpapers.com/pdf/341/rp_341_8.pdf.

Perkell, Christine, ed. *Reading Vergil's Aeneid: An Interpretive Guide*. Norman, OK: University of Oklahoma Press, 1997.

———. "*Aeneid* 1: An Epic Programme." In Perkell, *Reading Vergil's Aeneid*, 29–49.

Pharr, Mary. "In Medias Res: Harry Potter as Hero-in-Progress." In Whited, *Ivory Tower*, 53–66.

———. "A Paradox: The *Harry Potter* Series as Both Epic and Postmodern." In Steveker and Berndt, eds., *Heroism*, 9–23.

Pheasant-Kelly, Fran. "Bewitching, Abject, Uncanny: Other Spaces in the *Harry Potter* Films." In Hallett and Huey, *Rowling: Harry Potter*, 48–73.

Philostratus. *The Life of Apollonius of Tyana, translated from the Greek of Philostratus*. Translated by Edward Berwick. London: T. Payne, 1809.

Pollard, Tanya. *Drugs and Theater in Early Modern England*. Oxford: Oxford University Press, 2005.

Pottermore staff. "Lily, Petunia and the Language of Flowers." *Wizarding World*. January 30, 2016, https://www.wizardingworld.com/features/lily-potter-petunia-and-the-language-of-flowers.

Prady, Bill. "In Comedy Writing, Fear the 'Bono's' and 'Nakamura.' " Interview with Melissa Block. NPR, November 5, 2014. https://www.npr.org/2014/11/05/361820803/in-comedy-writing-fear-the-bonos-and-nakamura.

Pratt, Mary Louise. *Imperial Eyes: Travel Writing and Transculturation*. New York: Routledge, 1992.

Prinzi, Travis, ed. *Harry Potter for Nerds: Essays for Fans, Academics, and Lit Geeks*. Oklahoma City: Unlocking Press, 2001.

Provenzano, Danielle M., and Richard E. Heyman. "Harry Potter and the Resilience to Adversity." In *The Psychology of Harry Potter*, edited by Neil Mulholland, 105–19. Dallas, TX: BenBella Books, 2006.

Pugh, Tison, and Angela Jane Weisl. *Medievalisms: Making the Past in the Present*. London: Routledge, 2013.

Radcliffe, Daniel. "Daniel Radcliffe Responds to J. K. Rowling's Tweets on Gender Identity," Trevor Project, June 8, 2020. https://www.thetrevorproject.org/2020/06/08/daniel-radcliffe-responds-to-j-k-rowlings-tweets-on-gender-identity/.

Radulescu, R. L. " 'Oute of Mesure': Violence and Knighthood in Malory's *Morte Darthur*." In *Re-viewing Le Morte Darthur: Texts and Contexts, Characters and Themes*, edited by K. S. Whetter and R. L. Radulescu, 119–31. Cambridge: D. S. Brewer, 2005.

Bibliography

Ramachandran, Vilayanur S. "The Neurology and Evolution of Humor, Laughter, and Smiling: The False Alarm Theory." *Medical Hypotheses* 51, no. 4 (1998): 351–54. doi.org/10.1016/S0306-9877(98)90061-5.

Reuters staff. "JK Rowling Says Dumbledore Is Gay." Reuters, October 21, 2007, https://www.reuters.com/article/uk-rowling/jk-rowling-says-dumbledore-is-gay-idUKN2052004020071021.

Reynolds, Kimberley. *Modern Children's Literature: An Introduction*. Houndmills, UK: Palgrave Macmillan, 2004.

Rich, Adrienne. "Diving into the Wreck." *Diving into the Wreck and Other Poems*. New York: Norton, 1973.

Roback, Diane, and Joy Bean. "Adding up the Numbers." *Publisher's Weekly*, February 10, 2003. https://www.publishersweekly.com/pw/print/20030210/35543-adding-up-the-numbers.html.

Robinson, Joanna. "J. K. Rowling Addresses 'Racist' 'Idiot' Critics of the New Black Hermione." *Vanity Fair*, June 5, 2016. https://www.vanityfair.com/culture/2016/06/jk-rowling-defends-black-hermione-harry-potter-cursed-child.

Roger, Bernard. *The Initiatory Path in Fairy Tales: The Alchemical Secrets of Mother Goose*. Translated by Jon E. Graham. Rochester, VT: Inner Traditions, 2015.

Rogers, Brett M. "Orestes and the Half-Blood Prince: Ghosts of Aeschylus in the *Harry Potter* Series." In *Classical Traditions in Modern Fantasy*, edited by Brett M. Rogers and Benjamin Eldon Stevens, 209–32. Oxford: Oxford University Press, 2017.

Rojek, Chris. "Stuart Hall on Representation and Ideology." In *Media/Cultural Studies: Critical Approaches*, ed. Rhonda Hammer and Douglas Kellner. New York: Peter Lang, 2009, 49–62.

Root, Maria P. P. *The Multiracial Experience: Racial Borders as the New Frontier*. Thousand Oaks, CA: Sage, 1995.

Rowling, J. K. "Answers to Questions." *In My Own Words* (blog), November 12, 2018. https://www.jkrowling.com/opinions/latest-answers-to-frequently-asked-questions/.

———. *The Casual Vacancy*. New York: Little, Brown, 2012.

———. "Draco Malfoy." Wizarding World (originally Pottermore), August 10, 2015, https://www.wizardingworld.com/writing-by-jk-rowling/draco-malfoy.

———. *Fantastic Beasts and Where to Find Them*. New York: Scholastic Press, 2001.

———. *Fantastic Beasts and Where to Find Them*. Original screenplay. New York: Scholastic, 2015.

———. *Fantastic Beasts: The Crimes of Grindelwald*. Original screenplay. London: Little, Brown, 2018.

———. "Fourteenth to Seventeenth Centuries." Wizarding World. Accessed November 3, 2019. https://www.wizardingworld.com/writing-by-jk-rowling/fourteenth-century-to-seventeenth-century-en.

———. "Ghost Plots." Wizarding World. Accessed November 3, 2019. https://www.wizardingworld.com/writing-by-jk-rowling/ghost-plots.

Bibliography

———. "Grindelwald Casting." *In My Own Words* (blog), December 7, 2017. https://www.jkrowling.com/opinions/grindelwald-casting/.

———. *Harry Potter and the Chamber of Secrets*. London: Bloomsbury, 1998.

———. *Harry Potter and the Chamber of Secrets*. New York: Scholastic, 2000.

———. *Harry Potter and the Chamber of Secrets*. Illustrated by Jim Kay. London: Bloomsbury, 2016.

———. *Harry Potter and the Deathly Hallows*. New York: Scholastic, 2007.

———. *Harry Potter and the Goblet of Fire*. London: Bloomsbury, 2000.

———. *Harry Potter and the Goblet of Fire*. New York: Scholastic, 2000.

———. *Harry Potter and the Goblet of Fire*. Illustrated by Jim Kay. London: Bloomsbury, 2019.

———. *Harry Potter and the Half-Blood Prince*. London: Bloomsbury, 2005.

———. *Harry Potter and the Order of the Phoenix*. London: Bloomsbury, 2003.

———. *Harry Potter and the Philosopher's Stone*. Illustrated by Jim Kay. London: Bloomsbury, 2015.

———. *Harry Potter and the Prisoner of Azkaban*. London: Bloomsbury, 1999.

———. *Harry Potter and the Prisoner of Azkaban*. Illustrated by Jim Kay. London: Bloomsbury, 2017.

———. *Harry Potter and the Sorcerer's Stone*. New York: Scholastic, 1998.

———. *Hogwarts: An Incomplete and Unreliable Guide*. Pottermore Presents Book 3. Pottermore, 2016.

———. "Hogwarts Express." Wizarding World. Accessed November 3, 2019. https://www.wizardingworld.com/writing-by-jk-rowling/the-hogwarts-express.

———. "Hogwarts Ghosts." Wizarding World. Accessed November 3, 2019. https://www.wizardingworld.com/writing-by-jk-rowling/hogwarts-ghosts.

———. *The Ickabog*. New York: Scholastic, 2020.

———. "*The Ickabog*: Meet the Ickabog." *TheIckabog.com*. Accessed July 10, 2020. https://www.theickabog.com/en-us/home/.

———. "Ilvermorny School of Witchcraft and Wizardry." Wizarding World. Accessed November 3, 2019. https://www.wizardingworld.com/writing-by-jk-rowling/ilvermorny.

———. Interview by Christopher Lydon. *Connection*, National Public Radio (Boston), October 12, 1999. http://www.accio-quote.org/articles/1999/1099-connectiontransc2.htm.

———. Interview by Geordie Greig. *Tatler*, February 2006. http://www.accio-quote.org/articles/2006/0110-tatler-grieg.html.

———. "J. K. Rowling at the Edinburgh Book Festival." Interview by Lindsey Fraser. Edinburgh, August 15, 2004. Accio Quote. http://www.accio-quote.org/articles/2004/0804-ebf.htm.

———. "J. K. Rowling at the Royal Albert Hall." Interview by Stephen Fry, June 26, 2003. Accio Quote. http://www.accio-quote.org/articles/2003/0626-alberthall-fry.htm.

———. "J. K. Rowling Discusses Paris, Characters, Creatures, More in 'Fantastic Beasts' 2." Snitchseeker, March 11, 2018. https://www.snitchseeker.com/

Bibliography

harry-potter-news/j-k-rowling-discusses-paris-characters-creatures-more-in-fantastic-beasts-2-a-110752/.

———. "J. K. Rowling Introduces *The Ickabog*." *In My Own Words* (blog), May 26, 2020. https://www.jkrowling.com/j-k-rowling-introduces-the-ickabog/.

———. "JK Rowling Talks about Book Four." Interview with Lizo Mzimbo. *BBC Newsround*, July 8, 2000. http://www.accio-quote.org/articles/2000/0700-cbbc-mzimba.htm.

———. "J. K. Rowling Web Chat Transcript." Interview with Melissa Anelli, July 30, 2007. *Leaky Cauldron*. http://www.the-leaky-cauldron.org/2007/7/30/j-k-rowling-web-chat-transcript/.

———. "J. K. Rowling Writes about Her Reasons for Speaking out on Sex and Gender Issues." *In My Own Words* (blog), June 10, 2020,. https://www.jkrowling.com/opinions/j-k-rowling-writes-about-her-reasons-for-speaking-out-on-sex-and-gender-issues/.

———. "The Knight Bus." Wizarding World. Accessed November 3, 2019, https://www.wizardingworld.com/writing-by-jk-rowling/the-knight-bus.

———. "The Leaky Cauldron." Wizarding World. Accessed November 3, 2019. https://www.wizardingworld.com/writing-by-jk-rowling/the-leaky-cauldron.

———. "The Magical Congress of the United States of America." Wizarding World. Accessed November 3, 2019. https://www.wizardingworld.com/writing-by-jk-rowling/macusa.

———. "Mr. Ollivander." Wizarding World. Accessed November 3, 2019. https://www.wizardingworld.com/writing-by-jk-rowling/mr-ollivander.

———. "The Malfoy Family." Wizarding World. Accessed November 3, 2019. https://www.wizardingworld.com/writing-by-jk-rowling/the-malfoy-family.

———. "Nicholas Flamel." Pottermore, August 10, 2015. https://www.wizardingworld.com/writing-by-jk-rowling/nicolas-flamel.

———. "1920s Wizarding America." Wizarding World. Accessed March 11, 2016. https://www.wizardingworld.com/writing-by-jk-rowling/1920s-wizarding-america-enion.

———. "The Potter Family." Wizarding World. Accessed September 21, 2015. https://www.wizardingworld.com/writing-by-jk-rowling/the-potter-family.

———. "Professor McGonagall." Wizarding World. Accessed November 3, 2019. https://www.wizardingworld.com/writing-by-jk-rowling/professor-mcgonagall.

———. "Pure-Blood." Wizarding World. Accessed November 3, 2019. https://www.wizardingworld.com/writing-by-jk-rowling/pure-blood.

———. "Rappaport's Law." Wizarding World. Accessed November 3, 2019. https://www.wizardingworld.com/writing-by-jk-rowling/rappaports-law-en.

———. "Read the Full J. K. Rowling Interview." Transcript of press conference. *BBC Newsround*, July 18, 2005. http://news.bbc.co.uk/cbbcnews/hi/news-id_4690000/newsid_4690800/4690885.stm.

———. "Seventeenth Century and Beyond." Wizarding World. Accessed November 3, 2019. https://www.wizardingworld.com/writing-by-jk-rowling/seventeenth-century-and-beyond-en.

Bibliography

———. *Short Stories from Hogwarts of Heroism, Hardship, and Dangerous Hobbies.* Pottermore Presents Book 2. Pottermore, 2016.

———. *Short Stories from Hogwarts of Power, Politics, and Pesky Poltergeists.* Pottermore Presents Book 1. Pottermore, 2016.

———. "Sir Cadogan." Wizarding World. Accessed November 3, 2019. https://www.wizardingworld.com/writing-by-jk-rowling/sir-cadogan.

———. *The Tales of Beedle the Bard.* New York: Lumos, in association with Arthur A. Levine Books, 2017.

———. "Technology." Wizarding World. Accessed November 3, 2019. https://www.wizardingworld.com/writing-by-jk-rowling/technology.

———. "Text of J. K. Rowling's Speech." *Harvard Gazette*, January 5, 2018. https://news.harvard.edu/gazette/story/2008/06/text-of-j-k-rowling-speech/.

———. *Very Good Lives: The Fringe Benefits of Failure and the Importance of Imagination.* New York: Little, Brown, 2008.

Rowling, J. K., and Steve Kloves. *Fantastic Beasts: The Secrets of Dumbledore.* Complete screenplay. London: Little, Brown, 2022.

Sandwell, Ian. "What's All the Fuss about Fantastic Beasts: The Crimes of Grindelwald's Take on Nagini?" DigitalSpy, November 16, 2018. https://www.digitalspy.com/movies/a868497/fantastic-beasts-2-crimes-of-grindelwald-nagini-controversy-jk-rowling/.

Sanseverino, Gabriela Gruszynski, and Ana Gruszynski. "Representations of Journalism in the Potterverse." In Bell, *Transmedia Harry Potter*, 7–29. https://www.academia.edu/41836223/Representations_of_Journalism_in_the-Potterverse.

Saunders, Corinne. "Violent Magic in Middle English Romance." In Classen, *Violence*, 225–40.

Saunders, John H. *The Rhetorical Power of Children's Literature.* Lanham, MD: Lexington Books, 2018.

Saxena, Vandana. *The Subversive Harry Potter: Adolescent Rebellion and Containment in the J. K. Rowling Novels.* Jefferson, NC: McFarland, 2012.

Scamander, Newt. *Fantastic Beasts and Where to Find Them.* New York: Arthur A. Levine Books, 2001.

Scholastic. "Scholastic Announces Sales of More Than 3.3 Million Copies of Harry Potter and the Cursed Child Parts One and Two," August 10, 2016, http://mediaroom.scholastic.com/press-release/scholastic-announces-sales-more-33-million-copies-harry-potter-and-cursed-child-parts-.

Schott, Christine. "The House Elf Problem: Why Harry Potter is More Relevant Now Than Ever." *Midwest Quarterly* 61, no. 2 (2020): 259–73.

Schuck, Raymond I. "Harry Potter and the Anti-Racist-White-Hero Premise: Whiteness and the Harry Potter Series." In Bell, *Wizards vs. Muggles*, 9–26.

Scott. "Hermione's Family." *Harry Potter Lexicon.* Accessed November 1, 2019, https://www.hp-lexicon.org/2004/02/26/hermiones-family/.

Seden, Janet. "Parenting and the Harry Potter Stories: A Social Care Perspective." *Children and Society* 16, no. 5 (2002): 295–305. doi.org/10.1002/chi.715.

Bibliography

Segall, Mason. "Harry Potter: The 15 Worst Retcons JK Rowling Made to the Series (and the 8 Best)." *Screen Rant*, May 8, 2019. https://screenrant.com/harry-potter-jk-rowling-worst-best-retcons/.

Shakespeare, William. *The Norton Shakespeare*, 3rd Edition. Edited by Stephen Greenblatt et al. New York: W.W. Norton & Co., 2016.

Schanoes, Veronica L. "Cruel Heroes and Treacherous Texts: Educating the Reader in Moral Complexity and Critical Reading in J. K. Rowling's Harry Potter Books." In Anatol, *Reading Harry Potter*, 131–45.

Shippey, Tom. "Medievalisms and Why They Matter." In *Studies in Medievalism XVII: Defining Medievalism(s)*, edited by Karl Fugelso, 45–54. Cambridge: Boydell & Brewer, 2009.

Siegel, Tatiana, and Seth Abramovitch. "Universal Parks Responds to J. K. Rowling Tweets: 'Our Core Values Include Diversity, Inclusion and Respect.'" *Hollywood Reporter*, June 10, 2020, updated June 11, 2020, https://www.hollywoodreporter.com/news/ universal-parks-responds-jk-rowling-tweets-core-values-include-diversity-inclusion-respect-1297845.

Sims, Jennifer Patrice. "When the Subaltern Speaks Parseltongue: Orientalism, Racial RePresentation, and Claudia Kim as Nagini." In Dahlen and Thomas, eds., *Harry Potter and the Other*, 105–18.

Simpson, Anne. "Casting a Spell over Young Minds: Face to Face with J K Rowling." *The Herald* (Scotland), December 7, 1998, accessed October 30, 2019, https://www.heraldscotland.com/news/12021592.casting-a-spell-over-young-minds-anne-simpson-face-to-face-with-j-k-rowling/.

Sliter, Michael, Aron Kale, and Zhenyu Yuan. "Is Humor the Best Medicine? The Buffering Effect of Coping Humor on Traumatic Stressors in Firefighters." *Journal of Organizational Behavior* 35, no. 2 (2014): 257–72. doi.org/10.1002/job.1868

Smith, Dinitia. "The Times Plans a Children's Best-Seller List." *New York Times*, June 24, 2000. http://www.nytimes.com/2000/06/24/books/the-times-plans-a-children-s-best-seller-list.html.

Spindler, Audrey. "The Tales of Beedle the Bard." *Harry Potter for Seekers*. n.d., accessed October 31, 2019, http://www.harrypotterforseekers.com/articles/beedlethebardaudreyspindler.php.

Sommer, Marni, Virginia Kamowa, and Therese Mahon. "Opinion: Creating a More Equal Post-COVID-19 World for People Who Menstruate." *Devex*, May 28, 2020. https://www.devex.com/news/sponsored/opinion-creating-a-more-equal-post-covid-19-world-for-people-who-menstruate-97312#.XtwLnv0aEeR.twitter.

Sotheby's. "Autograph Manuscript of *The Tales of Beedle the Bard* Translated from the Original Runes by J. K. Rowling." Catalogue note, Lot 311a, December 13, 2007. Sotheby's. http://www.sothebys.com/en/auctions/ecatalogue/2007/english-literature-history-childrens-books-and-illustrations-l07411/lot.311A.html.

Spencer, Richard A. *Harry Potter and the Classical World: Greek and Roman Allusions in J. K. Rowling's Modern Epic*. Jefferson, NC: McFarland, 2015.

Bibliography

Stack, Liam. "J. K. Rowling Criticized after Tweeting Support for Anti-Transgender Researcher." *New York Times*, December 19, 2019. Updated May 26, 2020. https://www.nytimes.com/2019/12/19/world/europe/jk-rowling-maya-forstater-transgender.html.

Steggle, Matthew. "The Humours in Humour: Shakespeare and Early Modern Psychology." *Oxford Handbook of Shakespearean Comedy*. Edited by Heather Hirschfield, 220–35. Oxford: Oxford University Press.

Steveker, Lena, and Katrin Berndt, eds. *Heroism in the Harry Potter Series*. Farnham, UK: Ashgate, 2013.

Stotesbury, John A., and Susana Onega Jaén, eds., *London in Literature: Visionary Mappings of the Metropolis*, Heidelberg, Univ. of Heidelberg Press, 2002.

Strand, Emily. "Harry Potter and the Sacramental Principle." *Worship* 93 (October 2019): 345–65.

———. "The Second War was Won on the Quidditch Pitch of Hogwarts: Quidditch as a Symbol Set in the Harry Potter Series." In Prinzi, *Potter for Nerds*, 115–37.

Sturgill, Amanda, Jessica Winney, and Tina Libhart. "Harry Potter and Children's Perceptions of the News Media." *American Communication Journal* 10, no.1 (Spring 2008): 1–13. https://www.ijpc.org/uploads/files/1HarryPotter.pdf.

Sturgis, Amy H. "Hogwarts in America: In *Fantastic Beasts and Where to Find Them* J. K. Rowling Crosses the Atlantic and Makes a Hash of North American History and Culture." *Reason*, December 2016, https://reason.com/2016/11/18/hogwarts-in-america/.

Sundmark, Björn. "Of Memes and Muggles: *Harry Potter*, Facebook and the 2016 Presidential Campaign in the United States." In Firestone and Clark, eds., *Harry Potter and Convergence Culture*, 163–74.

Sutton-Ramspeck, Beth. *Harry Potter and Resistance*. Routledge, 2023.

Swank, Kris. "Harry Potter as Dystopian Literature." In McDaniel and Prinzi, *Harry Potter for Nerds II*, 157–74.

———. "House-Elves in Harlem: Stereotyping the Other in *Fantastic Beasts and Where to Find Them*." In Bell, *Transmedia Harry Potter*, 166–80.

Sweeney, Erin N. "Cracking the Planetary Code: Harry Potter, Alchemy, and the Seven Book Series as a Whole," in Prinzi, *Potter for Nerds*, 171–97.

Sweeney, Michelle. *Magic in Medieval Romance from Chrétien de Troyes to Geoffrey Chaucer*. Dublin: Four Courts Press, 2000.

Tarrant, Richard. "Aspects of Virgil's Reception in Antiquity." In *Cambridge Companion to Virgil*, 2nd edition, edited by Fiachra Mac Góráin and Charles Martindale, 43–62. Cambridge: Cambridge University Press, 2019.

Tatar, Maria, *Enchanted Hunters: The Power of Stories in Childhood*. New York: W.W. Norton, 2009.

Tate, Gregory. "Keats, Myth, and the Science of Sympathy." *Romanticism* 22, no.2 (2016), 191–202. doi.org/10.17613/M6XD0QX3W.

Telegraph reporters. "JK Rowling in 'Bleak Mode' as She Flies to America after Donald Trump's Presidential Election Victory for Fantastic Beasts Premiere." *Telegraph*

Bibliography

(London), November 10, 2016. https://www.telegraph.co.uk/news/2016/11/10/jk-rowling-in-bleak-mood-as-she-flies-to-america-after-donald-tr/.

Thevet, André. *The New Found Vvorlde . . . Written in the French Tong, by That Excellent Learned Man, Master Andrevve Theuet*. London: Henrie Bynneman, 1568.

Thomas, Ebony Elizabeth. *The Dark Fantastic: Race and the Imagination from Harry Potter to the Hunger Games*. New York University Press, 2019.

———. *Harry Potter and the Other: Race, Justice, and Difference in the Wizarding World*. Oxford: University of Mississippi, 2022.

Thomas, James W. *Repotting Harry Potter: A Professor's Book-by-book Guide for the Serious Re-Reader*. Allentown: Zossima Press, 2009.

———. *Rowling Revisited: Return Trips to Harry, Fantastic Beasts, Quidditch, and Beedle the Bard*. Hamden, CT: Zossima Press, 2010.

Thompson, Raymond H. "Modern Fantasy and Medieval Romance: A Comparative Study." In *The Aesthetics of Fantasy Literature and Art*, edited by Roger C. Schlobin, 211–25. Brighton: University of Notre Dame Press and Harvester Press, 1982.

Thorne Jack. *Harry Potter and the Cursed Child, Parts One and Two: Special Rehearsal Edition Script*. New York: Scholastic, 2016.

Ting, Nai-tung. "The Holy Man and the Snake-Woman: A Study of a Lamia Story in Asian and European Literature." *Fabula* 8, no.3 (1966): 145–91. doi.org/10.1515/fabl.1966.8.1.145.

Tolkien, J.R.R. "*Beowulf*: The Monsters and the Critics." In *The Monsters and the Critics and Other Essays*, edited by Christopher Tolkien, doi.org/10.1002/chi.715. Boston: Houghton Mifflin, 1984.

———. "On Fairy Stories." 1947, *FLIPHTML5*, accessed January 10, 2022, https://online.fliphtml5.com/srne/dwap/.

———, trans. *Sir Gawain and the Green Knight, Pearl, and Sir Orfeo*. Edited by Christopher Tolkien. London: HarperCollins, 1995.

Tosenberger, Catherine. "Homosexuality at the Online Hogwarts: Harry Potter Slash Fanfiction." *Children's Literature* 36, 2008: 185–207. doi.org/10.1353/chl.0.0017.

Tosh, John. *The Pursuit of History, 6th edition*. New York: Routledge, 2016.

Toswell, M.J. "The Tropes of Medievalism." In *Studies in Medievalism XVII: Defining Medievalism(s)*, edited by Karl Fugelso, 68–76. Cambridge: Boydell & Brewer, 2009.

Trachtenberg, Threa, and Lauren Sher. "J. K. Rowling's Personal Struggle with OCD Informed New Novel, *The Casual Vacancy*." *ABC News*, September 25, 2012. https://abcnews.go.com/Entertainment/jk-rowling-book-casual-vacancy-informed-personal-struggle/story?id=17321030#.UGSi3k3A9lk.

Trevarthen, Geo Athena. *The Seekers Guide to Harry Potter: The Unauthorized Course*. Winchester, UK: O Books, 2008.

Tuan, Yi-Fu. *Space and Place: The Perspective of Experience*. Minneapolis: University of Minnesota Press, 2001.

Üngör, Uğur Ümit, and Valerie Amandine Verkerke. «Funny as Hell: The Functions of Humour During and After Genocide.» *The European Journal of Humour Research* 3, no. 2/3 (2015): 80–101. doi.org/107592/EJHR2015.3.2.3.ungor.

Bibliography

Urban, Misty. "How the Dragon Ate the Woman: The Fate of Melusine in English." In Urban, Kemmis, and Elmes, *Melusine's Footprint*, 368–87.

———. *Monstrous Women in Middle English Romance: Representations of Mysterious Female Power*. Lewiston: Edwin Mellen Press, 2010.

Urban, Misty, Deva F. Kemmis, and Melissa Ridley Elmes, eds. *Melusine's Footprint: Tracing the Legacy of a Medieval Myth*. Leiden: Brill, 2017.

d'Urfe, Honoré. *The Third and Last Volume of Astrea a Romance*. Translated by John Davies. London: Hum. Moseley, Tho. Drink, and H. Herringman, 1658.

Valadão Lopes, Juliana. " 'All Was Well'?: The Sociopolitical Struggles of House-Elves, Goblins, and Centaurs." In Konchar Farr, *Open at the Close*, 178–87.

Verduin, Kathleen. "The Founding and the Founder: Medievalism and the Legacy of Leslie J. Workman." In *Studies in Medievalism XVII: Defining Medievalism(s)*, edited by Karl Fugelso, 1–27. Cambridge: Boydell & Brewer, 2009.

Vezzali, Loris, Sophia Stathi, Dino Giovanni, Dora Capozza, and Elena Trifiletti. "The Greatest Magic of Harry Potter: Reducing Prejudice." *Journal of Applied Social Psychology* 45, no. 2 (2014): 105–21, doi.org/10.1111/jasp.12279

Wade, James. *Fairies in Medieval Romance*. New York: Palgrave Macmillan, 2011.

Wade, Jasmine. "Harry Potter and Black Liberation Movements: Addressing the Imagination Gap with History." In Dahlen and Thomas, *Harry Potter and the Other*, 243–61.

Walde, Christine. "Graeco-Roman Antiquity and Its Productive Appropriation: The Example of Harry Potter." In *Our Mythical Childhood. . . The Classics and Literature for Children and Young Adults*, edited by Katarzyna Marciniak, 362–83. Leiden: Brill, 2016.

Wallin, Emmy. "The 20 Richest Authors in the World." *Wealthy Gorilla*. 7 June 2022. "https://wealthygorilla.com/richest-authors-world/.

Watson, Amy. "Harry Potter Unit Sales." *Statista*, December 3, 2020. https://www.statista.com/statistics/589978/harry-potter-book-sales/.

Westman, Karin E. "Perspective, Memory, and Moral Authority: The Legacy of Jane Austen in J. K. Rowling's Harry Potter." *Children's Literature* 35 (2007): 145–65. doi.org/10.1353/chl.2007.0021.

Whetter, K.S. "Warfare and Combat in *Le Morte Darthur*." In *Writing War: Medieval Literary Responses to Warfare*, edited by Corinne Saunders, Francoise Le Saux, and Neil Thomas, 169–86. Cambridge: Boydell & Brewer, 2004.

White, Hayden. *The Content of the Form*. Baltimore: Johns Hopkins University Press, 1987.

White, Roger. "Monsters Ink: How Maurice Sendak Made the World Safe for Monsters, and Vice-versa." *Boston.com*, October 4, 2009, http://archive.boston.com/bostonglobe/ideas/articles/2009/10/04/monsters_ink/.

White, T. H. *The Once and Future King*. New York: Ace Books, 1987.

Whited, Lana A. "From Hogwarts Academy to the Hero's Journey." In *Teaching with Harry Potter: Essays on Classroom Wizardry from Elementary School to College*, edited by Valerie Estelle Frankel, 4–20. Jefferson, N.C.: McFarland and Co., 2013.

———. "Harry Potter. From Craze to Classic?" Introduction to Whited, ed., *Ivory Tower*, 1–12.

———, ed. *The Ivory Tower and Harry Potter: Perspectives on a Literary Phenomenon*. Columbia: University of Missouri Press, 2002.

Whited, Lana A., and M. Katherine Grimes, eds. *Critical Insights: The Harry Potter Series*. Ipswich, MA: Salem Press, 2015.

Whitman, Walt. *Song of Myself*. *Leaves of Grass*. Boston: James R. Osgood, 1881.

Whyte, Pádraic and Keith O'Sullivan, eds, *Children's Literature and New York City*. New York: Routledge, 2014.

Willmott, Glenn. *Reading for Wonder: Ecology, Ethics, Enchantment*. New York: Palgrave Macmillan, 2018. doi.org/10.1007/978-3-319-70040-3.

Winters, Sarah Fiona. "Bubble-Wrapped Children and Safe Books for Boys: The Politics of Parenting in *Harry Potter*." *Children's Literature* 39, no. 1 (2011): 213–33. doi: 10.1353/chl.2011.0016.

Wiseman, T. P. "'At Figulus . . .': J. K. Rowling and the Ancient World." *Classical Outlook* 79, no. 3 (Spring 2002): 93–6. https://www.jstor.org/stable/i40162351.

Wolosky, Shira. *The Riddles of Harry Potter: Secret Passages and Interpretive Quests*. Basingstoke: Palgrave Macmillan, 2010.

Yates, David, dir. *Fantastic Beasts and Where to Find Them*. Burbank, CA: Warner Bros. Entertainment, 2016.

———, dir. *Fantastic Beasts: The Crimes of Grindelwald*. Burbank, CA: Warner Bros. Entertainment, 2018.

———, dir. *Fantastic Beasts: The Secrets of Dumbledore*. Burbank, CA: Warner Bros. Entertainment, 2022.

Young, Robert J. C. *Colonial Desire: Hybridity in Theory, Culture and Race*. New York: Routledge, 1995.

Zanger, Jules. "Heroic Fantasy and Social Reality: *Ex Nihilo Nihil Fit*." In *The Aesthetics of Fantasy Literature and Art*, edited by Roger C. Schlobin, 226–36. Brighton: University of Notre Dame Press and Harvester Press, 1982.

Zhao, Zifeng. "Metamorphoses of Snake Women: Melusine and Madam White." In Urban, Kemmis, and Elmes, eds, *Melusine's Footprint*, 282–300.

Zipes, Jack. *The Enchanted Screen: The Unknown History of Fairy-Tale Films*. New York: Routledge, 2011.

Contributors

Laurie Beckoff received her BA in English from the University of Chicago and MSc in medieval literatures and cultures from the University of Edinburgh. She serves as campaign manager for long-running Harry Potter fan site MuggleNet, created its academic section, produces the *Potterversity* podcast, coauthored *The Unofficial Harry Potter Hogwarts Handbook*, and regularly presents at the Harry Potter Academic Conference at Chestnut Hill College. Laurie hails from Queens, New York, and works as a digital editor and producer in public engagement with the humanities.

Leslie Bickford is an associate professor of English at Winthrop University in Rock Hill, SC, where she also serves as director of composition. Her research interests include twentieth-century American literature, African American literature, literary theory, and, of course, Harry Potter. She teaches a course on the literary merits of the Harry Potter novels and has attended numerous conferences to hear and deliver presentations on the Potterverse. Previous publications focus on American literature and fellowships advising, and she is thrilled to be included in this volume with so many excellent Potter scholars. Dr. Bickford earned a bachelor of arts in English and art history from the University of the South, an MA in English from the University of Mississippi, and a PhD from the University of South Carolina.

Rebecca Sutherland Borah earned her BSEd and MA in English at Northeast Missouri State University and her PhD in English from Southern Illinois University–Carbondale, where her major area was composition and rhetoric, with minor areas in nineteenth-century English literature and gender studies. She is an associate professor of English at the University of Cincinnati, where she teaches composition with service learning and the occasional monsters in literature or Tolkien course. Her publications include " 'Bruce Banner Can Be an Asshole': Using a FanFic to Break Down Privilege and Introduce Service-Learning Concepts," "Game Macabre: Fear as Essential Element in *The Hunger Games*," "Apprentice Wizards Welcome: Fan Communities and the Culture of Harry Potter," and "More than Girlfriends, Geekettes, and Gladiatrixes: Women, Feminism, and Fantasy Role-Playing Games," with Inez Schaechterle. Borah is the author of the ongoing fan fiction *Special Needs: A Bruce and Natasha FanFic*, *Body and Soul: The Endgame Fix*, and many shorter works found on Archive of Our Own. She is a pop culture expert frequently interviewed by media about fan culture, monsters, comic books, and superheroes.

Molly L. Burt is a graduate of Kansas State University, where she received her BS in secondary education (2018) and her MA in English children's literature (2020). The work featured here is a product of her ultimate master's writing project, which investigates the portrayal of cultural hybridity in contemporary young adult fantasy. Earlier versions of the work received the 2019 Honor Essay Award from the Children's Literature Association, and the 2019 K-State Children's Literature Critical Essay Award. Her other academic interests include midwestern literature, film adaptation, and picture book theory. She now teaches high school English language arts in Manhattan, Kansas, where she lives with her husband and too many dogs.

Louise M. Freeman is a professor emerita of psychology at Mary Baldwin University, where she taught for twenty-three years, and a licensed behavior analyst. She has provided in-home services for special needs children since 2017. She is a behavioral neuroscientist by training, and her scholarship also includes psychological themes in young adult literature and the role of reading in the development of social cognition in children and adolescents. Her work on the Harry Potter series and other young adult novels has been published in the *ALAN Review*, *Study and Scrutiny: Research on Young Adult Literature*, *Critical Insights: The Hunger Games*, and *Potterversity: Essays Exploring the World of Harry Potter*. Dr. Freeman has written for multiple websites dedicated to the study of young adult literature and currently blogs at the *Farting Sofa Faculty Lounge (http://www.farting sofafaculty.blogspot.com*. She presents at a variety of fan festivals, podcasts, conventions, and scholarly conferences, including the annual Harry Potter Academic Conference at Chestnut Hill. She received her undergraduate degree in biology from Emory University and her master's and doctorate in biological psychology from the University of California at Berkeley.

Tagged the "Dean of Harry Potter Scholars" by *Time* magazine's Lev Grossman, **John Granger** writes and speaks on the intersection of literature, philosophy, faith, and culture. The author or editor of eight books, the "Hogwarts Professor" has been a keynote and featured speaker at more than twenty academic and fan conferences and spoken at twenty-five major universities and colleges, from Princeton and Pepperdine to Yale and the University of Chicago. He is the author of eight books, including *Unlocking Harry Potter* (Zossima, 2007), *How Harry Cast His Spell* (Tyndale, 2008), *The Deathly Hallows Lectures* (Zossima, 2008), *Harry Potter's Bookshelf* (Penguin, 2009), and *Harry Potter as Ring Composition and Ring Cycle* (Zossima, 2010). Dr. Granger was also a finalist in the 2016 *Witch Weekly* "Most Winning Smile," house-elf division. He completed his doctorate from the University of Swansea in spring 2023, having written his dissertation on Rowling's work. He lives in Oklahoma City with his wife Mary and the last of their seven Harry, Narnia, and Redwall–loving children. Keep up with John on Substack at https://hogwartsprofessor.substack.com/ or at his blog *Hogwarts Professor*, https://www.hogwartsprofessor.com/.

M. Katherine Grimes is a professor of English and former English program coordinator at Ferrum College. In April 2023 she became the first recipient of the Sam Lionberger Jr. Trustee Faculty Award. She contributed "Harry Potter as Real Boy, Fairy-Tale Prince, and Archetypal Hero" to Lana A. Whited's first anthology of essays on the Harry Potter series, *The Ivory Tower and Harry Potter*. She is editor of *Critical Insights: "The Outsiders"* and coeditor, with Lana A. Whited, of *Critical Insights: The Harry Potter Series*. A proud native North Carolinian, she holds a PhD from the University of North Carolina at Greensboro, an MA from the University of North Carolina at Chapel Hill, and a BA from Catawba College.

Beatrice Groves, PhD, Research Fellow and Lecturer in Renaissance English at Trinity College, Oxford, has published three monographs and a wide number of articles and book chapters on Shakespeare, Renaissance literature, and literary allusion. Since publishing *Literary Allusion in Harry Potter* (Routledge, 2017), her work has engaged with Harry Potter on a variety of platforms. She has published journal articles on Dickens, Shakespeare, and Arthurian myth in Harry Potter in *The Use of English* and the *English Review*. She also has a book chapter, "Communities of Interpretation in Jane Austen and Harry Potter," in *Open at the Close: Literary Essays on Harry Potter*, edited by Cecilia Koncharr Farr (University of Mississippi Press, 2022). Groves has a dedicated blog, *Bathilda's Notebook*, on Mugglenet, and regularly writes for The Leaky Cauldron and *Hogwarts Professor*. She is also a regular guest expert on the podcast *Potterversity* (formerly *Reading, Writing, Rowling*) and gives Harry Potter tours at the Ashmolean Museum in Oxford.

Elizabeth Baird Hardy is author of *Milton, Spenser, and the Chronicles of Narnia: Literary Sources for the C. S. Lewis Novels* (McFarland, 2007) and a senior instructor of English at Mayland Community College, where she was awarded the 2006 Teaching Excellence Award. She teaches composition and literature courses as well as Myth in Human Culture, Introduction to Film, and classes in Appalachian culture and storytelling. She also guest-lectures at other schools, colleges, and universities. In addition to the works of Lewis, Milton, and Spenser, Hardy's areas of expertise and interest include Harry Potter, the Hunger Games books, and a diverse array of literature and works of popular culture. Hardy has presented at several national conferences, including C. S. Lewis: The Man and His Work, the Women of Appalachia Conference, the Carolina Mountains Literary Festival, the Witching Hour, LeakyCon, and Infinitus. She writes regularly for *Carolina Mountain Life* and has been a frequent contributor to *Hogwarts Professor* for over a decade. She has published chapters in several volumes, including *Critical Insights: The Hunger Games* (Salem, 2016), *Star Trek and History* (Wiley, 2013), *Harry Potter for Nerds* (Unlocking Press, 2012), and *Twilight and History* (Wiley, 2010).

Caitlin Elizabeth Harper is a writer and communication and organizational culture consultant and the founder of the change management consultancy Commcoterie. She received her MFA in fiction from the New

School and is the author of the young adult novel *It Will Set You Free*. Her nonfiction work has appeared in many outlets, including the Harry Potter Alliance's *Wizard Activist News Dispatch*. She presents annually at the Harry Potter Academic Conference at Chestnut Hill on topics ranging from Quidditch to an analysis of the Weasley children represented as the Seven Deadly Sins; has delivered her signature Quidditch talk at LeakyCon; and has appeared on MuggleNet's *Reading, Writing, Rowling* (now *Potterversity*) podcast to discuss both Quidditch and humor in the Harry Potter series.

Carsten Kullmann is a lecturer and PhD candidate at Otto von Guericke University in Magdeburg, Germany. His scholarship and teaching focuses on contemporary fantasy literature and film, and he is currently working on his dissertation about London urban fantasy in the twenty-first century. He has contributed to the study of J. K. Rowling's Wizarding world with articles about the portrayal of racism and fascism in the series (*The Allure of Harry Potter*, Inklings Yearbook 35, Peter Lang, 2017) and the Patronus Charm's use of Christian animal symbolism (*Flora and Fauna in Fantastic Worlds*, Inklings Yearbook 37, Peter Lang, 2020).

Alyssa Magee Lowery is associate professor of children's literature and young learners in the Department of Teacher Education at the Norwegian University of Science and Technology (NTNU). Dr. Lowery has a long-standing interest in critical media literacy and popular children's media, and she is currently writing a book that explores typologies and thematic categories in Disney animated features in the context of the death of the Disney vault.

Patrick McCauley received a PhD in philosophical theology and literature from the University of Iowa in conjunction with the University of Glasgow and its Centre for the Study of Literature, Theology and the Arts. He teaches philosophy, religion, and literature at Chestnut Hill College in Philadelphia. Along with Karen Wendling, PhD, he created and co-ordinates the Harry Potter Academic Conference, held every October at Chestnut Hill. He is the author of *Into the Pensieve: The Philosophy and Mythology of Harry Potter* (Schiffer, 2015).

Contributors

Kathryn N. McDaniel is the Andrew U. Thomas Professor of History and chair of the Department of History, Philosophy, Religion, and Gender and Sexuality Studies at Marietta College, Marietta, Ohio. She holds a BA in history from Davidson College and MA and PhD degrees from Vanderbilt University and has published and presented on the intersections of history and popular culture. McDaniel is the editor of *Virtual Dark Tourism: Ghost Roads* (Palgrave, 2018), for which she wrote the essay "Through the Looking Glass Darkly: The Convergence of Past and Present in Connie Willis's Time Travel Novels," and coeditor, with Travis Prinzi, of *Harry Potter for Nerds 2* (Unlocking Press, 2015) and, with Emily Strand, of *Potterversity: Essays Exploring the World of Harry Potter* (McFarland, 2023), as well as co-hosting (with Strand) MuggleNet's *Potterversity* podcast. She is also the author of several Harry Potter papers, including "The Elfin Mystique," "Dumbledore's Uncertain Past," "Harry Potter and the Ghost Teacher," and "Dumbledore's Army and the White Rose Society."

After completing an MA in English with a dissertation on the Harry Potter series and the city of London at King's College London in 2017, **Madison McLeod** has recently completed her PhD in digital humanities and children's literature at the University of Cambridge. Her research interests center around digital mapping, mythology, and the intersection of feminist studies and children's literature. Her publications include "An Initial Foray into the Digital Mapping of London in Children's and Young Adult Literature" in *International Research Society for Children's Literature* special issue 14.1, edited by Blanka Grzeogorcsyk and Farah Mendlesohn, and "Architecture and Magic: Mapping the London of Children's Fantasy Fiction" in *Building Children's Worlds: The Representation of Architecture and Modernity in Picturebooks*, edited by Torsten Schmiedeknecht, Jill Rudd, and Emma Hayward.

Heather Murray has taught literature and composition at colleges and universities in Pennsylvania and Georgia for more than two decades, and published biographical essays on early modern women writers. In addition, she has given more than two dozen conference presentations on such diverse topics as revenge in early modern drama, Shakespeare and pedagogy, and teaching composition to dual-enrollment high school students.

Catherine Olver is an ecocritic, fantasy scholar, and children's poet. She recently completed a PhD at the Centre for Research in Children's Literature at the University of Cambridge, with a doctoral thesis titled "Ecoconscious: Skilful Sensing in Young Adult Fantasy Literature." Drawing from a corpus of 160 novels published between 1994 and 2021, her thesis combines ecocriticism with sensory studies to analyse common sensory motifs that, when developed, model how humans can perceive and participate in the more-than-human world ecoconsciously. Its first chapter extends her work in this volume, investigating how focalization in J. K. Rowling's Harry Potter series and Nnedi Okorafor's Nsibidi Scripts trilogy presents sight as an embodied, relational skill. Catherine's poetry for children also considers how literature can help children and adults participate in their environments sensitively. Her poems have appeared recently in *The Caterpillar*, *Tyger Tyger*'s "Refrains and Animals" issues, *PaperBound*'s issue on magic, and the anthology *Chasing Clouds*.

Mitchell H. Parks received his PhD in classics from Brown University and teaches at Knox College in Galesburg, Illinois, offering a wide range of courses on the ancient Mediterranean world, including one on Harry Potter and its Greco-Roman antecedents. Apart from this volume, his published work on Harry Potter consists of an article, "Epigraphs and Epitaphs: Raising the Dead in *The Deathly Hallows*," in the online classics journal *Eidolon* (2017). On the classics side, his favorite subjects are Athenian democracy and Latin epic. He lives in Illinois with his family and dedicates his chapter in this volume to them: *Tempus fugit, amor manet*.

Emily Strand has taught religion at the collegiate level for nearly twenty years and authored two books on Catholic sacraments (Liguori, 2013, 2014). Her essay on the symbolic function of Quidditch appeared in *Harry Potter for Nerds 2* (Unlocking, 2015) and several more peer-reviewed publications have followed, including "Harry Potter and the Sacramental Principle" (*Worship*, October 2019) and "Dobby the Robot: The Science Fiction in *Harry Potter*" (*Mythlore*, 2019). More recently, Emily has coedited scholarly anthologies on the Star Wars films (Vernon, 2023) and Harry Potter (McFarland, 2023). She is a proud member of the 501st and Rebel Legions, charitable international Star Wars costuming associations. Her official website is emilystrand.com; she writes about religion and popular culture at *Liturgy and Life*.

Kris Swank is a librarian at Pima Community College, Tucson, Arizona, and a member of the Signum University faculty. A PhD candidate in English literature at the University of Glasgow, she holds an MA in language and literature from Signum. Kris has taught courses on the Harry Potter series at both Pima and Signum. Her two series, *Harry Potter Numerology* and *Harry Potter and The Hunger Games*, ran on the now-defunct blog *The Hog's Head* from 2012 to 2013, and are now available on her Academia.edu site. She is the author of "Harry Potter as Dystopian Literature" in *Harry Potter for Nerds II*, edited by Travis Prinzi and Kathryn N. McDaniel (Unlocking Press, 2015), and "House-Elves in Harlem: Stereotyping the Other in *Fantastic Beasts and Where to Find Them*" in *Transmedia Harry Potter: Essays on Storytelling Across Platforms*, edited by Christopher E. Bell (McFarland, 2019).

Lana Whited is editor of the first published essay collection on the Harry Potter novels, *The Ivory Tower and Harry Potter* (Missouri, 2002). She also edited Critical Insights volumes on the Harry Potter series (Salem, 2015, with M. Katherine Grimes) and the Hunger Games trilogy (Salem, 2016). Her essay "Here Be Dragons and Phoenixes: A Thematic Direction for *Fantastic Beasts*" appears in *Potterversity: The Book* (McFarland, 2023). Dr. Whited is professor of English and director of the Boone Honors Program at Ferrum College in Ferrum, Virginia, where she serves as faculty marshall. She earned degrees at Emory & Henry College (BA), College of William & Mary (MA), Hollins (MA), and UNC Greensboro (PhD). She has received the Exemplary Teaching Award from the Council of Higher Education of the United Methodist Church and was a 2016 nominee for the Outstanding Faculty Awards of the State Council of Higher Education of Virginia. Her most recent book is *Murder, in Fact: Death and Disillusionment in the American True Crime Novel* (McFarland, 2020).

Index

Achilles, 71–73, 76, 80n24
Adam and Eve, 44, 354
Aeneas, 67–68, 70–78, 80n20, 80n23
Aeneid, The, 15, 67–79. 80n14, 80n16, 80n18, 80n24
   parallels with *Deathly Hallows*, 72–75, 78
alchemy, 14, 239–51, 251n7, 252n42, 345
Andersen, Hans Christian, 14, 241, 249
antiracism, 11, 15, 115–16, 127–28, 235n57
Anzaldúa, Gloria, 222, 233–34
Aragog, 195, 351, 353
Archive of Our Own (AO3), 368–69
Aristotle, 214, 259
Arthur (King of Britain), 15, 23, 50, 83, 85–95
Authoritarianism, 4, 55–56

B

Bagshot, Bathilda, 289, 300
Barthes, Roland, 10, 18n35, 375–76
basilisk, 174, 181, 190
Battle of Hogwarts, 71, 110–11, 118, 182, 233, 277, 282
Beamish, Bert, 342–44, 348, 350–51, 356
Beamish, Major, 342, 344, 348, 351, 355
Beedle the Bard, 14, 205, 227, 239, 244, 249
Bellchapel, 254–55, 260, 263
Beowulf, 170, 251n21, 260, 353
Berger, John, 187–89
Bettelheim, Bruno, 46, 353, 358–59n62
bin Laden, Osama, 5
Black (family), 16, 22, 33n2

Black, Sirius
   as Animagus, 227–28
   death of, 93, 133–34, 176, 285n14
   father of, 22, 33n2
   as fugitive, 143, 160
   gift of Firebolt, 176, 178
   as Marauder, 21
   as pureblood, 21
   relationship with Harry Potter, 94, 147, 176, 327
   rescue of, 164, 174, 176, 179–80, 191
   treatment of house elves, 117
boggart, 16, 24, 136, 202–3, 208–9
borderlands, 219–20, 222, 225, 229
Borgin and Burkes, 30–31, 34, 273
Brown, Jake, 5, 383
brownies (folkloric creatures), 122–24
Buckbeak, 164, 175, 190–91, 197, 351
Byatt, A.S., 14, 18, 294–95

C

Campbell, Joseph, 47n41, 329, 353–54
Campbell, Charlotte, 329. 333
Carroll, Lewis, 343
Casual Vacancy, The, 3, 13, 206, 253–56, 258, 259–65, 333, 365n10, 365n14, 366n32, 366n35, 366nn40–41
Central Park Five, 4, 17n9
Chamber of Secrets (location), 30, 174, 181
Charing Cross Road, 38
chiasmus. *See* Ring Composition
Chiswell family, 329–30, 334–36
Chiswell, Jasper, 329–30, 335–36
Chouxville, 344, 347–48, 350

415

Index

Christianity, 240, 261–64, 266n35, 266n41, 269, 277, 279, 281, 287n65
Christie, Agatha, 16
Christmas Pig, The, 3
Cogsworth, 349
colonialism, 50, 57, 59, 61–62, 220
Cormoran Strike detective novels, 3, 12–13, 339n12, 339n13
    as ring composition, 325–27, 339n12
    as series-in-parallel with Harry Potter, 325–38
Cornucopia, 290, 343–45, 349–50, 352, 356
critical reading, 15, 119, 129, 155–67, 227
Crouch, Barty, Sr., 116–17, 123–24, 330–31, 335–36
Crouch, Barty, Jr., 27–28, 204, 330, 334
Cursed Child, The, 3, 14, 78, 108, 269–84, 288nn87–88, 370–72

D

Dark Other, 372
death
    of Albus Dumbledore, 30, 139, 180
    alchemical symbolism for, 244–48, 250
    as theme of the Harry Potter series, 194–95, 281
    barrier between life and, 32, 42–45
    of Barry Fairbrother, 253–56, 258–59, 261, 265
    of Barty Crouch, Sr., 330, 335
    of Catherine Weedon, 257
    of Cedric Diggory, 192, 194, 335
    of Dobby, 93, 196–97
    of Dora Dovetail, 350
    of Fred Weasley, 133, 149, 277
    of Gautama Buddha, 264
    of Guru Nanak, 263
    of Harry Potter (as sacrifice) 8, 32, 43–44, 72–73, 76, 183, 187, 197, 278, 280
    of Hedwig, 148, 197
    of James and Lily Potter, 72, 92
    of Jasper Chiswell, 329, 335
    of Jesus, 259, 264
    of Krystal Weedon, 259, 264
    of Leda Strike, 333
    of Lily Potter, 38, 194, 277–79
    of Lula Landry, 328–29
    of Mad–Eye Moody, 146
    of Major Beamish, 344, 348, 351, 355
    mysterious nature of, 192–97
    of Nagini, 197
    of Robbie Weedon, 258–59, 264, 265n10
    of Severus Snape, 223
    of Sirius Black, 93, 176, 285n14
    of Voldemort, 342
Death Eaters, 24, 30, 45, 63n27, 75, 90, 146, 160, 162, 166, 169, 177–80, 182, 223, 228, 230, 253, 284, 322, 330–31, 336
"death of the author," 10, 18n35, 321, 375–76
Deathly Hallows (magical objects), 32, 91, 93, 162, 182, 194–96, 247–48, 280
    Elder Wand, 89, 91, 93, 182, 194, 248
    Invisibility Cloak, 28, 91, 188, 163, 194–95, 248, 278–79, 327
    Philosopher's (or Resurrection or Sorcerer's) Stone, 24, 39, 76, 92, 165, 173, 182, 227, 239–42, 244–46, 248–49, 287n80
deconstruction, 222, 306, 314, 317, 319–20
Delacour, Fleur, 231,
Derrida, Jacques, 186–88, 196
Diagon Alley, 22–23, 27, 29, 31, 36–40, 45–46, 46n13, 135, 143–45, 172, 224
Diggory, Cedric, 31, 134,143, 174, 177, 192, 194, 197, 210, 335
Discworld (series), 28, 34
Dobby, 93, 116–18, 123–24, 130, 134, 140, 142, 195–97, 210, 215, 413
Dougal the Demiguise, 27
Douglas, Mary, 176, 325, 339n12
Dovetail, Daisy, 343–48, 350, 352
Dovetail, Dora, 350
Draco Trilogy, 370
Dumbledore, Albus Percival Wulfric Brian, 8, 22, 33, 79, 115, 155, 163, 172, 178, 207, 220, 225, 233, 253, 327, 339n6
    and *The Daily Prophet*, 155, 159, 161
    death of, 30, 44, 139, 180, 285n27

Index

Dumbledor (*continued*)
   and the Dursley family, 136, 139–42, 150n32, 204, 271
   and Gellert Grindelwald, 232, 311–12, 317, 342, 372
   and Harry Potter, 8, 29, 44–45, 93, 104, 166, 176, 179, 206, 223, 277, 280–83, 285n8, 334, 336
   and Hermione Granger, 110
   and humor, 136, 139–42
   magical ability, 24–25, 28–29, 163, 327, 334
   and Newt Scamander, 309–10, 317–19
   quotations of, 23, 33, 44–45, 81n38, 176, 343, 357n12
   and Remus Lupin, 229–31
   sexual orientation of, 366, 372
   and Sirius Black, 228
   and Tom Riddle, 103–4, 180, 196–197, 206, 223, 271, 288n95, 291
Dumbledore's Army, 24, 100, 161–62, 178, 181, 210, 250, 254,
Dursley, Dudley, 136, 138–39, 142–43, 145–48, 158, 187–89, 270, 272, 349
Dursley family, 141, 146–47, 150n31
Dursley, Petunia, 140–42, 145–48, 271, 278, 287n65
Dursley, Vernon, 41, 136, 138–41, 144–48, 271, 283, 285n8, 349

E

Eden, 43, 291, 297–98, 301
Elder Wand. *See* Deathly Hallows
Elizabeth I (Queen), 50
"Emperor's New Clothes, The," 14, 349, 358
enslavement, slavery, 110, 115, 117, 119–21, 124, 126, 128, 130, 376
epic, 15, 67–68, 70–71, 73, 75–77, 80, 83, 260, 302n22
European Union, 13, 305
Eve and Adam. *See* Adam and Eve

F

Facebook 260, 364, 378n4
Fairbrother, Barry, 253–59, 261–66, 266n32

Fairbrother, Mary, 254–55, 257–58, 261
fandom, 12, 16, 289, 337, 363–78
fanfiction, 78, 81n36, 368–70, 377
Fantastic Beasts and Where to Find Them (book), 34n13, 124–25, 129, 305–06, 310, 314, 317, 372, 379
Fantastic Beasts (film series), 3, 13–14, 21, 25, 240. 290, 293, 295, 305, 319–20, 321n, 342, 351–52, 358n56
Fantastic Beasts and Where to Find Them (film), 56, 60, 125–26, 305–10, 314, 317, 372
Fantastic Beasts: The Crimes of Grindelwald, 34n17, 126–27, 289–301, 302n7, 303n44, 305–06, 309–12, 316–19, 322n22, 321–22n5, 363, 372
Fantastic Beasts: The Secrets of Dumbledore 292–93, 306, 312–14, 317, 320
fantasy, 13, 41, 45, 49, 62, 89–90, 94–95, 129, 192, 220, 276, 337, 342, 351–53
   medievalist, 84–95
   portal, 36–37, 42
Farr, Cecilia Konchar, 8–9, 18n29
Faulkner, William, 253
Fellowship of the Ring, The, 354–55
Fiendfyre, 30, 139
Flapoon, Lord, 343–44, 348–49, 356
Flitwick, Filius, 25
Floo Powder, 23, 30
focalization, 185–86, 193, 198
Forbidden Forest, 32, 43, 72, 137, 183, 302, 363
Fountain of Fair Fortune, 14, 74, 239–46, 249–50
Frank the Thunderbird, 27, 317
Frankenstein (novel), 354
Fred the Fearless (King), 341, 344, 346, 348–51, 355
Freeman, Louise, 13–4, 234n, 285n5, 285n11, 330–31, 337, 345
Freytag's pyramid, 253

G

Gawain (character), 85, 90, 92, 94. See also *Sir Gawain and the Green Knight*

gaze, 186–92, 194–95, 197–98, 206–9, 212, 214–15
gender identity, 6–9, 12, 320–21n
Generation Hex, 11
Generation Z, 5
Genesis, 79, 127, 266n32, 290–91, 298
ghost plots, 49–50, 57, 60, 62, 62n1, 62n7
Gierzynski, Anthony (Jack), 4–5, 70, 80n15, 161, 305, 321n4, 373
Gilgamesh (character), 354
Gog and Magog, 347, 358n34
Goldsmith, Amber, 365, 367
Goldstein, Porpentina (Tina), 32, 127, 307–8, 313, 315–18
Good Samaritan, 257, 262
Granger family, 225, 273–74
Granger, Hermione, 39, 42, 104, 106, 143, 174, 176–83, 189, 210–11, 227, 231, 246, 260, 273, 277–78, 285n14, 363
  black Hermione, 371–72
  critical-thinking abilities of, 26, 110, 158–59, 161, 163–64, 227
  magic and magical objects (use of), 16, 23, 25–29, 172–73
  as Muggle-born, 21, 26, 62n10, 106, 222–27, 273–74
  as social activist, 15, 110, 115–19, 127–30, 130n5, 331–32, 376
  relationship with Harry Potter, 115–16, 211–15, 233, 333, 368
  relationship with Ron Weasley, 15, 75, 106–11, 223, 246, 333
Granger, John, 12–13, 49, 68, 137, 170, 240, 256, 265n10, 266n35, 325, 327, 329, 331, 335, 337, 339, 358
Grendel, 260, 353
Greyback, Fenrir, 207
Grimes, M. Katherine, 8, 13, 68, 216, 357n9
Grimmauld Place, 22, 36, 38, 131, 143, 145, 202, 228
Grindelwald, Gellert, 34, 126, 132, 232, 289–93, 295–96, 300–02, 304–17, 320, 322–23, 342–43, 351–53, 358, 363, 372, 379
Gringotts Bank, 22–23, 29, 39–40, 75, 198, 272, 366

Griphook, 39
Guru Granth Sahib, 263
Guru Nanak, 253, 260–63, 266

H

Hagrid, Rubeus
  and animals and creatures, 189–90, 195
  attitude toward house elves, 117
  attitude toward Ministry of Magic, 159
  and Azkaban, 144
  and Battle of Hogwarts, 75
  and Chamber of Secrets, 29
  dialect (use of), 123
  and Dursley family, 147
  and Forbidden Forest, 137
  as half-giant, 136, 179, 225, 229–31, 233
  as mentor to Harry Potter, 22, 25, 36–40, 43, 75, 172, 224, 226, 233, 272
  and Time-Turner sequence, 163–64
Hardy, Thomas, 259
Harry Potter and the Chamber of Secrets (book), 8, 29–30, 34n20, 75, 100, 107, 124, 137, 170, 190, 196, 225, 273, 275
  parallels with *Half-Blood Prince*, 137–42, 170, 181
Harry Potter and the Deathly Hallows
  book publication and sales, 3, 5, 337, 363, 366, 371–72
  film adaptation, 3, 6, 81n38
  parallels with *The Aeneid*, 72–75, 78
  parallels with *Goblet of Fire*, 137–39, 146–48
  parallels with *Half-Blood Prince*, 123, 204
  parallels with *Sorcerer's Stone*, 137, 146–48, 170, 181–82, 203–4
Harry Potter and the Goblet of Fire (book)
  parallels with *Deathly Hallows*, 137–39, 146–48
  parallels with *Lethal White*, 13, 329–37
  parallels with *Sorcerer's Stone*, 137–38, 146–48
  as series' turning-point, 13, 137–38, 170, 176–78, 330
Harry Potter and the Half-Blood Prince (book)
  parallels with *Chamber of Secrets*, 34n20, 137–42, 170, 204

Index

Harry Potter and the Half-Blood Prince (continued)
  parallels with *Deathly Hallows*, 123, 204
  parallels with *Goblet of Fire*, 204
  parallels with *Sorcerer's Stone*, 203–4
Harry Potter and the Order of the Phoenix (book)
  film adaptation, 366
  parallels with *Prisoner of Azkaban*, 137, 142–46, 170
Harry Potter and the Philosopher's Stone
  audio edition, 341
  book publication, 3, 28, 45
  as ring composition, 326–27
  See also *Harry Potter and the Sorcerer's Stone*
Harry Potter and the Prisoner of Azkaban
  boggart lesson in, 202
  parallels with *Order of the Phoenix*, 137, 142–46, 170
  Time-Turner (use of), 16, 21, 163
Harry Potter and the Sorcerer's Stone
  book publication and sales, 3, 45
  parallels with *Deathly Hallows*, 137–38, 146–48, 170–74, 181–82, 203–04
  parallels with *Goblet of Fire*, 137–38, 146–48
  parallels with *Order of the Phoenix*, 181–82
Harry Potter at Home, 341
Harry Potter Lexicon, 274, 364, 366–67
Harry Potter Wizarding Alamanac, The, 3
Hedwig, 72–73, 134, 148, 197
Henderson, Tolonda, 7, 10
hippogriff, 190–91
history
  as academic subject, 21, 49, 54, 57–62, 63n28, 64n39
  of the Wizarding world, 49–64, 126, 227
"History of Magic in North America" (essay by Rowling), 57, 61–62
Hogwarts, Battle of, 40, 71, 110–11, 118, 182, 223, 233, 277
Hogwarts, a History, 227, 277,
Hogwarts Express, 43, 53, 100, 108, 175, 276, 326, 363, 368–69
Homer, 144

Horcrux, 24–25, 29, 32, 39, 182, 223, 260, 293
house elves 109–11, 115–30, 130n2, 130n3, 130n5, 131n42, 221
  dialect (use of), 115, 117, 123
humor (general), 14, 91, 99, 111, 133–39, 139, 141–42, 144–46, 148–49, 150, 173
  benign violation, 139
  disclosure, 135–37, 141, 145, 149–50
  distortion, 135–37, 139, 142, 144–45, 148–49
hybridity, 14, 219–33, 234n20

I

Ickabog (creature), 290, 301n5, 342–56
Ickabog, The (book) 3, 14, 290, 341–56
Ilvermorny, 56, 58, 63n29, 372
immortality (as theme), 87, 166, 269, 281–84, 287n80, 354
International Statute of Wizarding Secrecy, 50–62
Invisibility Cloak. *See* Deathly Hallows
Isolt, 58–59

J

"Jabberwocky," 343
Jawanda, Parminder, 256–57, 262–63, 265n14, 266n40
Jawanda, Sukhvinder, 254–64, 265n14n 266n32
Jawanda, Vikram, 261, 261, 265n14
Jenkins, Henry, 16, 364, 366, 369
Jesus, 253, 256, 259–62, 264, 266n41, 279, 287n66, 356
Johnson, Boris, 178, 341
Joseph (father of Jesus), 287n66

K

Kalsi, M.S., 263, 266
Kay, Jim, 188. 295
Keats, John, 14, 290–91, 296–99, 300–1
Kim, Claudia, 290–93
Kim, Lorrie, 10
King's Cross Station 40–45, 100, 280
knights, 83–88, 91–93

419

Index

Kreacher, 116–18, 123–24, 126, 129–30, 142, 163, 347

L
Lady Eslanda, 344, 350
Lamia (character), 290, 297–300
lamia (creature), 290, 293, 296–300, 303n40
Lamia, The (painting by Draper), 302n7
Lamia (work by Keats), 14, 290, 296–300
Landry, Lula, 328–29
Last Battle, The, 34
Leaky Cauldron, The, 22, 31, 36–7, 50, 364, 367
LeStrange family, 126–27, 295–96, 303n44
LeStrange, Leta, 32, 126, 295–96, 352
Lethal White
 parallels with *Cuckoo's Calling*, 329–30
 parallels with *Goblet of Fire*, 13, 330–37
 as ring writing, 325, 328
Lewis, Clive Staples (C.S.), 11, 30–31, 84, 281, 357
Life and Lies of Albus Dumbledore, The, 227, 280
liminality, 32, 42, 295–96, 303, 306, 314, 317, 319
Lion, the Witch, and the Wardrobe, The, 30, 34n21, 357
London, 3, 14, 34n21, 35–46, 78, 193, 319, 331, 347, 370
Longbottom, Neville, 24, 75, 136–37, 144–45, 171, 189, 258, 260, 352
love poetry, 100–1, 109
love potions, 100, 103–5
love tokens, 103
Lovegood, Luna, 137, 162, 179, 194
Lovegood, Xenophilius, 162, 194, 248–49
luggage (magical), 27–9, 146
Luggage, The (Discworld series), 28–9, 34n18
Lupin, Remus, 21, 24, 160, 175, 202, 225, 230–31, 233, 271, 277, 282, 368

M
Mabinogion, The, 29, 347
Magical Congress of the United States of America (MACUSA), 55–56, 59–61, 63n29, 64n39, 64n43, 125, 306–10, 313–14, 318
Maledictus, 291–91, 294, 300, 303n31
Malfoy, Draco, 30, 107, 123, 171, 173–75, 178, 181–82, 223, 225, 258, 272–73, 285n26, 285n27, 287n84, 347, 368, 370
Malfoy family, 30, 50–1, 53, 117, 225, 269, 272–73, 275, 282, 347
Malfoy, Lucius, 157, 173, 181, 196, 225, 272–73, 285n26, 286, 286n45, 347, 370
Malfoy, Narcissa, 94, 287
Malfoy, Scorpius, 282
Malory, Thomas, 85, 89, 91–4
Marshlands, 342, 344–45, 351, 354
Martha (character in *The Ickabog*), 345–48
Martin, George R.R., 84
Mary (mother of Jesus), 279
Mary Magdalene, 256
McGonagall, Minerva, 53, 63, 172, 204, 227–28, 372
Medievalism in literature, *see* fantasy, medieval
Melusine (character), 290–91, 293–97, 303n29, 303n48
Melusine (folktale), 14, 18n43, 291–300, 302n27, 302n28, 303n40, 303n47
Mendlesohn, Farah, 11–13, 35, 119
Merleau–Ponty, Maurice, 188
Merlin, 86–91
millennials, 4–6, 80, 155, 161, 321n4, 365, 379
Milton, John, 297, 304n54
Ministry of Magic, 4, 126, 229
 battle with Death Eaters in, 90, 93, 179–80
 complicity with *The Daily Prophet*, 159–60
 as employer, 166, 275
 in England (British Ministry), 22–23, 36, 38, 55–56, 60–1, 90, 100, 110, 306, 309–13
 in France, 296, 311–12
 in Germany, 306, 312–14
 as magical location, 224
 as political entity, 159–61, 220
 regulation of underage wizards, 136–37, 140, 143, 145, 157, 176, 228

Index

Ministry of Magic (*continued*)
   in the United States of America (*see* Magical Congress of the United States of America [MACUSA])
Mirror of Erised, 24, 92, 173, 326
Modern Language Association, 8–9
Modern novel, 253–54, 258–59
monsters and monstrosity, 14, 33, 83–4, 290, 298–300, 341–59
Montague, Graham, 30–31
Moody, Alastor ("Mad-Eye"), 27–9, 34n7, 103, 134, 144–45, 148, 330, 332, 334–35, 337
Morte Darthur, 85–87, 92, 95
Moses, 141, 260–61, 264
MuggleNet, 12, 13, 170, 364, 367
Muggles, 12, 22, 34, 41, 49, 50–4, 58–60, 111, 135, 139, 221, 224–27, 240, 275, 278, 287, 315, 321
myth, 6, 42, 71, 83–4, 214, 343, 345–46, 356, 358, 375
   Chinese, 289, 290, 292, 293, 300, 301
   French, 289, 290, 294, 294, 295, 296, 301, 303
   Greek and Roman, 68, 71, 246, 287n84, 290, 297, 300
   Indian, 289–90, 292, 294, 301
   snake woman (*see* snake-woman myth)

N

Naga. *See* snake-woman myth
Nagini, 14, 127, 194, 197, 266n41, 289–93, 299–301, 302n7, 303n29, 353, 372
Naturalism, Naturalistic novel, 259, 266n24
Nearly Headless Nick, 30, 50, 62n7, 123
Niffler, 27, 34, 307
No-Maj, 56, 58–60, 63, 307, 315, 318
Nurmengard, 351

O

O'Connor, Flannery, 26
Obama, Barack, 4–5
Odysseus, 73, 76, 80n24
Odyssey, The, 68, 71–3, 80n24, 170
Onomastics, 241–44, 250

Order of the Phoenix (organization), 22, 33n2, 38, 160, 162, 178–79, 182, 228, 230, 232, 250, 277
ornamentalism, 57, 63
Other, Otherness, 12, 188, 209–10, 212, 220, 223, 227–29, 231–32, 235n57

P

Pagford, 254–55, 259–61
Paradise Lost, 170, 297, 304n51
Parallel Series theory, 13, 325–38, 339n10
parenting (as theme), 37, 76–77, 80, 138–39, 141–43, 255–56, 259, 265n13, 269–84, 284n, 284n3, 286n51, 287n82, 288n88, 327, 345–47
parody, 50, 56–57, 135, 291, 302n14
participatory culture, 364, 369
Patronus charm, 91, 143, 145, 164, 174–76, 203, 206, 215, 249, 270
Pensieve, 29n, 155–56, 158, 160, 162–67
Perkins (Arthur Weasley's co-worker), 23
Pevensie family, 31
Pevensie, Lucy, 30
Peverell family, 287n64
Philosopher's Stone. *See* Deathly Hallows
Picquery, Madam Seraphina, 308–9, 314
Pius Thicknesse, 23
Platform Nine and Three-Quarters, 21–22, 27, 29, 38, 40–43, 135, 224, 282
Poppins, Mary, 29
populism, 12, 305, 320–21
Potter family, 24, 38, 63, 287n64
Potter, Harry (character)
   and Albus Potter, 288n88, 288n91
Potter, Harry (character)
   death of, 8, 32, 43–44, 72–73, 76, 183, 187, 197, 278, 280
   glasses of, 186, 204–5, 207
   interactions with animals, 185–98
   as media celebrity, 155–56, 158–62
   parallels with Aeneas, 67–79
   parallels with (King) Arthur, 83–95
   parallels with Newt Scamander, 32
   as point of view, 185–98, 203–16
   Quidditch career, 169–83

Index

Potter, Harry (character) (*continued*)
  relationship with Albus Dumbledore, 8, 29, 44–45, 93, 104, 166, 176, 179, 206, 223, 277, 280–83, 285n8, 334, 336
  relationship with Dursleys, 139–48, 270–72
  relationship with Ginny Weasley, 100–106, 111
  relationship with Hermione Granger, 107, 115, 211–15, 333
  relationship with London, 35–46
  relationship with Ron Weasley, 326
  relationship with Rubeus Hagrid, 37
  relationship with Severus Snape, 8
  relationship with Sirius Black, 94, 147, 176, 327
  search for horcruxes, 75
Potter, James, 8, 21, 72, 76, 92, 144, 164, 171, 175, 203, 205, 249, 278–80, 287n64, 368
Potter, Lily Evans, 8, 37, 46n16, 72, 76–77, 92, 205–6, 277–79, 282, 285n11, 287n64, 379n23
Pottermore. See *Wizarding World*
Potterversity podcast, 12–13
Price, Andrew, 255–57, 258, 264
Price, Simon, 255–58, 262, 264–65, 265n5
Prince Caspian, 31, 34
Prydain, 29
pureblood, 53–6, 106, 110, 127, 223, 226, 235, 316, 331
Puritans, 51, 63n29

Q

quest, 71, 75, 87, 93, 162, 182, 196, 198, 213, 239–41, 243–44, 247–50, 260, 269, 281, 287n80, 295
  esoteric, 239–40, 245
Quibbler, The, 63, 162
Quidditch, 15, 31, 57, 63, 124, 131, 139, 157, 169–84, 226, 276, 331, 336, 363, 377
  in *Chamber of Secrets*, 173–74
  in *Deathly Hallows*, 181–83
  in *Goblet of Fire*, 176–78
  in *Half-Blood Prince*, 180–81
  in *Order of the Phoenix*, 178–80
  in *Prisoner of Azkaban*, 174–76
  and soccer, 234n41
  in *Sorcerer's Stone*, 171–73
Quidditch Through the Ages, 57
Quixote, Don, 349
Quora, 365, 367

R

race, racism, 12, 54–55, 72, 81, 119–21, 129, 199, 212, 221, 256, 279, 282, 303, 346, 368, 371, 376
Radcliffe, Daniel, 321n, 375
Rappaport's Law, 56, 63n29, 307, 314, 318
RDR Books, 367, 378
religion (thematic use of), 261–65, 277–84
resistance, 12, 14, 22, 94, 120, 139, 181, 219–20, 222, 224, 311, 348
Resurrection Stone (*see* Deathly Hallows)
Riddle, Tom, Jr., 8, 29, 80n29, 137, 165–66, 173–75, 204, 206–7, 214, 283, 288n95, 327, 351. *See also* Voldemort
Riddle, Tom, Sr., 103–4, 165, 271, 288n95
ring composition, 13, 15, 73, 149, 169–71, 176, 325–30, 338–39, 339n12, 339n13
Roach, Roderick, 343–48, 350
Romantic comedy, 99–111
Room of Requirement, 24–25, 30–31, 75–76
Rowling, Joanne Kathleen (J. K.)
  as author of fairy tales and folktales, 341–57
  commercial success of, 3–4
  as comic writer, 99–111, 133–49, 259, 332
  family of, 9
  gender identity (views on), 6–8, 12, 320–21n, 372–75
  as historian of the Wizarding world, 49–62, 64n39
  lawsuits involving, 366–68
  oeuvre, 3
  online activity, 6–7, 364–65, 372–75
  as parodist, 49–50. 56–57, 135. 291, 302n14
  as social realist, 253–65

422

Index

Rowling, J. K. (continued)
  portrayal of news media and journalists, 155–62, 307,
  relationships with fans, 6–9, 363–78
  See also titles of specific works

S

Salem, 50–52, 54–55, 57, 60–61
Sartre, Jean–Paul, 189
Satan, 297, 301, 304
Scamander, Newt, 16, 25–26, 125, 253, 306–14, 317–20, 352, 372
Scholastic (publisher), 366, 371, 375
Scots (language), 3, 122, 131n33
Segregation, 49–56, 58–62, 64, 313–14, 317
September 11, 2001 terrorist attacks, 5
Shakespeare, William
  All's Well that Ends Well, 104
  As You Like It, 100–101
  Midsummer Night's Dream, A, 101–5, 104
  Much Ado about Nothing, 106–9
  Romeo and Juliet, 104
  Taming of the Shrew, The, 106
  Twelfth Night, 100, 106
  Two Gentlemen of Verona, 100
Shelley, Mary, 354
sight, 22, 105, 170, 182, 185–86, 188–95, 198, 214
Sikh, Sikhism, 253, 260–64
Sir Gawain and the Green Knight, 85, 90, 92–94
slavery. *See* enslavement
snake, 74–75, 174–75, 187–89, 194–95, 197, 211, 289–92, 297–98, 301, 302n22, 304n54, 342, 351
snake-woman myth, 14, 289–301, 302n7, 302n26
Snape, Severus, 230, 233, 285n11, 287n82, 370
  animosity with Harry Potter, 8, 135–36, 285n11
  as ambiguous character, 163, 172–73, 180, 370
  as Death Eater 223
  detention given by, 136–37, 181
  love for Lily Evans Potter, 8, 76, 106, 206, 287n82
  as Occlumency teacher, 32, 72, 76, 93, 223
  as Potions teacher, 107
  as protector of Harry Potter, 137, 172–73
Society for the Promotion of Elfish Welfare (S.P.E.W.), 15, 115–30, 331–32, 376
Sorcerer's Stone (*see* Deathly Hallows)
Sorting Hat, 101, 177, 204, 346, 377
Spittleworth, 341, 343–45, 348–51, 353, 356
St. Mungo's Hospital, 22–23, 34n7, 224
Strike, Cormoran, 253, 325, 328, 331, 333–35, 336, 338
Strike, Leda, 333
Superman, 253, 337

T

Tales of Beedle the Bard, The, 14, 205, 227, 239, 244, 249
TERF (Trans-Exclusionary Radical Feminist), 7, 17n22, 373, 375
thestrals, 180, 186, 192–94, 197, 200
Thomas, Ebony Elizabeth, 12, 120, 368, 371
Tolkien, J.R.R., 11, 62n3, 78, 84, 353–54
Totalitarianism, 55, 305–06, 313, 315–16, 321n3
tragicomedy, 258–59
Trans-Exclusionary Radical Feminist. *See* TERF
Triwizard Tournament, 28, 80n29, 101, 134, 156, 170, 176–78, 183, 189, 191, 229, 231, 240, 245, 334
Trump, Donald, 4, 12–13, 17n9, 155, 305, 321n4, 341
Tuan, Yi-Fu, 36
Twitter, 321n, 326, 364, 364–65, 370, 373–75, 378n4, 380n45
Twoflower, 28

U

Umbridge, Dolores, 30, 136, 159, 161–62, 178, 206, 220, 285, 343, 376
Uncle Tom's Cabin, 5

V

Vanishing Cabinet, 30–31, 34, 163

Index

Vezzali, Loris, 5, 70, 80n15, 209, 373
Virgil, 69–70, 73, 79–80
Voldemort
   ability to talk to snakes, 289
   betrayal by Narcissa Malfoy, 94
   in *Cursed Child*, 283–84
   defeat of, 45, 76, 111, 169, 175, 194, 250
   and horcruxes, 24, 31–32, 29, 44, 87–88, 93, 166, 195, 223, 301
   humor as weapon against, 134, 136
   as hybrid or half-blood, 219–20, 227–28
   killing of James and Lily Potter, 37
   killing of Hedwig, 148
   and Ministry of Magic, 55
   Nagini (relationship with), 197, 291
   and Occlumency, 93, 232
   parallels with Spittleworth, 343
   parents of, 103–4
   Philosopher's Stone and immortality (desire for), 39, 269, 281, 287n80
   physical form (return to), 158–60, 162, 178, 333, 335and Priori Incantatem spell, 92
   as symbol for evil, 5, 110, 334, 353
   as threat to Harry Potter, 37, 43–44, 75–76, 87, 89, 93–95, 105–6, 170–73, 182–83, 253, 278–79, 285n11
   as totalitarian leader, 305, 320

W

Warner Brothers, 320, 320–21n, 366–67, 375
Weasley, Arthur, 23, 139, 141, 148, 157–58, 211, 224–25, 274–77, 353
Weasley, Bill, 106, 202, 231, 246, 275–76
Weasley, Charlie, 275–76
Weasley family, 16, 40, 100, 148–49, 203, 223, 225–26, 231–32, 274–77, 281, 326
Weasley, Fred, 21, 24, 30, 133–34, 136, 139, 147–49, 173–74, 202, 275–77, 286n51, 336
Weasley, George, 21, 24, 30, 133–34, 136, 139, 147–49, 173–74, 202, 275–76, 286n51, 336

Weasley, Ginny, 100–106, 111, 137, 173–74, 179–80, 214, 231, 276, 286n52, 368
Weasley, Molly, 16, 148, 160, 182, 202–03, 226, 231, 275–77
Weasley, Percy, 116, 133, 136, 202, 275–76, 335–36
Weasley, Ron, 139, 143, 163, 171–74, 177–83, 189, 202, 212–14, 220, 223, 225–27, 229–30, 234n41, 246, 260, 274–76, 333, 353, 363
   abandonment of Harry and Hermione, 212–13
   heteronormative reactions, 201–12
   house elves (attitude toward), 110, 117, 130n5
   humor (use of), 133, 139
   jealousy of Viktor Krum, 108
   lack of confidence, 276
   as mediocre student, 107
   and Mirror of Erised, 24, 326
   prejudices of, 229–30
   relationship with Hermione Granger, 15, 75, 106–11, 214, 223, 226–27, 246, 333
   relationship with Lavender Brown, 104
   and Quidditch, 171–73, 178–83, 234n41
   and *Tales of Beedle the Bard*, 110–11
   and Triwizard Tournament, 177
Weedon, Catherine, 256–7
Weedon family, 256–59, 261–62
Weedon, Krystal, 254–57, 259, 261, 264–65
Weedon, Robbie, 255–61, 264–65
White, Madam, 290, 292–93, 299–300
Whited, Lana A., 110, 266n24, 275
Winky, 24, 116–17, 124, 130, 335
Wizarding World (website, formerly *Pottermore*), 14, 49, 121, 125–26, 287, 367, 370
Wood between the Worlds, 31

Z

Zipes, Jack, 43